I ENVY YOU

I.N.V.U.

Innocent Nice Vivid Unique

ALSO AVAILABLE FROM ⊙ TOKYOPOP®

MANGA

ANGELIC LAYER*
BABY BIRTH* (September 2003)
BATTLE ROYALE*
BRAIN POWERD* (June 2003)
BRIGADOON* (August 2003)
CARDCAPTOR SAKURA
CARDCAPTOR SAKURA: MASTER OF THE CLOW*
CLAMP SCHOOL DETECTIVES*
CHOBITS*
CHRONICLES OF THE CURSED SWORD (July 2003)
CLOVER
CONFIDENTIAL CONFESSIONS* (July 2003)
CORRECTOR YUI
COWBOY BEBOP*
COWBOY BEBOP: SHOOTING STAR* (June 2003)
DEMON DIARY (May 2003)
DIGIMON
DRAGON HUNTER (June 2003)
DRAGON KNIGHTS*
DUKLYON: CLAMP SCHOOL DEFENDERS* (September 2003)
ERICA SAKURAZAWA* (May 2003)
ESCAFLOWNE* (July 2003)
FAKE*(May 2003)
FLCL* (September 2003)
FORBIDDEN DANCE* (August 2003)
GATE KEEPERS*
G-GUNDAM* (June 2003)
GRAVITATION* (June 2003)
GTO*
GUNDAM WING
GUNDAM WING: ENDLESS WALTZ*
GUNDAM: THE LAST OUTPOST*
HAPPY MANIA*
HARLEM BEAT
INITIAL D*
I.N.V.U.
ISLAND
JING: KING OF BANDITS* (June 2003)
JULINE
KARE KANO*
KINDAICHI CASE FILES* (June 2003)
KING OF HELL (June 2003)

KODOCHA*
LOVE HINA*
LUPIN III*
MAGIC KNIGHT RAYEARTH* (August 2003)
MAGIC KNIGHT RAYEARTH II* (COMING SOON)
MAN OF MANY FACES* (May 2003)
MARMALADE BOY*
MARS*
MIRACLE GIRLS
MIYUKI-CHAN IN WONDERLAND* (October 2003)
MONSTERS, INC.
NIEA_7* (August 2003)
PARADISE KISS*
PARASYTE
PEACH GIRL
PEACH GIRL: CHANGE OF HEART*
PET SHOP OF HORRORS* (June 2003)
PLANET LADDER
PLANETS* (October 2003)
PRIEST
RAGNAROK
RAVE MASTER*
REAL BOUT HIGH SCHOOL*
REALITY CHECK
REBIRTH
REBOUND*
SABER MARIONETTE J* (July 2003)
SAILOR MOON
SAINT TAIL
SAMURAI DEEPER KYO* (June 2003)
SCRYED*
SHAOLIN SISTERS*
SHIRAHIME-SYO* (December 2003)
THE SKULL MAN*
SORCERER HUNTERS
TOKYO MEW MEW*
UNDER THE GLASS MOON (June 2003)
VAMPIRE GAME* (June 2003)
WILD ACT* (July 2003)
WISH*
X-DAY* (August 2003)
ZODIAC P.I.* (July 2003)

CINE-MANGA™

AKIRA*
CARDCAPTORS
JIMMY NEUTRON (COMING SOON)
KIM POSSIBLE
LIZZIE McGUIRE
SPONGEBOB SQUAREPANTS (COMING SOON)
SPY KIDS 2

NOVELS

SAILOR MOON
KARMA CLUB (COMING SOON)

TOKYOPOP KIDS

STRAY SHEEP (September 2003)

ART BOOKS

CARDCAPTOR SAKURA*
MAGIC KNIGHT RAYEARTH*

ANIME GUIDES

GUNDAM TECHNICAL MANUALS
COWBOY BEBOP
SAILOR MOON SCOUT GUIDES

I.N.V.U.

by
Kim Kang Won

Los Angeles • Tokyo

Translator - Lauren Na
English Adaptation - Mark Paniccia
Retouch - Milissa Hackett
Lettering - Tomas Montalvo-Lagos & Mark Paniccia
Graphic Design - Mark Paniccia
Cover Layout - Gary Shum

Editor - Mark Paniccia
Managing Editor - Jill Freshney
Production Manager - Jennifer Miller
Art Director - Matthew Alford
Editorial Director - Jeremy Ross
VP of Production & Manufacturing - Ron Klamert
President & C.O.O. - John Parker
Publisher & C.E.O. - Stuart Levy

Email: editor@TOKYOPOP.com
Come visit us online at www.TOKYOPOP.com

A ⚙️ TOKYOPOP® Manga
TOKYOPOP® is an imprint of Mixx Entertainment Inc.
5900 Wilshire Blvd. Suite 2000, Los Angeles, CA 90036

ISBN: 1-59182-002-2

First TOKYOPOP® printing: Feb 2003

10 9 8 7 6 5 4 3 2 1
Printed in Canada

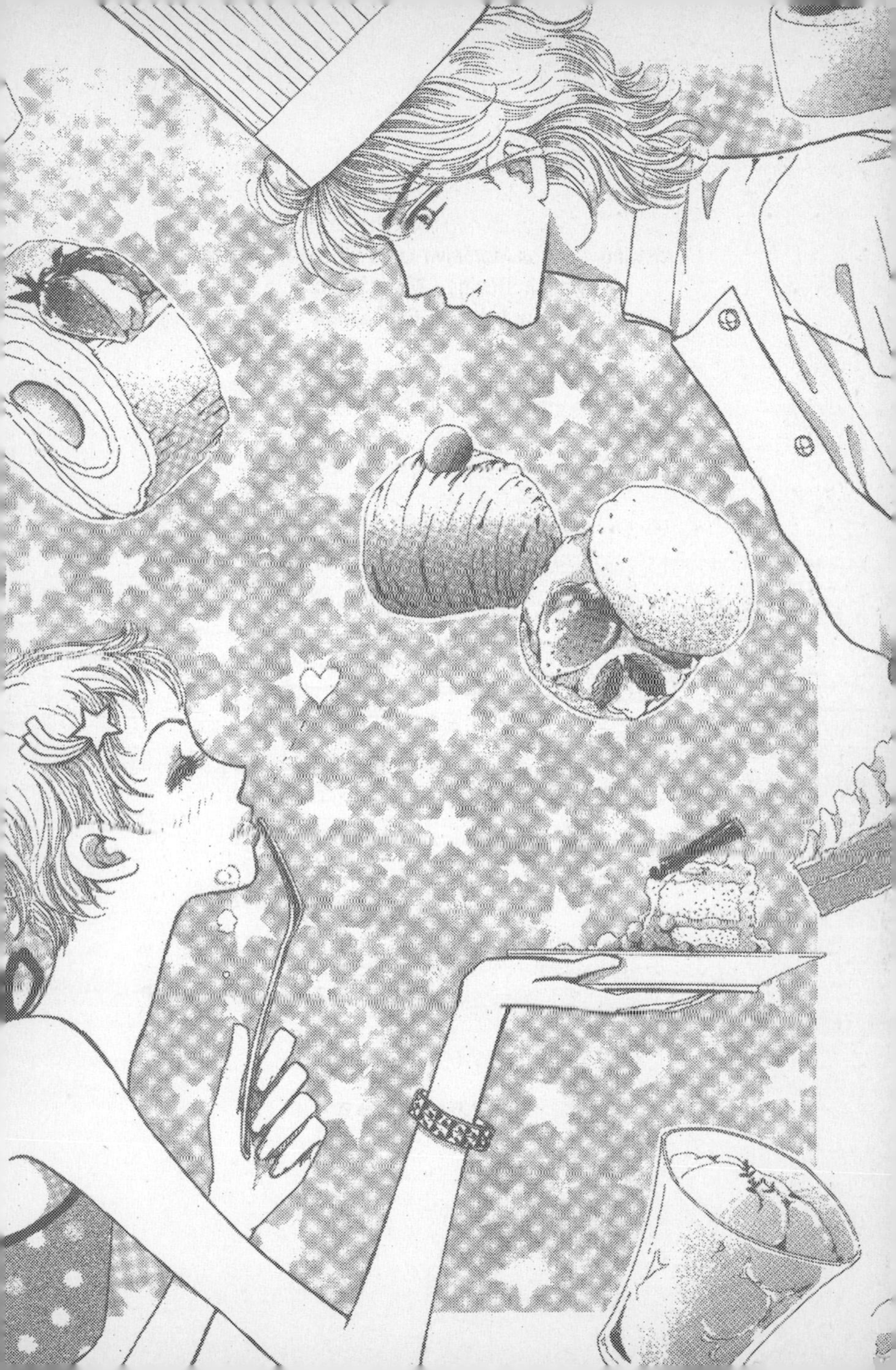

THE STORY THUS FAR

Sey Hong is a skittish teenage girl whose mom—a somewhat famous writer— has left her in the care of an old friend while travelling abroad. Now living in what appears to be the perfect family, Sey finds out that Terry, the son of the house, is really Hali, a daughter. Hali impersonates her dead brother to keep her mom from suffering a mental breakdown. Things continue to get more complicated as Sey finds out that Hali is in love with the same teacher that Sey has had a crush on for years. The flirtatious Rea Yoo's boyfriend, Siho Lee, finds himself intrigued with Sey and helps get her a part-time job at a gas station. He quickly ends things with Rea but begins to get suspiciuos of Sey's relationship with Hajun Cho.

OUR CHARACTERS

SEY HONG: A rather cheerful girl who grew up only with her mother. Sey has endured a lot of emotional heartache due to her mother's liberal, free-spirited, uninhibited lifestyle. With her mother's sudden departure to Italy, Sey, living with Hali, is encountering endless problems. She's had a crush on Hajun Cho, her homeroom teacher and childhood friend, but with the arrival of Siho it looks as if there might be a change.

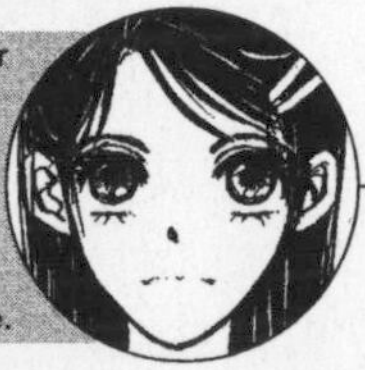

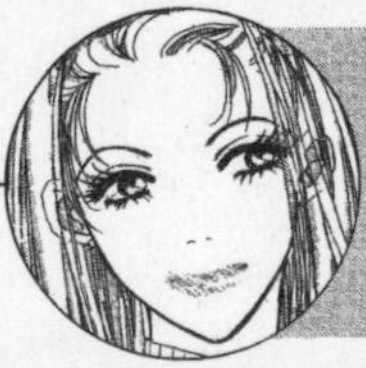

REA YOO: Sey's friend. Pretty, slim and a big-time flirt, though she is steadfast in what she wants. Rea's dream is to make it big in the entertainment world. At the moment, she is modeling for magazines. She was dating Siho for a little while, but once she realized that Siho was interested in Sey, she made a clean break! For now, she is putting boys aside and focusing on molding her career.

HALI KANG: After an accident that took the life of her brother Terry, she has taken on the role of the lost son to keep her mother from going into shock. Although she's a little tight-lipped because of her pride, more than anyone else, she is fragile and sensitive. While she was in Junior high, she confessed her love to her tutor, Hajun Cho, who refused her advances. But no matter what anyone says, her love is real!

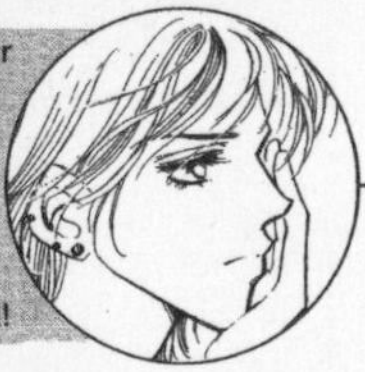

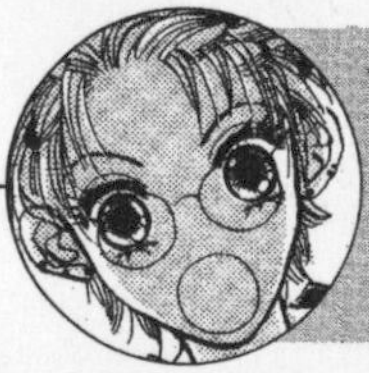

JEA EUN: Sey's very best friend. She likes comic books and Cosplay, and has a carefree and happy personality. After meeting Simon, who was working part time at a cake shop, she's been ditching her after-school tutorials to take lessons from him at the Cultural Center. She listens to Sey's problems and is very understanding. After hearing about Hali from Sey, she has become interested in Hali!

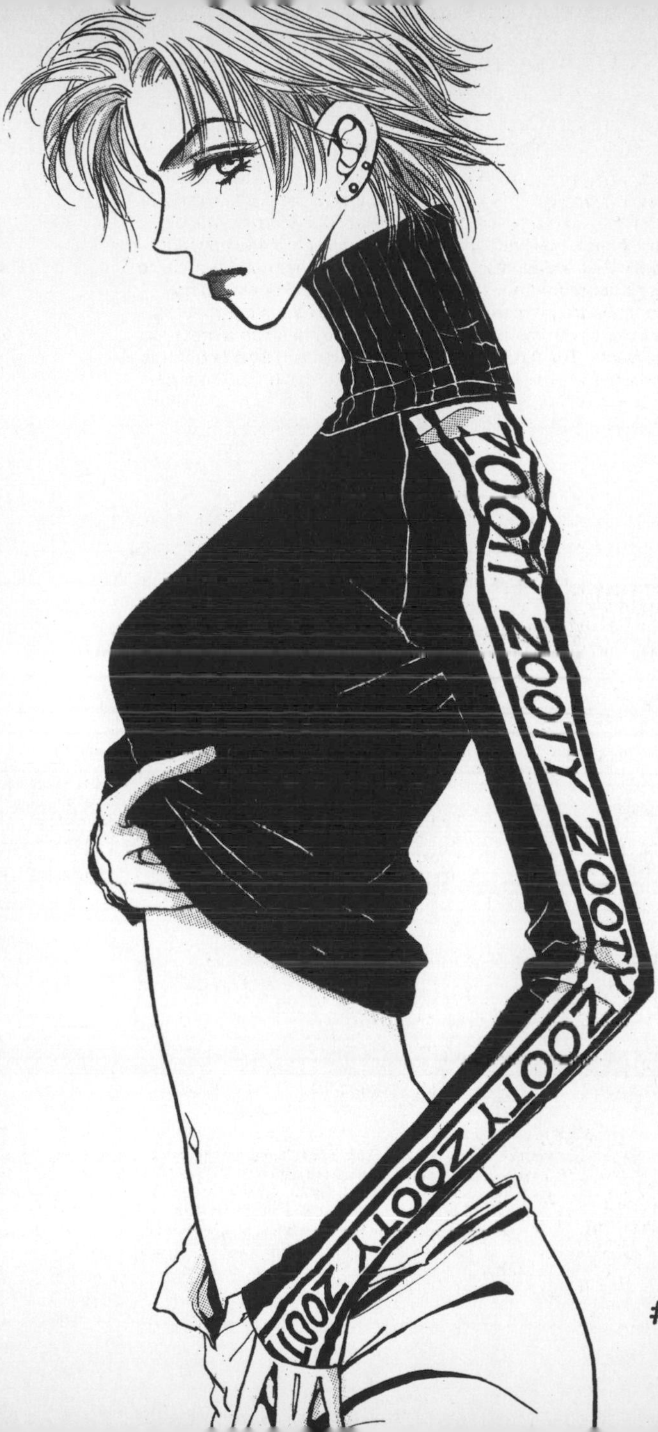
ZOOTY ZOOTY ZOOTY ZOOTY ZOOTY

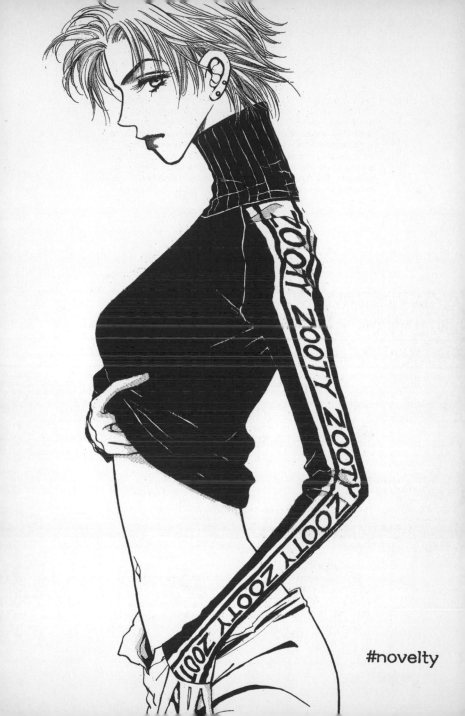

#novelty

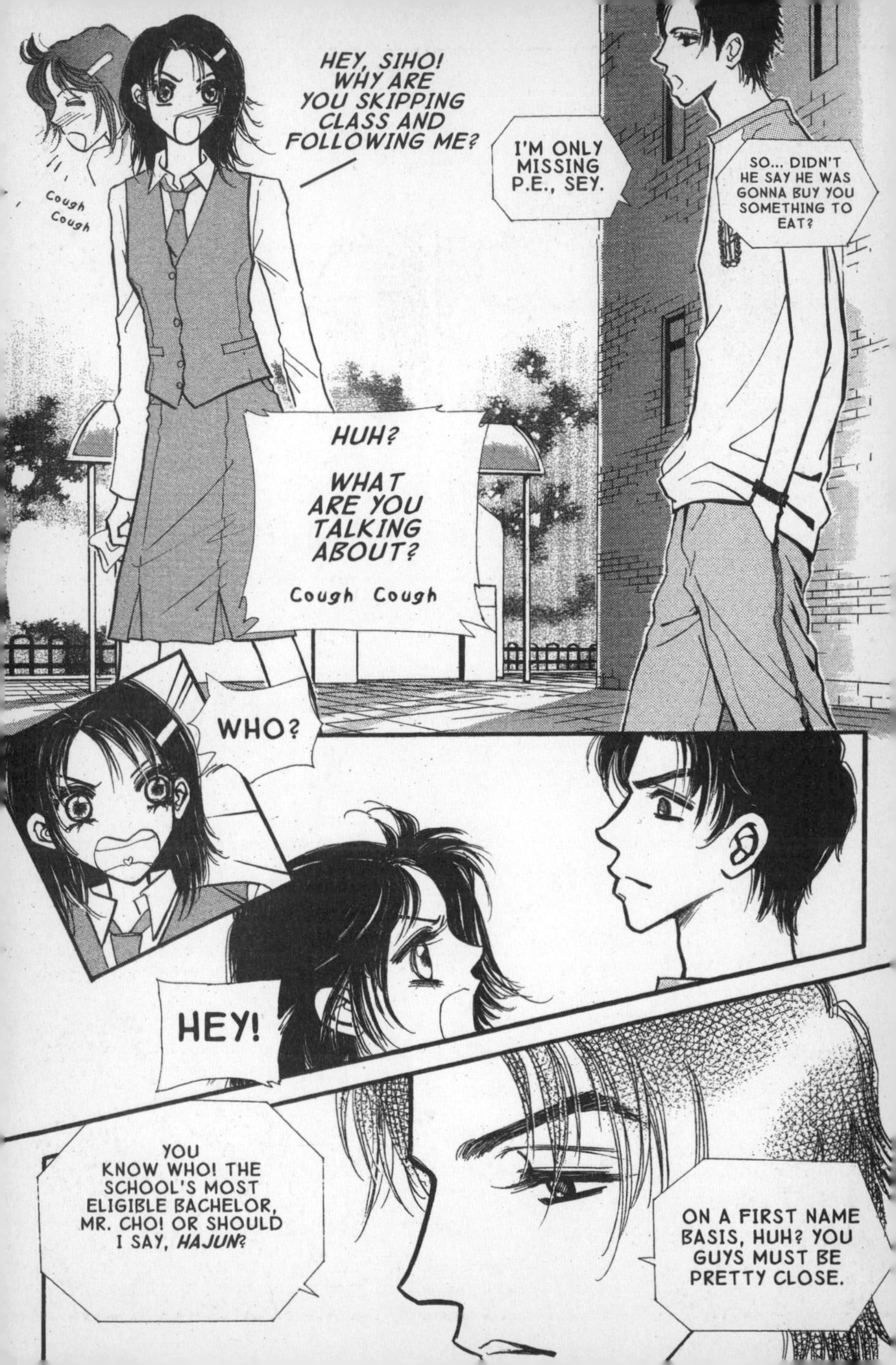
HEY, SIHO! WHY ARE YOU SKIPPING CLASS AND FOLLOWING ME?
Cough Cough
I'M ONLY MISSING P.E., SEY.
SO... DIDN'T HE SAY HE WAS GONNA BUY YOU SOMETHING TO EAT?
HUH?
WHAT ARE YOU TALKING ABOUT?
Cough Cough
WHO?
HEY!
YOU KNOW WHO! THE SCHOOL'S MOST ELIGIBLE BACHELOR, MR. CHO! OR SHOULD I SAY, *HAJUN*?
ON A FIRST NAME BASIS, HUH? YOU GUYS MUST BE PRETTY CLOSE.

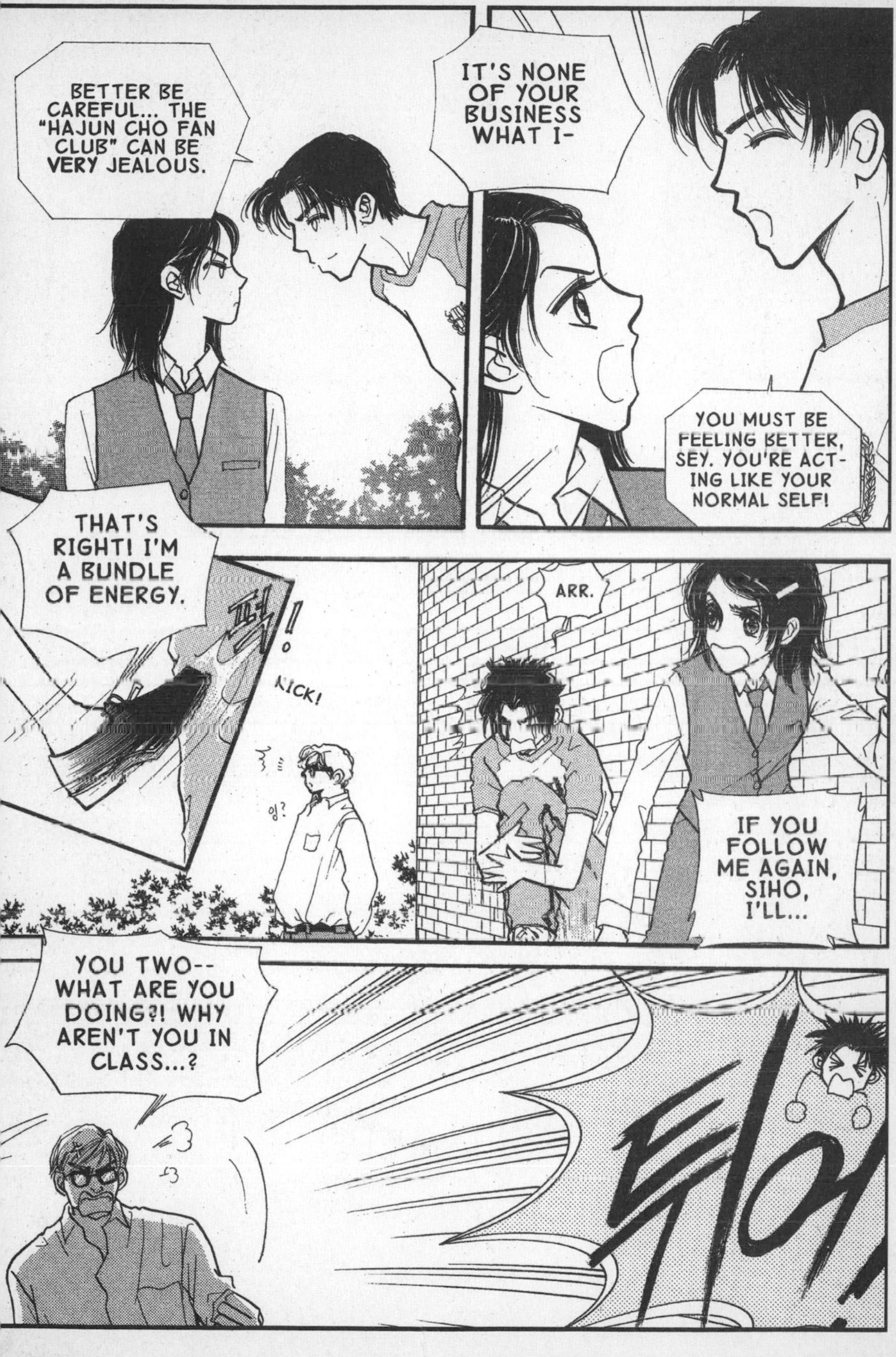
BETTER BE CAREFUL... THE "HAJUN CHO FAN CLUB" CAN BE VERY JEALOUS.
IT'S NONE OF YOUR BUSINESS WHAT I-
YOU MUST BE FEELING BETTER, SEY. YOU'RE ACT-ING LIKE YOUR NORMAL SELF!
THAT'S RIGHT! I'M A BUNDLE OF ENERGY.
KICK!
잉?
ARR.
IF YOU FOLLOW ME AGAIN, SIHO, I'LL...
YOU TWO-- WHAT ARE YOU DOING?! WHY AREN'T YOU IN CLASS...?

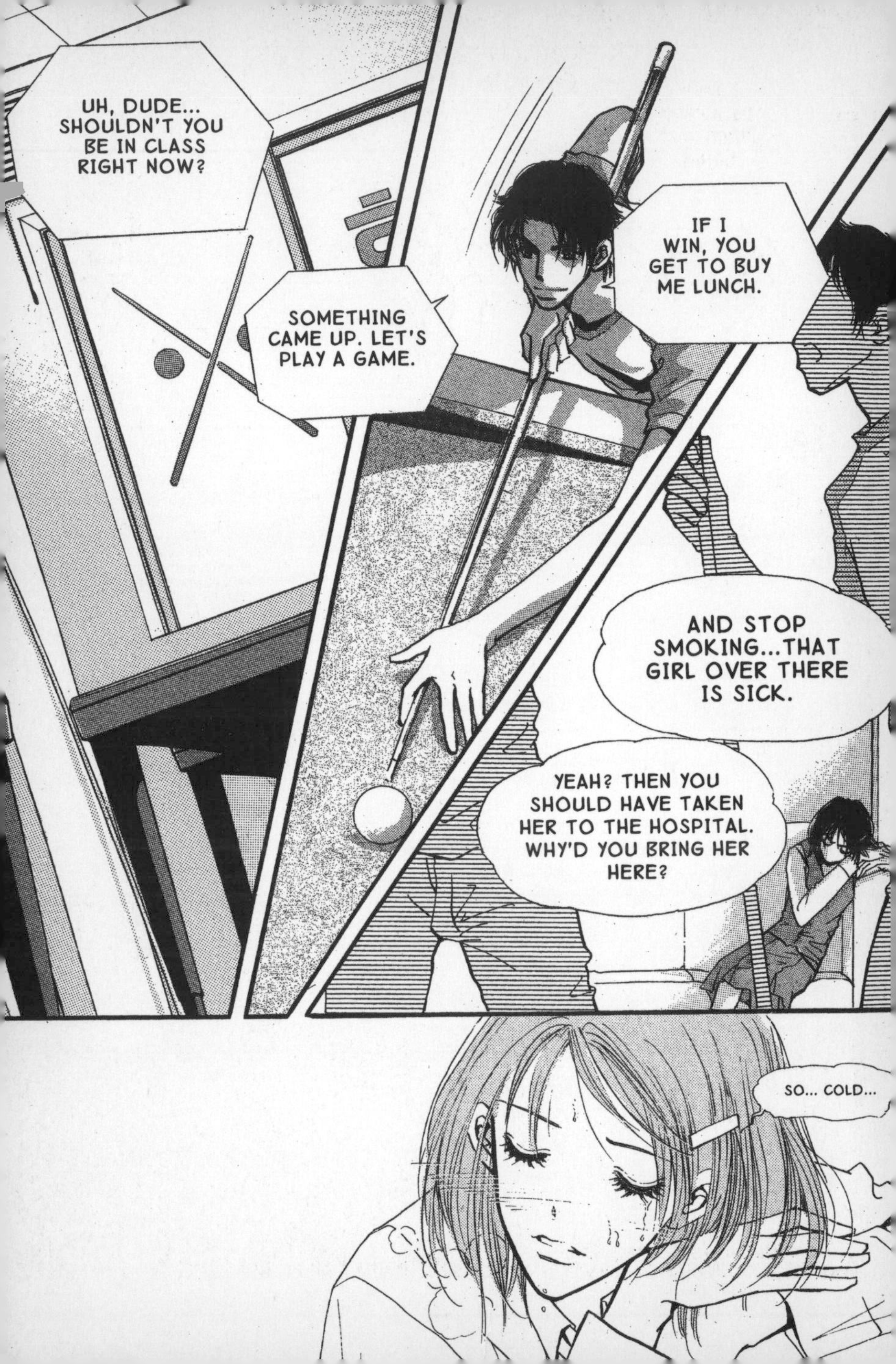
UH, DUDE... SHOULDN'T YOU BE IN CLASS RIGHT NOW?
SOMETHING CAME UP. LET'S PLAY A GAME.
IF I WIN, YOU GET TO BUY ME LUNCH.
AND STOP SMOKING...THAT GIRL OVER THERE IS SICK.
YEAH? THEN YOU SHOULD HAVE TAKEN HER TO THE HOSPITAL. WHY'D YOU BRING HER HERE?
SO... COLD...

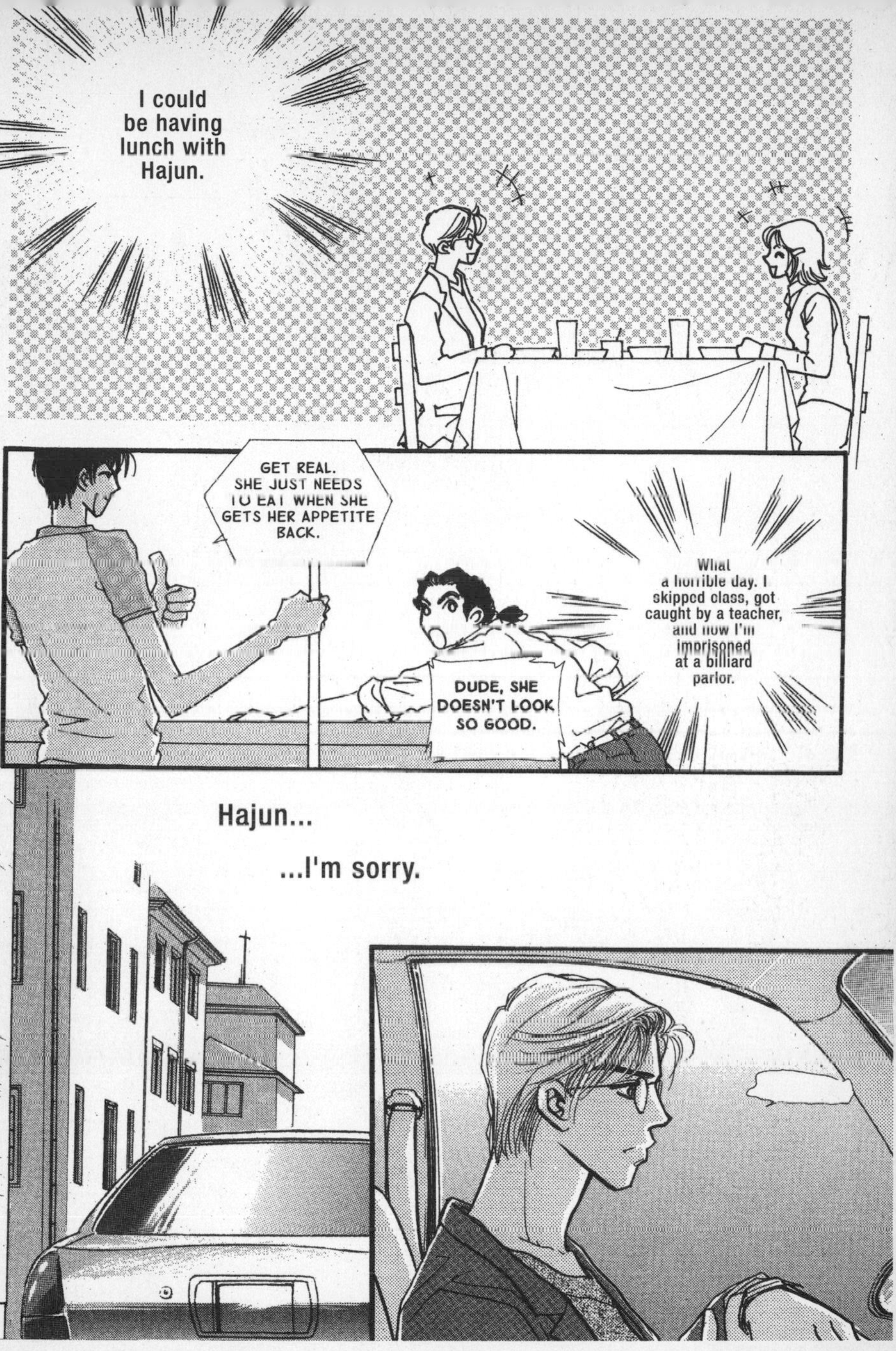
I could be having lunch with Hajun.
GET REAL. SHE JUST NEEDS TO EAT WHEN SHE GETS HER APPETITE BACK.
DUDE, SHE DOESN'T LOOK SO GOOD.
What a horrible day. I skipped class, got caught by a teacher, and now I'm imprisoned at a billiard parlor.
Hajun...
...I'm sorry.

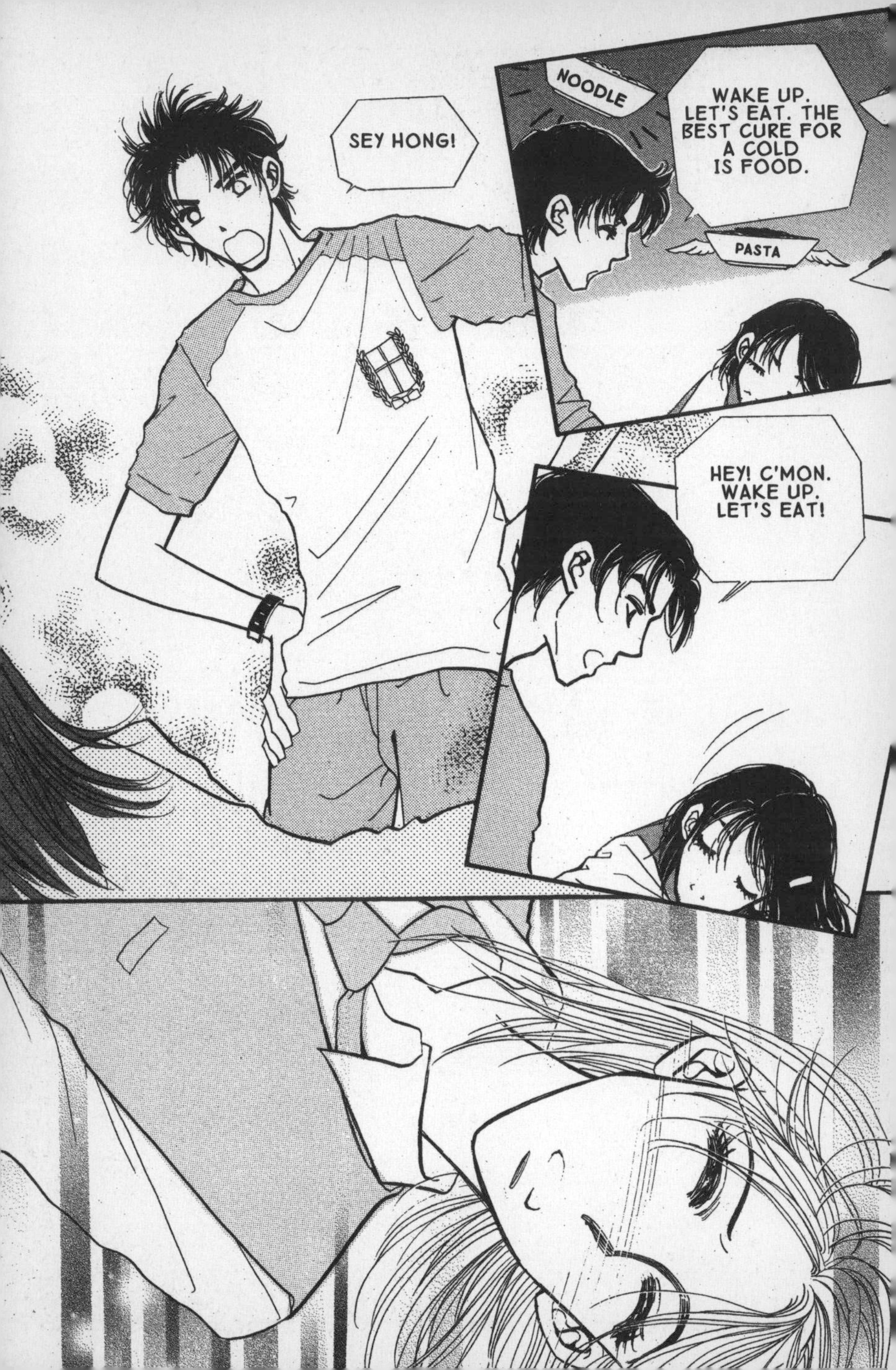
SEY HONG!
NOODLE
WAKE UP. LET'S EAT. THE BEST CURE FOR A COLD IS FOOD.
PASTA
HEY! C'MON. WAKE UP. LET'S EAT!

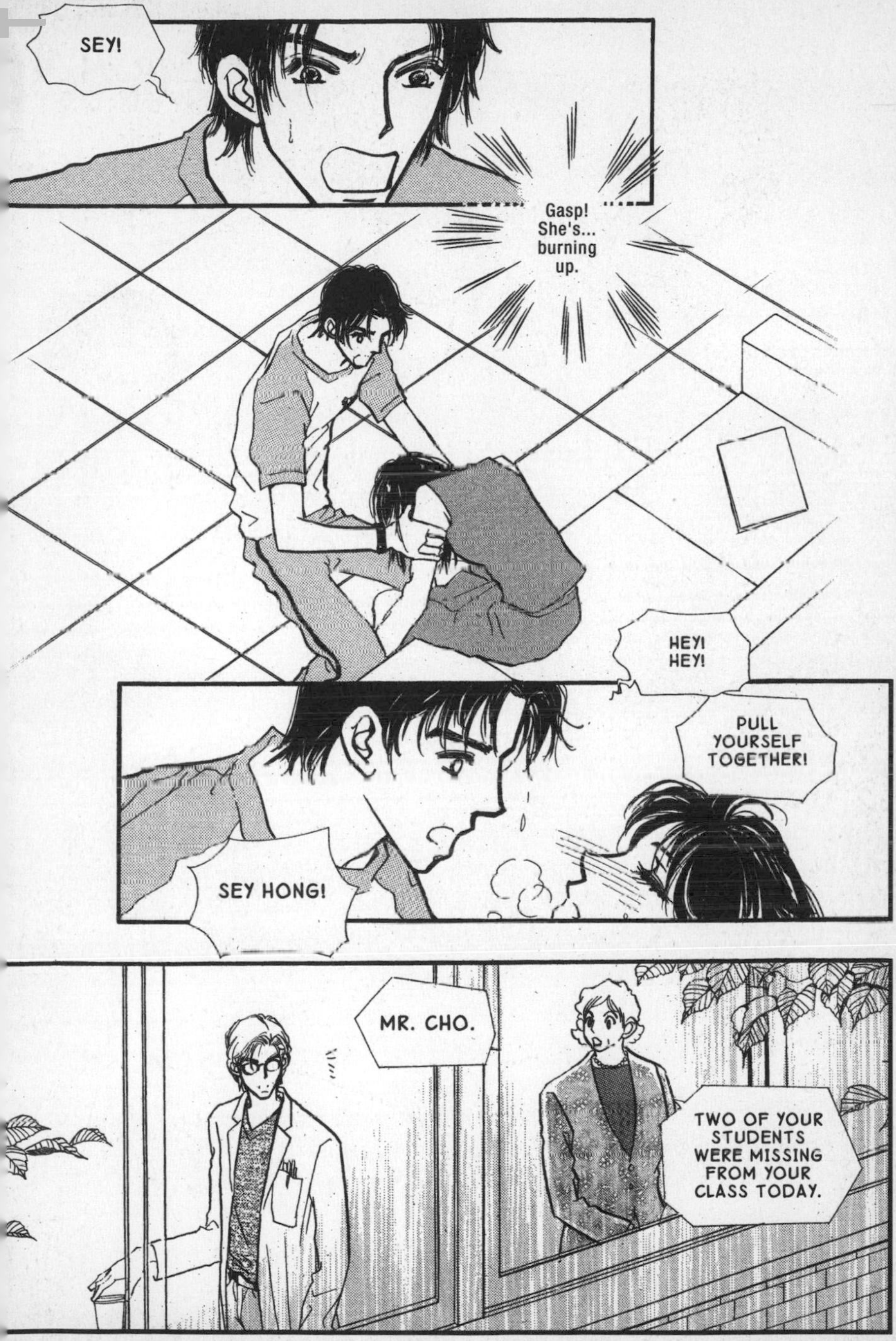
SEY!
Gasp! She's... burning up.
HEY! HEY!
PULL YOURSELF TOGETHER!
SEY HONG!
MR. CHO.
TWO OF YOUR STUDENTS WERE MISSING FROM YOUR CLASS TODAY.

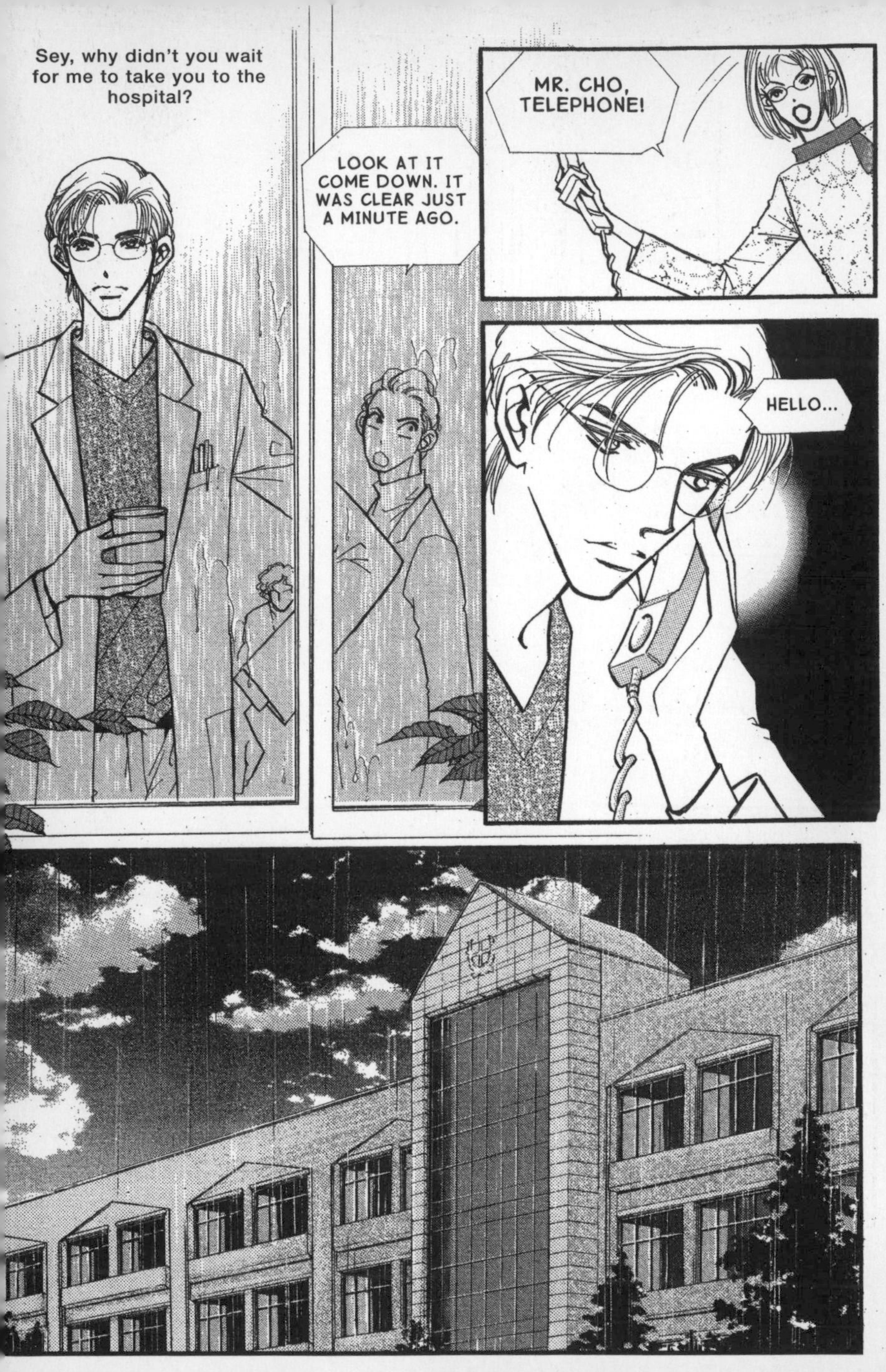
Sey, why didn't you wait for me to take you to the hospital?
LOOK AT IT COME DOWN. IT WAS CLEAR JUST A MINUTE AGO.
MR. CHO, TELEPHONE!
HELLO...

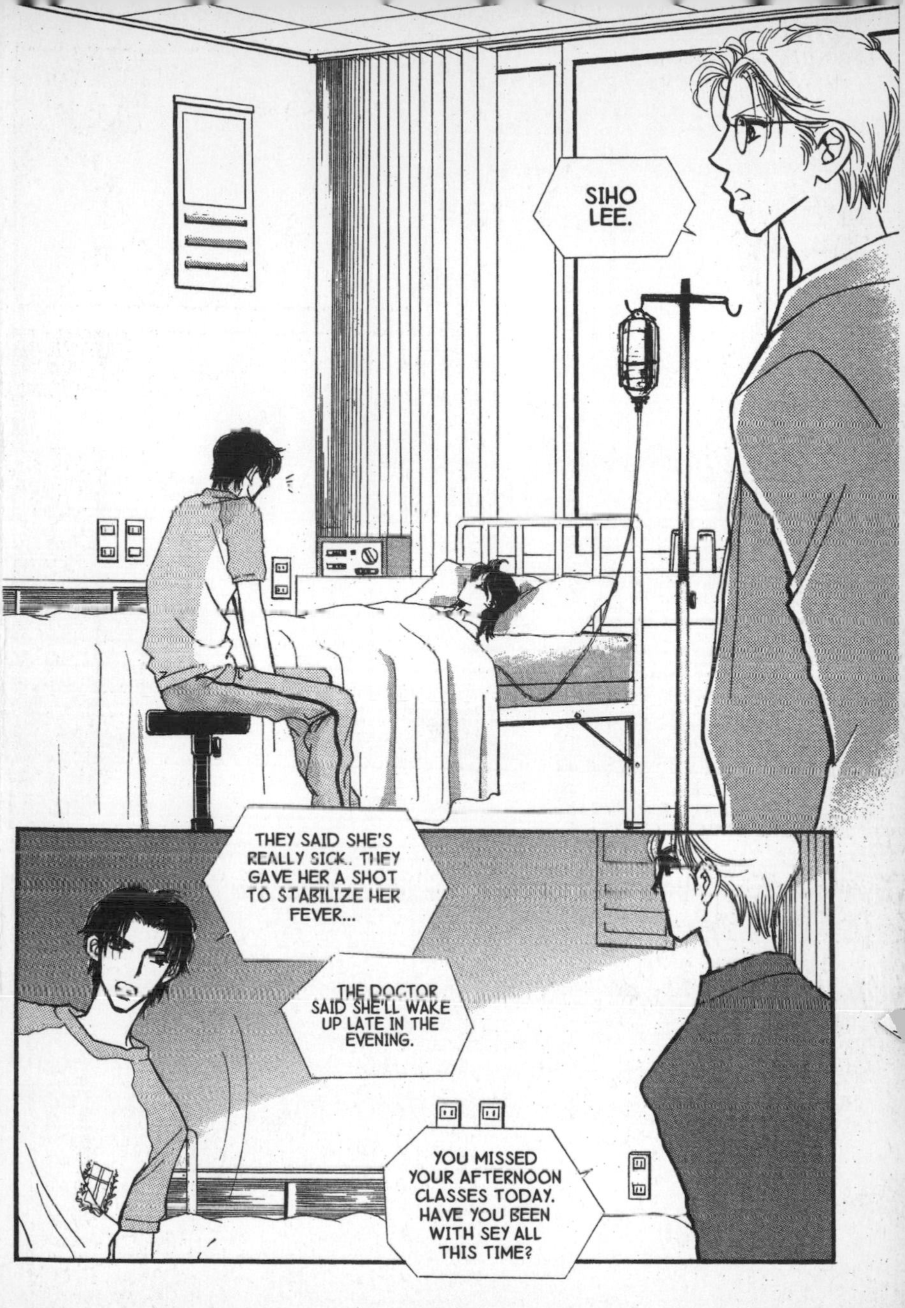

SIHO LEE.
THEY SAID SHE'S REALLY SICK. THEY GAVE HER A SHOT TO STABILIZE HER FEVER...
THE DOCTOR SAID SHE'LL WAKE UP LATE IN THE EVENING.
YOU MISSED YOUR AFTERNOON CLASSES TODAY. HAVE YOU BEEN WITH SEY ALL THIS TIME?

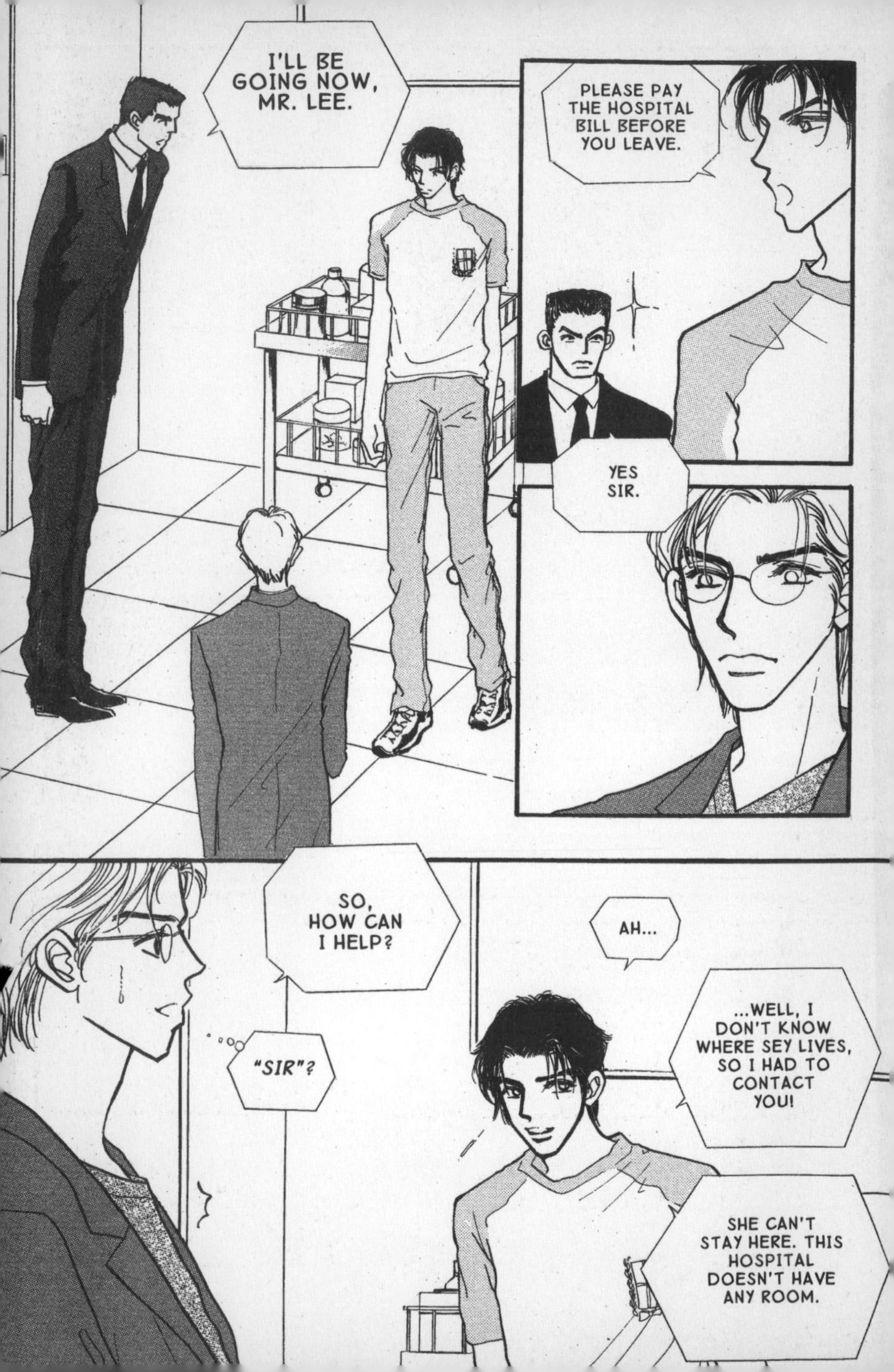
I'LL BE GOING NOW, MR. LEE.
PLEASE PAY THE HOSPITAL BILL BEFORE YOU LEAVE.
YES SIR.
SO, HOW CAN I HELP?
"SIR"?
AH...
...WELL, I DON'T KNOW WHERE SEY LIVES, SO I HAD TO CONTACT YOU!
SHE CAN'T STAY HERE. THIS HOSPITAL DOESN'T HAVE ANY ROOM.

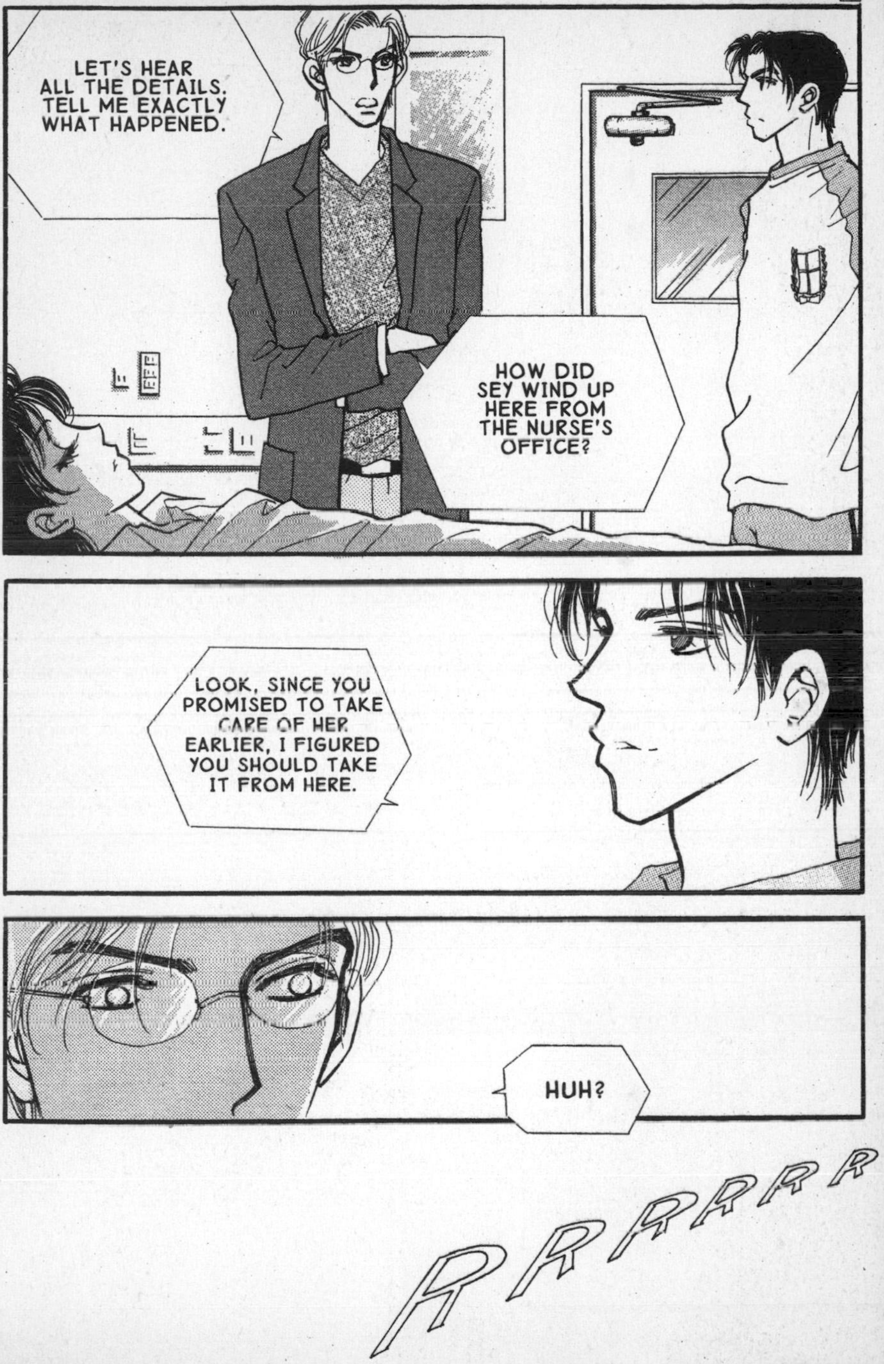
LET'S HEAR ALL THE DETAILS. TELL ME EXACTLY WHAT HAPPENED.
HOW DID SEY WIND UP HERE FROM THE NURSE'S OFFICE?
LOOK, SINCE YOU PROMISED TO TAKE CARE OF HER EARLIER, I FIGURED YOU SHOULD TAKE IT FROM HERE.
HUH?
RRRRRRR

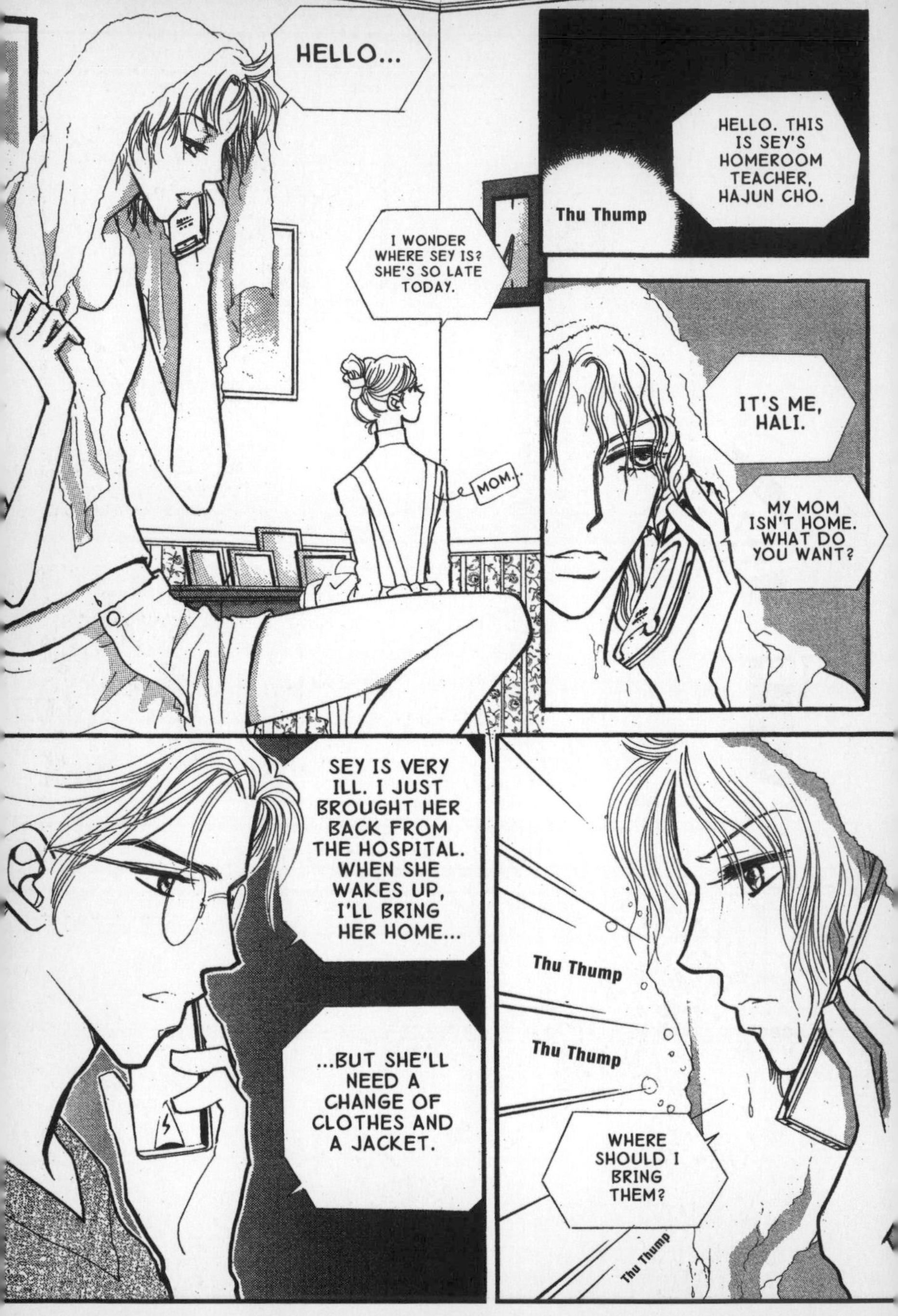
HELLO...
I WONDER WHERE SEY IS? SHE'S SO LATE TODAY.
MOM...
Thu Thump
HELLO. THIS IS SEY'S HOMEROOM TEACHER, HAJUN CHO.
IT'S ME, HALI.
MY MOM ISN'T HOME. WHAT DO YOU WANT?
SEY IS VERY ILL. I JUST BROUGHT HER BACK FROM THE HOSPITAL. WHEN SHE WAKES UP, I'LL BRING HER HOME...
...BUT SHE'LL NEED A CHANGE OF CLOTHES AND A JACKET.
Thu Thump
Thu Thump
WHERE SHOULD I BRING THEM?
Thu Thump

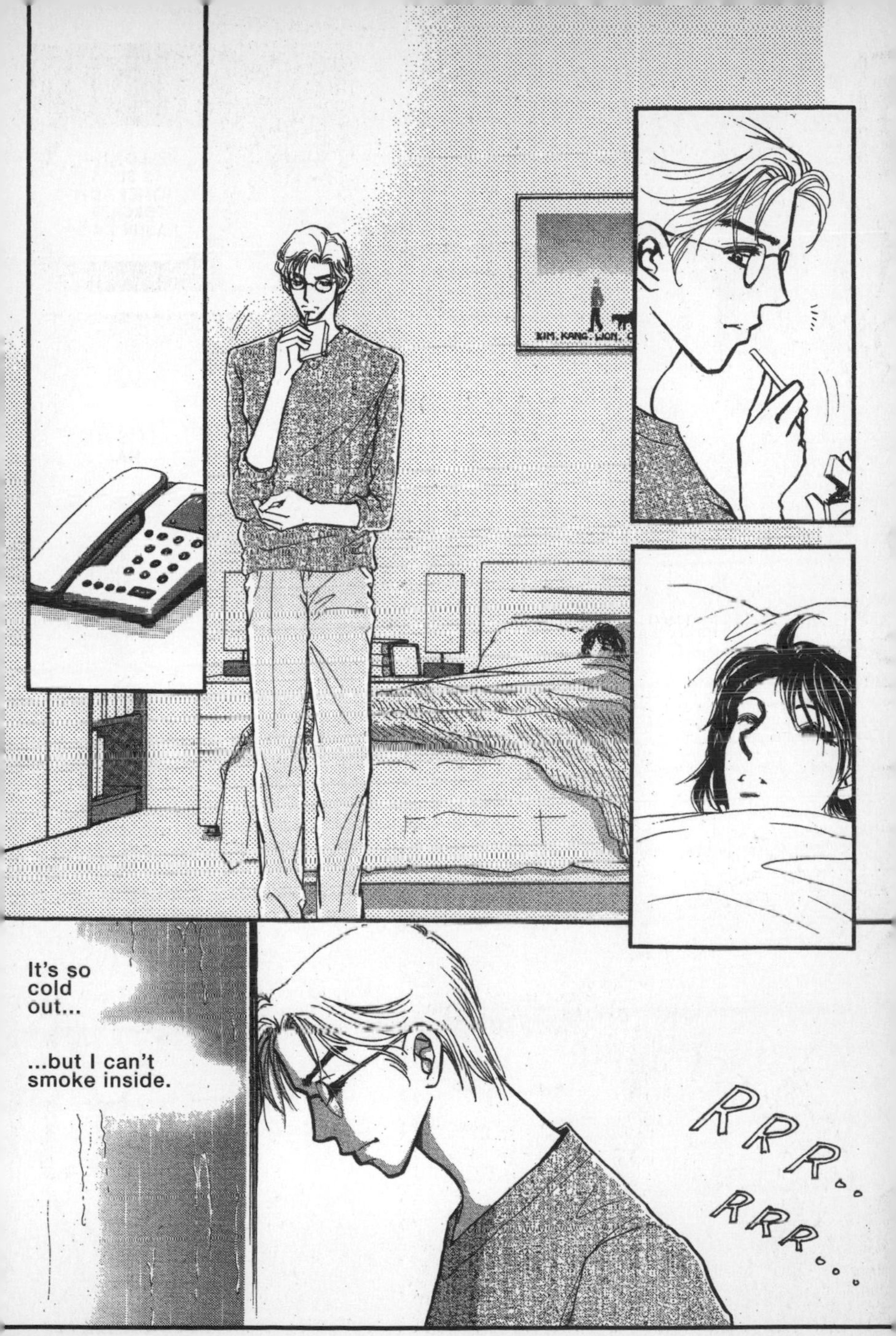
KIM. KANG. WON.
It's so cold out...
...but I can't smoke inside.
RRR...
RRR...

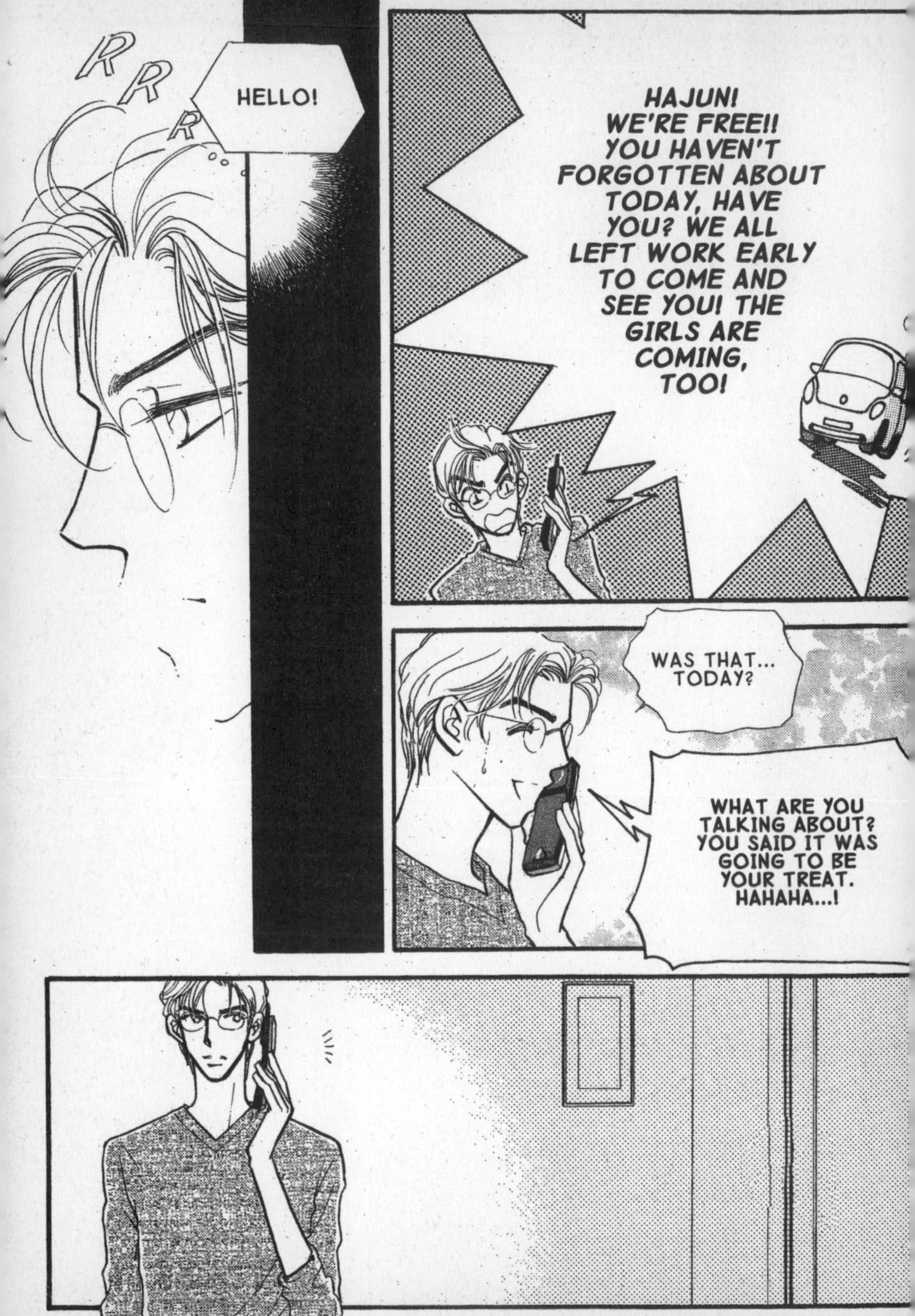
RRR
HELLO!
HAJUN! WE'RE FREE!! YOU HAVEN'T FORGOTTEN ABOUT TODAY, HAVE YOU? WE ALL LEFT WORK EARLY TO COME AND SEE YOU! THE GIRLS ARE COMING, TOO!
WAS THAT... TODAY?
WHAT ARE YOU TALKING ABOUT? YOU SAID IT WAS GOING TO BE YOUR TREAT. HAHAHA...!

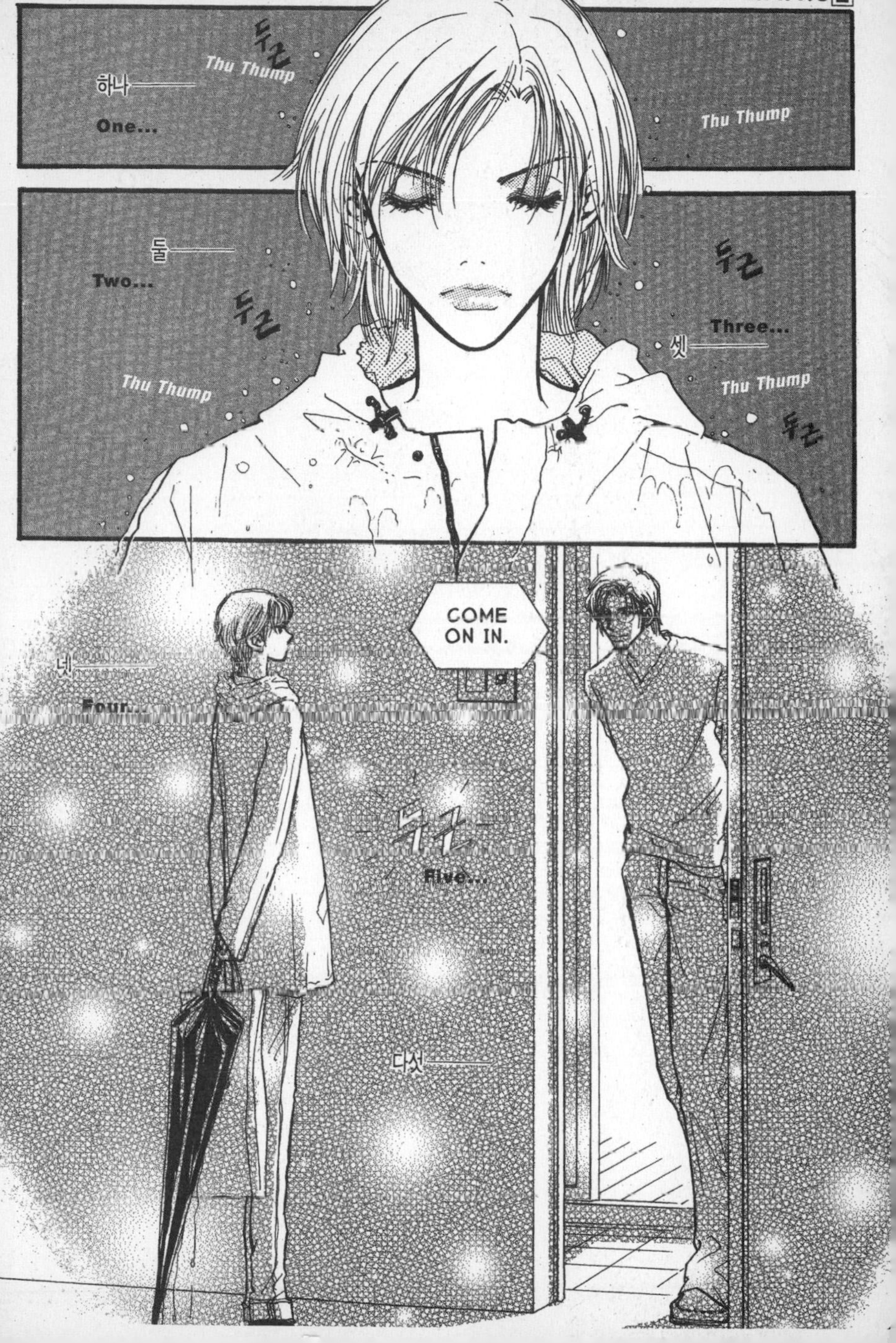
두근
Thu Thump
하나
One...
Thu Thump
둘
Two...
두근
Thu Thump
두근
Three...
셋
Thu Thump
두근
넷
Four...
COME ON IN.
두근
Five...
다섯

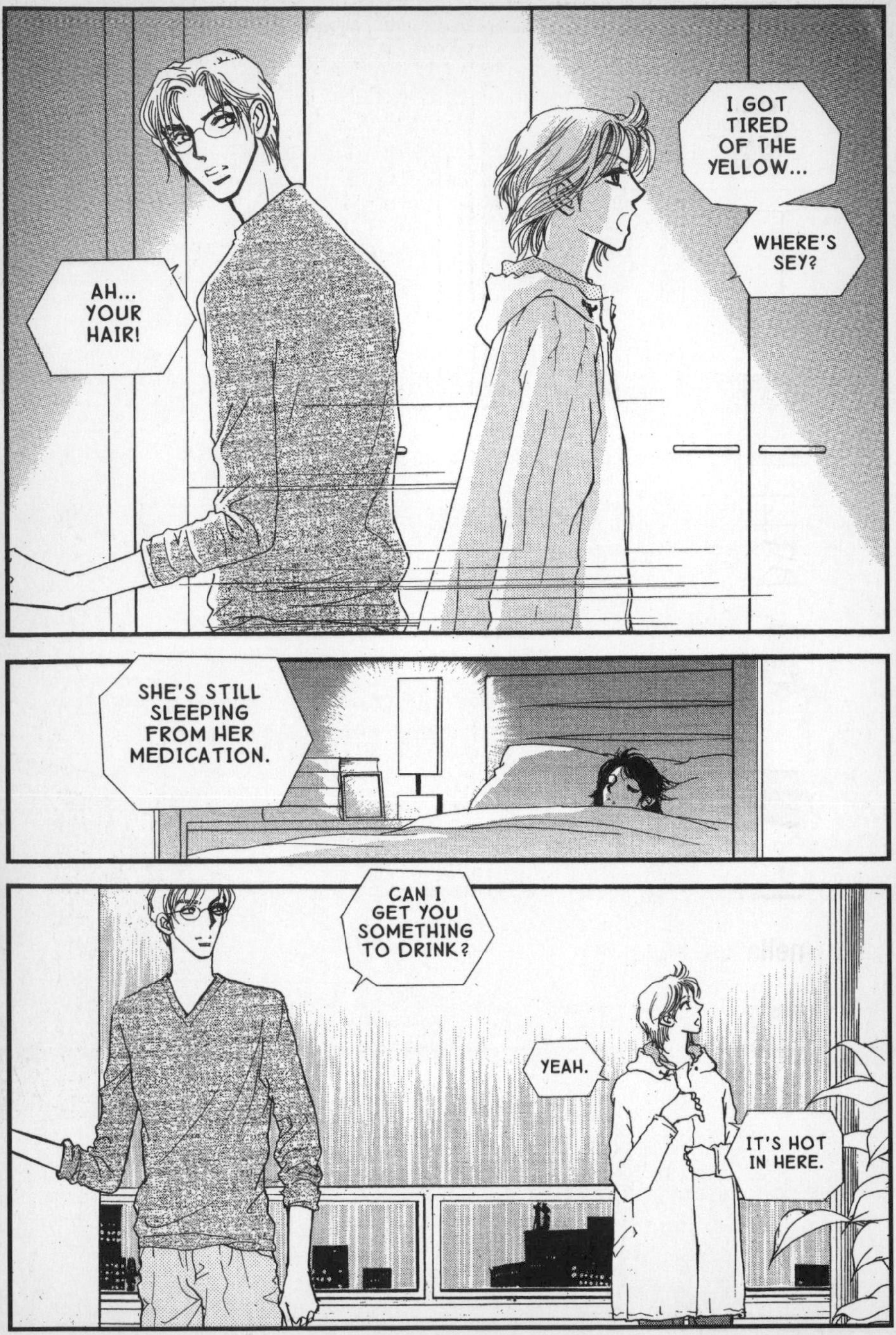
AH... YOUR HAIR!
I GOT TIRED OF THE YELLOW...
WHERE'S SEY?
SHE'S STILL SLEEPING FROM HER MEDICATION.
CAN I GET YOU SOMETHING TO DRINK?
YEAH.
IT'S HOT IN HERE.

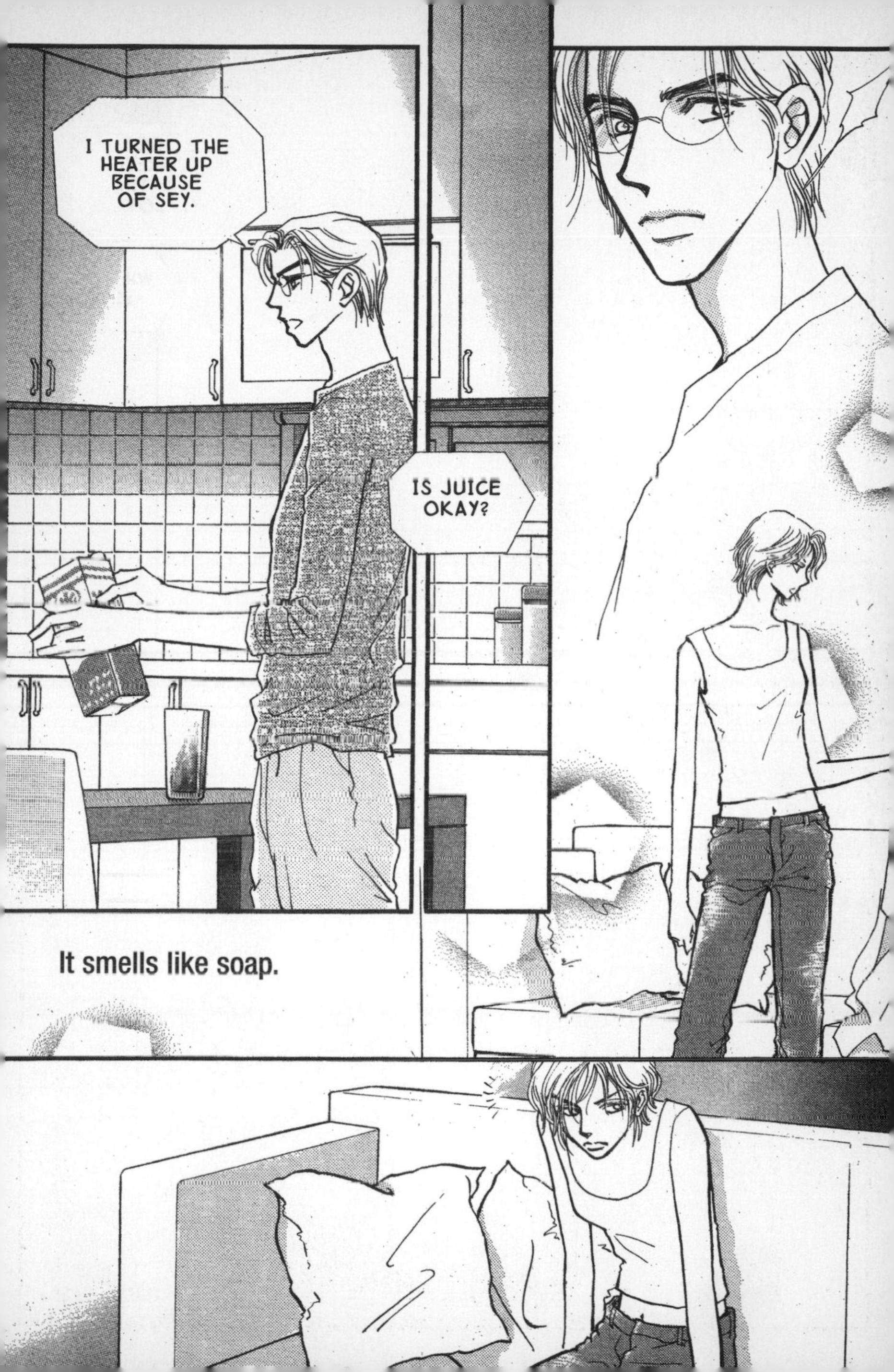
I TURNED THE HEATER UP BECAUSE OF SEY.
IS JUICE OKAY?
It smells like soap.

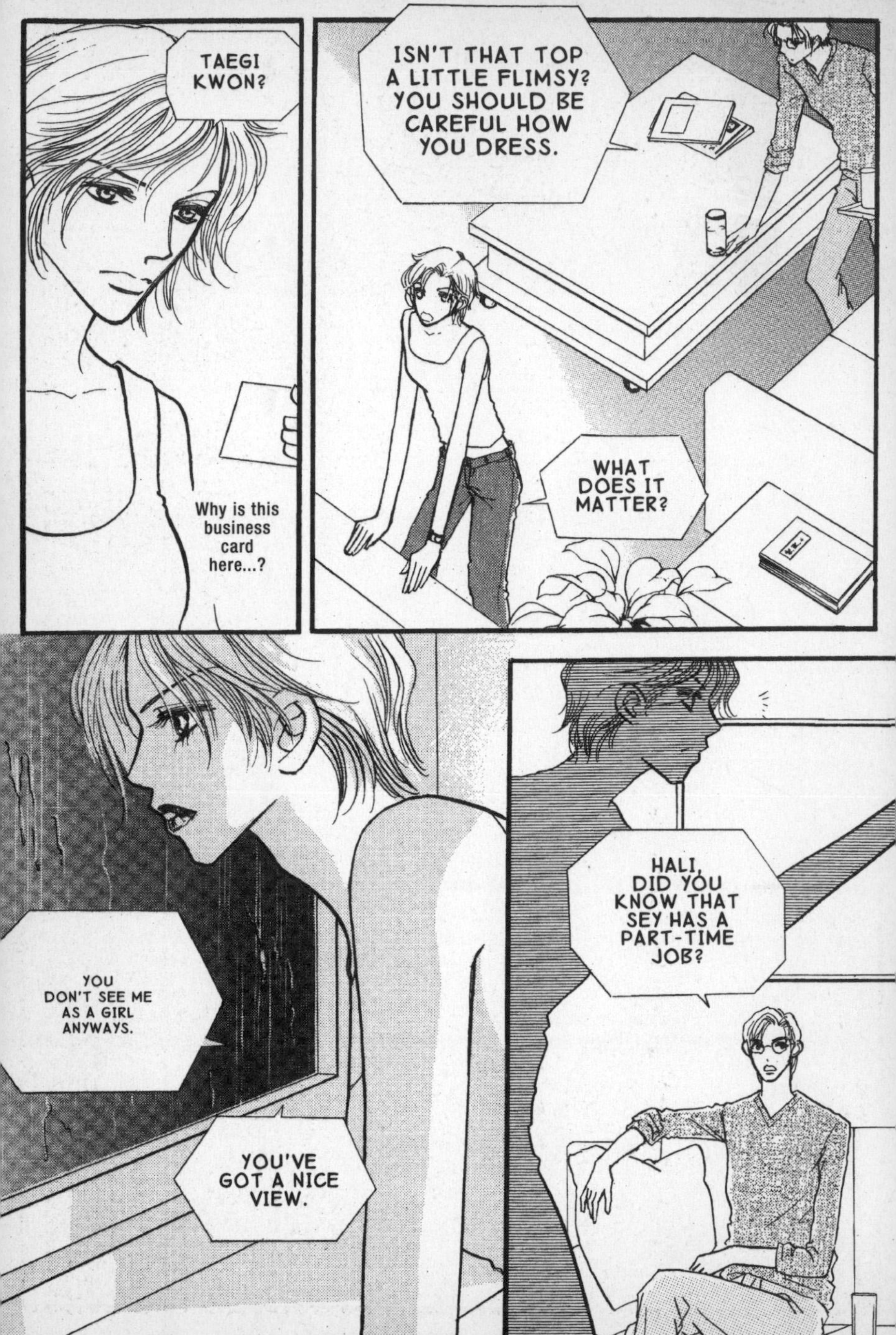
TAEGI KWON?
Why is this business card here...?
ISN'T THAT TOP A LITTLE FLIMSY? YOU SHOULD BE CAREFUL HOW YOU DRESS.
WHAT DOES IT MATTER?
YOU DON'T SEE ME AS A GIRL ANYWAYS.
YOU'VE GOT A NICE VIEW.
HALI, DID YOU KNOW THAT SEY HAS A PART-TIME JOB?

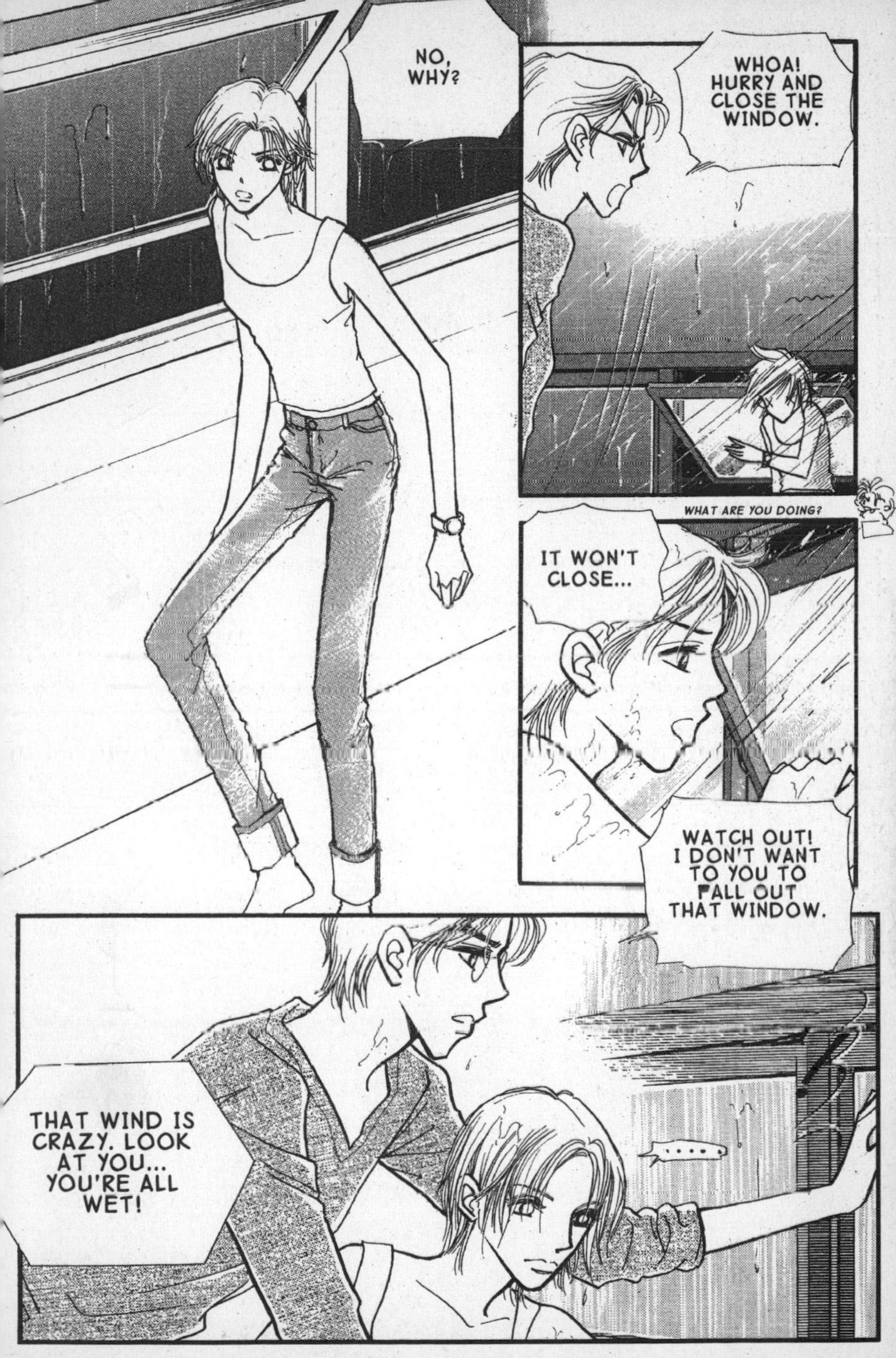
NO, WHY?
WHOA! HURRY AND CLOSE THE WINDOW.
WHAT ARE YOU DOING?
IT WON'T CLOSE...
WATCH OUT! I DON'T WANT TO YOU TO FALL OUT THAT WINDOW.
THAT WIND IS CRAZY. LOOK AT YOU... YOU'RE ALL WET!
.....

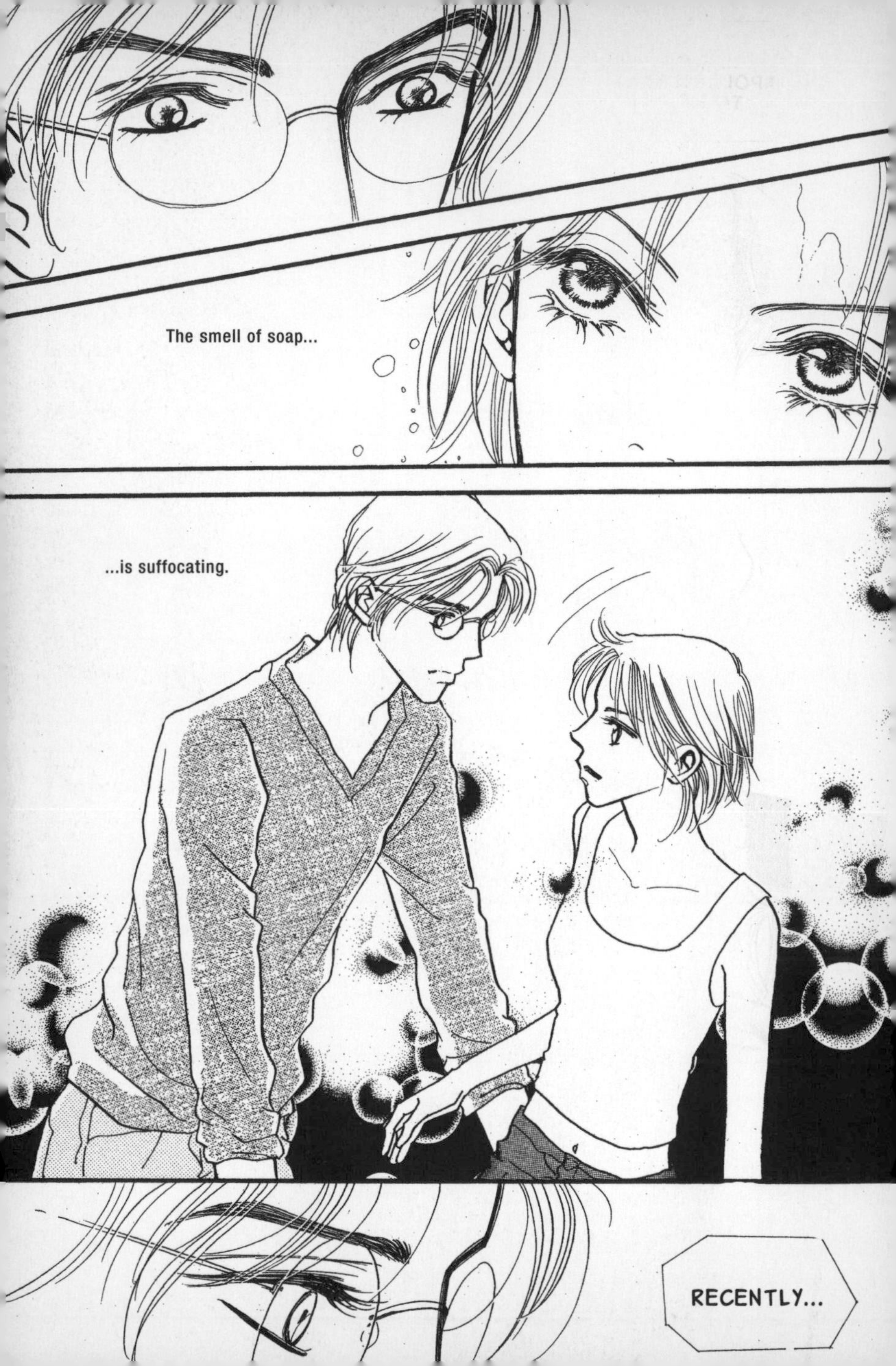
The smell of soap...
...is suffocating.
RECENTLY...

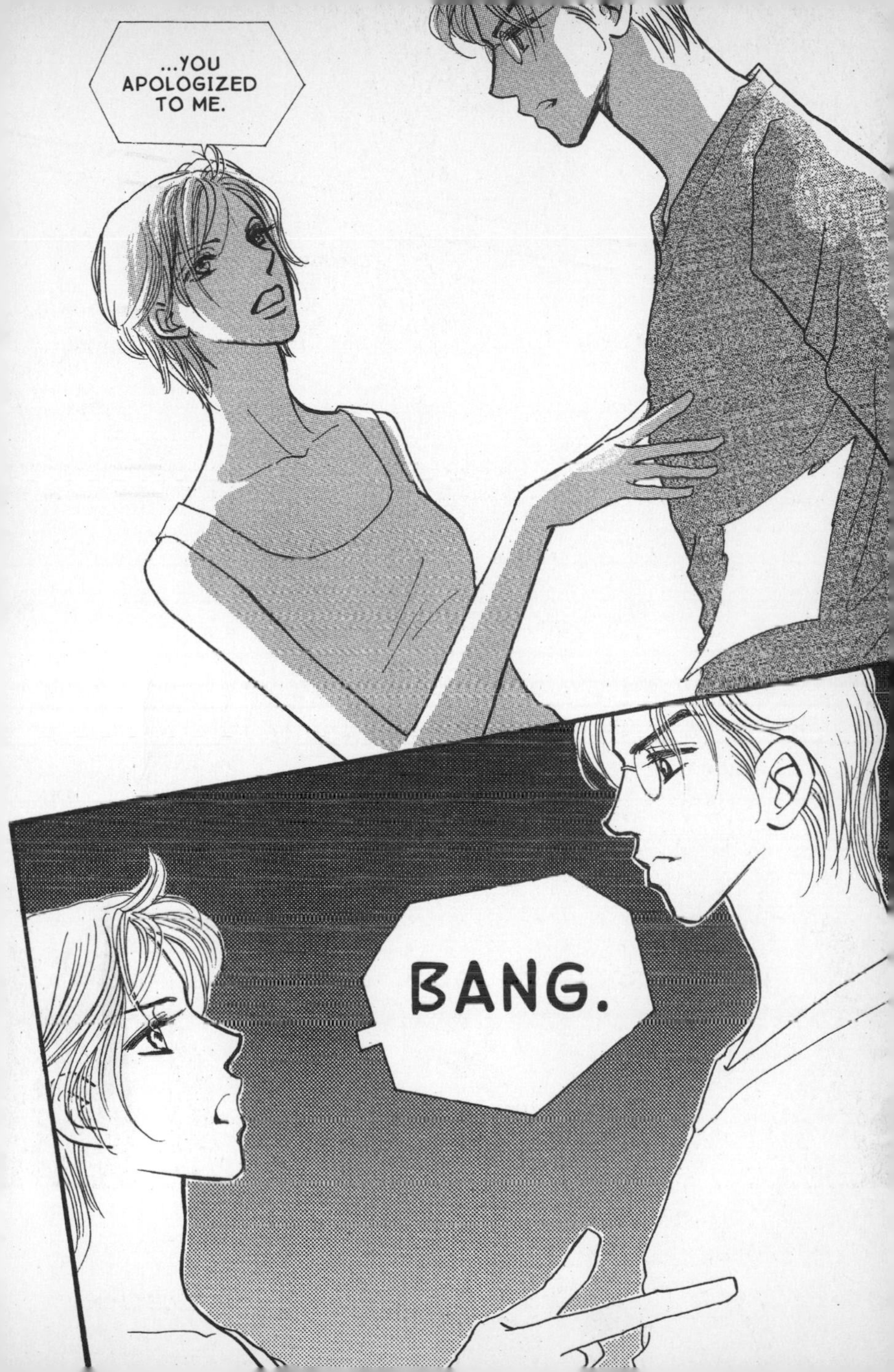
...YOU APOLOGIZED TO ME.
BANG.

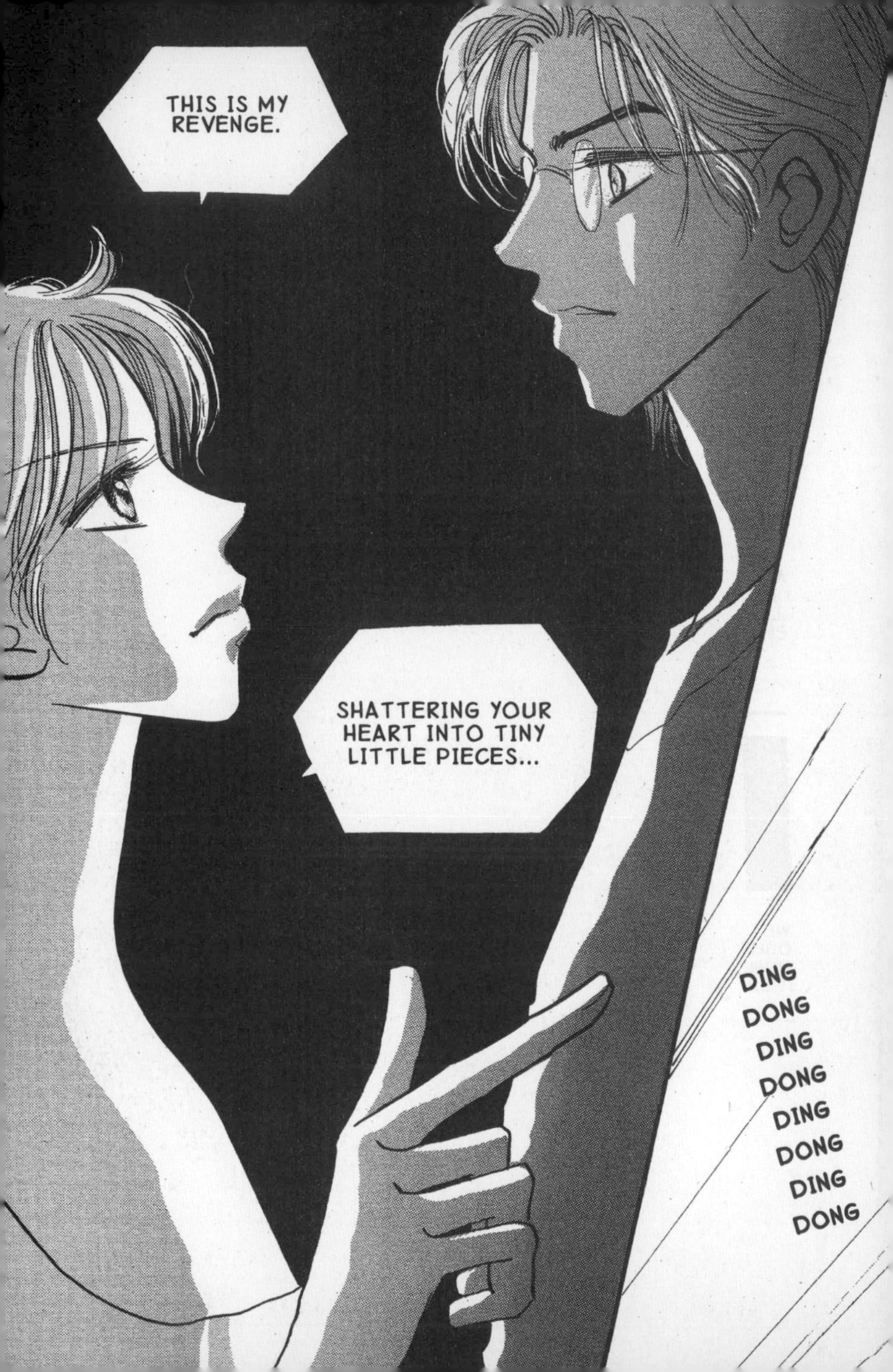
THIS IS MY REVENGE.
SHATTERING YOUR HEART INTO TINY LITTLE PIECES...
DING DONG DING DONG DING DONG DING DONG

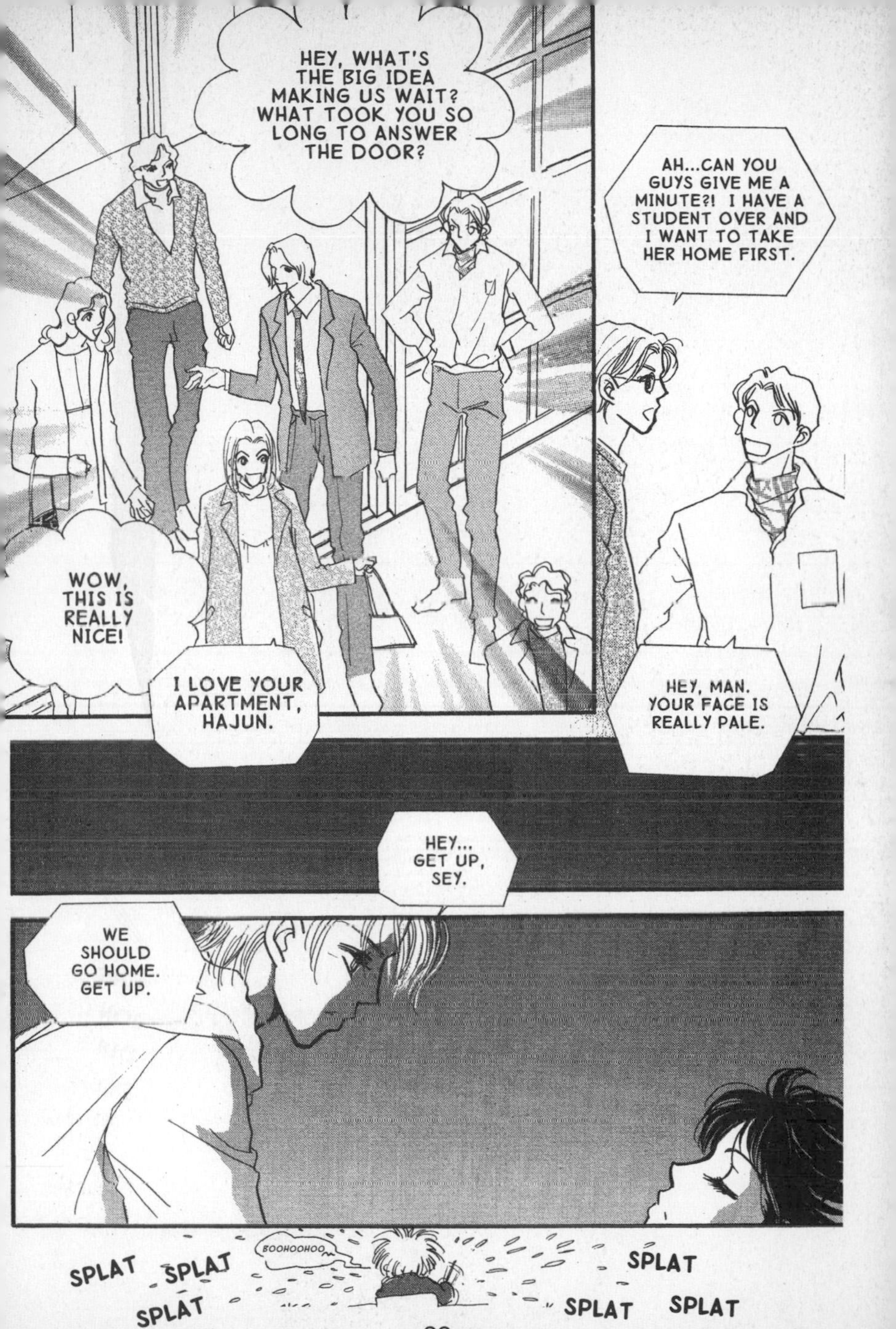
HEY, WHAT'S THE BIG IDEA MAKING US WAIT? WHAT TOOK YOU SO LONG TO ANSWER THE DOOR?
WOW, THIS IS REALLY NICE!
I LOVE YOUR APARTMENT, HAJUN.
AH...CAN YOU GUYS GIVE ME A MINUTE?! I HAVE A STUDENT OVER AND I WANT TO TAKE HER HOME FIRST.
HEY, MAN. YOUR FACE IS REALLY PALE.
HEY... GET UP, SEY.
WE SHOULD GO HOME. GET UP.
SPLAT
SPLAT
SPLAT
BOOHOOHOO
SPLAT
SPLAT
SPLAT

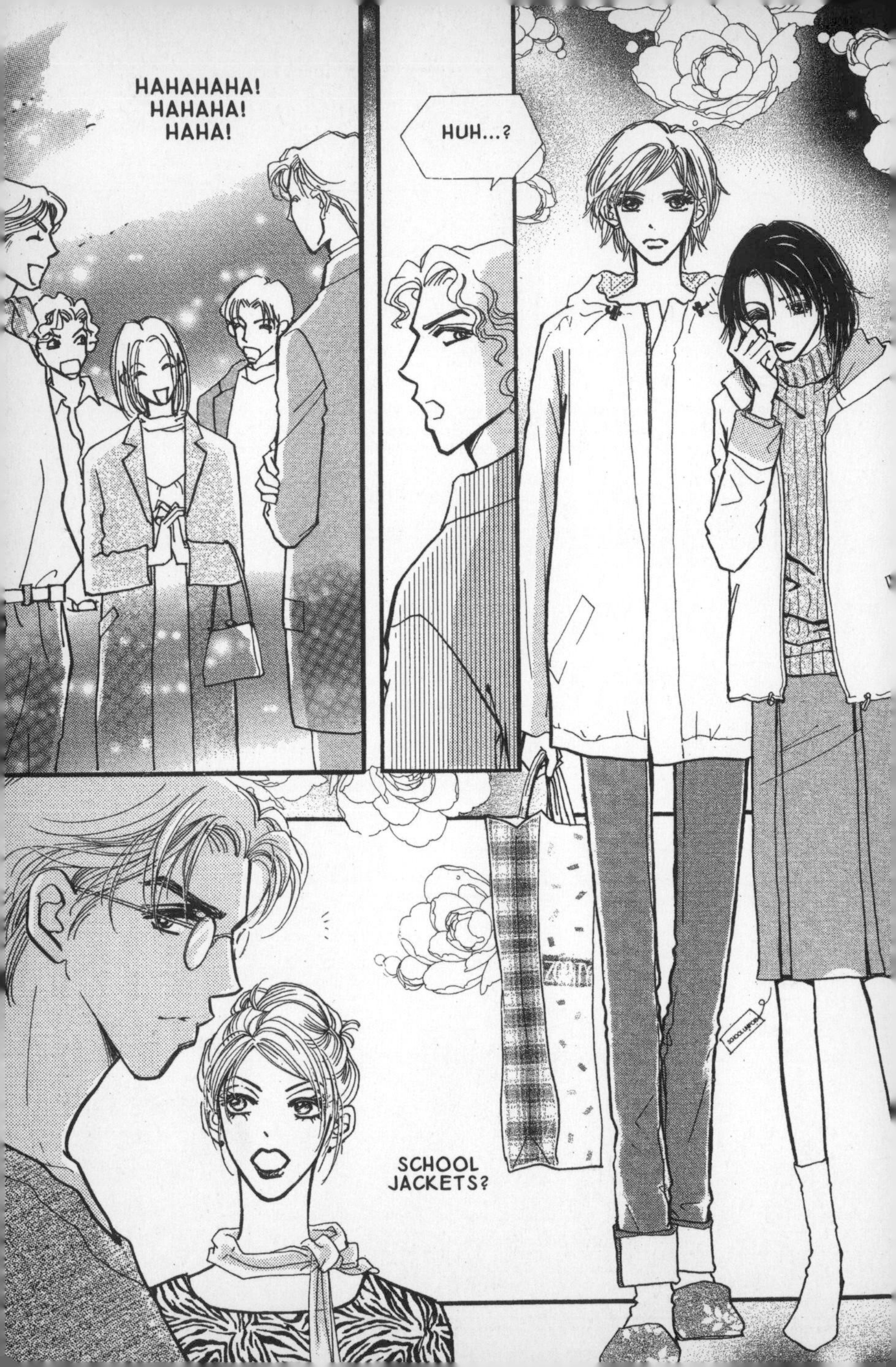
HAHAHAHA!
HAHAHA!
HAHA!
HUH...?
SCHOOL
JACKETS?

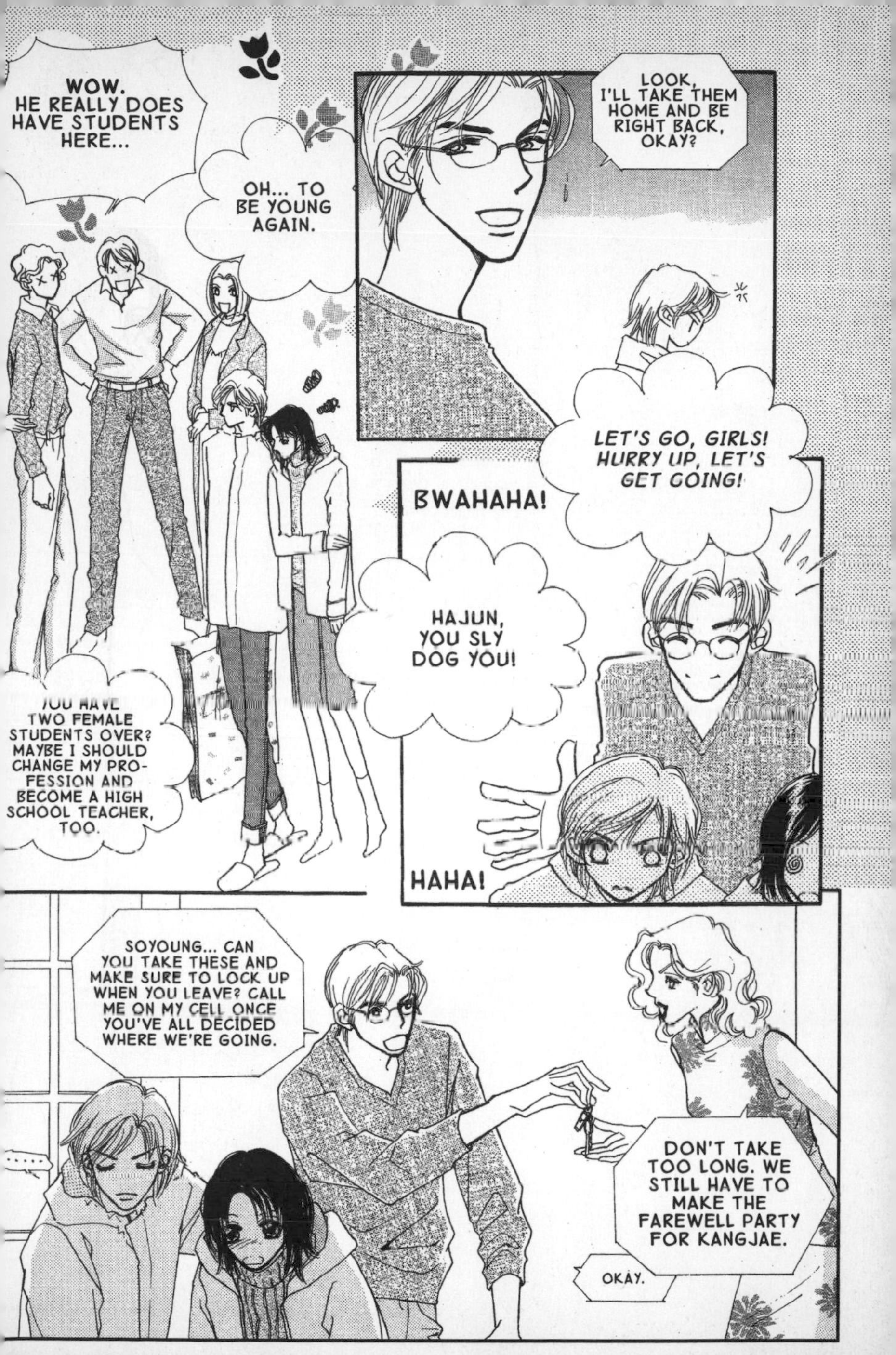
WOW. HE REALLY DOES HAVE STUDENTS HERE...
OH... TO BE YOUNG AGAIN.
YOU HAVE TWO FEMALE STUDENTS OVER? MAYBE I SHOULD CHANGE MY PRO-FESSION AND BECOME A HIGH SCHOOL TEACHER, TOO.
LOOK, I'LL TAKE THEM HOME AND BE RIGHT BACK, OKAY?
LET'S GO, GIRLS! HURRY UP, LET'S GET GOING!
BWAHAHA!
HAJUN, YOU SLY DOG YOU!
HAHA!
SOYOUNG... CAN YOU TAKE THESE AND MAKE SURE TO LOCK UP WHEN YOU LEAVE? CALL ME ON MY CELL ONCE YOU'VE ALL DECIDED WHERE WE'RE GOING.
......
DON'T TAKE TOO LONG. WE STILL HAVE TO MAKE THE FAREWELL PARTY FOR KANGJAE.
OKAY.

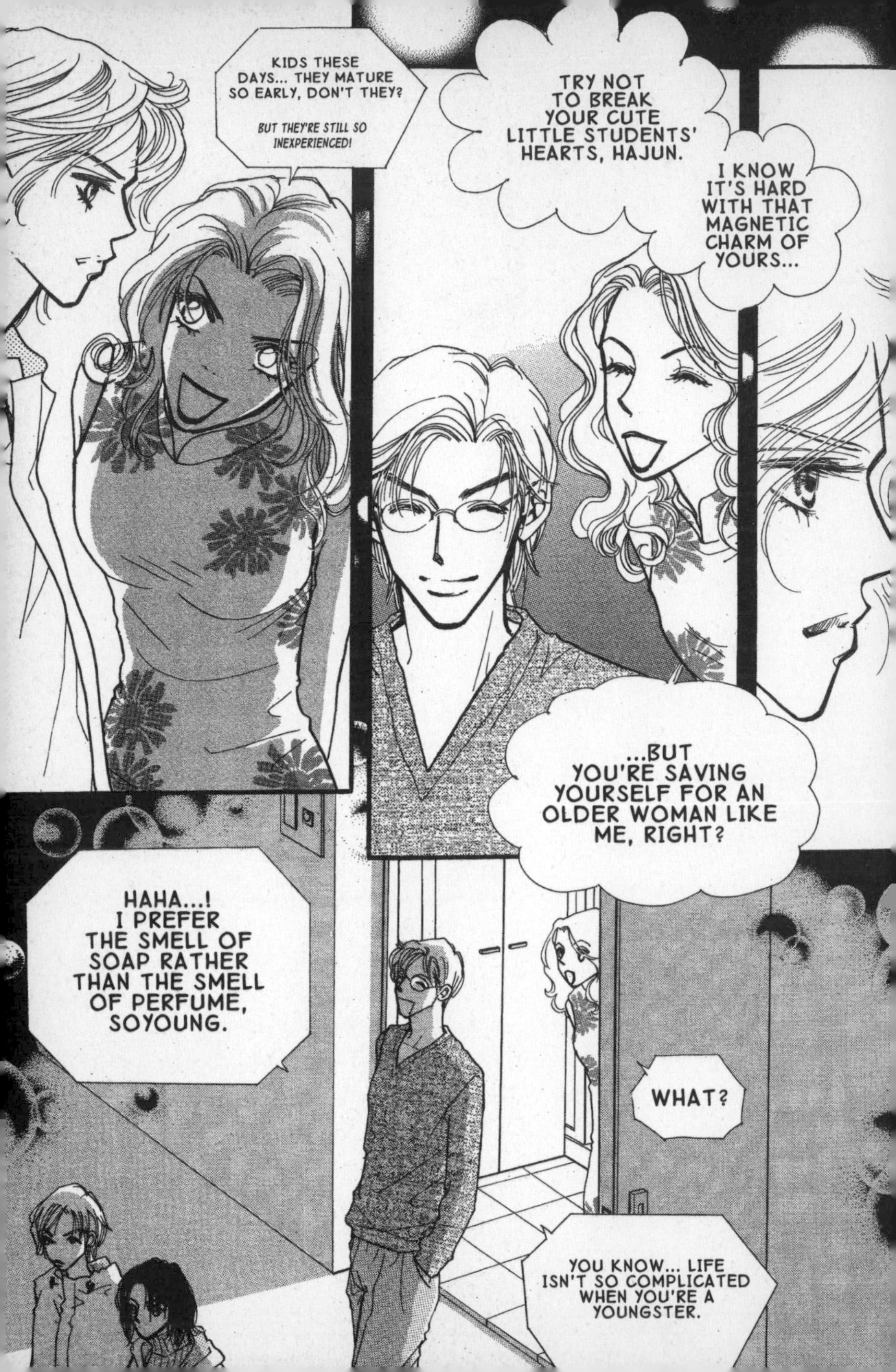
KIDS THESE DAYS... THEY MATURE SO EARLY, DON'T THEY?
BUT THEY'RE STILL SO INEXPERIENCED!
TRY NOT TO BREAK YOUR CUTE LITTLE STUDENTS' HEARTS, HAJUN.
I KNOW IT'S HARD WITH THAT MAGNETIC CHARM OF YOURS...
...BUT YOU'RE SAVING YOURSELF FOR AN OLDER WOMAN LIKE ME, RIGHT?
HAHA...! I PREFER THE SMELL OF SOAP RATHER THAN THE SMELL OF PERFUME, SOYOUNG.
WHAT?
YOU KNOW... LIFE ISN'T SO COMPLICATED WHEN YOU'RE A YOUNGSTER.

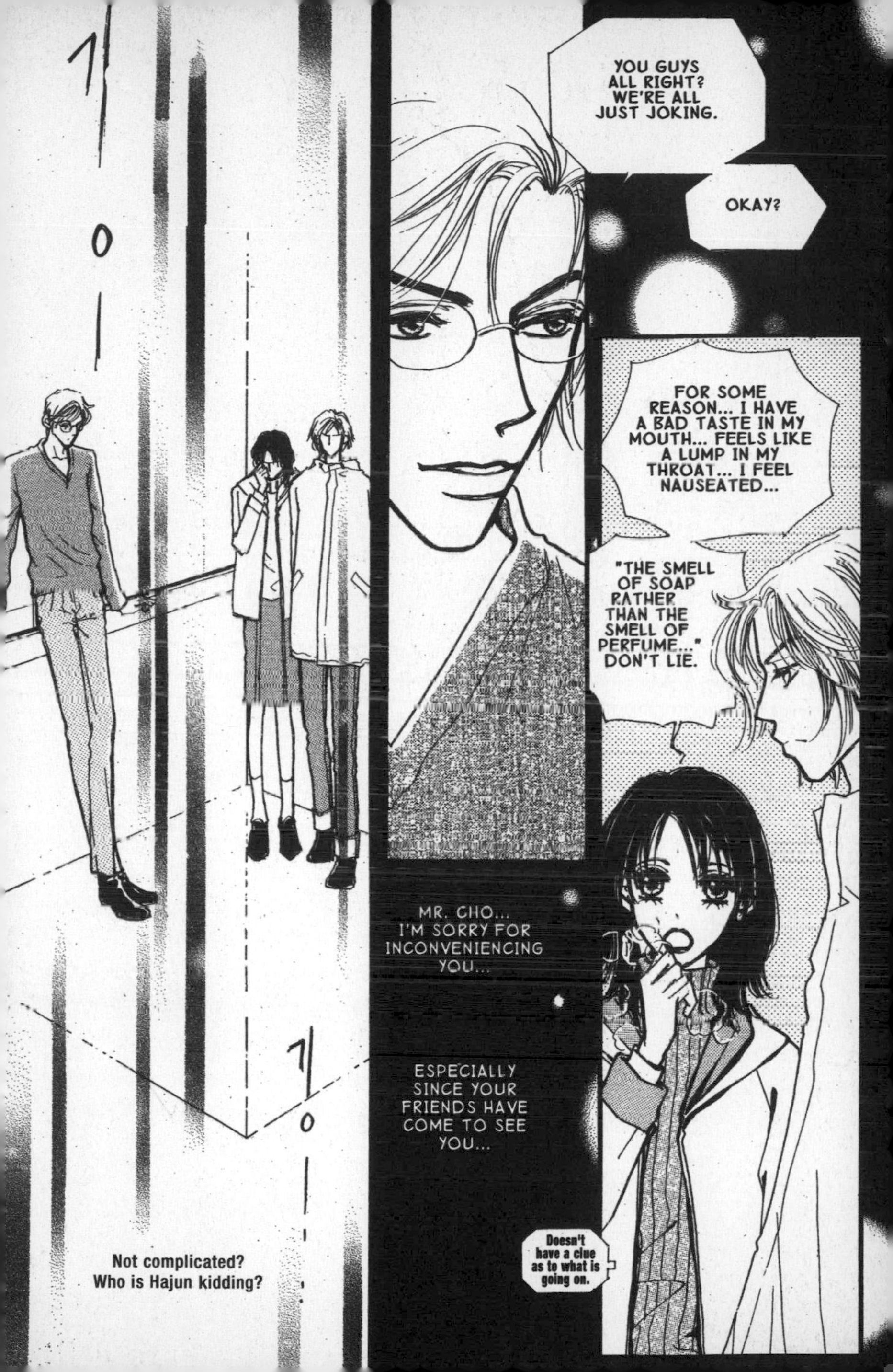

Not complicated?
Who is Hajun kidding?
YOU GUYS ALL RIGHT? WE'RE ALL JUST JOKING.
OKAY?
FOR SOME REASON... I HAVE A BAD TASTE IN MY MOUTH... FEELS LIKE A LUMP IN MY THROAT... I FEEL NAUSEATED...
"THE SMELL OF SOAP RATHER THAN THE SMELL OF PERFUME..." DON'T LIE.
MR. CHO... I'M SORRY FOR INCONVENIENCING YOU...
ESPECIALLY SINCE YOUR FRIENDS HAVE COME TO SEE YOU...
Doesn't have a clue as to what is going on.

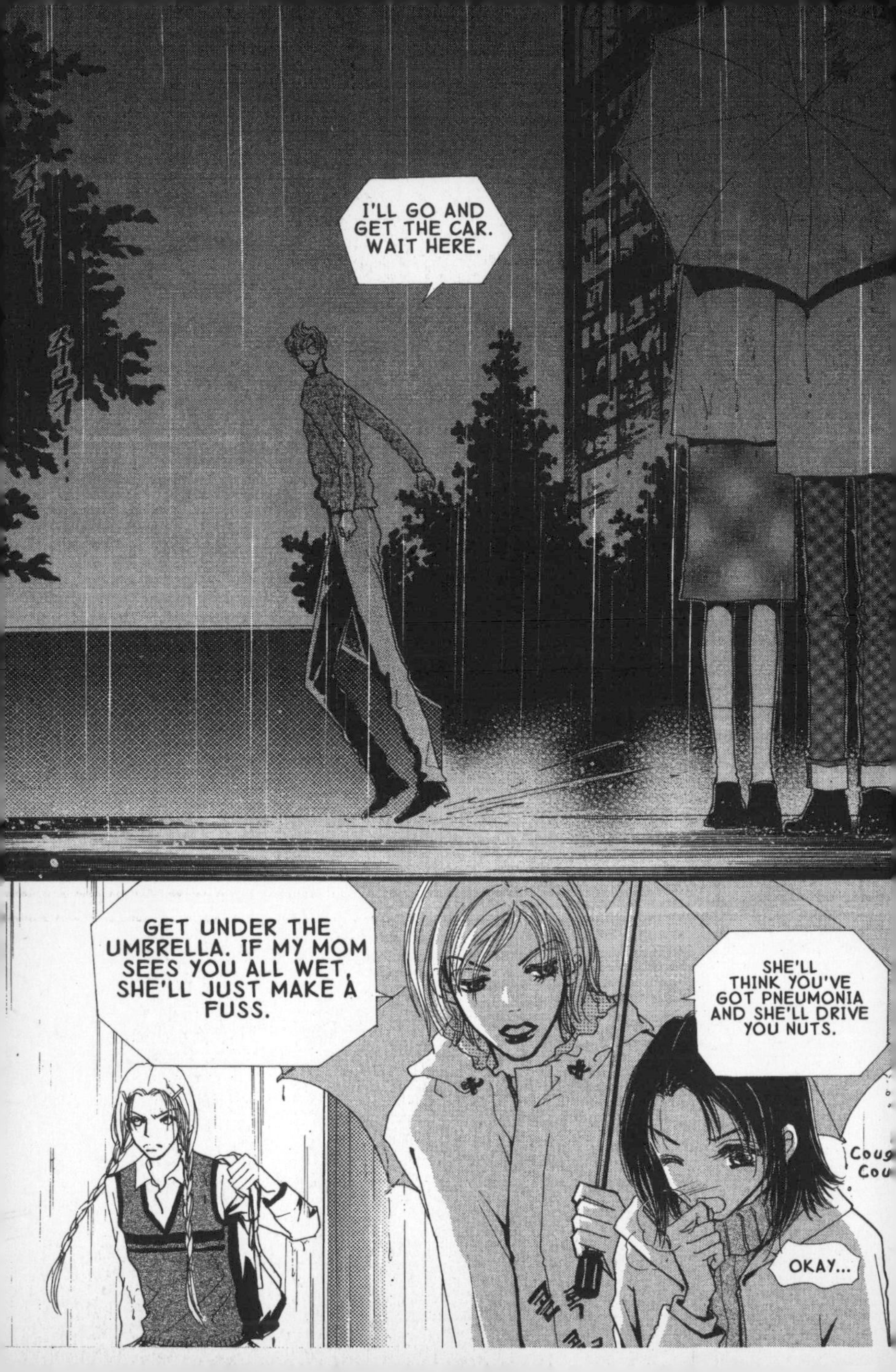
I'LL GO AND GET THE CAR. WAIT HERE.
GET UNDER THE UMBRELLA. IF MY MOM SEES YOU ALL WET, SHE'LL JUST MAKE A FUSS.
SHE'LL THINK YOU'VE GOT PNEUMONIA AND SHE'LL DRIVE YOU NUTS.
Coug
Cou
OKAY...

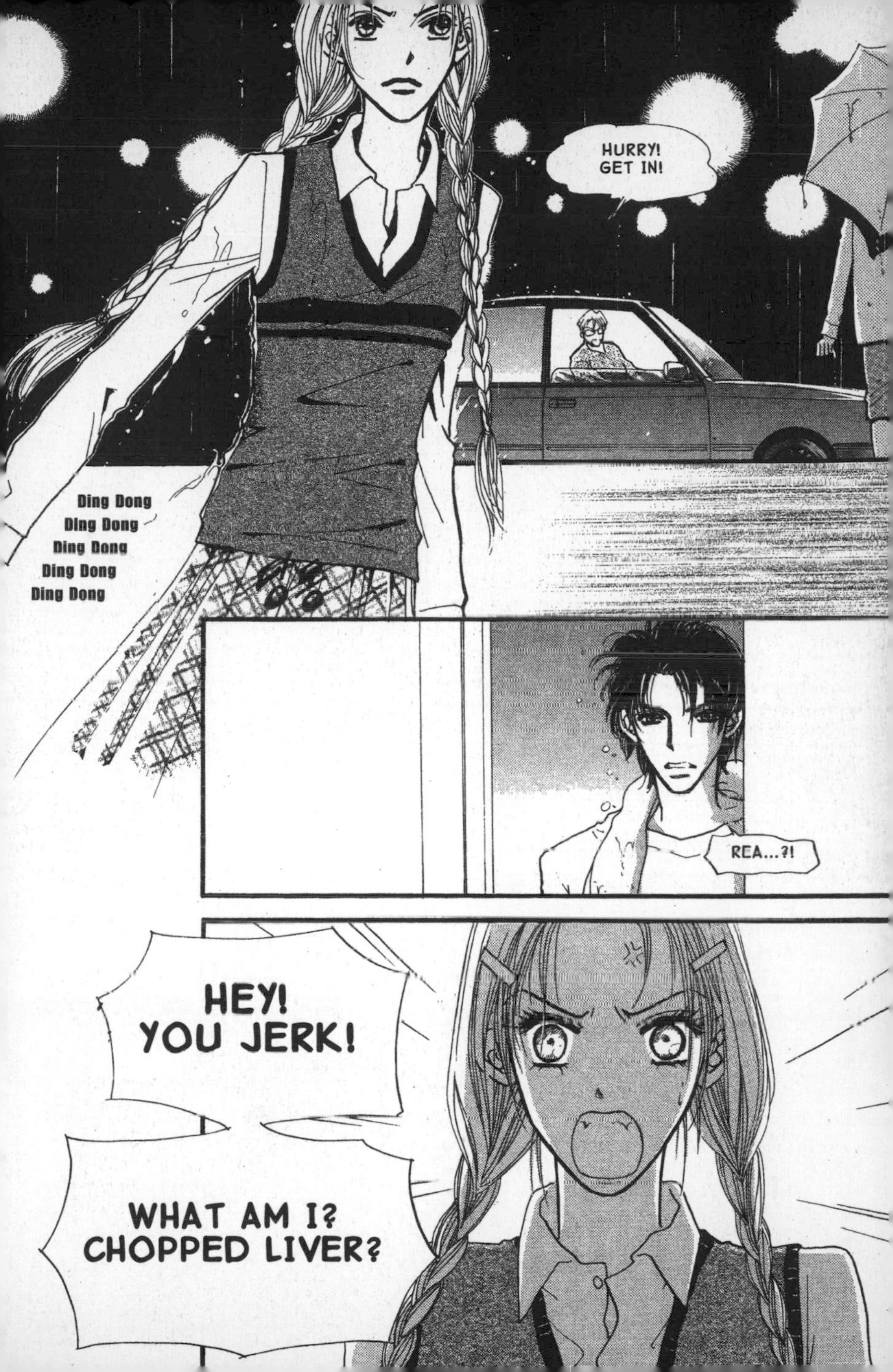
HURRY! GET IN!
Ding Dong
Ding Dong
Ding Dong
Ding Dong
Ding Dong
REA...?!
HEY! YOU JERK!
WHAT AM I? CHOPPED LIVER?

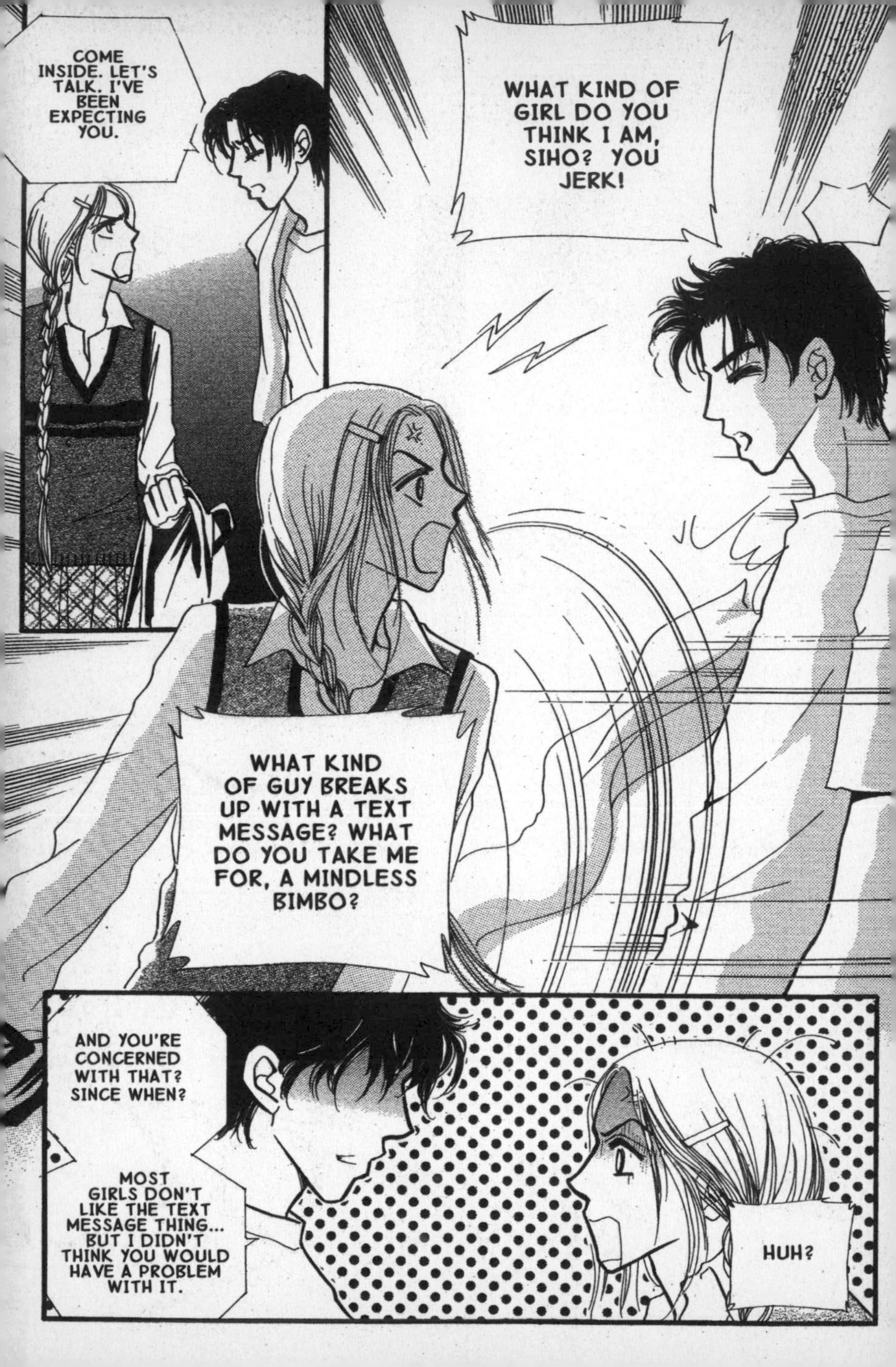
COME INSIDE. LET'S TALK. I'VE BEEN EXPECTING YOU.
WHAT KIND OF GIRL DO YOU THINK I AM, SIHO? YOU JERK!
WHAT KIND OF GUY BREAKS UP WITH A TEXT MESSAGE? WHAT DO YOU TAKE ME FOR, A MINDLESS BIMBO?
AND YOU'RE CONCERNED WITH THAT? SINCE WHEN?
MOST GIRLS DON'T LIKE THE TEXT MESSAGE THING... BUT I DIDN'T THINK YOU WOULD HAVE A PROBLEM WITH IT.
HUH?

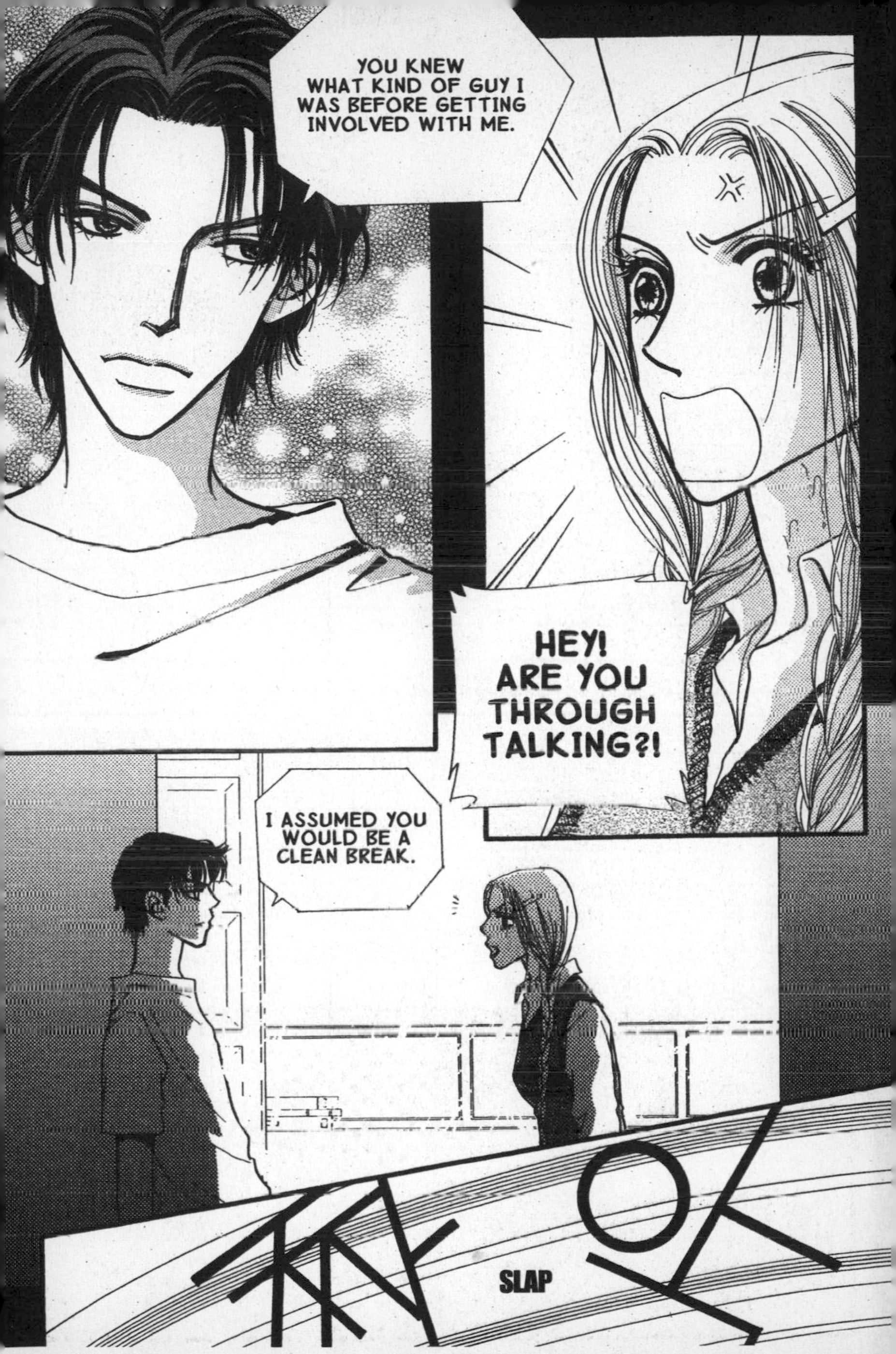
YOU KNEW WHAT KIND OF GUY I WAS BEFORE GETTING INVOLVED WITH ME.
HEY! ARE YOU THROUGH TALKING?!
I ASSUMED YOU WOULD BE A CLEAN BREAK.
SLAP

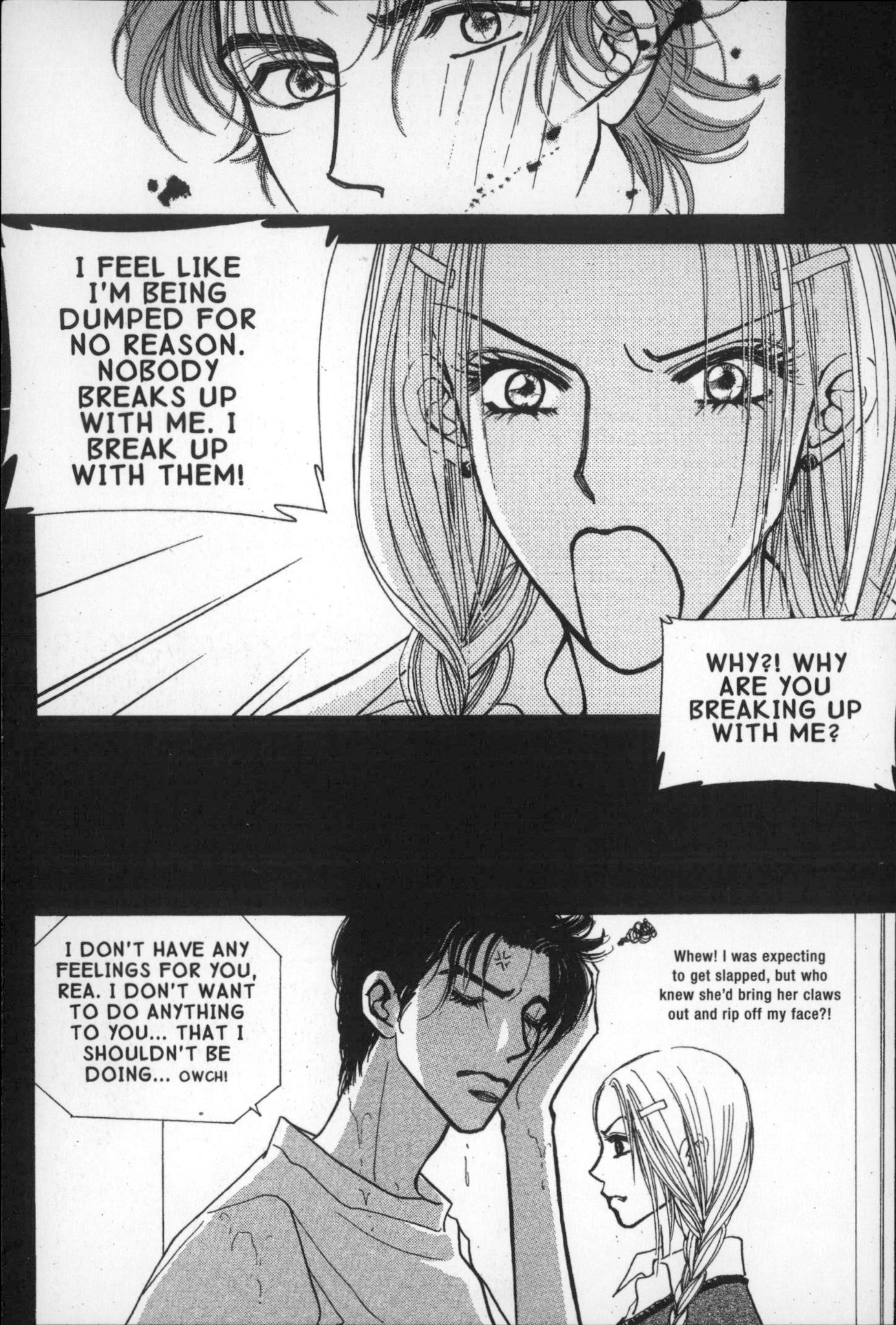
I FEEL LIKE I'M BEING DUMPED FOR NO REASON. NOBODY BREAKS UP WITH ME. I BREAK UP WITH THEM!
WHY?! WHY ARE YOU BREAKING UP WITH ME?
I DON'T HAVE ANY FEELINGS FOR YOU, REA. I DON'T WANT TO DO ANYTHING TO YOU... THAT I SHOULDN'T BE DOING... OWCH!
Whew! I was expecting to get slapped, but who knew she'd bring her claws out and rip off my face?!

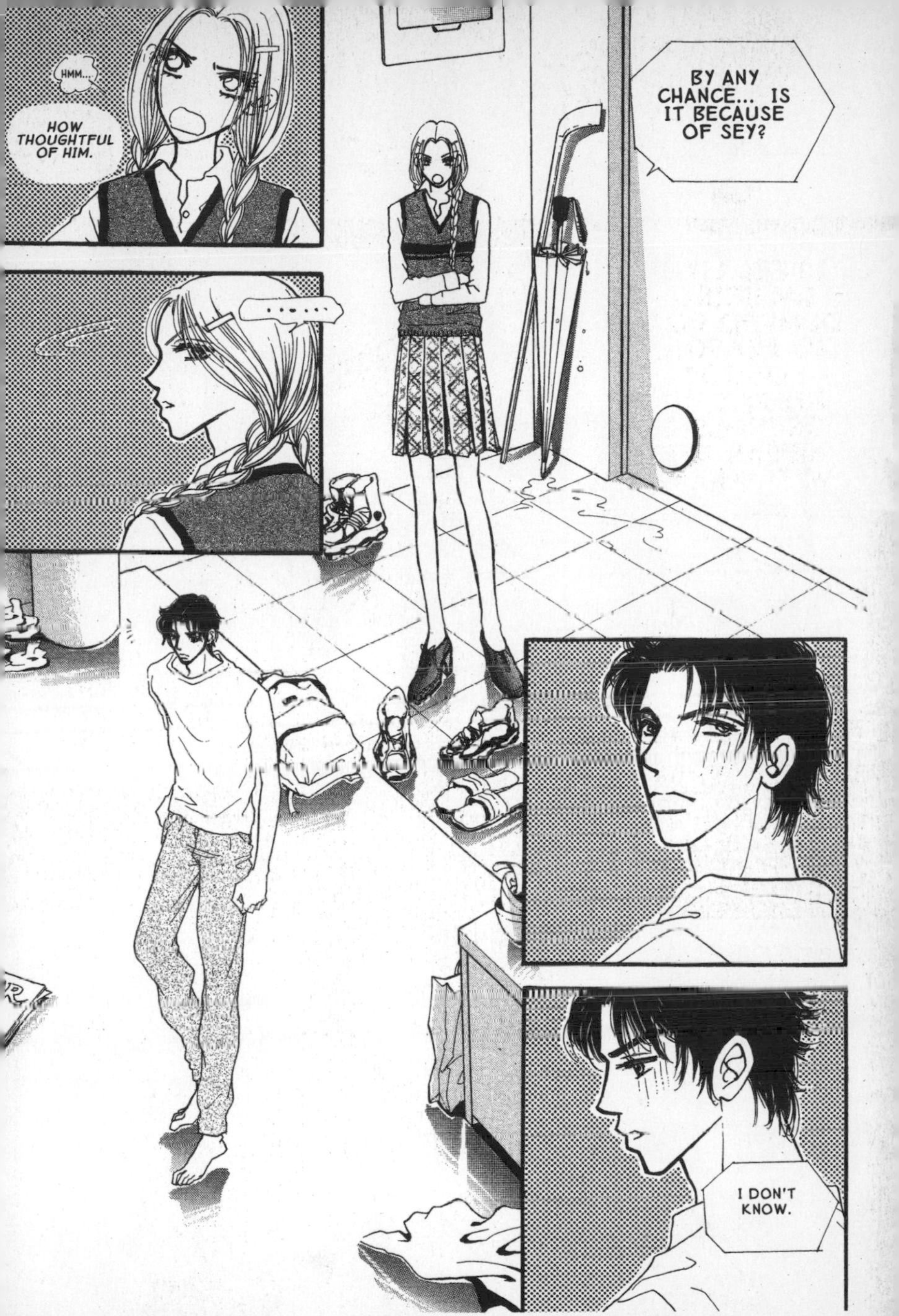
HMM...
HOW THOUGHTFUL OF HIM.
.....
BY ANY CHANCE... IS IT BECAUSE OF SEY?
I DON'T KNOW.

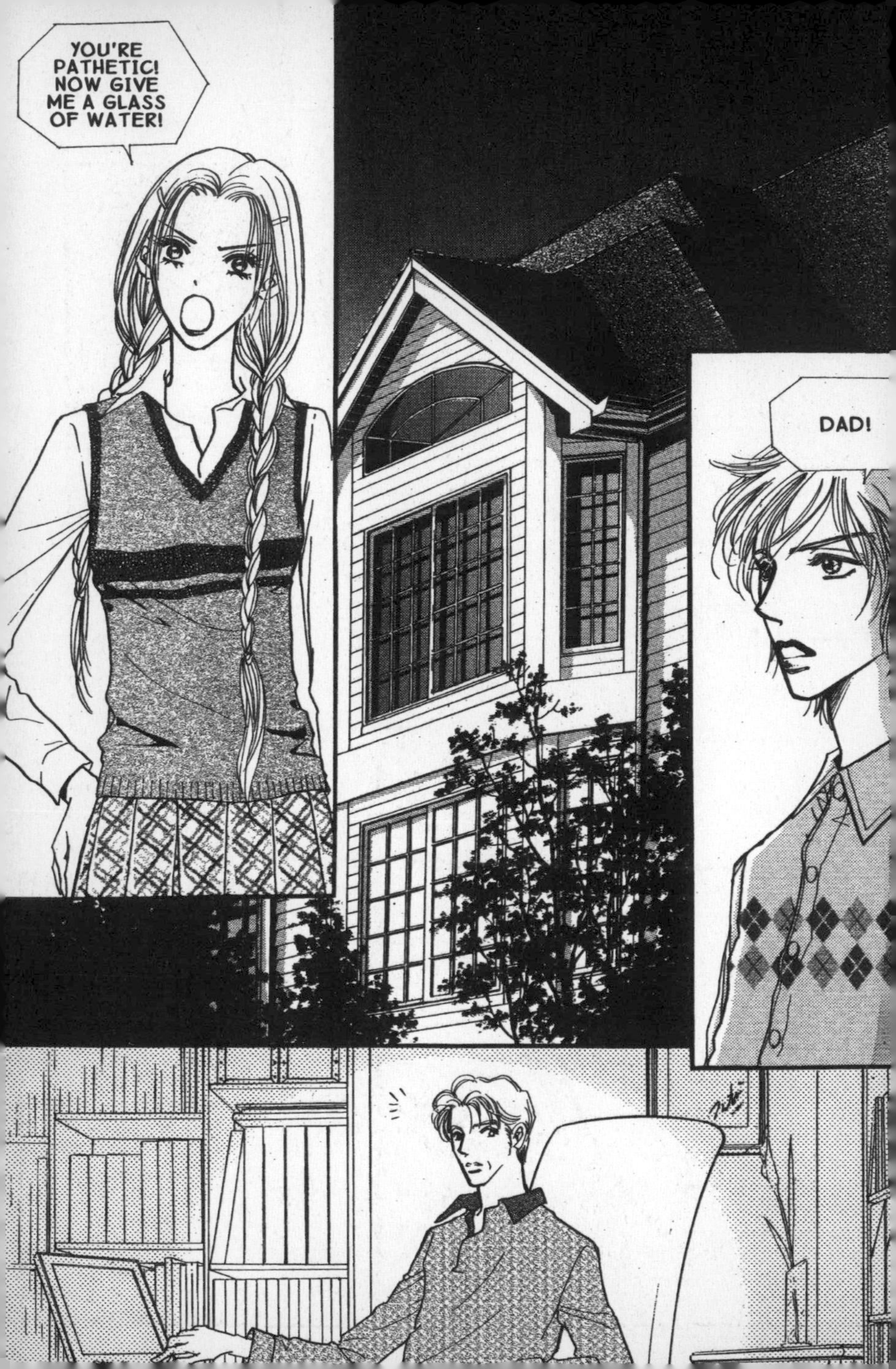
YOU'RE PATHETIC! NOW GIVE ME A GLASS OF WATER!
DAD!

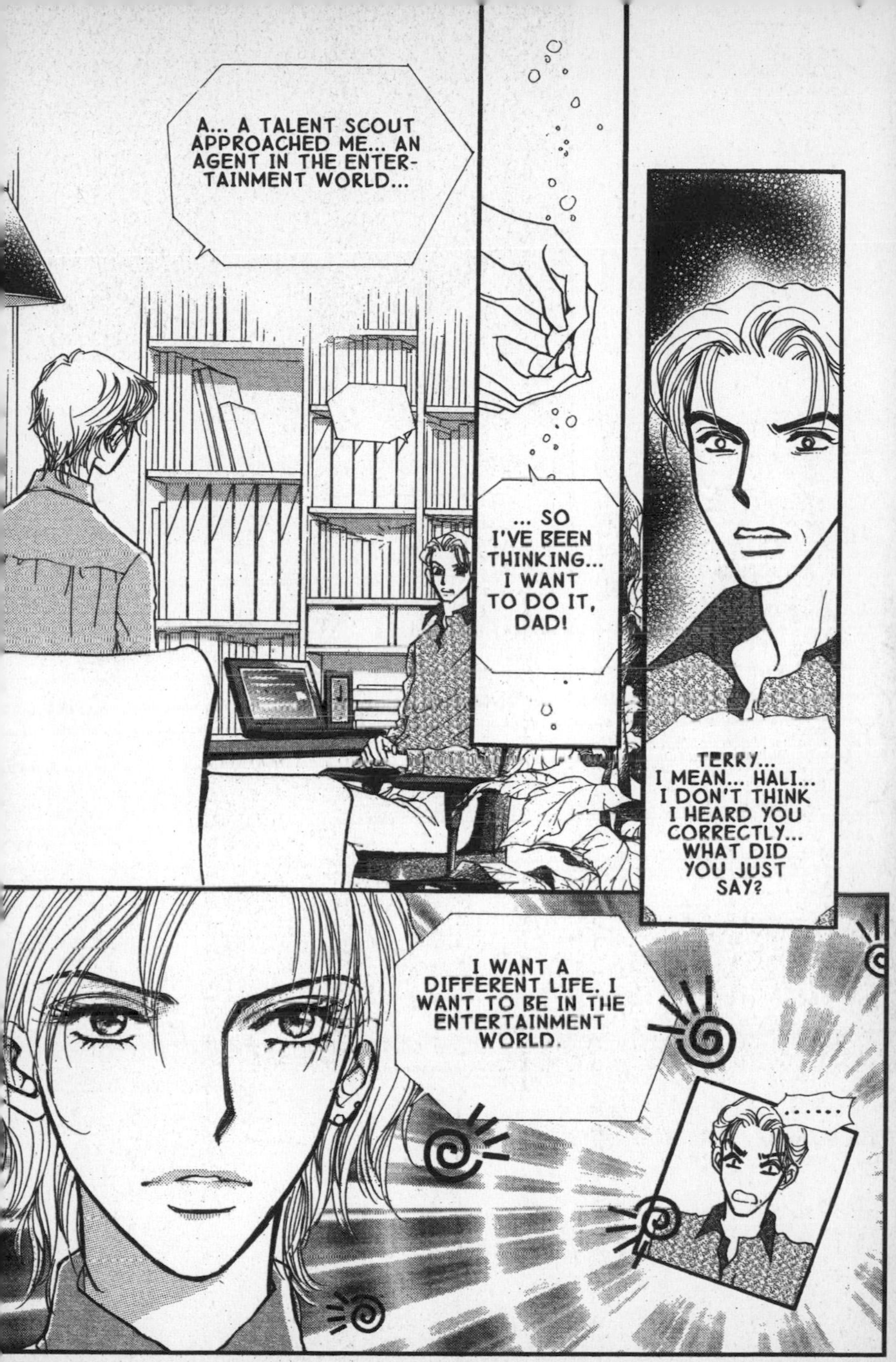
A... A TALENT SCOUT APPROACHED ME... AN AGENT IN THE ENTERTAINMENT WORLD...
... SO I'VE BEEN THINKING... I WANT TO DO IT, DAD!
TERRY... I MEAN... HALI... I DON'T THINK I HEARD YOU CORRECTLY... WHAT DID YOU JUST SAY?
I WANT A DIFFERENT LIFE. I WANT TO BE IN THE ENTERTAINMENT WORLD.
......

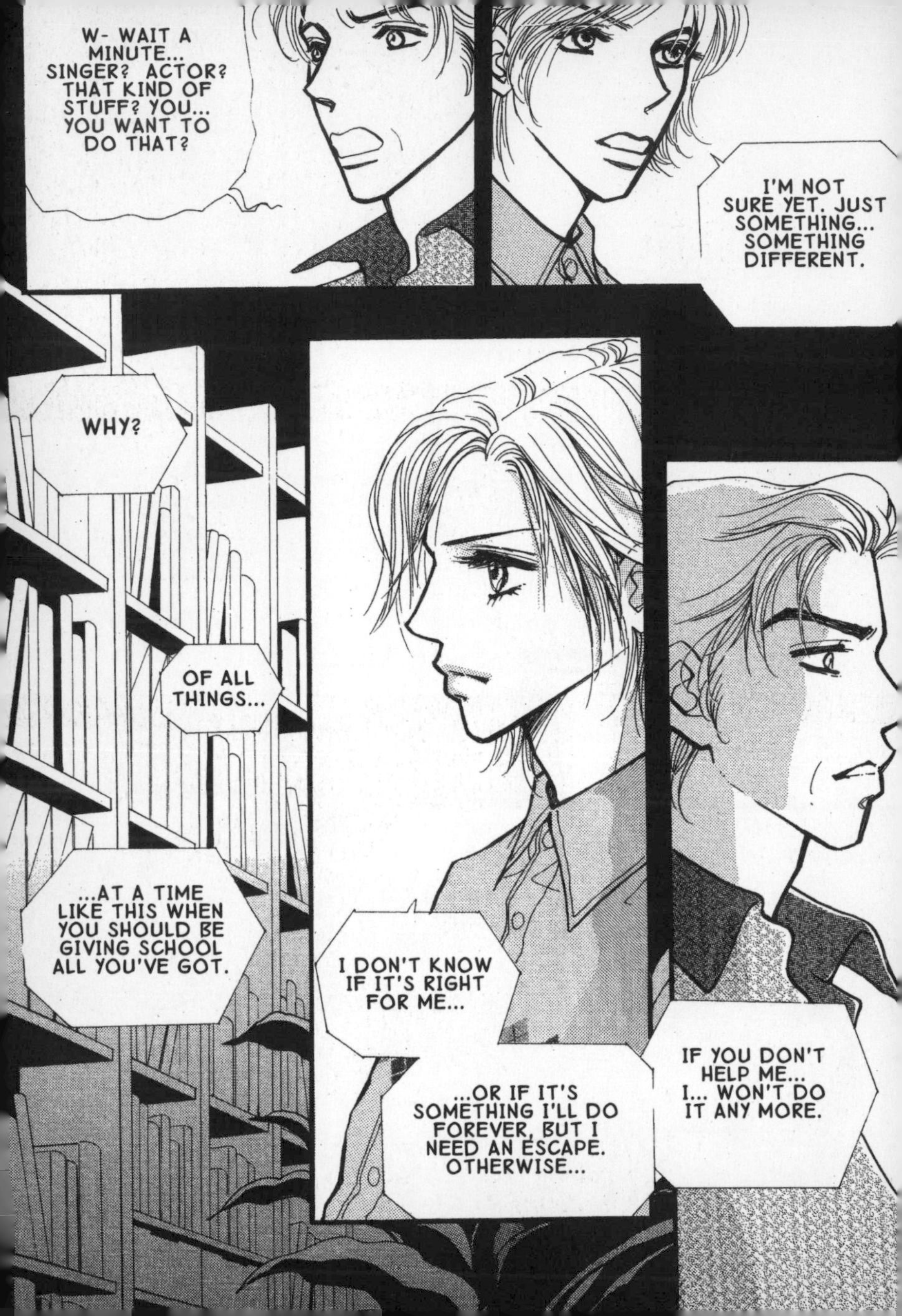
W- WAIT A MINUTE... SINGER? ACTOR? THAT KIND OF STUFF? YOU... YOU WANT TO DO THAT?
I'M NOT SURE YET. JUST SOMETHING... SOMETHING DIFFERENT.
WHY?
OF ALL THINGS...
...AT A TIME LIKE THIS WHEN YOU SHOULD BE GIVING SCHOOL ALL YOU'VE GOT.
I DON'T KNOW IF IT'S RIGHT FOR ME...
...OR IF IT'S SOMETHING I'LL DO FOREVER, BUT I NEED AN ESCAPE. OTHERWISE...
IF YOU DON'T HELP ME... I... WON'T DO IT ANY MORE.

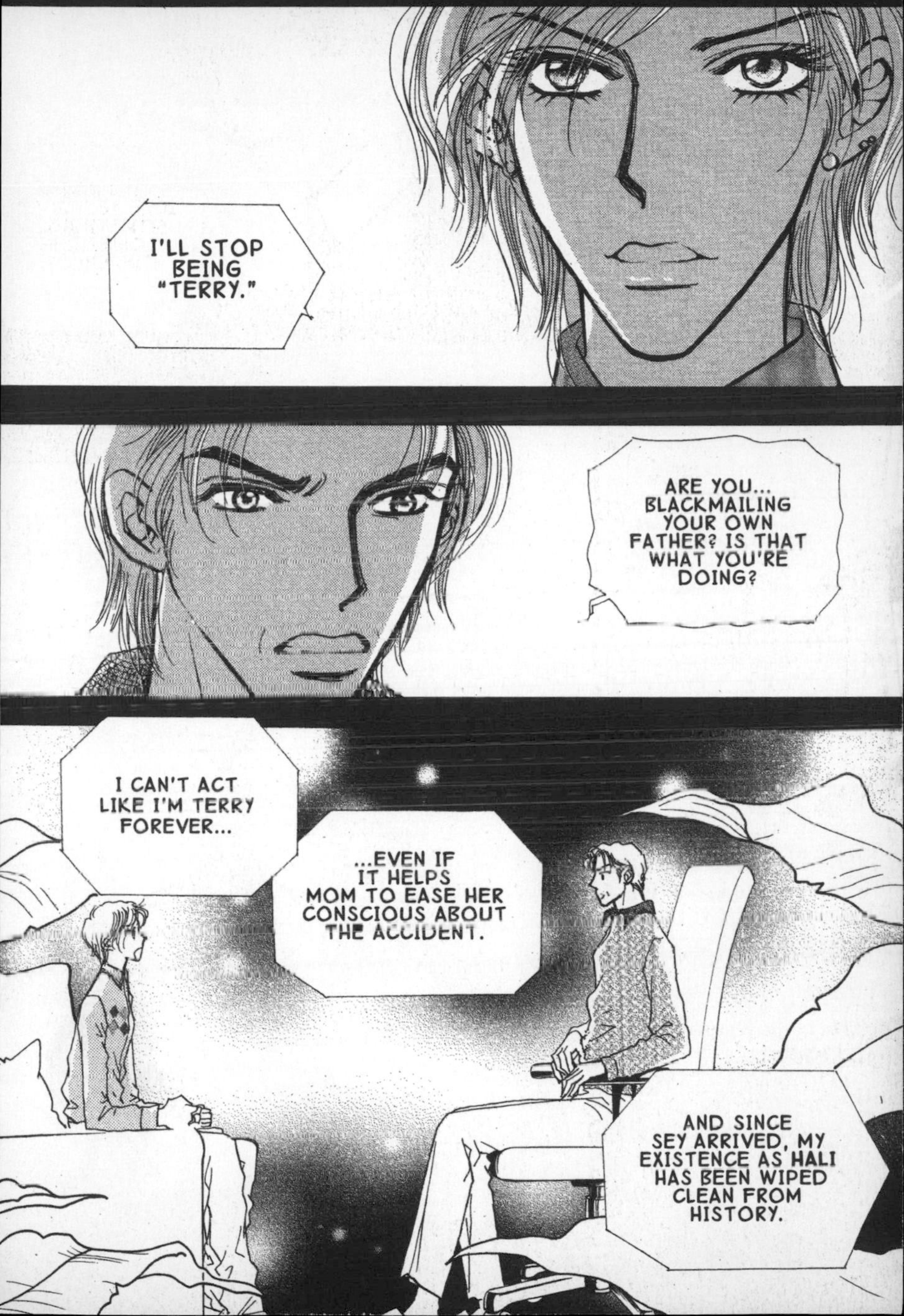
I'LL STOP BEING "TERRY."
ARE YOU... BLACKMAILING YOUR OWN FATHER? IS THAT WHAT YOU'RE DOING?
I CAN'T ACT LIKE I'M TERRY FOREVER...
...EVEN IF IT HELPS MOM TO EASE HER CONSCIOUS ABOUT THE ACCIDENT.
AND SINCE SEY ARRIVED, MY EXISTENCE AS HALI HAS BEEN WIPED CLEAN FROM HISTORY.

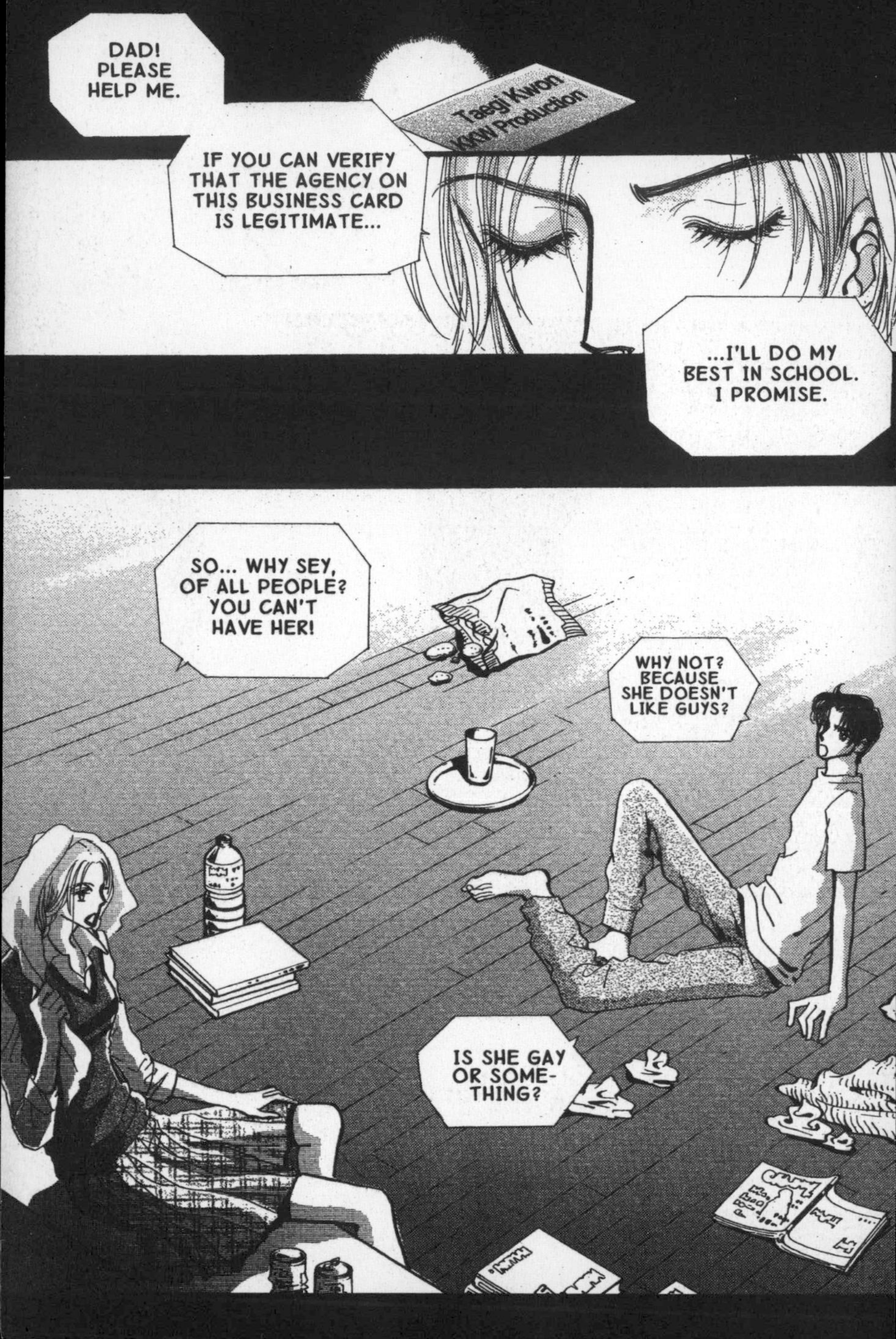
DAD! PLEASE HELP ME.
Taegi Kwon
KWN Production
IF YOU CAN VERIFY THAT THE AGENCY ON THIS BUSINESS CARD IS LEGITIMATE...
...I'LL DO MY BEST IN SCHOOL. I PROMISE.
SO... WHY SEY, OF ALL PEOPLE? YOU CAN'T HAVE HER!
WHY NOT? BECAUSE SHE DOESN'T LIKE GUYS?
IS SHE GAY OR SOME-THING?

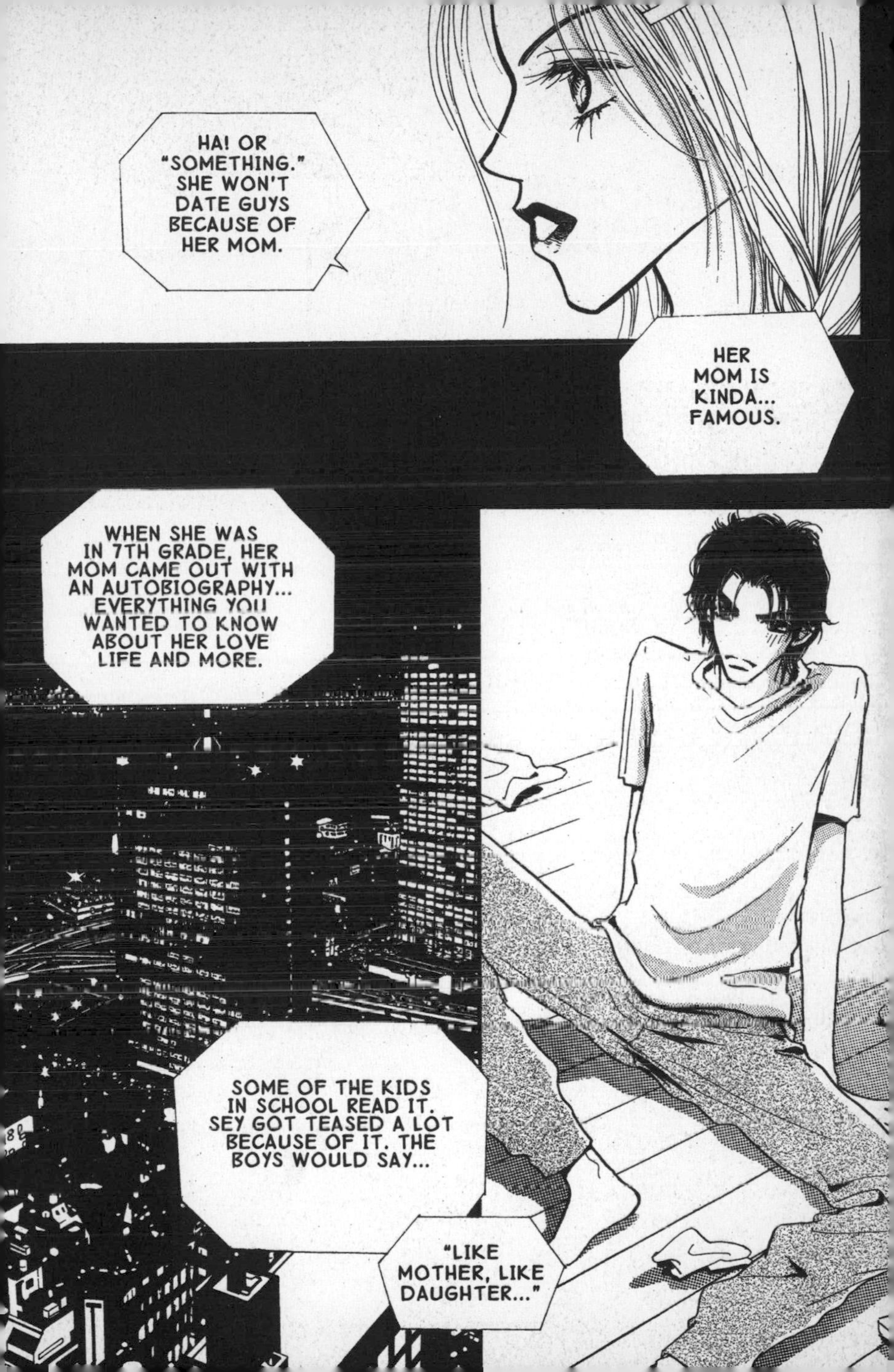
HA! OR "SOMETHING." SHE WON'T DATE GUYS BECAUSE OF HER MOM.
HER MOM IS KINDA... FAMOUS.
WHEN SHE WAS IN 7TH GRADE, HER MOM CAME OUT WITH AN AUTOBIOGRAPHY... EVERYTHING YOU WANTED TO KNOW ABOUT HER LOVE LIFE AND MORE.
SOME OF THE KIDS IN SCHOOL READ IT. SEY GOT TEASED A LOT BECAUSE OF IT. THE BOYS WOULD SAY...
"LIKE MOTHER, LIKE DAUGHTER..."

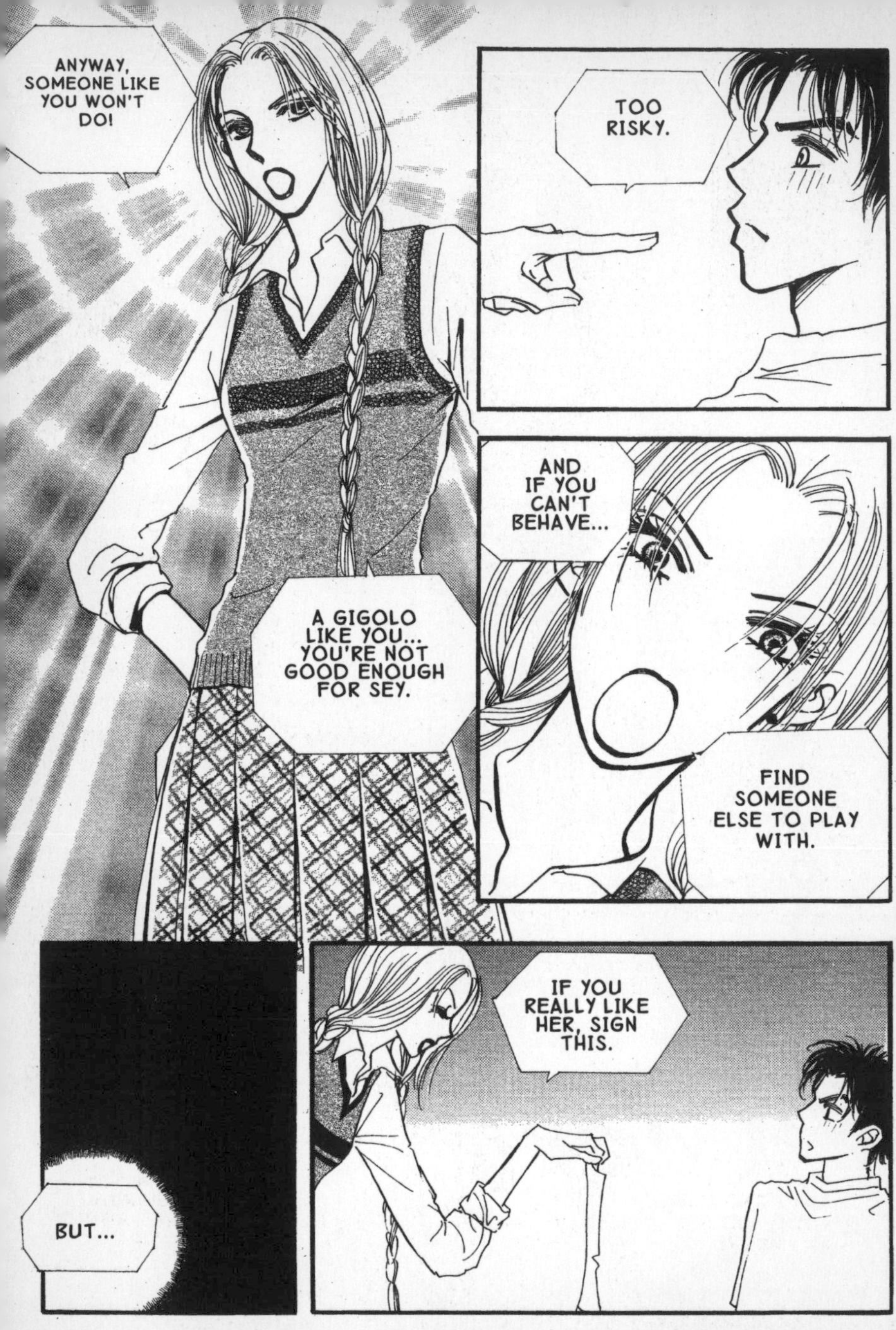

ANYWAY, SOMEONE LIKE YOU WON'T DO!
A GIGOLO LIKE YOU... YOU'RE NOT GOOD ENOUGH FOR SEY.
TOO RISKY.
AND IF YOU CAN'T BEHAVE...
FIND SOMEONE ELSE TO PLAY WITH.
BUT...
IF YOU REALLY LIKE HER, SIGN THIS.

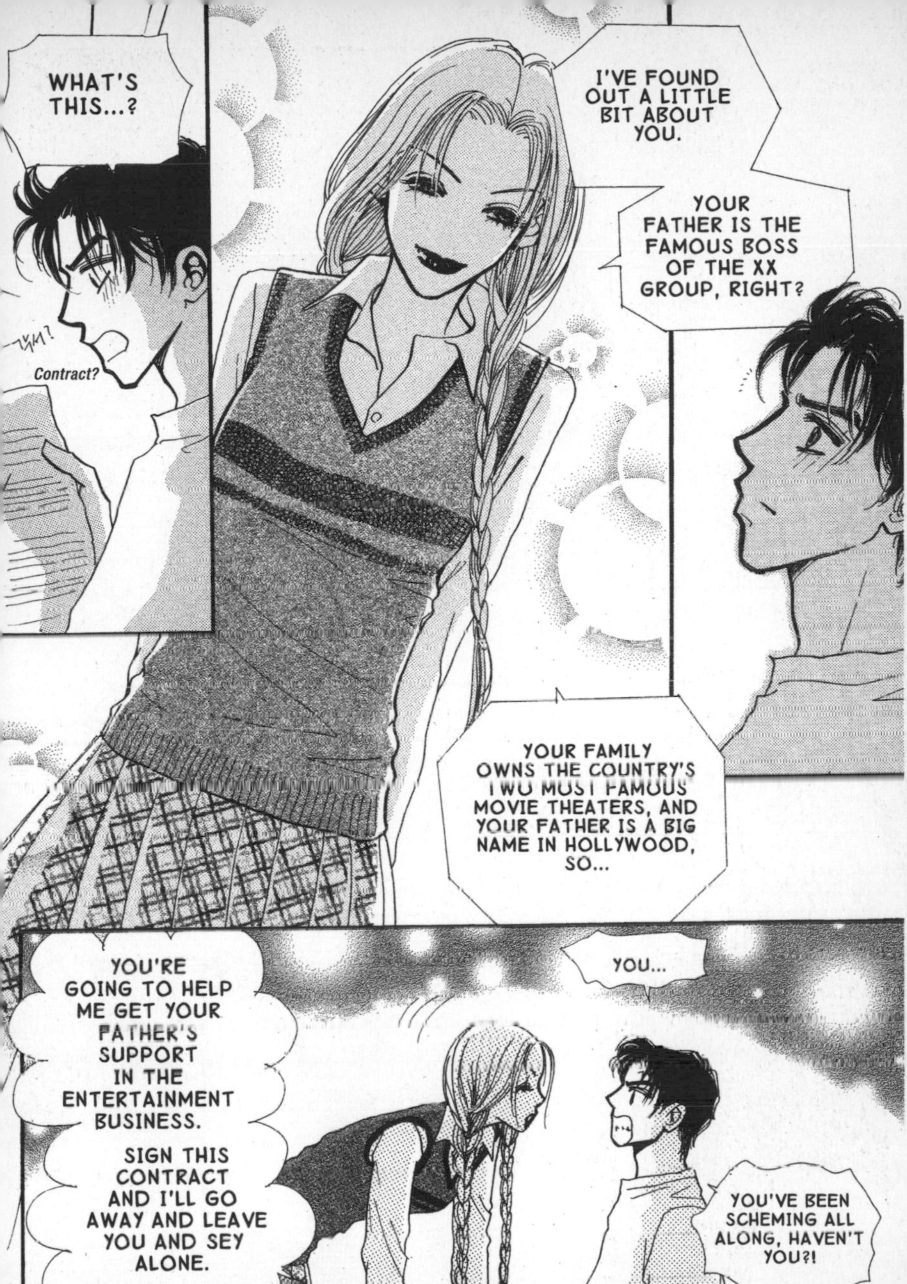
WHAT'S THIS...?
Contract?
I'VE FOUND OUT A LITTLE BIT ABOUT YOU.
YOUR FATHER IS THE FAMOUS BOSS OF THE XX GROUP, RIGHT?
YOUR FAMILY OWNS THE COUNTRY'S TWO MOST FAMOUS MOVIE THEATERS, AND YOUR FATHER IS A BIG NAME IN HOLLYWOOD, SO...
YOU'RE GOING TO HELP ME GET YOUR FATHER'S SUPPORT IN THE ENTERTAINMENT BUSINESS.
SIGN THIS CONTRACT AND I'LL GO AWAY AND LEAVE YOU AND SEY ALONE.
YOU...
YOU'VE BEEN SCHEMING ALL ALONG, HAVEN'T YOU?!

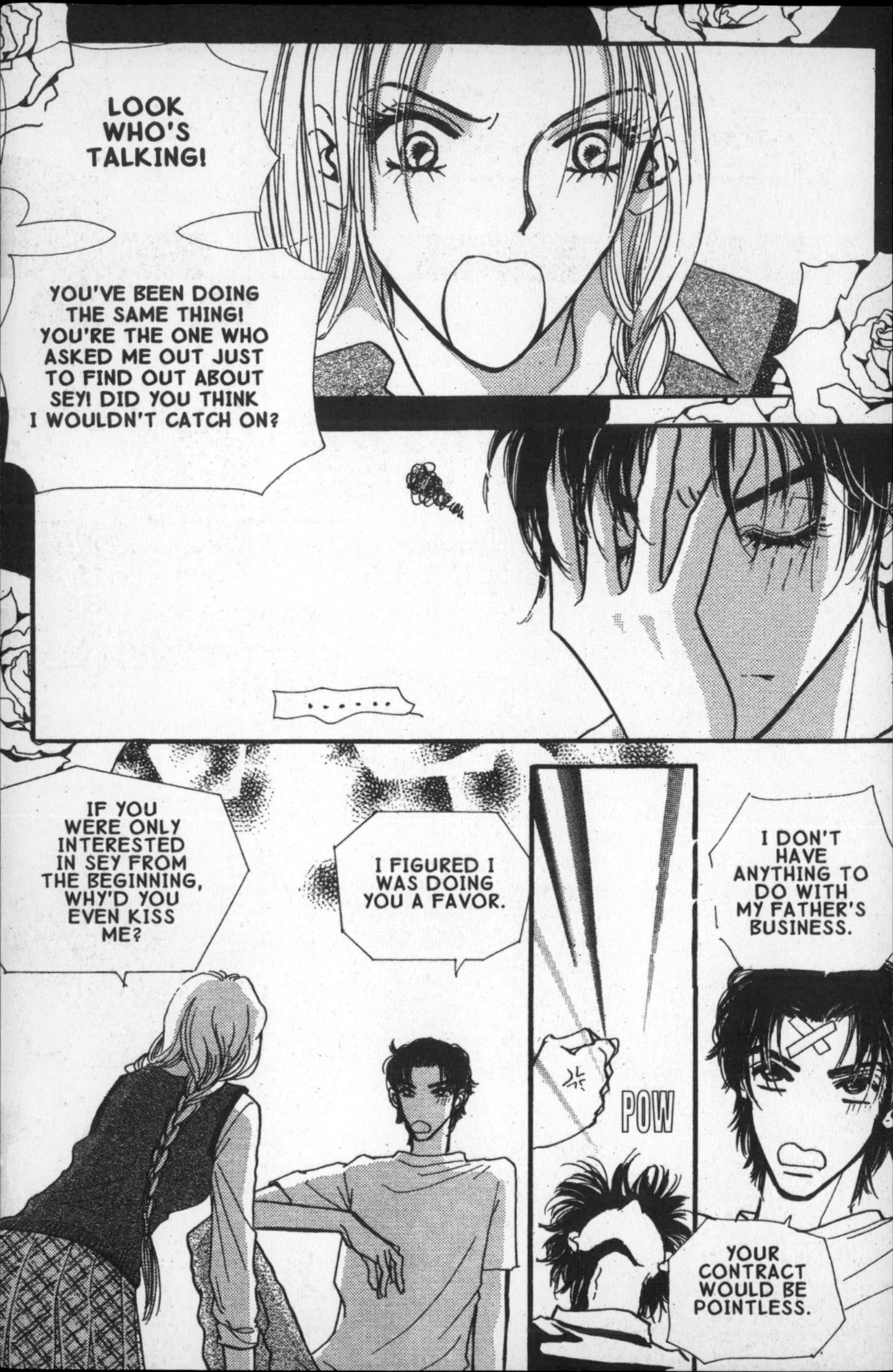
LOOK WHO'S TALKING!
YOU'VE BEEN DOING THE SAME THING! YOU'RE THE ONE WHO ASKED ME OUT JUST TO FIND OUT ABOUT SEY! DID YOU THINK I WOULDN'T CATCH ON?
......
IF YOU WERE ONLY INTERESTED IN SEY FROM THE BEGINNING, WHY'D YOU EVEN KISS ME?
I FIGURED I WAS DOING YOU A FAVOR.
POW
I DON'T HAVE ANYTHING TO DO WITH MY FATHER'S BUSINESS.
YOUR CONTRACT WOULD BE POINTLESS.

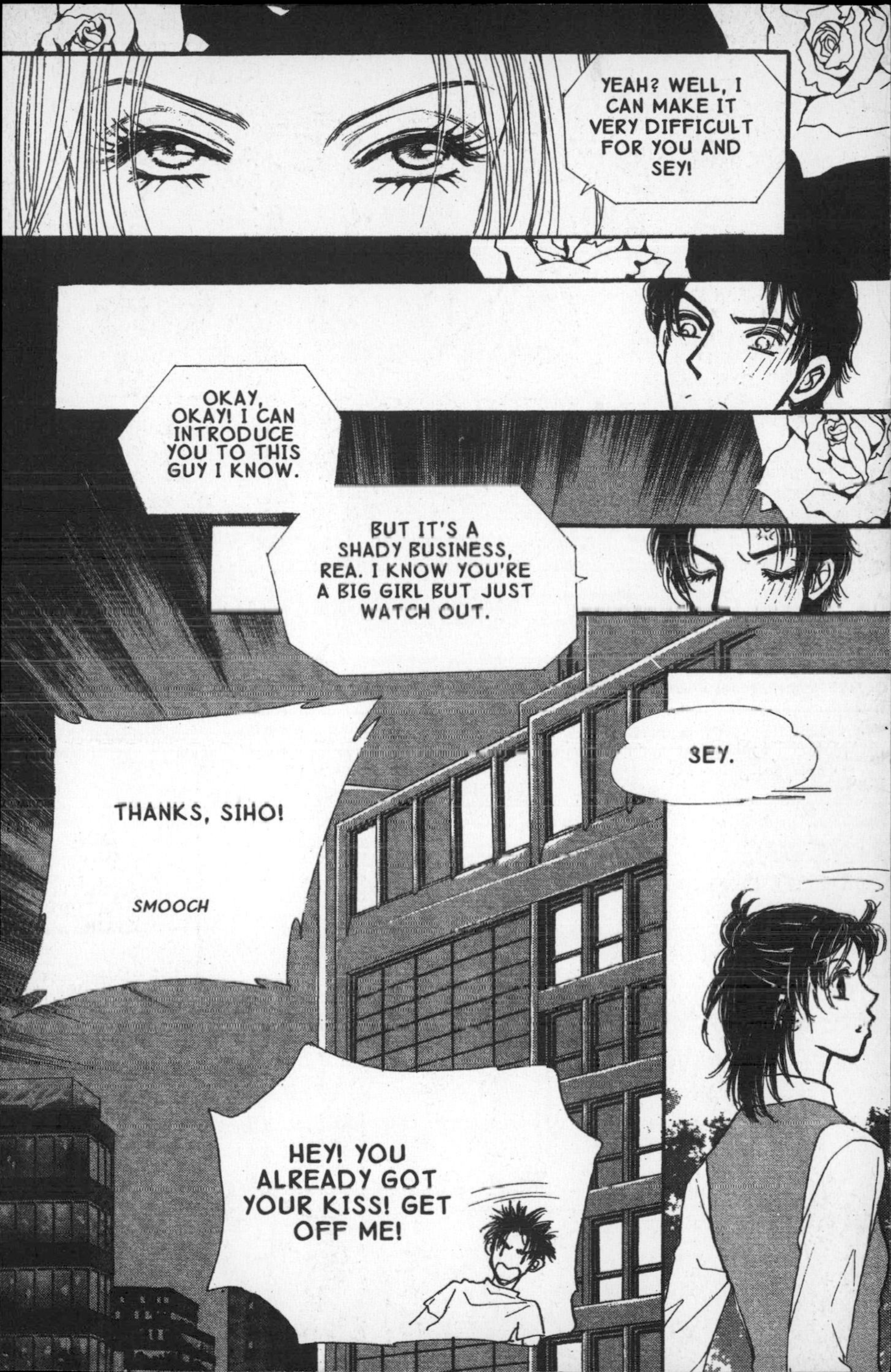
YEAH? WELL, I CAN MAKE IT VERY DIFFICULT FOR YOU AND SEY!
OKAY, OKAY! I CAN INTRODUCE YOU TO THIS GUY I KNOW.
BUT IT'S A SHADY BUSINESS, REA. I KNOW YOU'RE A BIG GIRL BUT JUST WATCH OUT.
THANKS, SIHO!
SMOOCH
SEY.
HEY! YOU ALREADY GOT YOUR KISS! GET OFF ME!

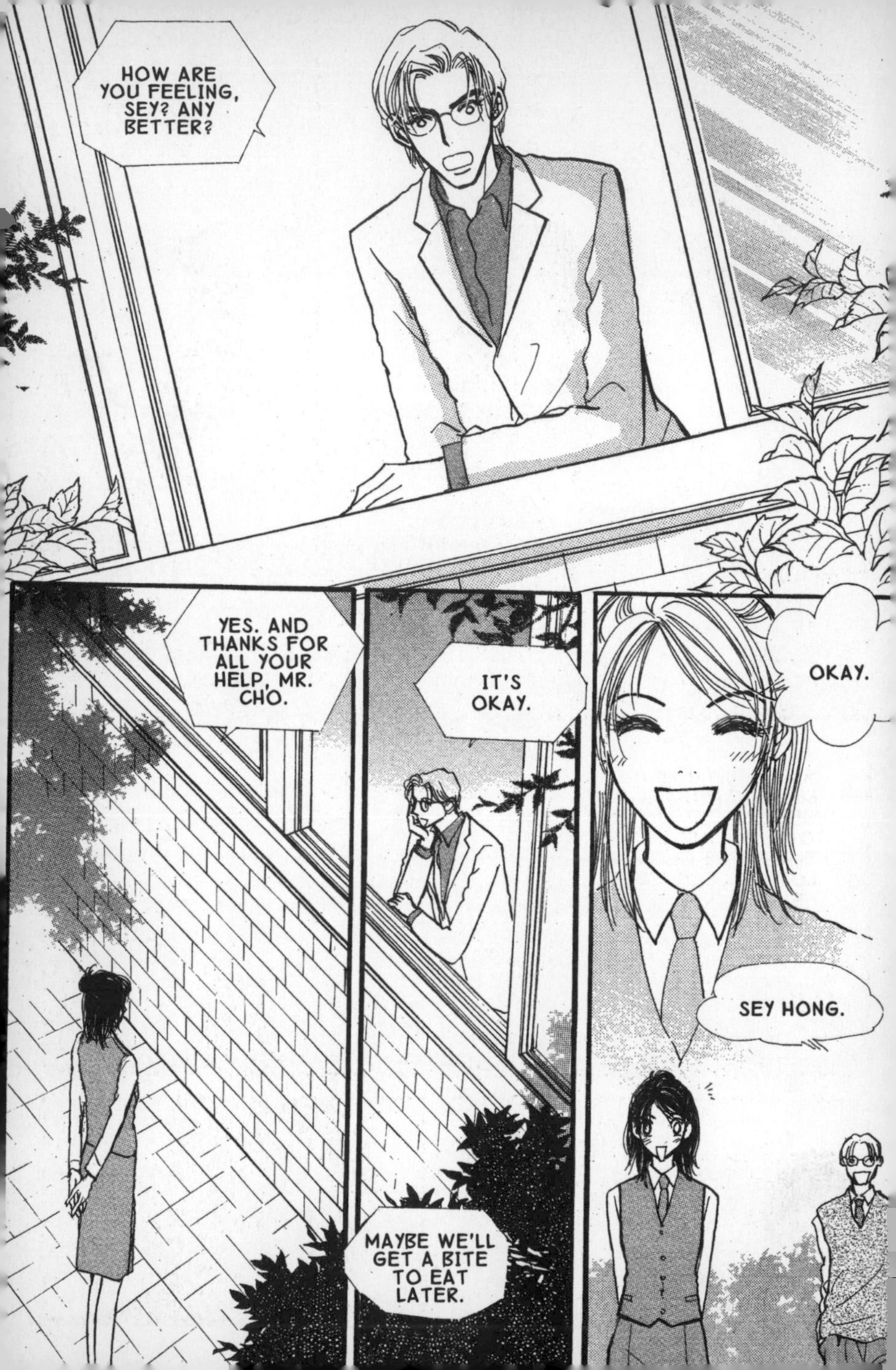
HOW ARE YOU FEELING, SEY? ANY BETTER?
YES. AND THANKS FOR ALL YOUR HELP, MR. CHO.
IT'S OKAY.
MAYBE WE'LL GET A BITE TO EAT LATER.
OKAY.
SEY HONG.

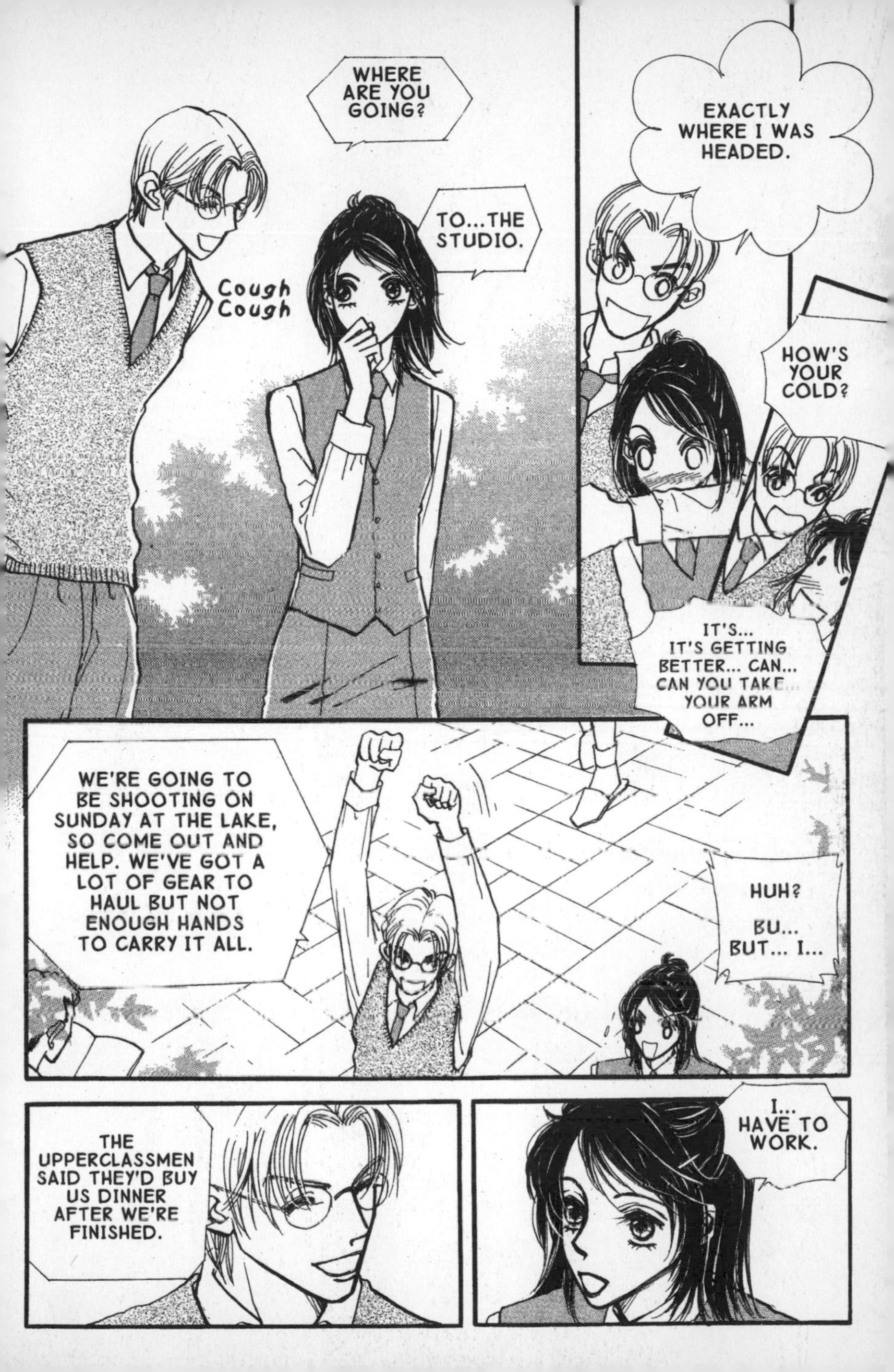
WHERE ARE YOU GOING?
Cough Cough
TO...THE STUDIO.
EXACTLY WHERE I WAS HEADED.
HOW'S YOUR COLD?
IT'S... IT'S GETTING BETTER... CAN... CAN YOU TAKE... YOUR ARM OFF...
WE'RE GOING TO BE SHOOTING ON SUNDAY AT THE LAKE, SO COME OUT AND HELP. WE'VE GOT A LOT OF GEAR TO HAUL BUT NOT ENOUGH HANDS TO CARRY IT ALL.
HUH?
BU... BUT... I...
THE UPPERCLASSMEN SAID THEY'D BUY US DINNER AFTER WE'RE FINISHED.
I... HAVE TO WORK.

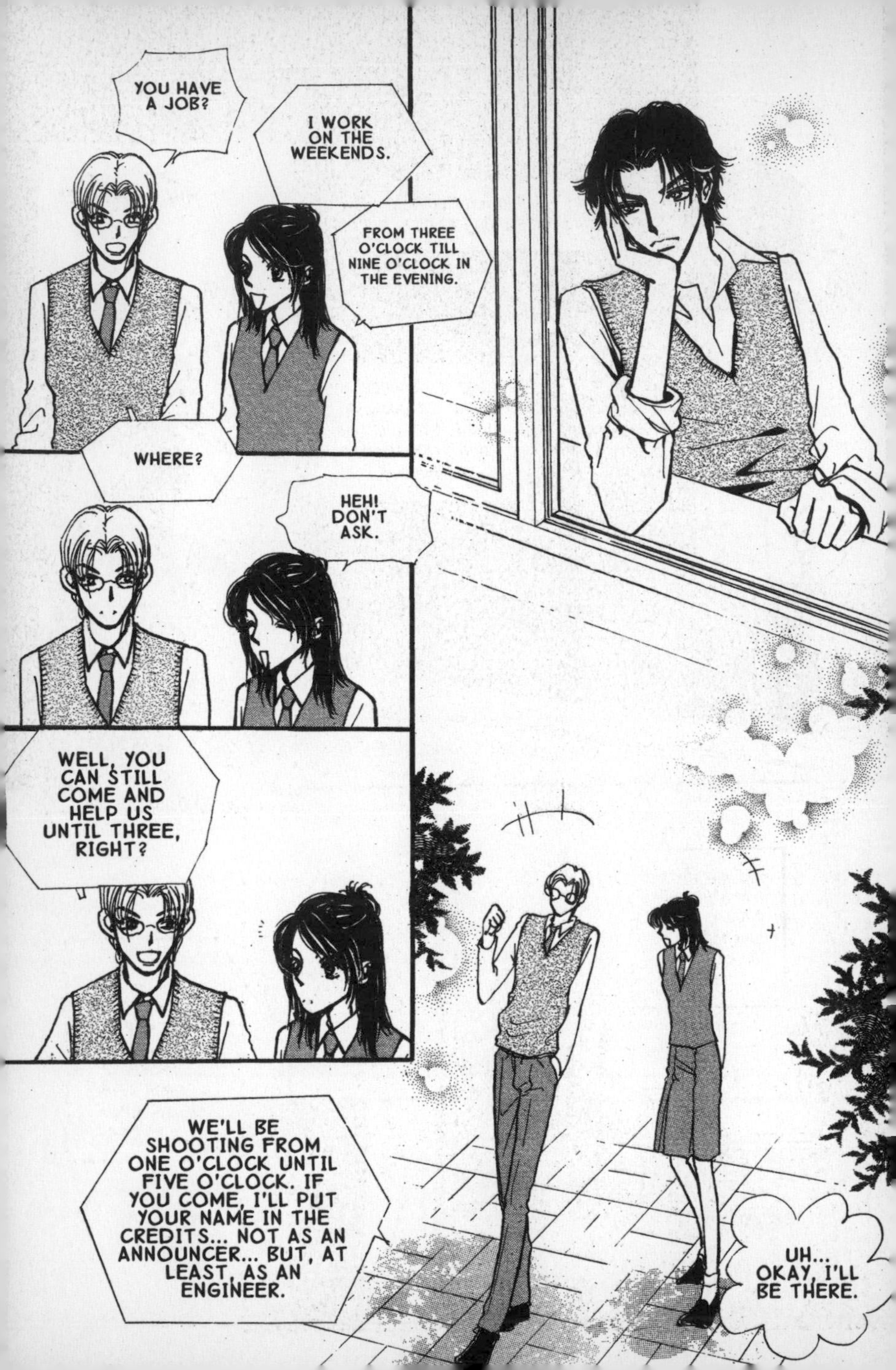
YOU HAVE A JOB?
I WORK ON THE WEEKENDS.
FROM THREE O'CLOCK TILL NINE O'CLOCK IN THE EVENING.
WHERE?
HEH! DON'T ASK.
WELL, YOU CAN STILL COME AND HELP US UNTIL THREE, RIGHT?
WE'LL BE SHOOTING FROM ONE O'CLOCK UNTIL FIVE O'CLOCK. IF YOU COME, I'LL PUT YOUR NAME IN THE CREDITS... NOT AS AN ANNOUNCER... BUT, AT LEAST, AS AN ENGINEER.
UH... OKAY, I'LL BE THERE.

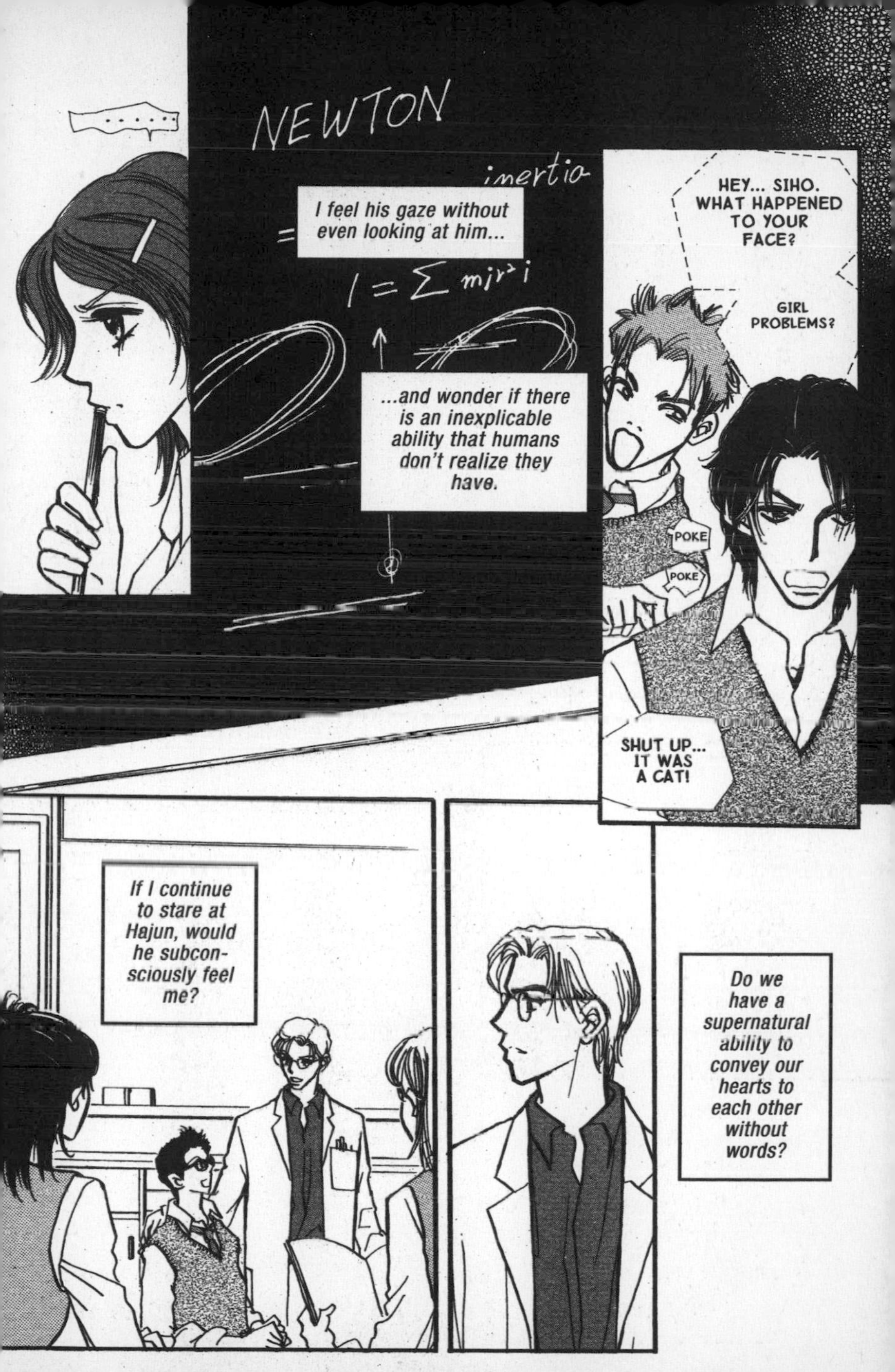
......
NEWTON
inertia
I feel his gaze without even looking at him...
...and wonder if there is an inexplicable ability that humans don't realize they have.
HEY... SIHO. WHAT HAPPENED TO YOUR FACE?
GIRL PROBLEMS?
POKE
POKE
SHUT UP... IT WAS A CAT!
If I continue to stare at Hajun, would he subconsciously feel me?
Do we have a supernatural ability to convey our hearts to each other without words?

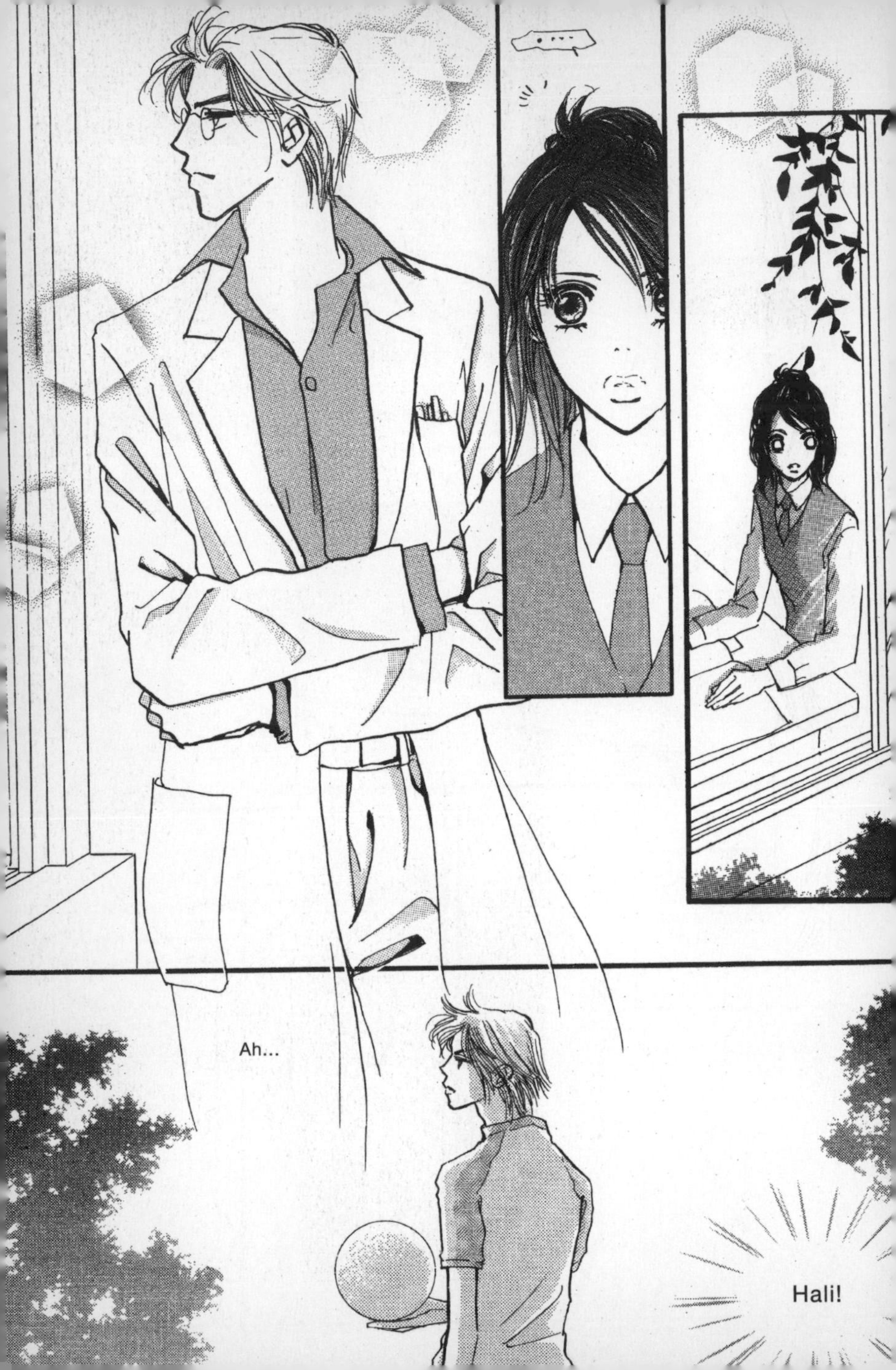
Hali!
Ah...

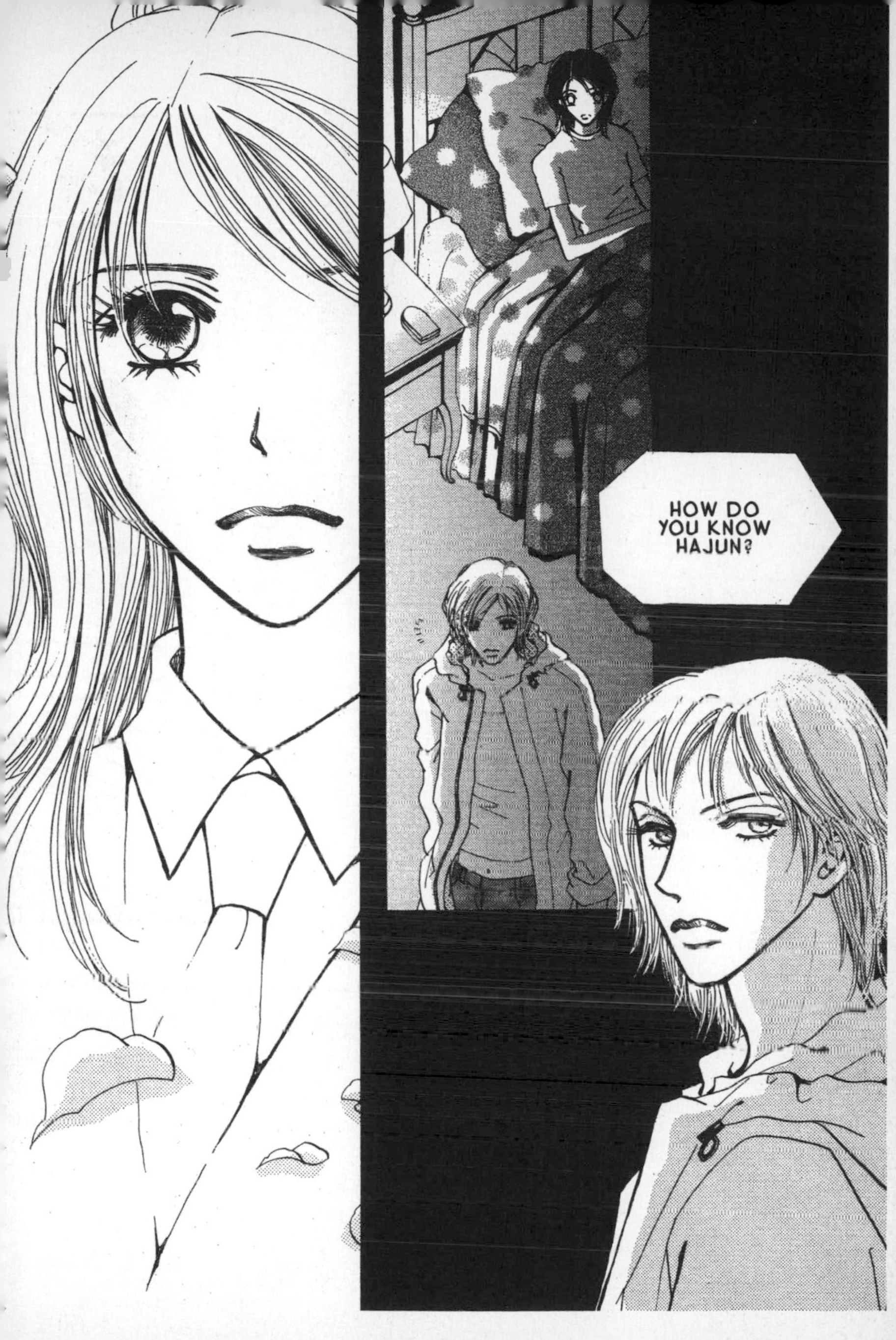
HOW DO YOU KNOW HAJUN?

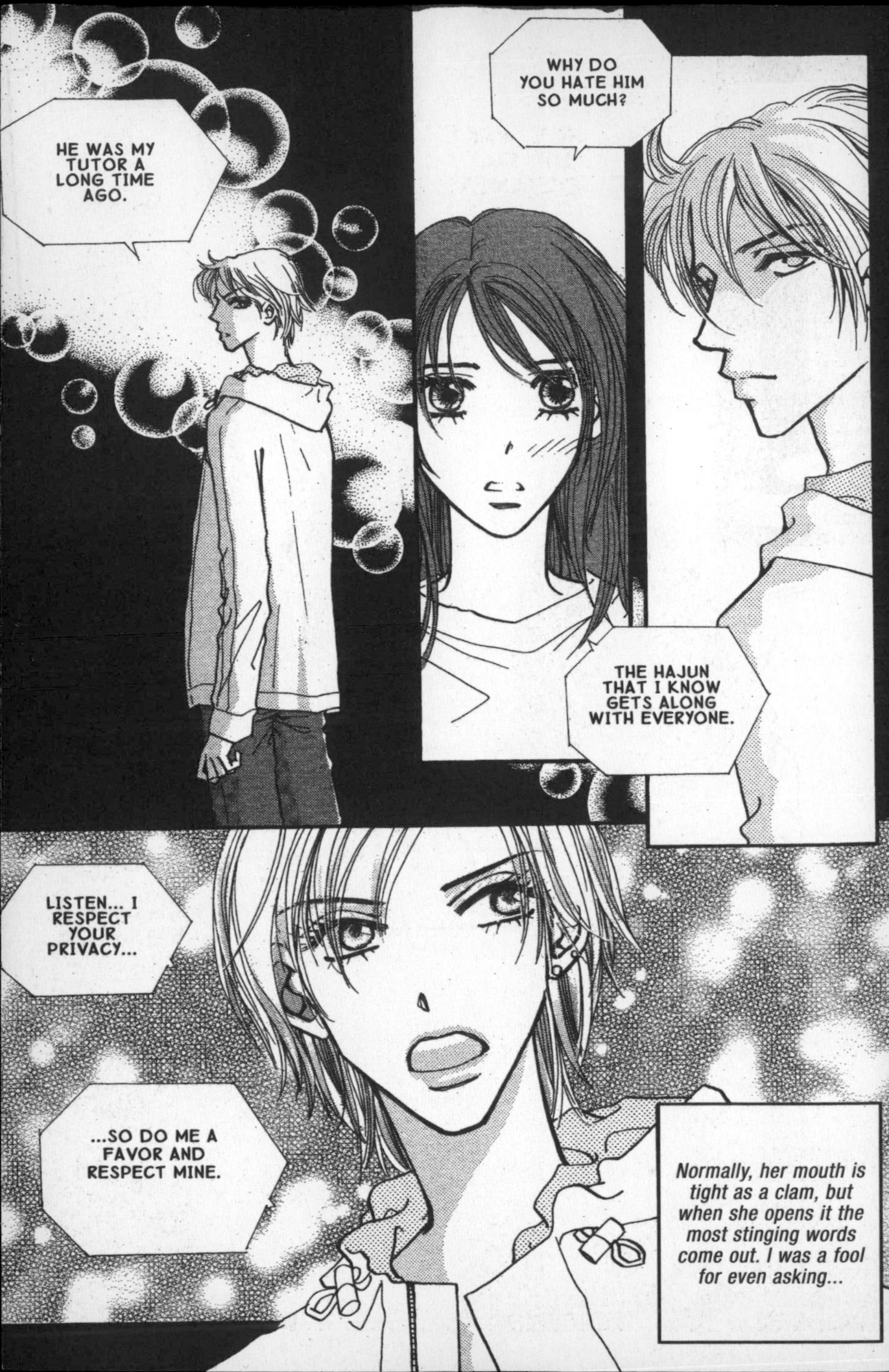
HE WAS MY TUTOR A LONG TIME AGO.
WHY DO YOU HATE HIM SO MUCH?
THE HAJUN THAT I KNOW GETS ALONG WITH EVERYONE.
LISTEN... I RESPECT YOUR PRIVACY...
...SO DO ME A FAVOR AND RESPECT MINE.
Normally, her mouth is tight as a clam, but when she opens it the most stinging words come out. I was a fool for even asking...

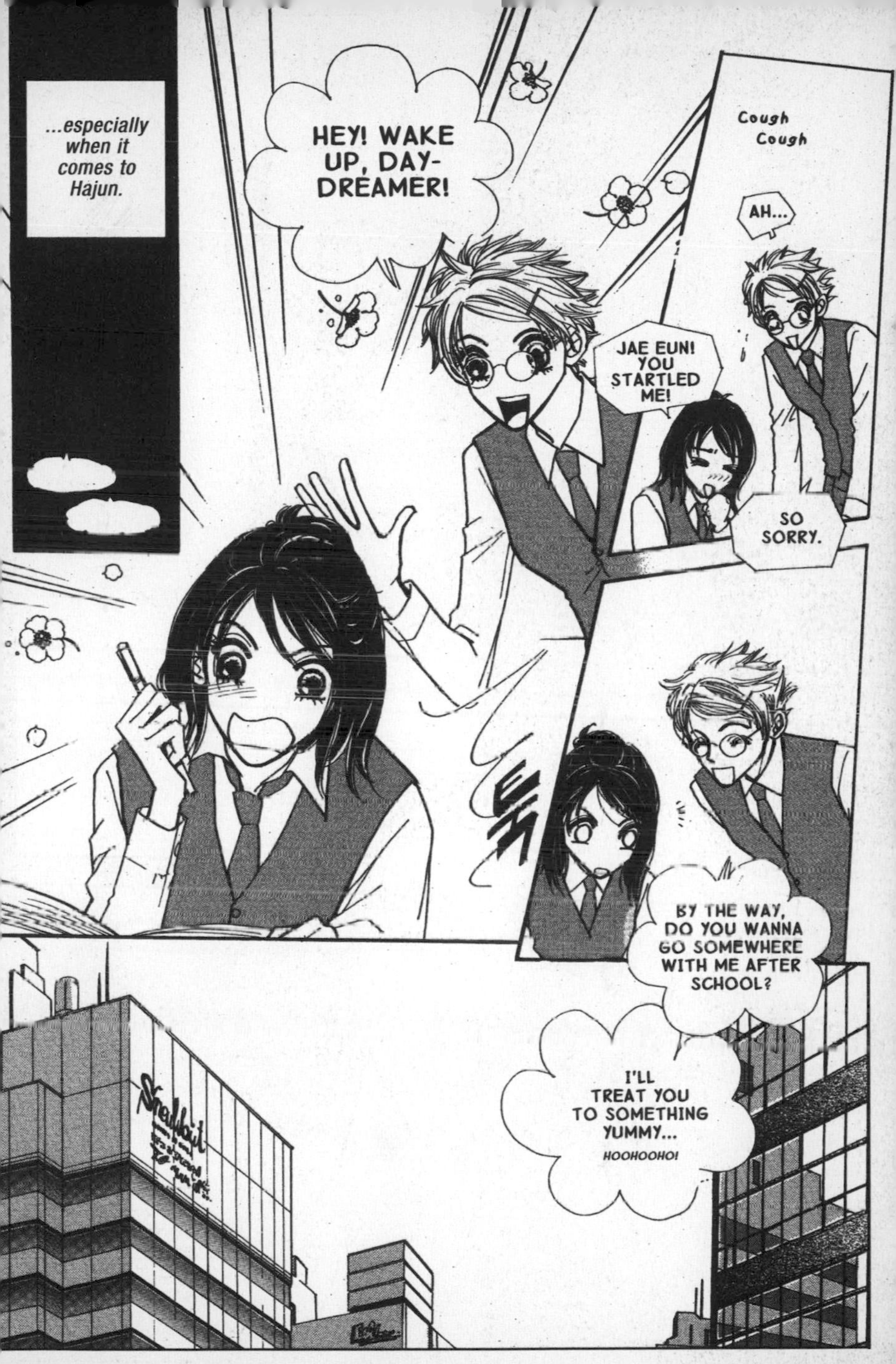
...especially when it comes to Hajun.
HEY! WAKE UP, DAY-DREAMER!
Cough Cough
AH...
JAE EUN! YOU STARTLED ME!
SO SORRY.
BY THE WAY, DO YOU WANNA GO SOMEWHERE WITH ME AFTER SCHOOL?
I'LL TREAT YOU TO SOMETHING YUMMY...
HOOHOOHO!

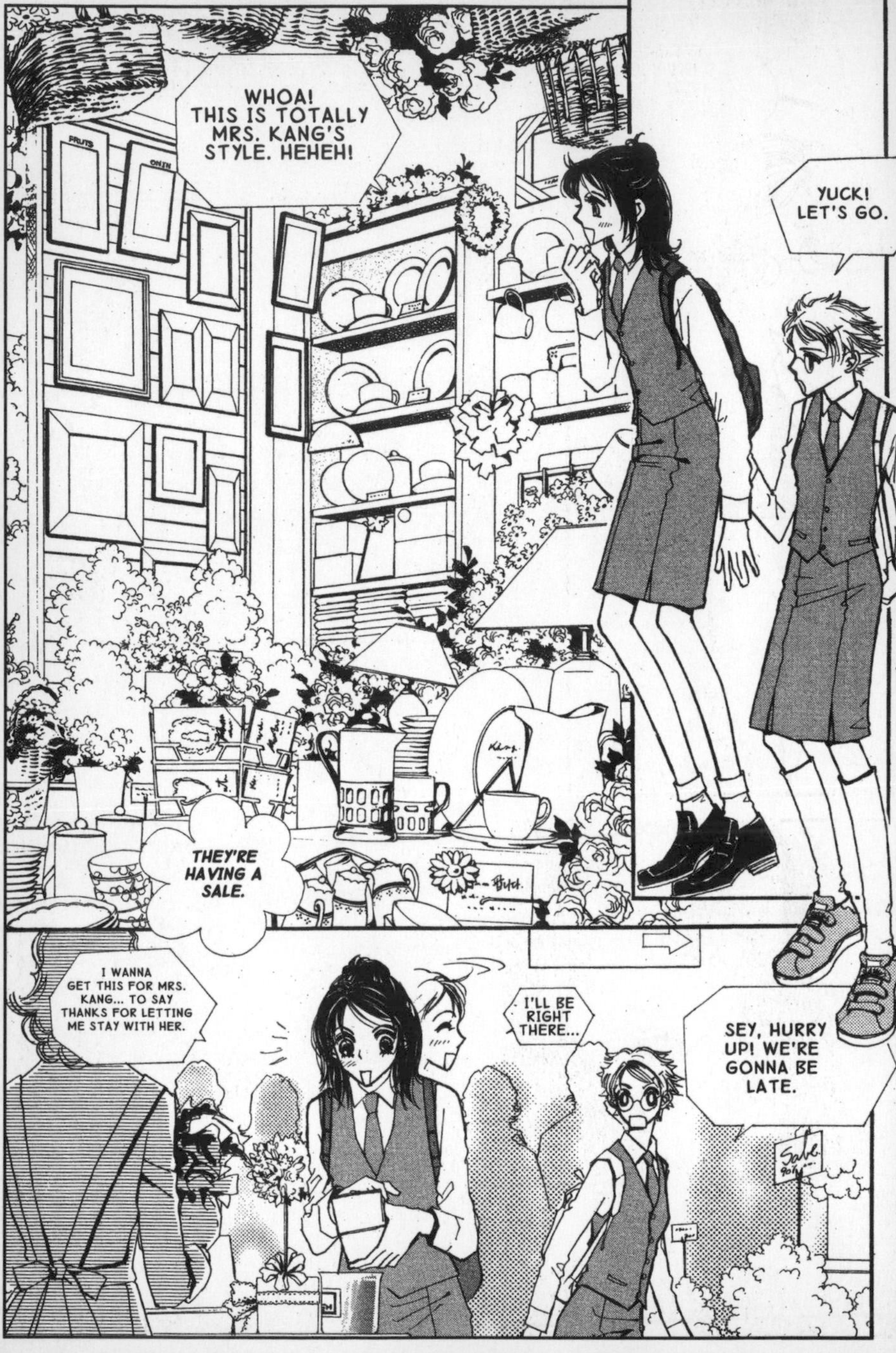
WHOA! THIS IS TOTALLY MRS. KANG'S STYLE. HEHEH!
YUCK! LET'S GO.
THEY'RE HAVING A SALE.
I WANNA GET THIS FOR MRS. KANG... TO SAY THANKS FOR LETTING ME STAY WITH HER.
I'LL BE RIGHT THERE...
SEY, HURRY UP! WE'RE GONNA BE LATE.

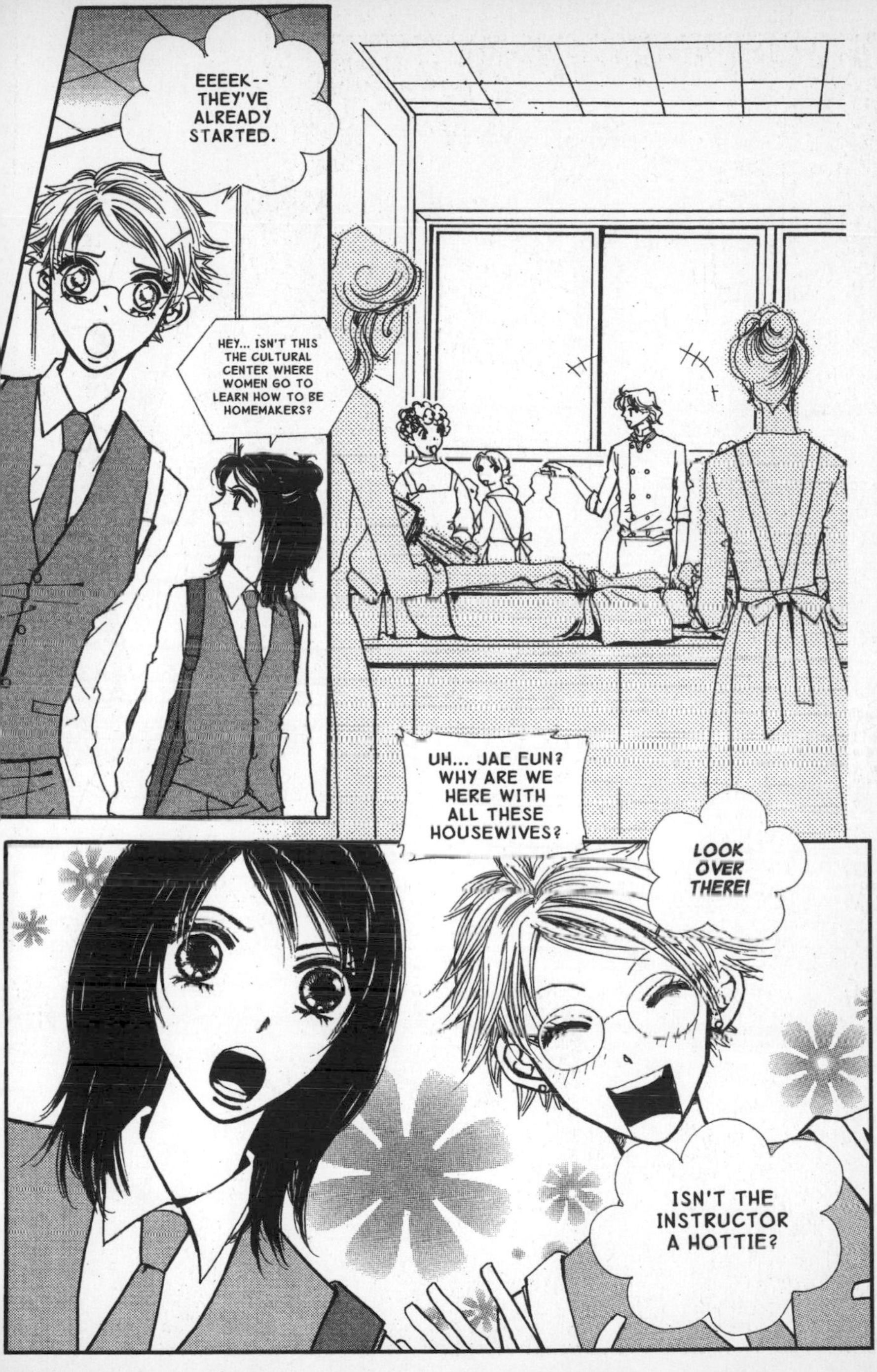
EEEEK--
THEY'VE
ALREADY
STARTED.
HEY... ISN'T THIS
THE CULTURAL
CENTER WHERE
WOMEN GO TO
LEARN HOW TO BE
HOMEMAKERS?
UH... JAE EUN?
WHY ARE WE
HERE WITH
ALL THESE
HOUSEWIVES?
LOOK
OVER
THERE!
ISN'T THE
INSTRUCTOR
A HOTTIE?

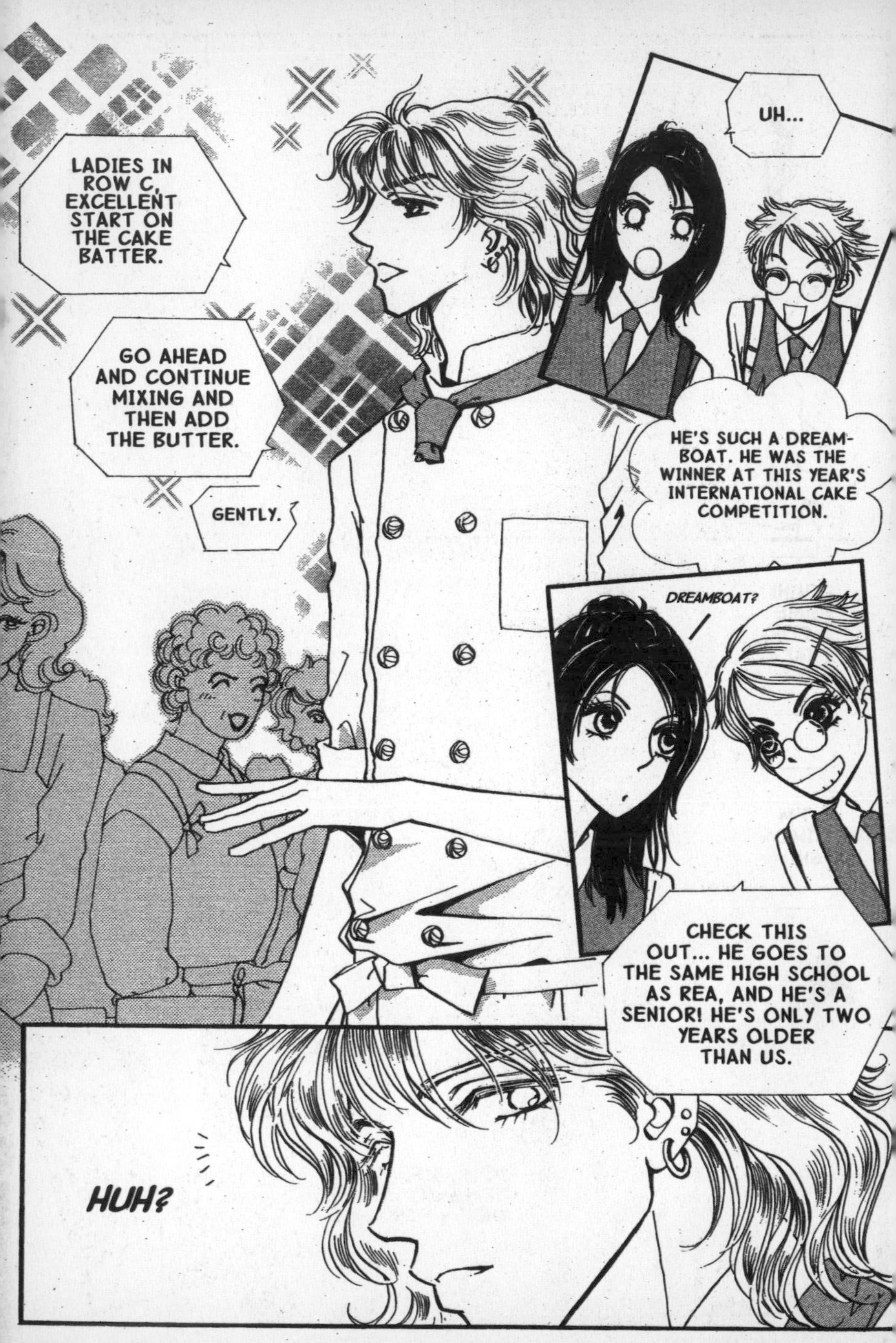
LADIES IN ROW C, EXCELLENT START ON THE CAKE BATTER.
GO AHEAD AND CONTINUE MIXING AND THEN ADD THE BUTTER.
GENTLY.
UH...
HE'S SUCH A DREAM-BOAT. HE WAS THE WINNER AT THIS YEAR'S INTERNATIONAL CAKE COMPETITION.
DREAMBOAT?
CHECK THIS OUT... HE GOES TO THE SAME HIGH SCHOOL AS REA, AND HE'S A SENIOR! HE'S ONLY TWO YEARS OLDER THAN US.
HUH?

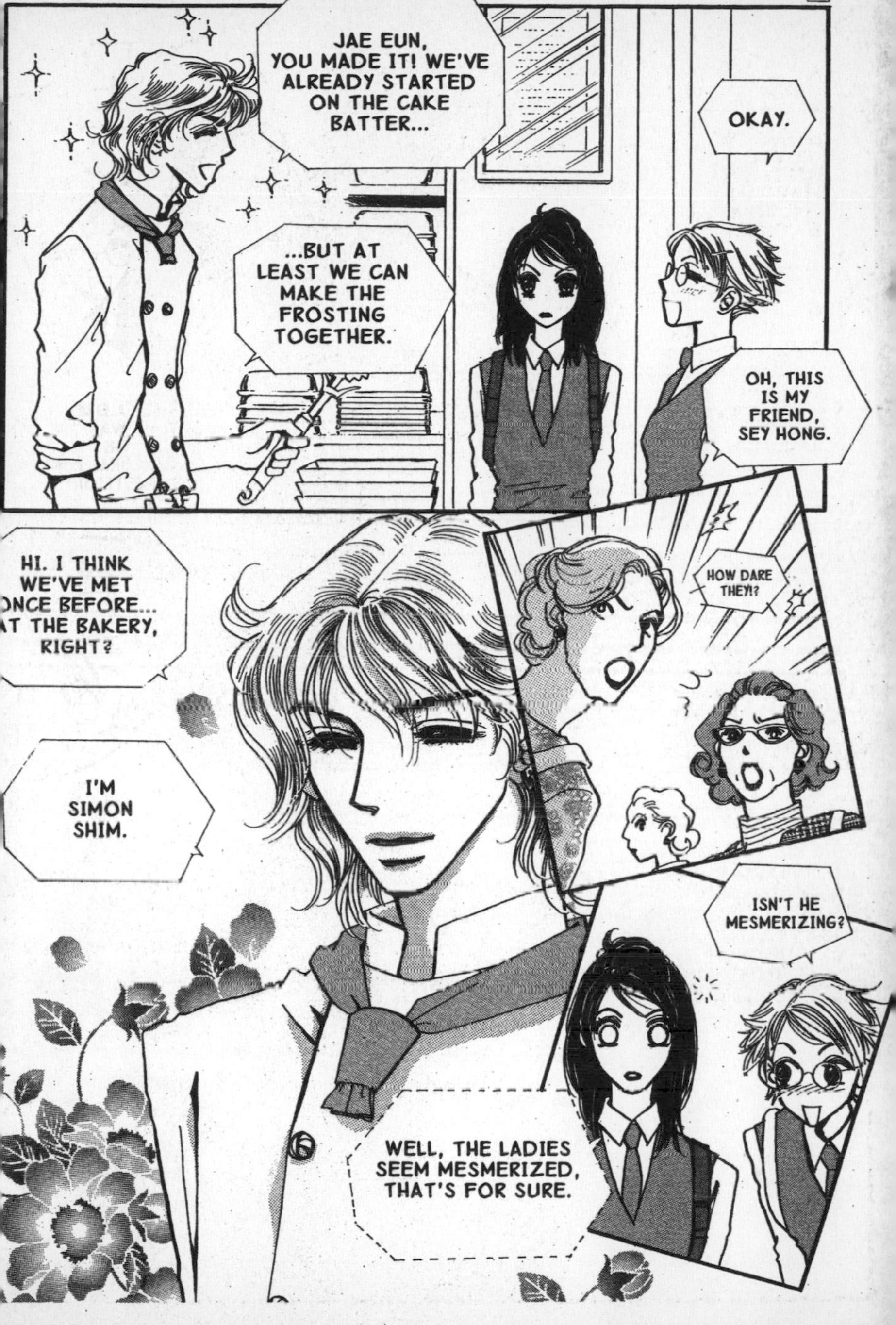
JAE EUN, YOU MADE IT! WE'VE ALREADY STARTED ON THE CAKE BATTER...
...BUT AT LEAST WE CAN MAKE THE FROSTING TOGETHER.
OKAY.
OH, THIS IS MY FRIEND, SEY HONG.
HI. I THINK WE'VE MET ONCE BEFORE... AT THE BAKERY, RIGHT?
I'M SIMON SHIM.
HOW DARE THEY!?
ISN'T HE MESMERIZING?
WELL, THE LADIES SEEM MESMERIZED, THAT'S FOR SURE.

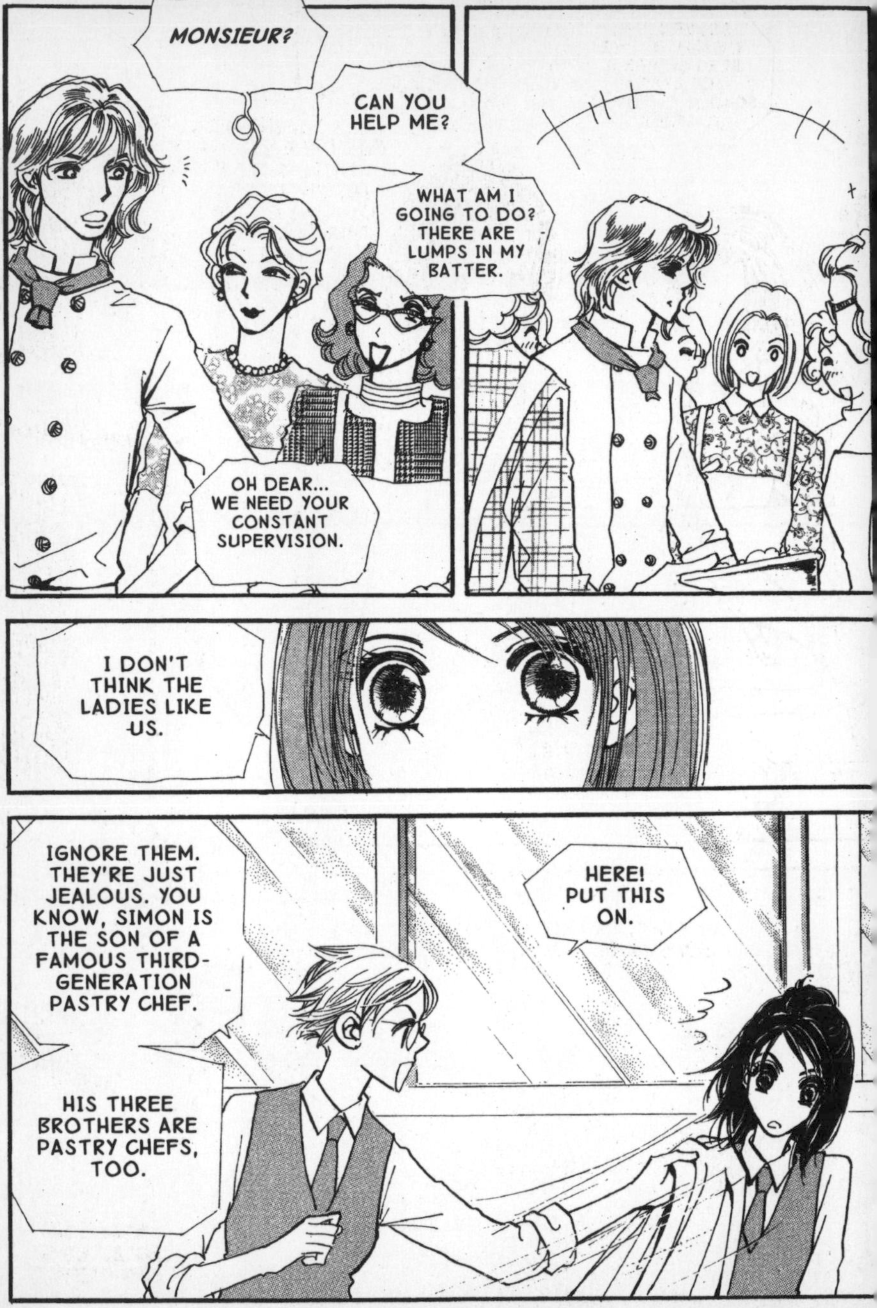
MONSIEUR?
CAN YOU HELP ME?
WHAT AM I GOING TO DO? THERE ARE LUMPS IN MY BATTER.
OH DEAR... WE NEED YOUR CONSTANT SUPERVISION.
I DON'T THINK THE LADIES LIKE US.
IGNORE THEM. THEY'RE JUST JEALOUS. YOU KNOW, SIMON IS THE SON OF A FAMOUS THIRD-GENERATION PASTRY CHEF.
HIS THREE BROTHERS ARE PASTRY CHEFS, TOO.
HERE! PUT THIS ON.

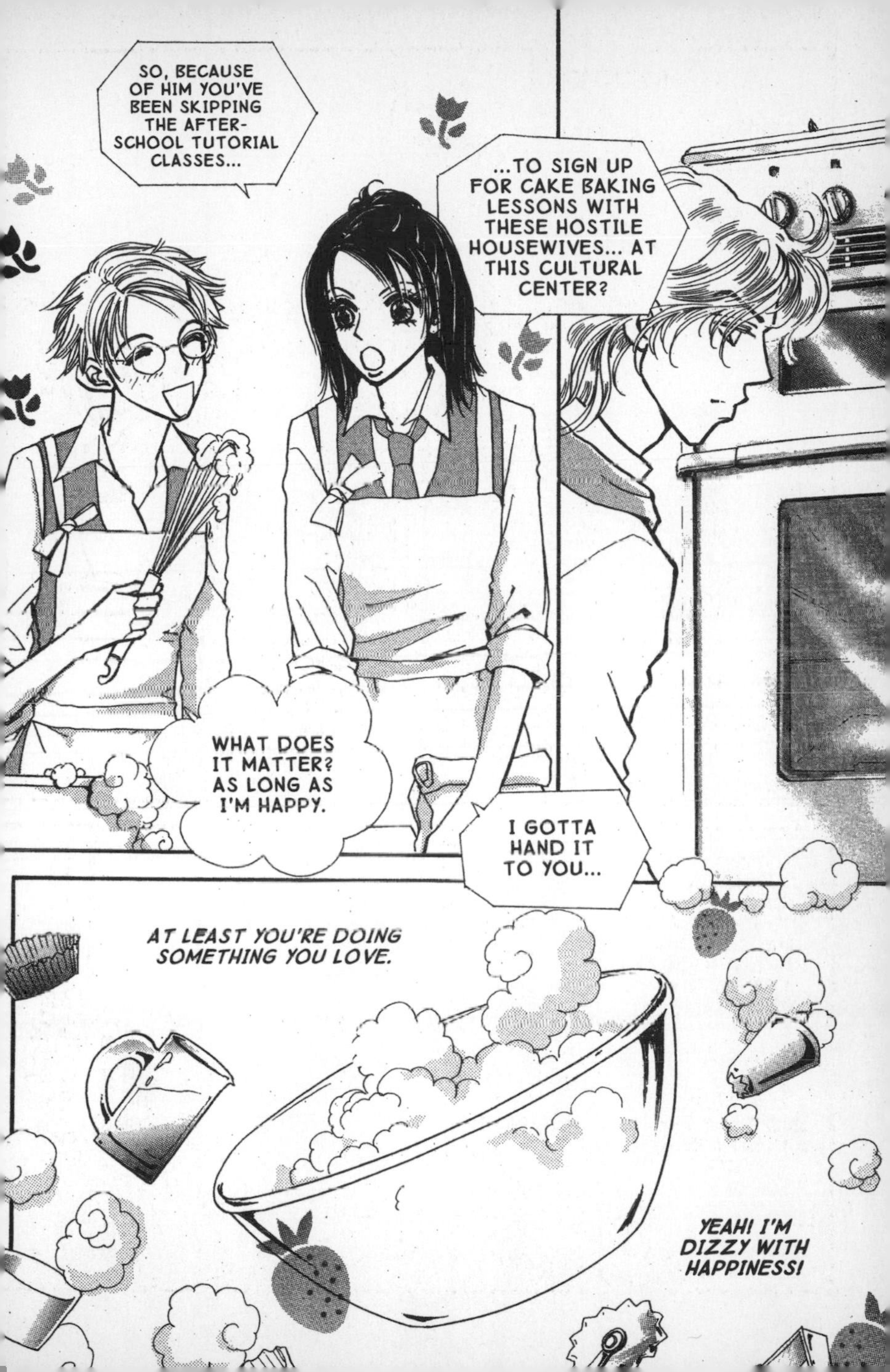
SO, BECAUSE OF HIM YOU'VE BEEN SKIPPING THE AFTER-SCHOOL TUTORIAL CLASSES...
...TO SIGN UP FOR CAKE BAKING LESSONS WITH THESE HOSTILE HOUSEWIVES... AT THIS CULTURAL CENTER?
WHAT DOES IT MATTER? AS LONG AS I'M HAPPY.
I GOTTA HAND IT TO YOU...
AT LEAST YOU'RE DOING SOMETHING YOU LOVE.
YEAH! I'M DIZZY WITH HAPPINESS!

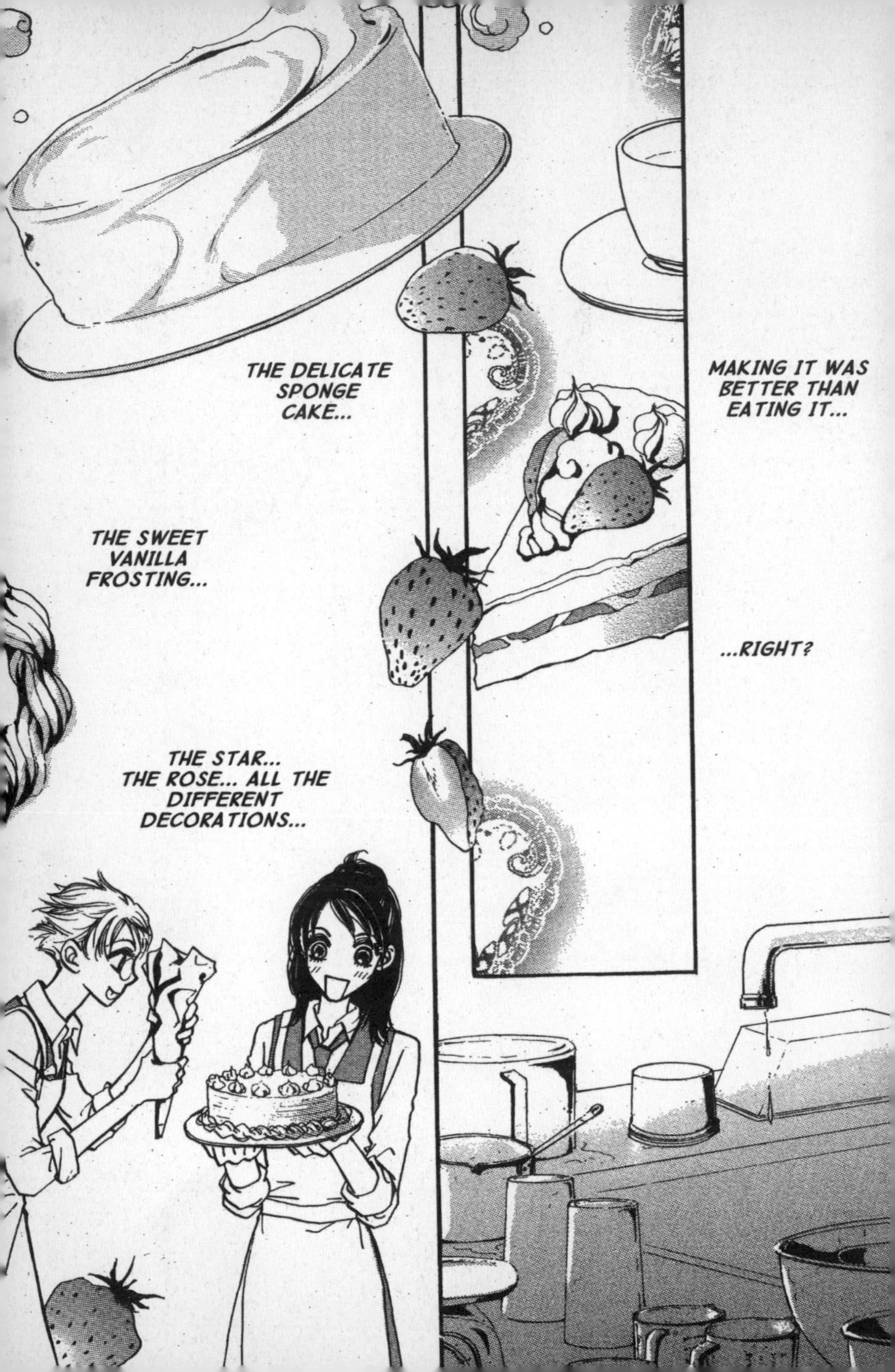
THE DELICATE SPONGE CAKE...
THE SWEET VANILLA FROSTING...
THE STAR... THE ROSE... ALL THE DIFFERENT DECORATIONS...
MAKING IT WAS BETTER THAN EATING IT...
...RIGHT?

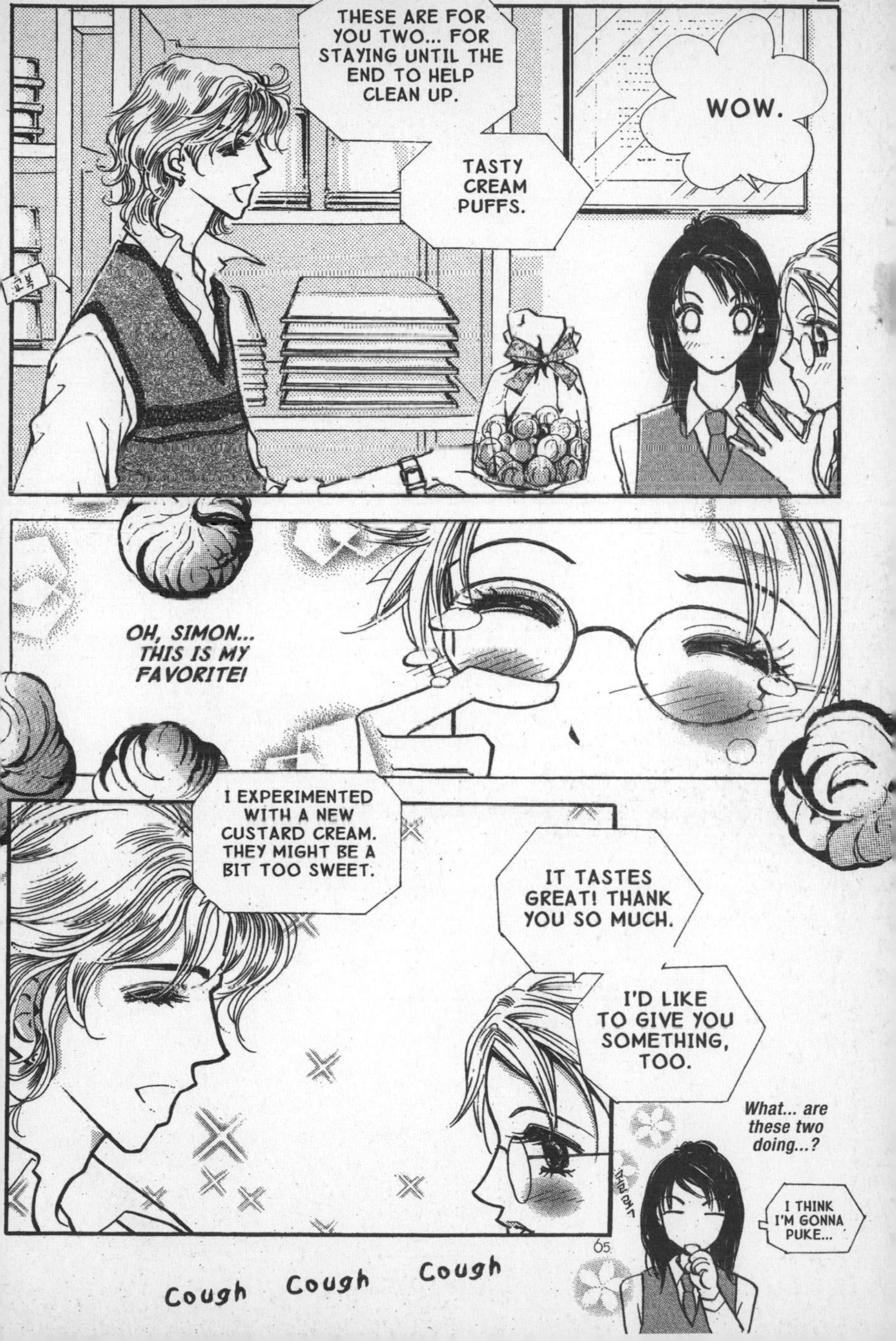
THESE ARE FOR YOU TWO... FOR STAYING UNTIL THE END TO HELP CLEAN UP.
TASTY CREAM PUFFS.
WOW.
OH, SIMON... THIS IS MY FAVORITE!
I EXPERIMENTED WITH A NEW CUSTARD CREAM. THEY MIGHT BE A BIT TOO SWEET.
IT TASTES GREAT! THANK YOU SO MUCH.
I'D LIKE TO GIVE YOU SOMETHING, TOO.
What... are these two doing...?
I THINK I'M GONNA PUKE...
Cough Cough Cough

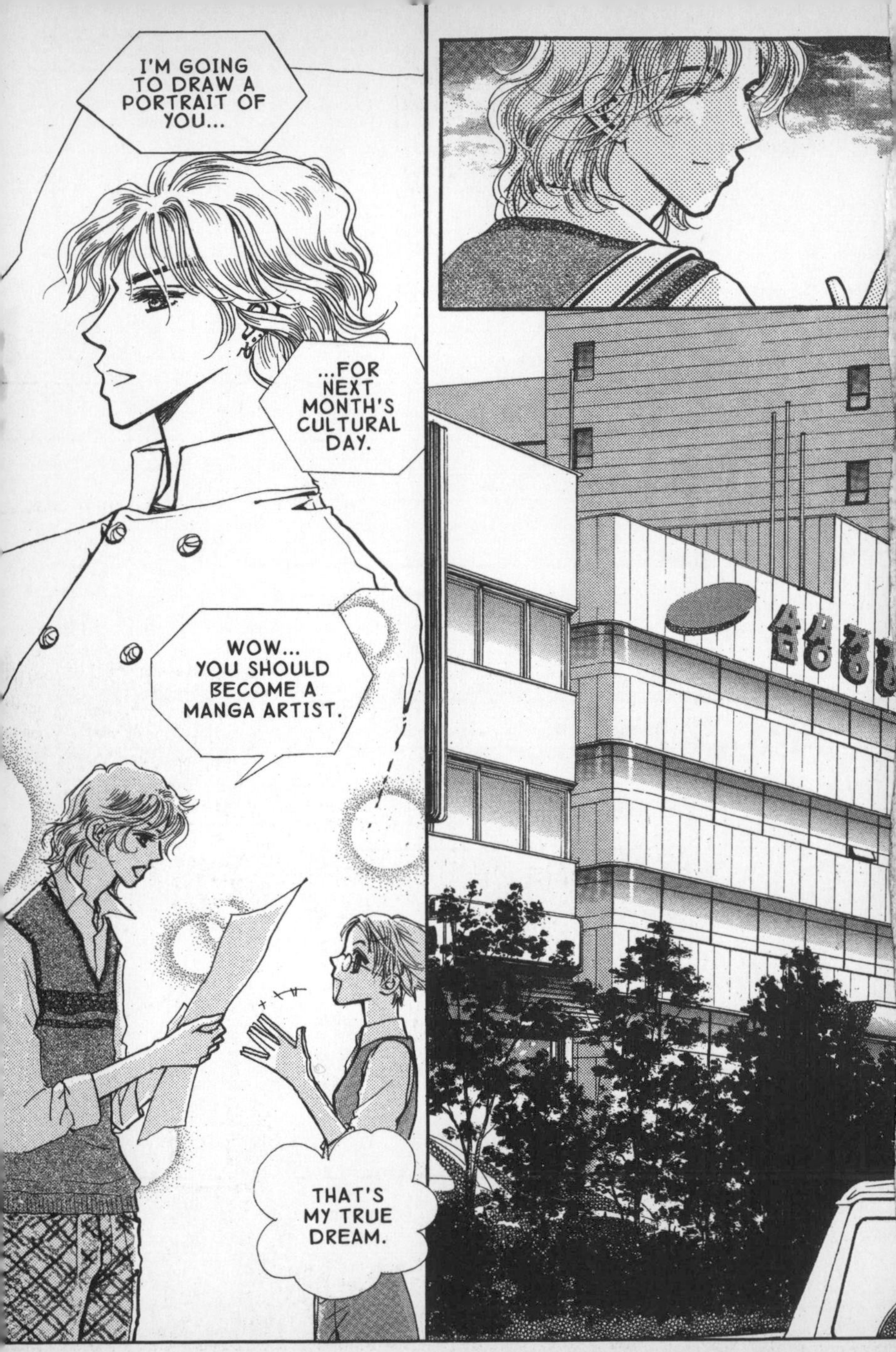
I'M GOING TO DRAW A PORTRAIT OF YOU...
...FOR NEXT MONTH'S CULTURAL DAY.
WOW... YOU SHOULD BECOME A MANGA ARTIST.
THAT'S MY TRUE DREAM.

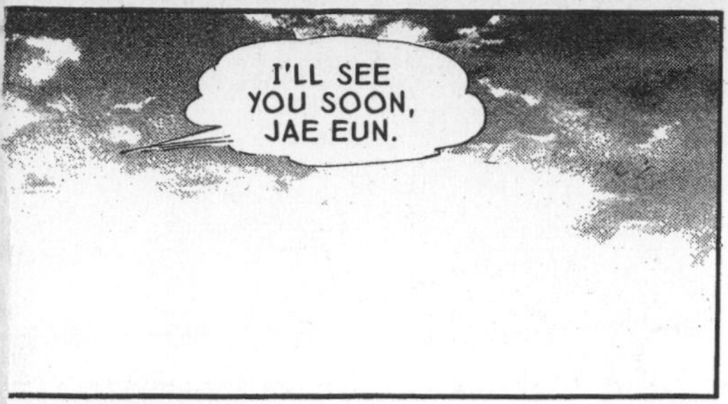
I'LL SEE YOU SOON, JAE EUN.

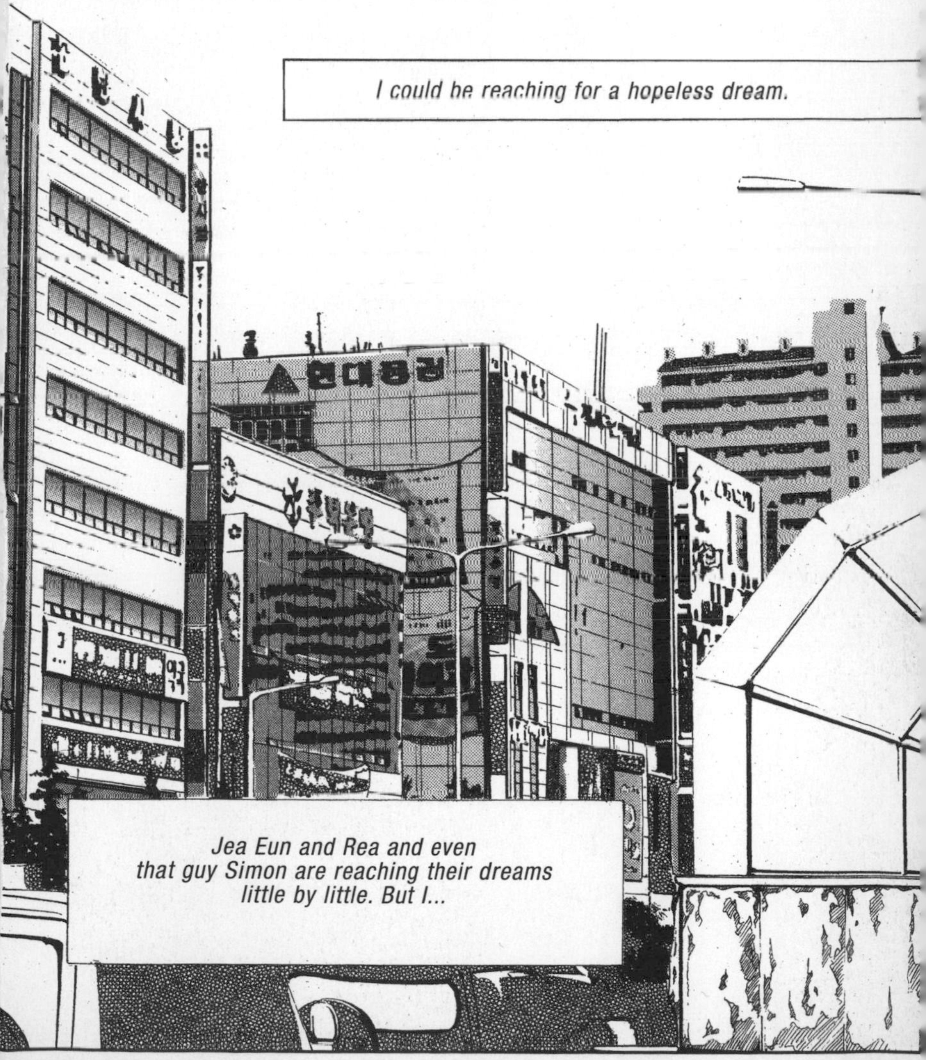
I could be reaching for a hopeless dream.
Jea Eun and Rea and even that guy Simon are reaching their dreams little by little. But I...

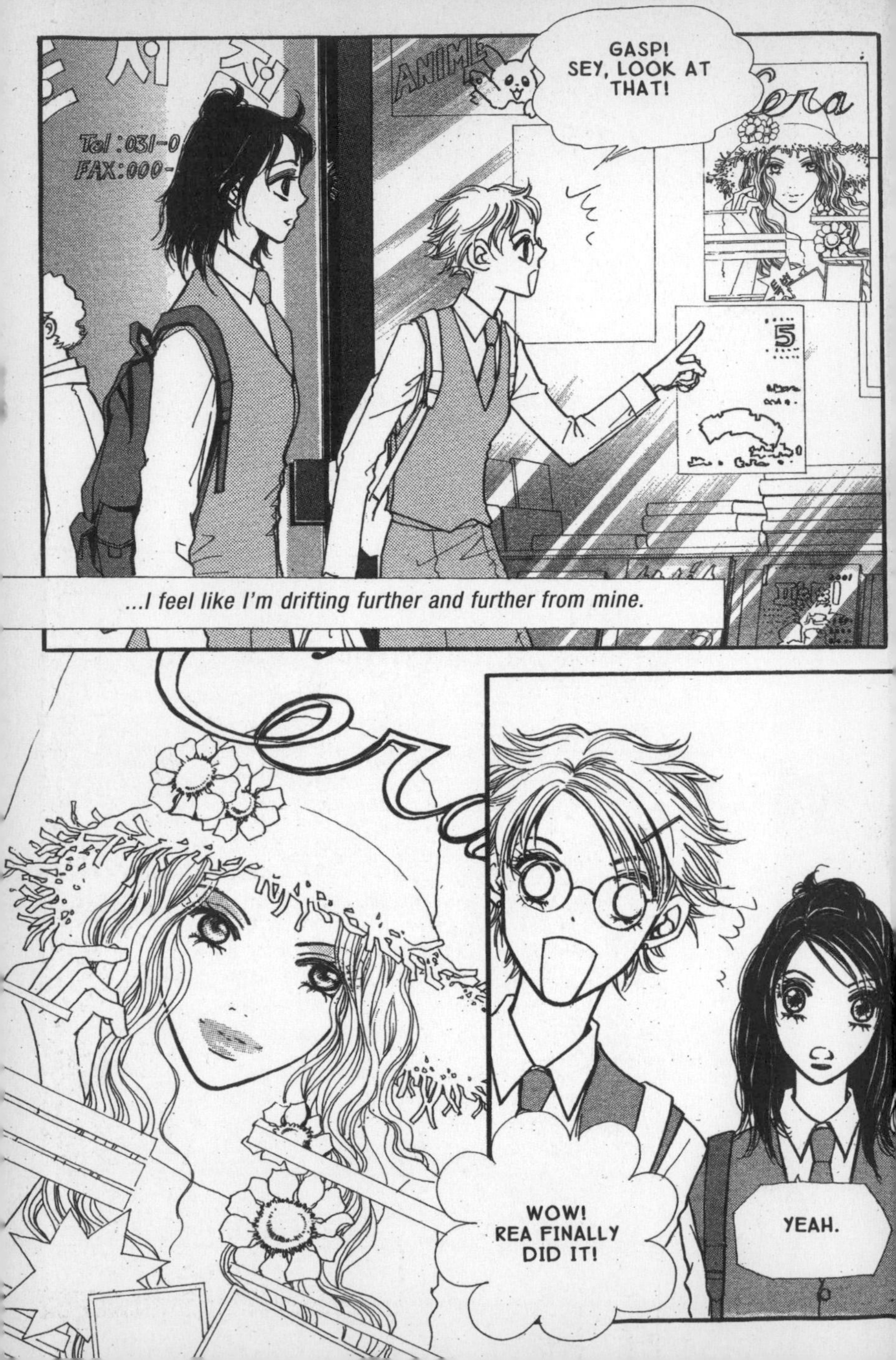
Tel :031-0
FAX:000-
ANIME
GASP!
SEY, LOOK AT THAT!
...I feel like I'm drifting further and further from mine.
WOW! REA FINALLY DID IT!
YEAH.

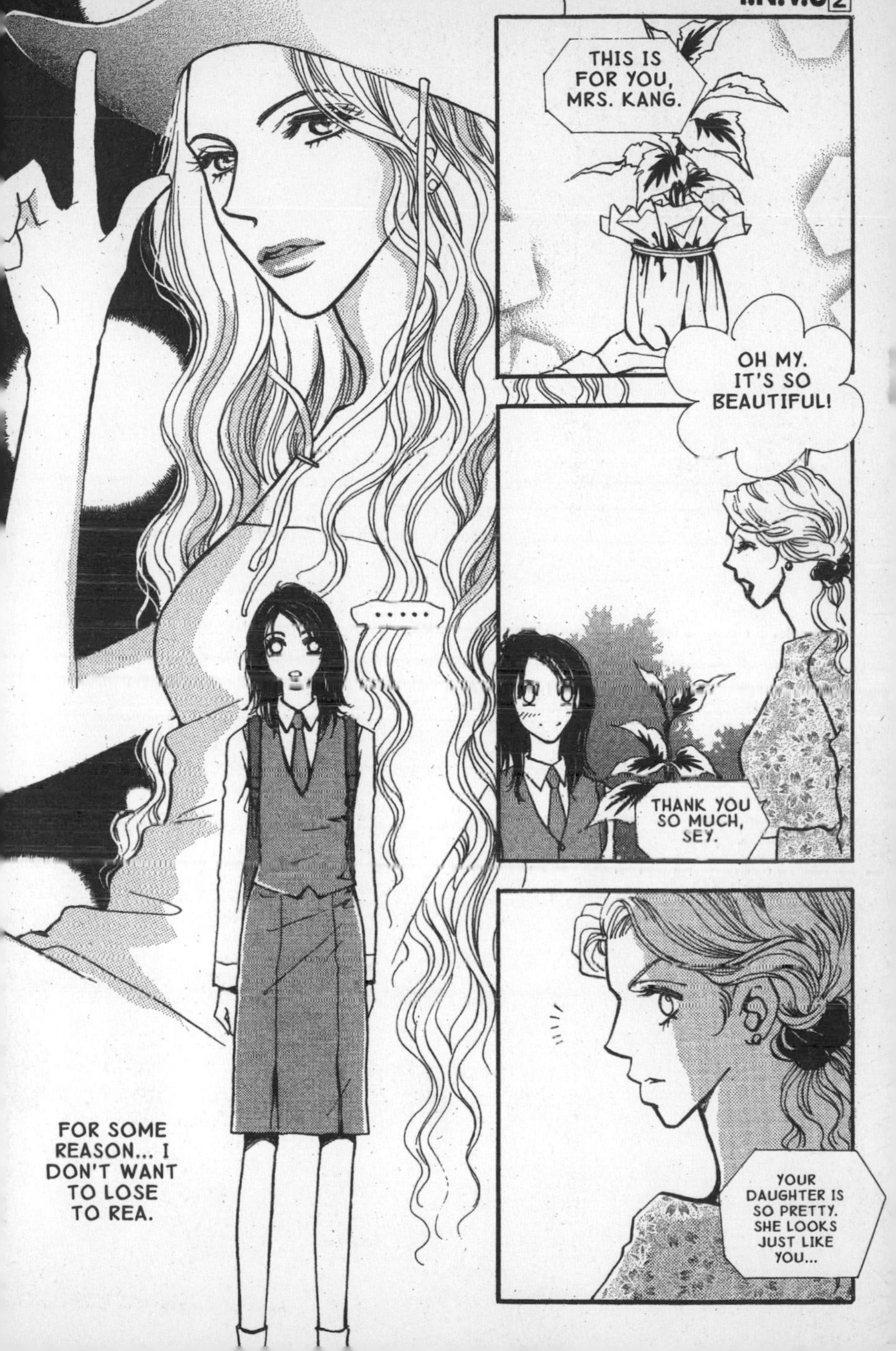
......
FOR SOME REASON... I DON'T WANT TO LOSE TO REA.
THIS IS FOR YOU, MRS. KANG.
OH MY. IT'S SO BEAUTIFUL!
THANK YOU SO MUCH, SEY.
YOUR DAUGHTER IS SO PRETTY. SHE LOOKS JUST LIKE YOU...

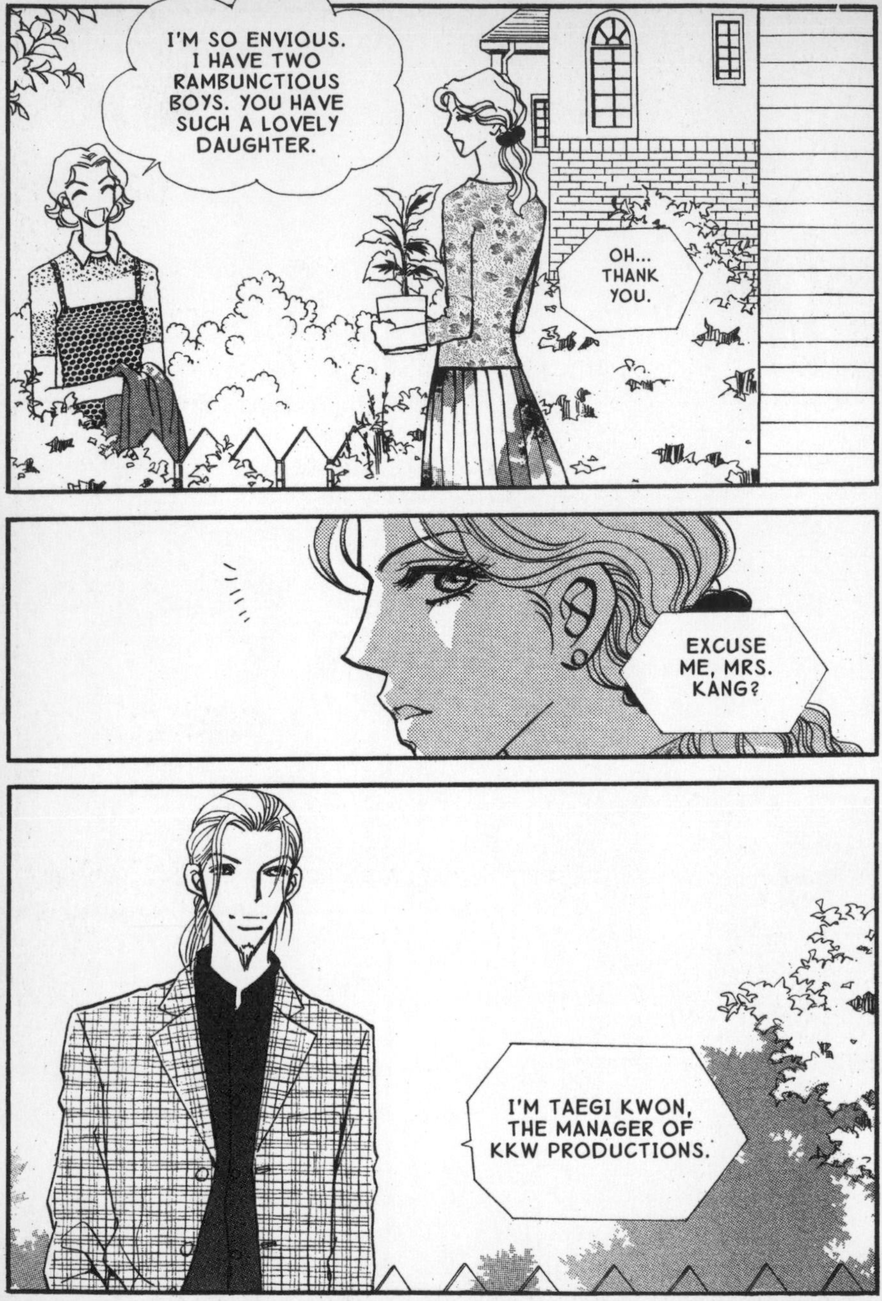
I'M SO ENVIOUS. I HAVE TWO RAMBUNCTIOUS BOYS. YOU HAVE SUCH A LOVELY DAUGHTER.
OH... THANK YOU.
EXCUSE ME, MRS. KANG?
I'M TAEGI KWON, THE MANAGER OF KKW PRODUCTIONS.

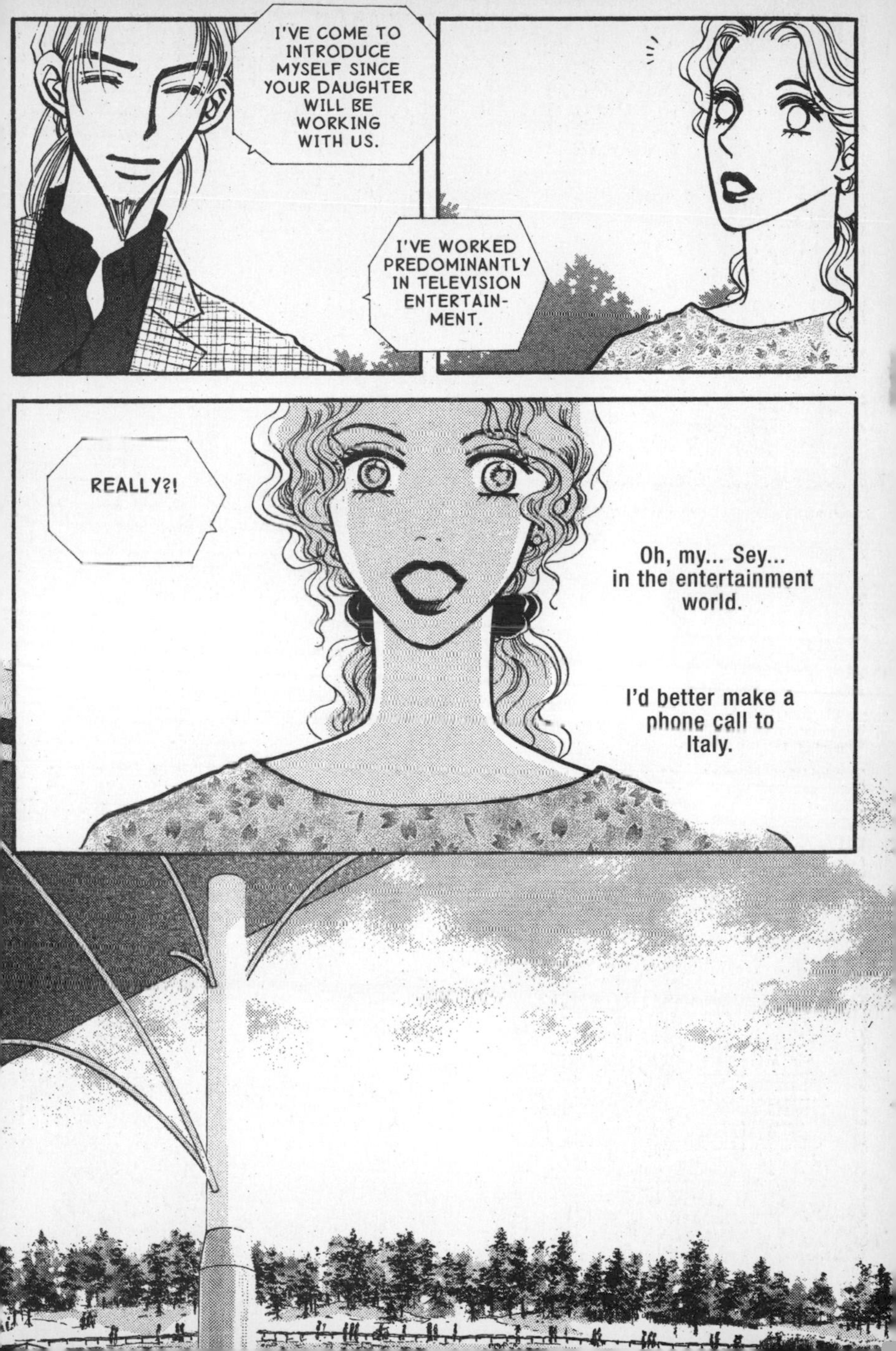
I'VE COME TO INTRODUCE MYSELF SINCE YOUR DAUGHTER WILL BE WORKING WITH US.
I'VE WORKED PREDOMINANTLY IN TELEVISION ENTERTAIN-MENT.
REALLY?!
Oh, my... Sey... in the entertainment world.
I'd better make a phone call to Italy.

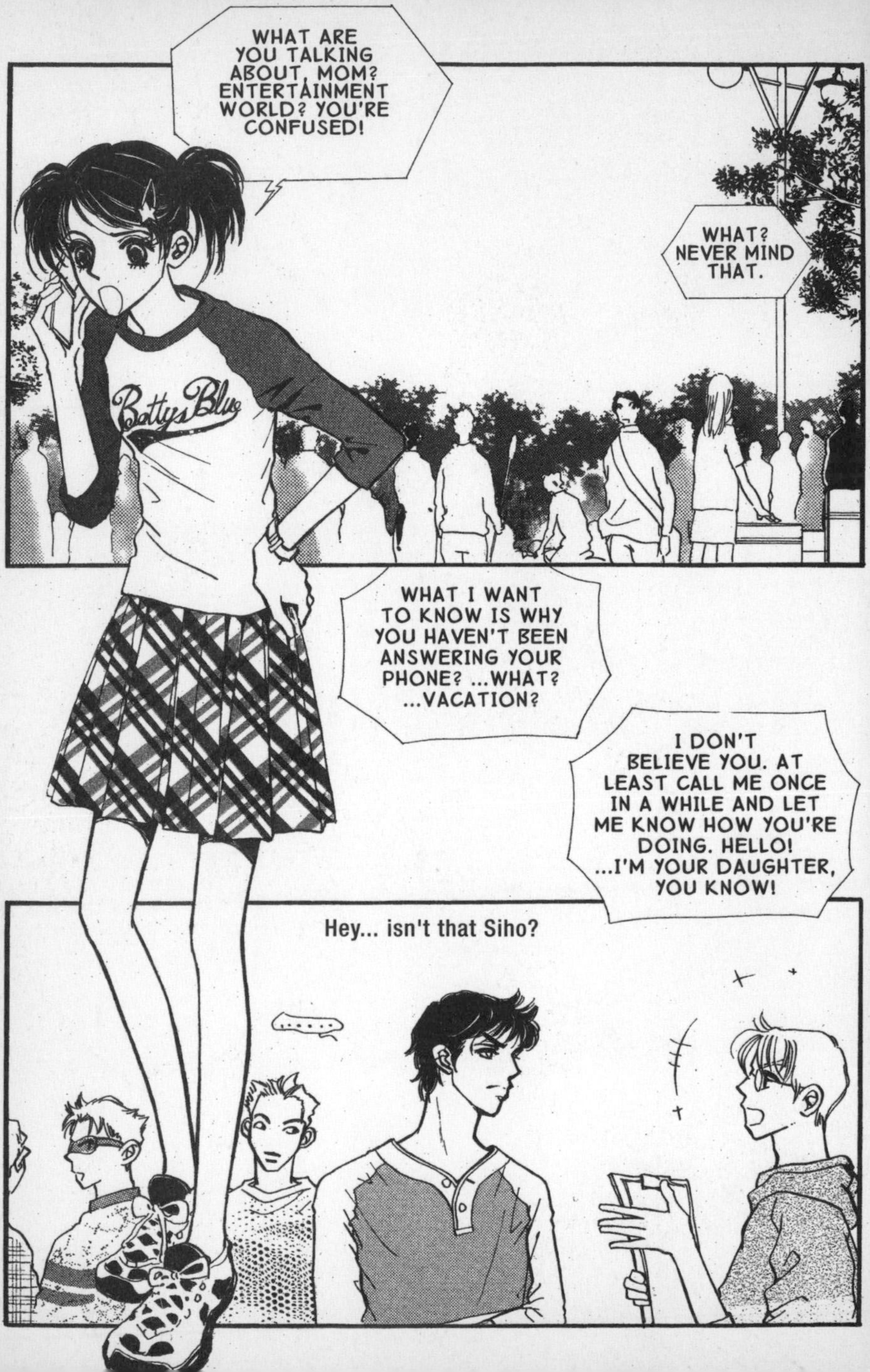
WHAT ARE YOU TALKING ABOUT, MOM? ENTERTAINMENT WORLD? YOU'RE CONFUSED!
Battys Blue
WHAT? NEVER MIND THAT.
WHAT I WANT TO KNOW IS WHY YOU HAVEN'T BEEN ANSWERING YOUR PHONE? ...WHAT? ...VACATION?
I DON'T BELIEVE YOU. AT LEAST CALL ME ONCE IN A WHILE AND LET ME KNOW HOW YOU'RE DOING. HELLO! ...I'M YOUR DAUGHTER, YOU KNOW!
Hey... isn't that Siho?
.....

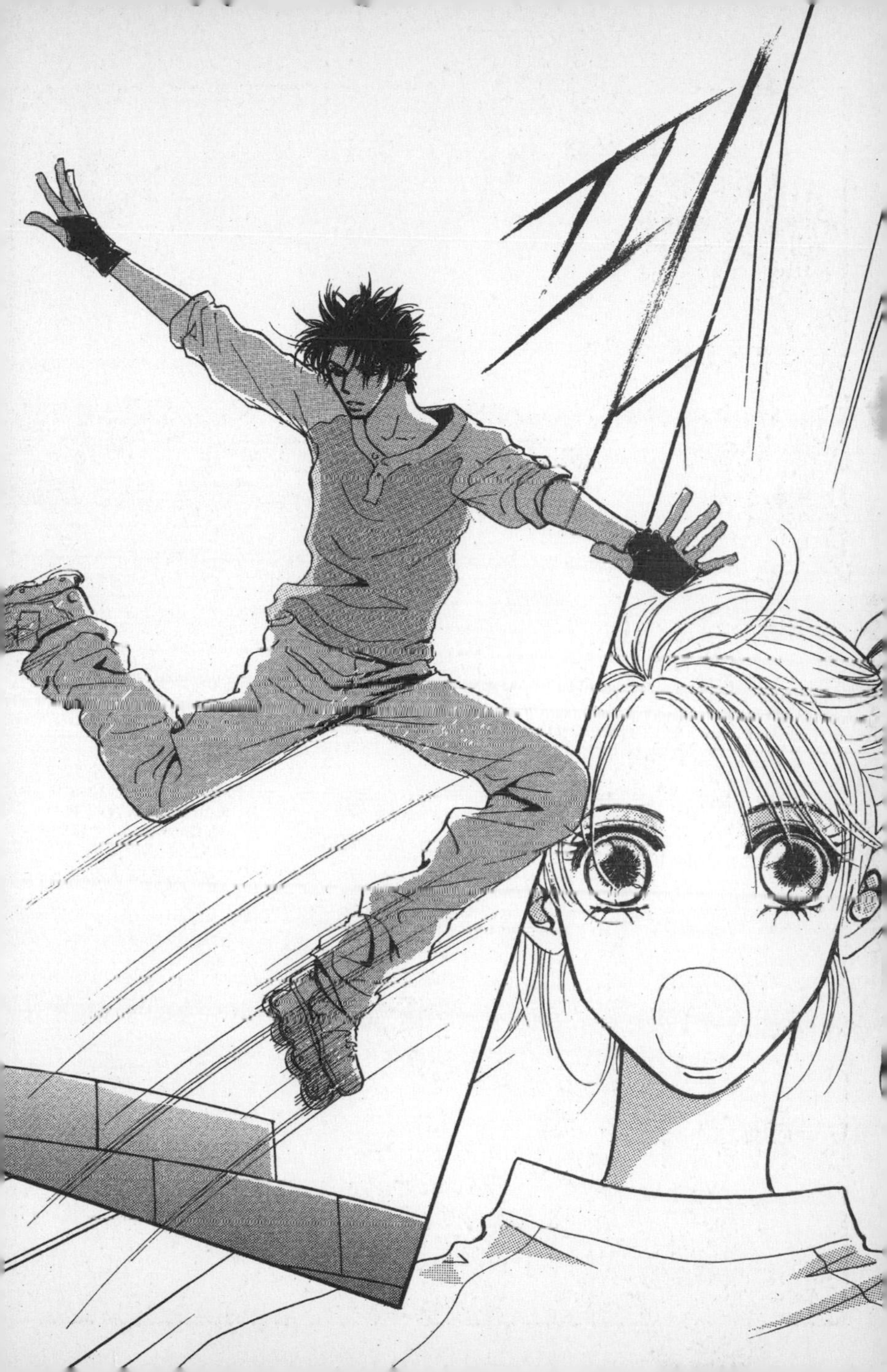

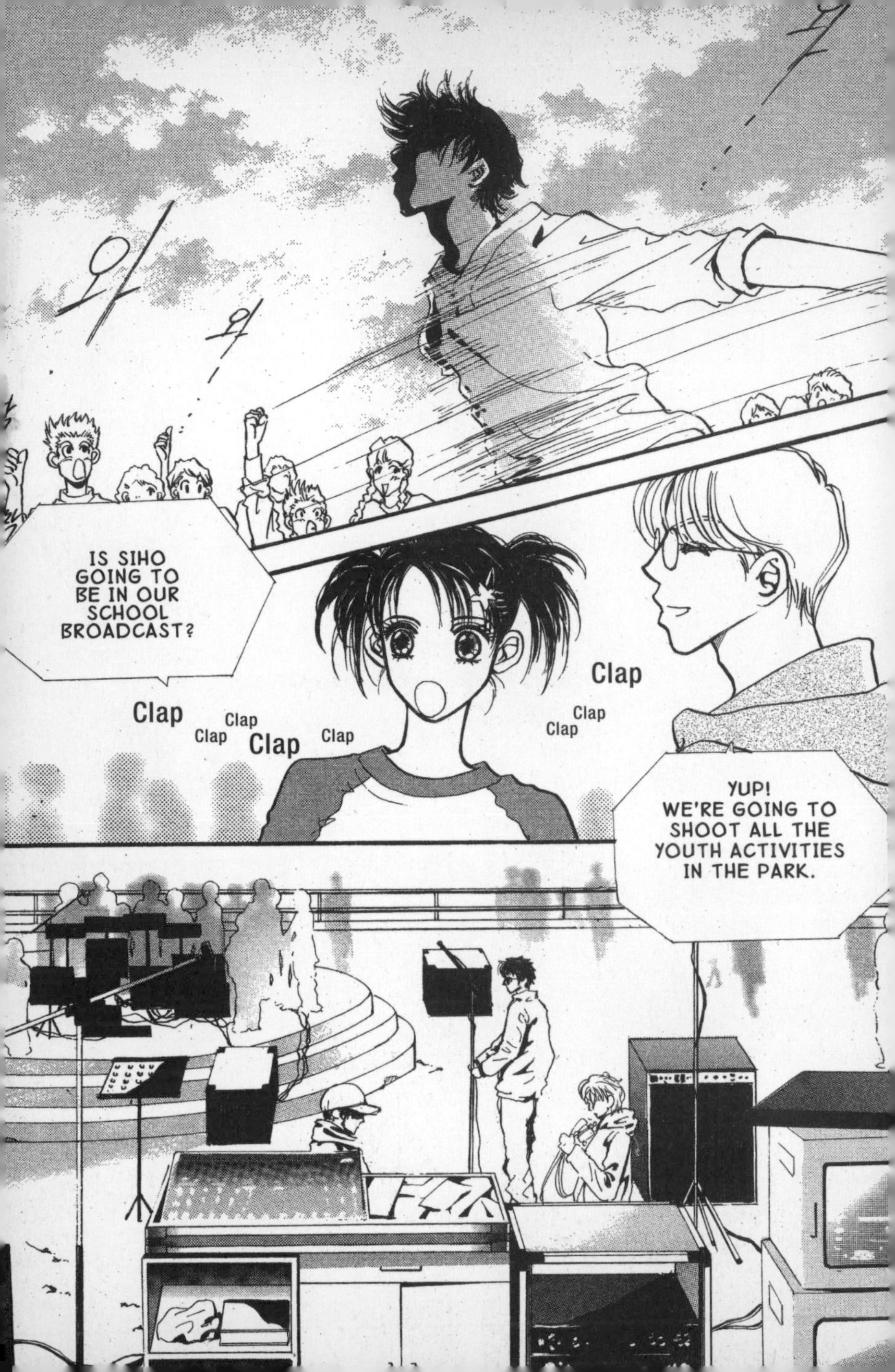
IS SIHO GOING TO BE IN OUR SCHOOL BROADCAST?
Clap
Clap
Clap
Clap
Clap
Clap
Clap
Clap
YUP! WE'RE GOING TO SHOOT ALL THE YOUTH ACTIVITIES IN THE PARK.

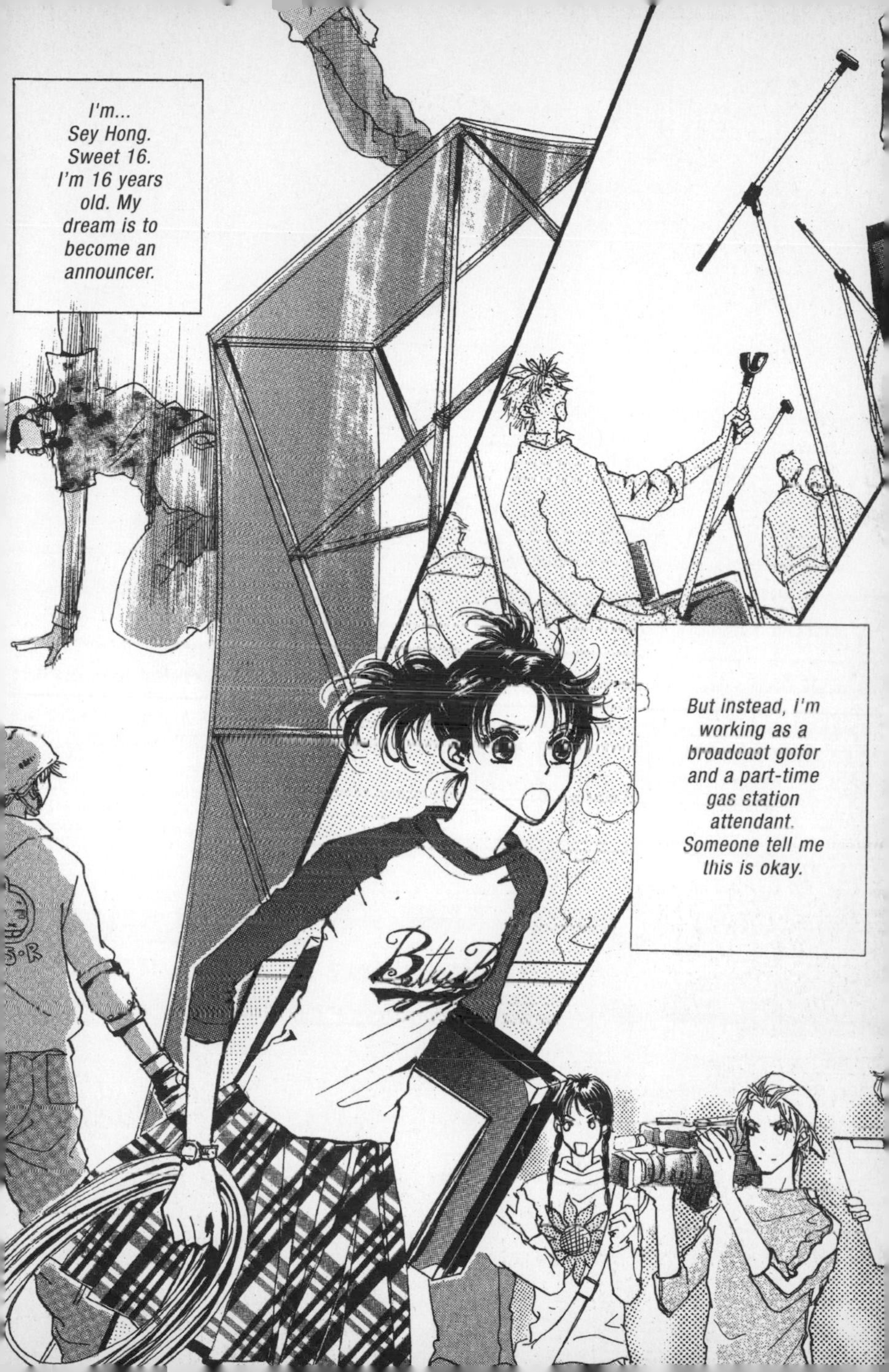
I'm...
Sey Hong.
Sweet 16.
I'm 16 years
old. My
dream is to
become an
announcer.
But instead, I'm
working as a
broadcast gofor
and a part-time
gas station
attendant.
Someone tell me
this is okay.

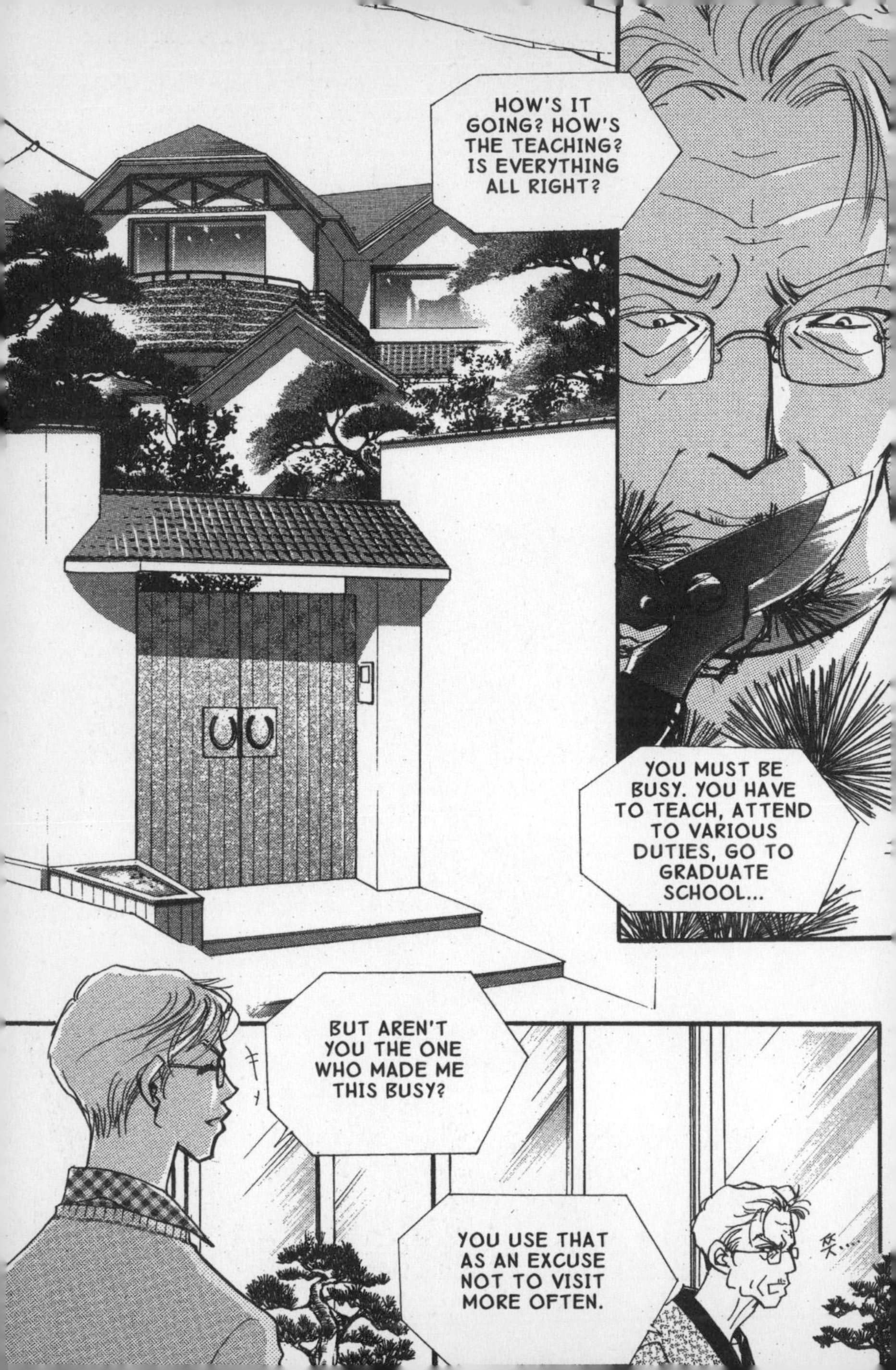
HOW'S IT GOING? HOW'S THE TEACHING? IS EVERYTHING ALL RIGHT?
YOU MUST BE BUSY. YOU HAVE TO TEACH, ATTEND TO VARIOUS DUTIES, GO TO GRADUATE SCHOOL...
BUT AREN'T YOU THE ONE WHO MADE ME THIS BUSY?
YOU USE THAT AS AN EXCUSE NOT TO VISIT MORE OFTEN.

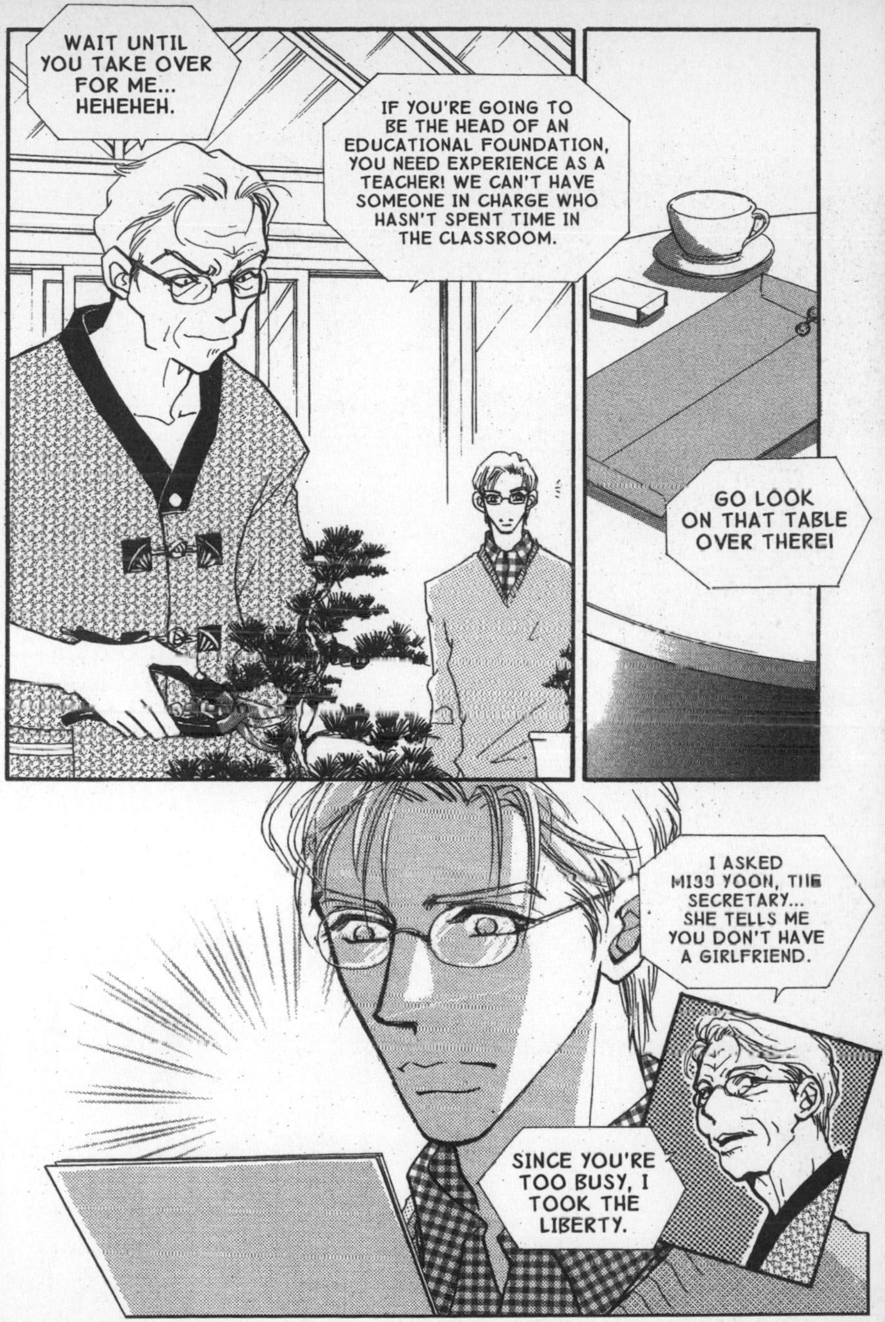
WAIT UNTIL YOU TAKE OVER FOR ME... HEHEHEH.
IF YOU'RE GOING TO BE THE HEAD OF AN EDUCATIONAL FOUNDATION, YOU NEED EXPERIENCE AS A TEACHER! WE CAN'T HAVE SOMEONE IN CHARGE WHO HASN'T SPENT TIME IN THE CLASSROOM.
GO LOOK ON THAT TABLE OVER THERE!
I ASKED MISS YOON, THE SECRETARY... SHE TELLS ME YOU DON'T HAVE A GIRLFRIEND.
SINCE YOU'RE TOO BUSY, I TOOK THE LIBERTY.

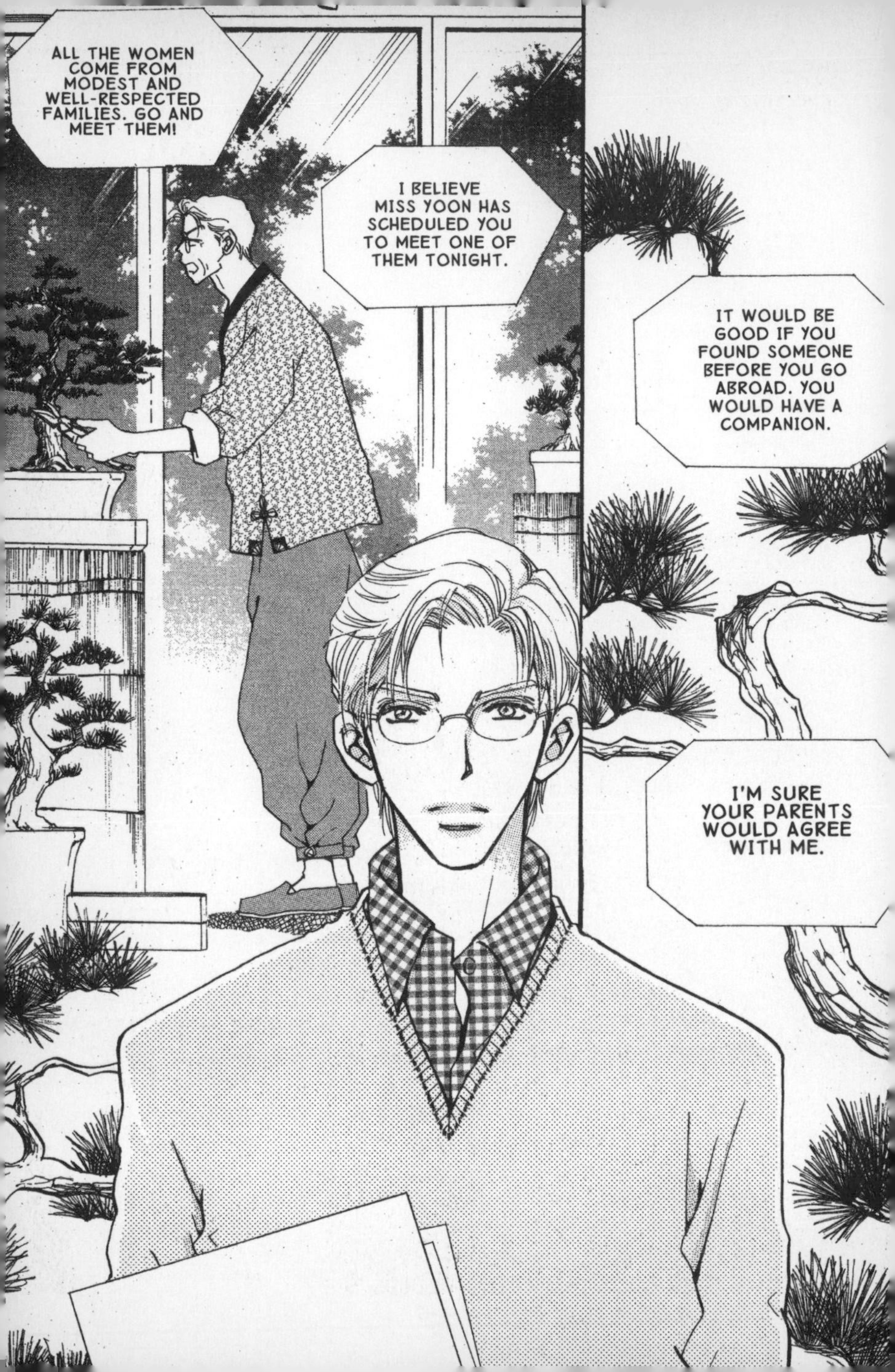
ALL THE WOMEN COME FROM MODEST AND WELL-RESPECTED FAMILIES. GO AND MEET THEM!
I BELIEVE MISS YOON HAS SCHEDULED YOU TO MEET ONE OF THEM TONIGHT.
IT WOULD BE GOOD IF YOU FOUND SOMEONE BEFORE YOU GO ABROAD. YOU WOULD HAVE A COMPANION.
I'M SURE YOUR PARENTS WOULD AGREE WITH ME.

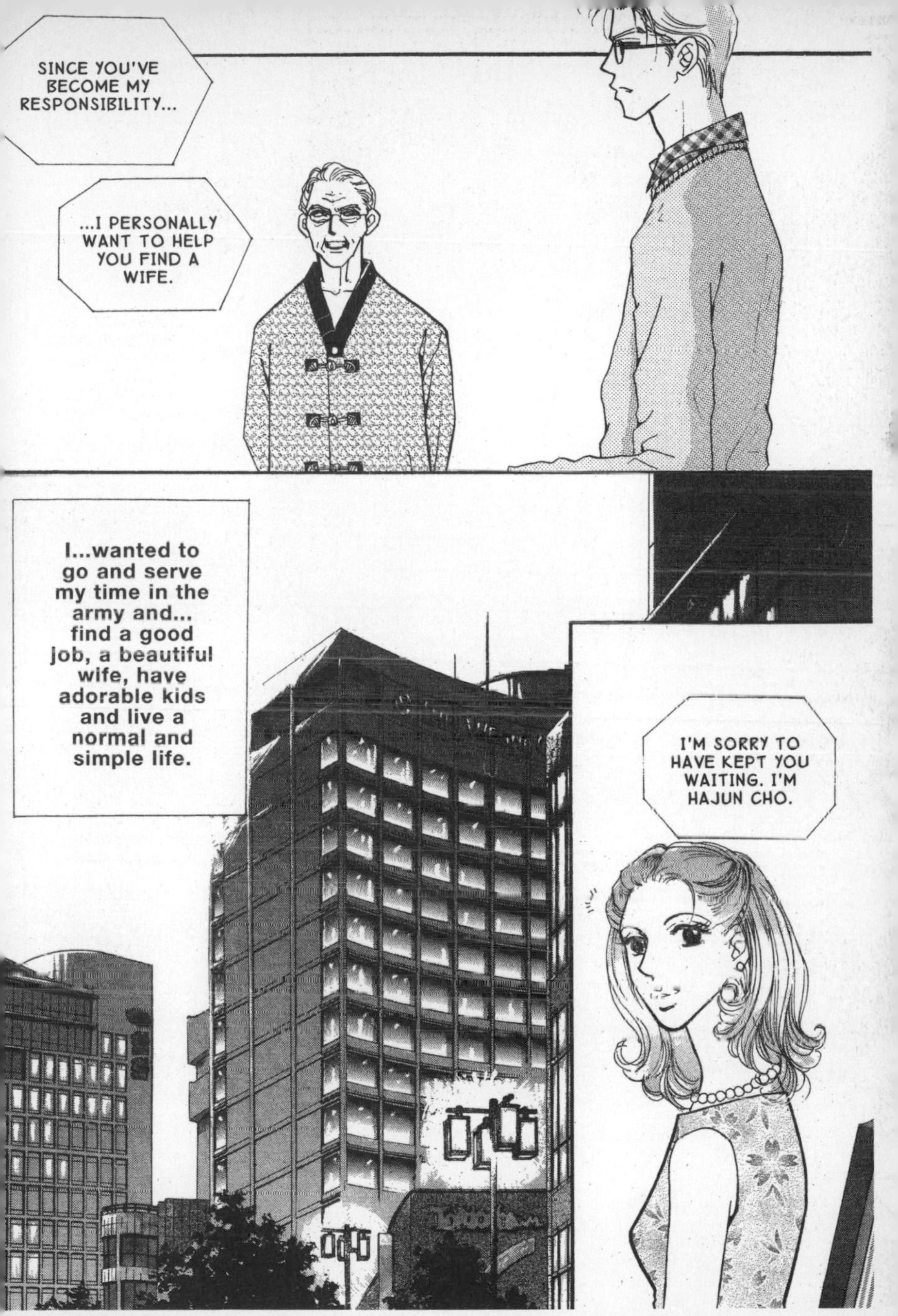
SINCE YOU'VE BECOME MY RESPONSIBILITY...
...I PERSONALLY WANT TO HELP YOU FIND A WIFE.
I...wanted to go and serve my time in the army and... find a good job, a beautiful wife, have adorable kids and live a normal and simple life.
I'M SORRY TO HAVE KEPT YOU WAITING. I'M HAJUN CHO.

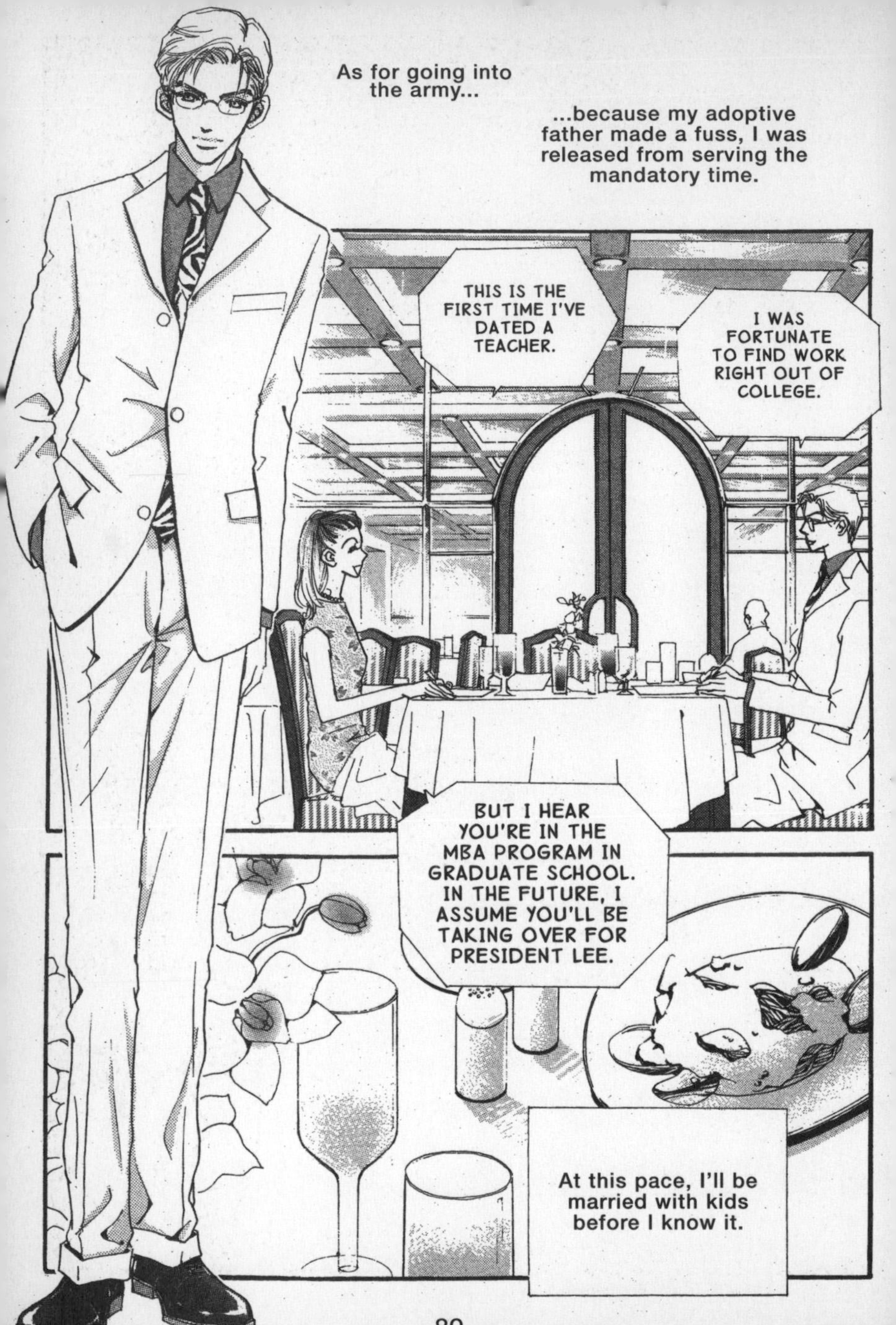
As for going into the army...
...because my adoptive father made a fuss, I was released from serving the mandatory time.
THIS IS THE FIRST TIME I'VE DATED A TEACHER.
I WAS FORTUNATE TO FIND WORK RIGHT OUT OF COLLEGE.
BUT I HEAR YOU'RE IN THE MBA PROGRAM IN GRADUATE SCHOOL. IN THE FUTURE, I ASSUME YOU'LL BE TAKING OVER FOR PRESIDENT LEE.
At this pace, I'll be married with kids before I know it.

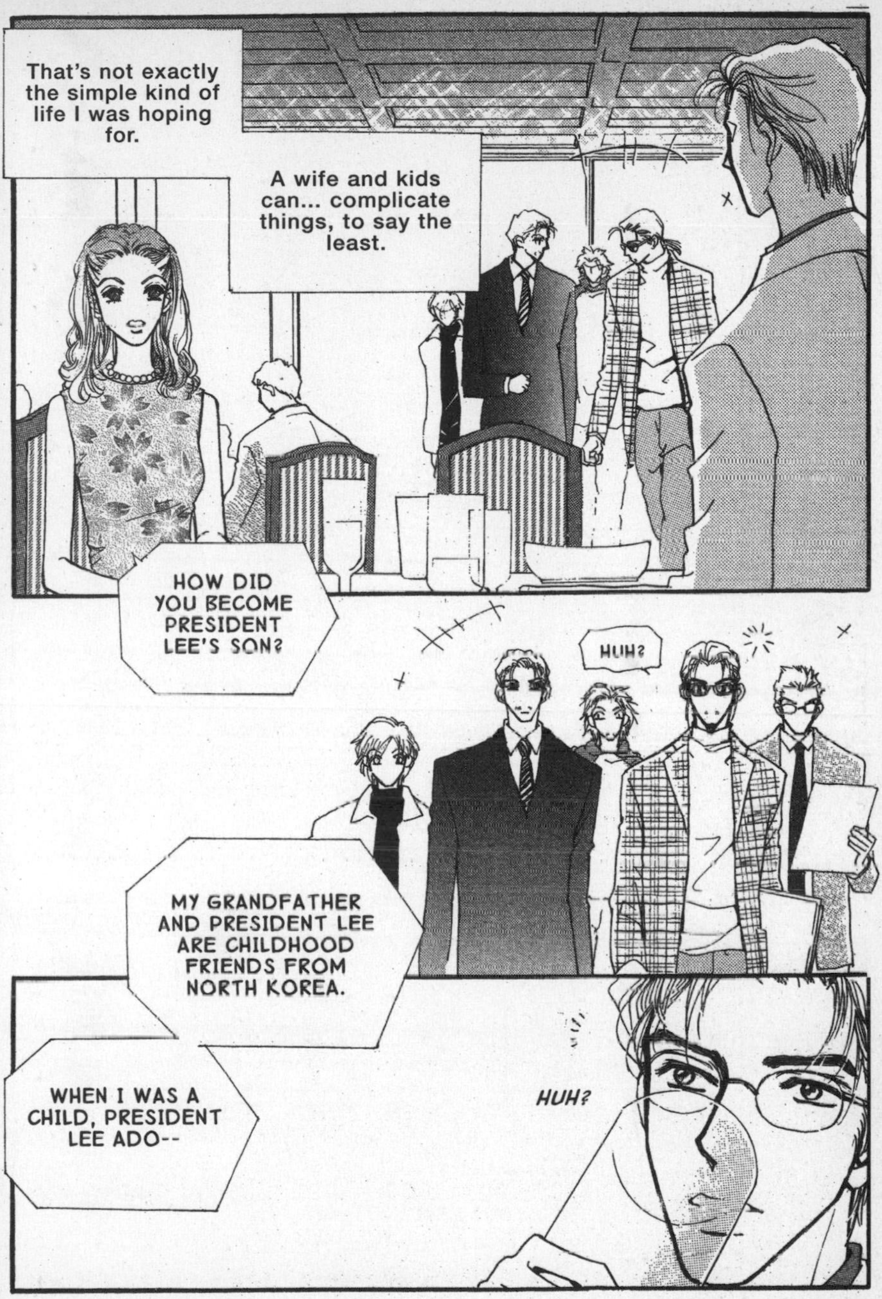
That's not exactly the simple kind of life I was hoping for.
A wife and kids can... complicate things, to say the least.
HOW DID YOU BECOME PRESIDENT LEE'S SON?
HUH?
MY GRANDFATHER AND PRESIDENT LEE ARE CHILDHOOD FRIENDS FROM NORTH KOREA.
WHEN I WAS A CHILD, PRESIDENT LEE ADO--
HUH?

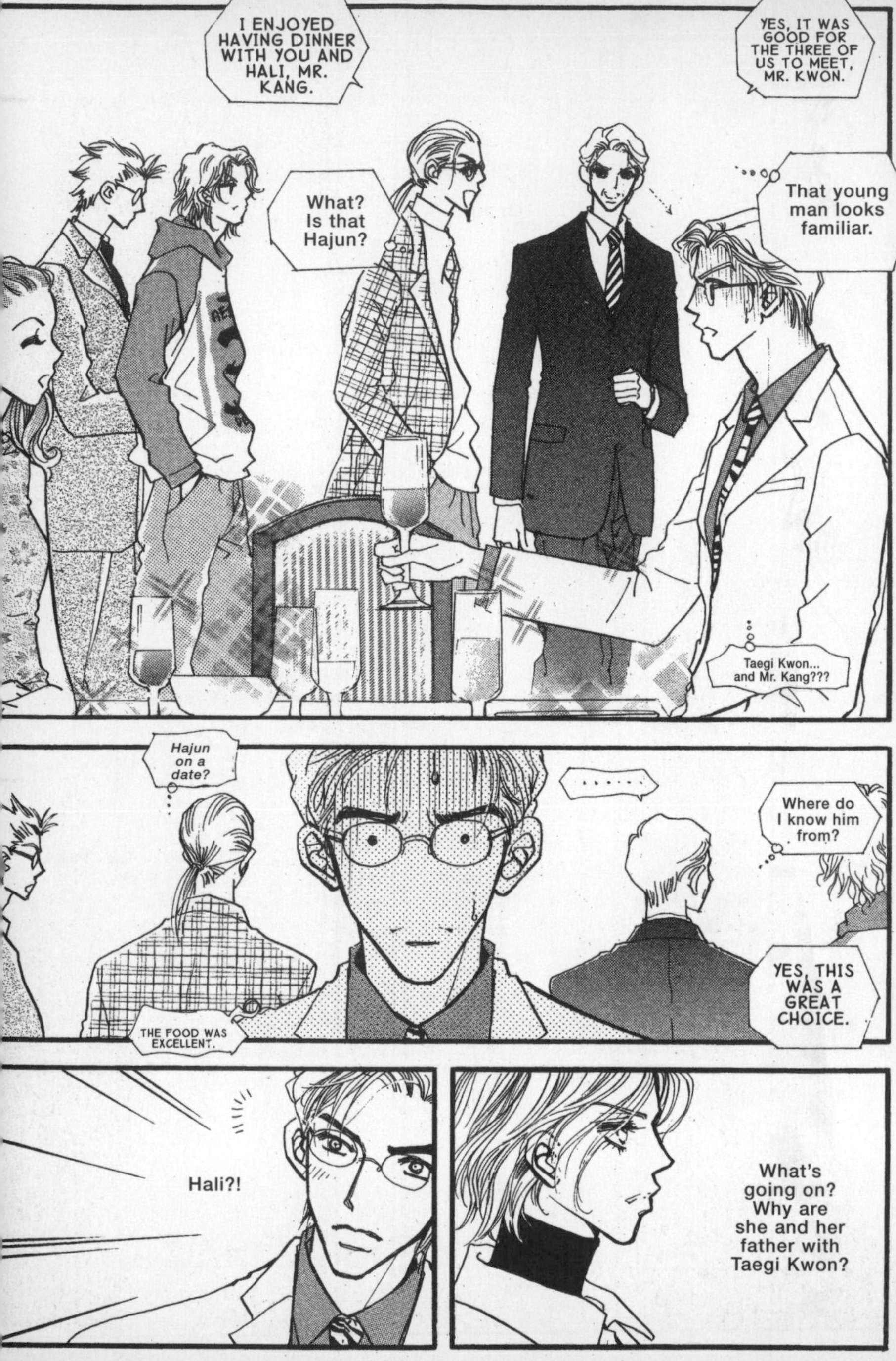
I ENJOYED HAVING DINNER WITH YOU AND HALI, MR. KANG.
YES, IT WAS GOOD FOR THE THREE OF US TO MEET, MR. KWON.
What? Is that Hajun?
That young man looks familiar.
Taegi Kwon... and Mr. Kang???
Hajun on a date?
......
Where do I know him from?
THE FOOD WAS EXCELLENT.
YES, THIS WAS A GREAT CHOICE.
Hali?!
What's going on? Why are she and her father with Taegi Kwon?

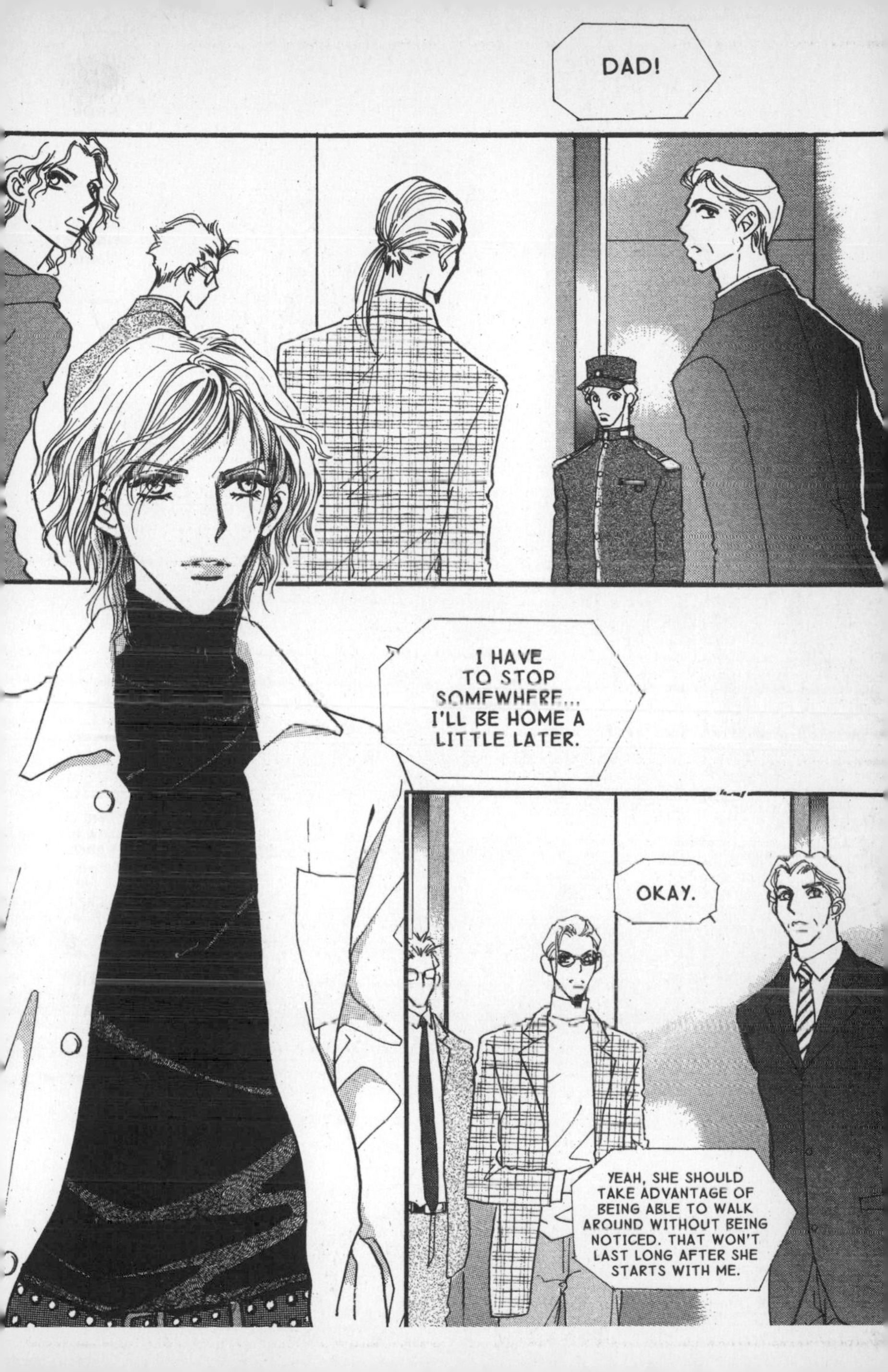
DAD!
I HAVE TO STOP SOMEWHERE... I'LL BE HOME A LITTLE LATER.
OKAY.
YEAH, SHE SHOULD TAKE ADVANTAGE OF BEING ABLE TO WALK AROUND WITHOUT BEING NOTICED. THAT WON'T LAST LONG AFTER SHE STARTS WITH ME.

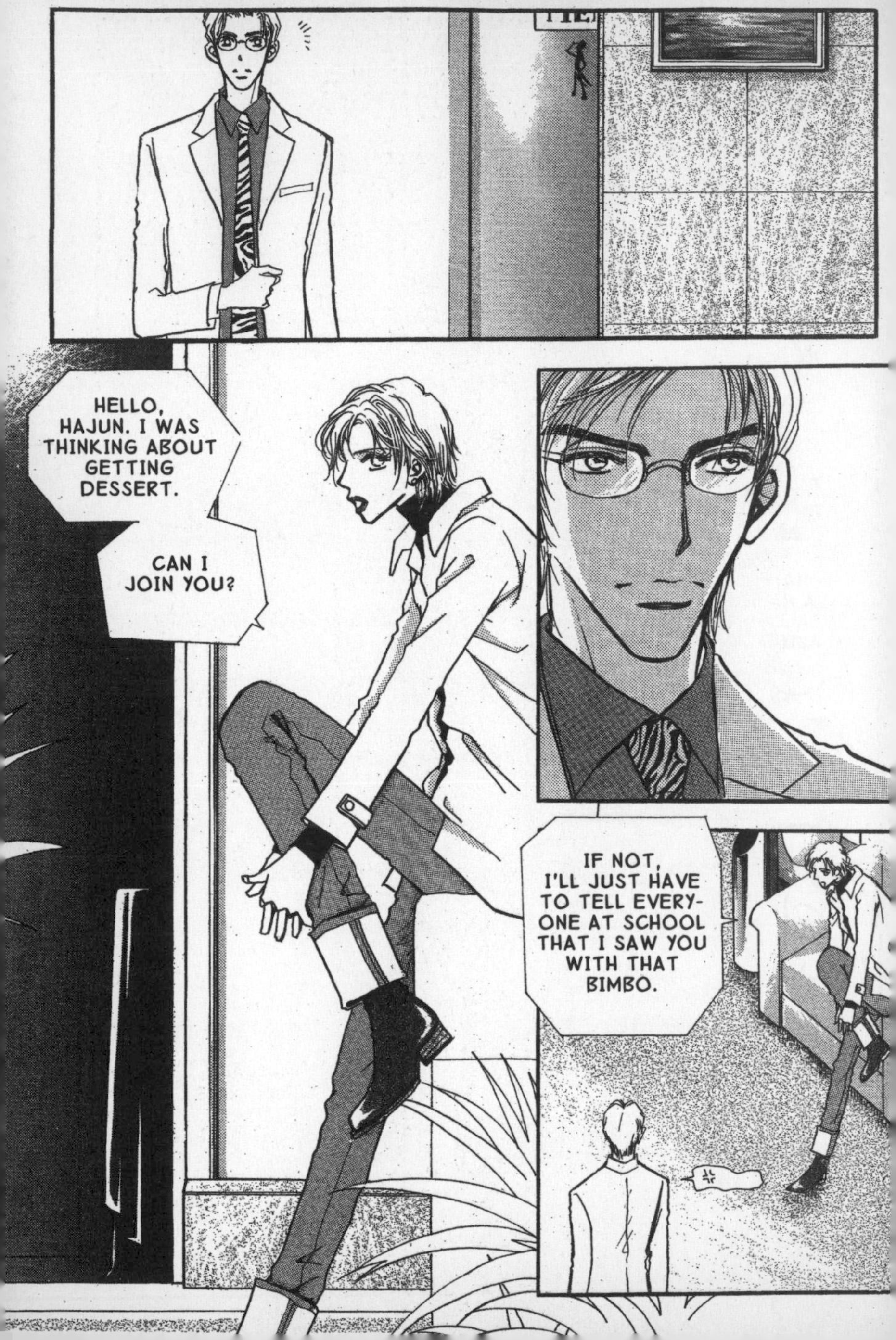
HELLO, HAJUN. I WAS THINKING ABOUT GETTING DESSERT.
CAN I JOIN YOU?
IF NOT, I'LL JUST HAVE TO TELL EVERY-ONE AT SCHOOL THAT I SAW YOU WITH THAT BIMBO.

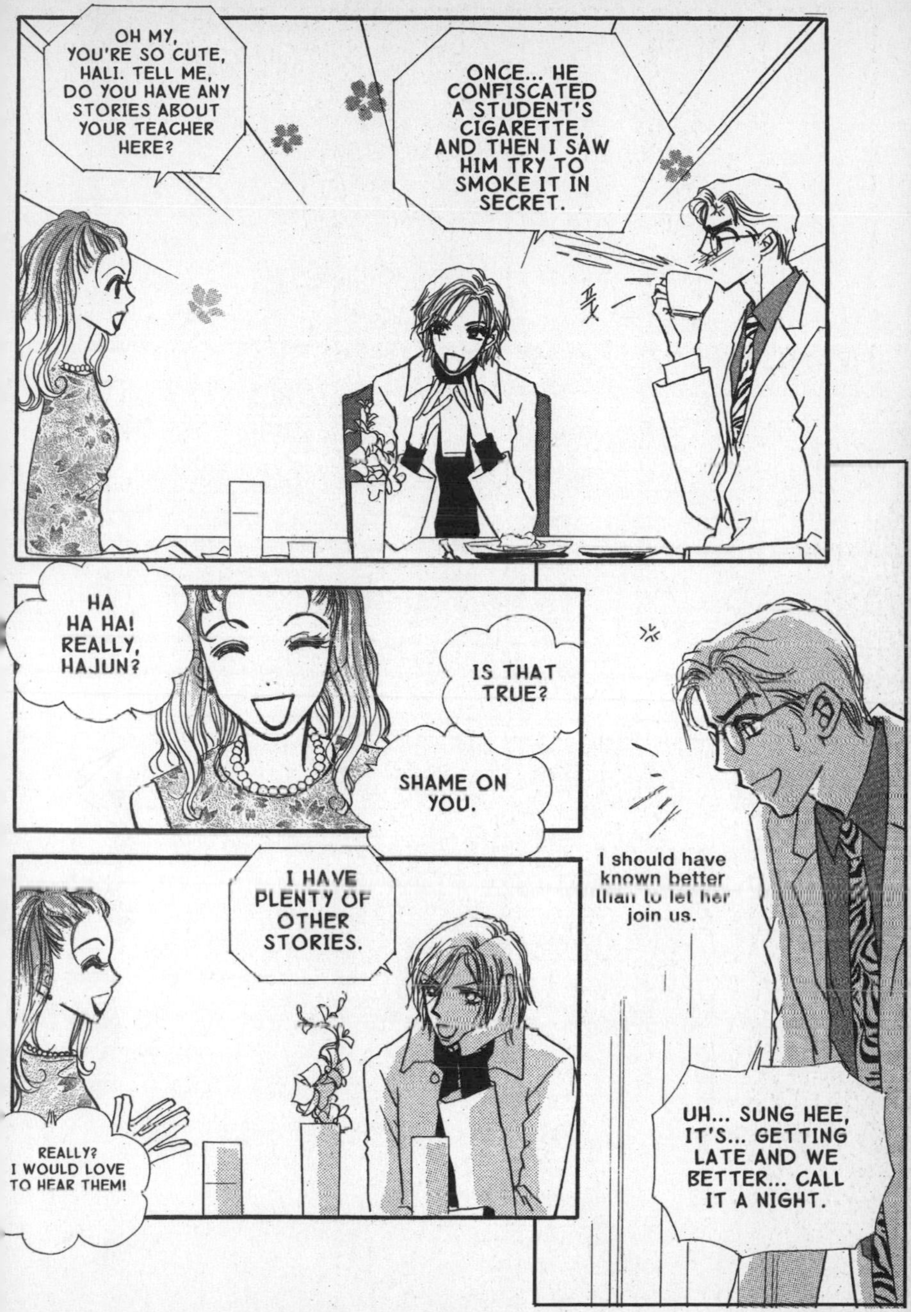
OH MY, YOU'RE SO CUTE, HALI. TELL ME, DO YOU HAVE ANY STORIES ABOUT YOUR TEACHER HERE?
ONCE... HE CONFISCATED A STUDENT'S CIGARETTE, AND THEN I SAW HIM TRY TO SMOKE IT IN SECRET.
HA HA HA! REALLY, HAJUN?
IS THAT TRUE?
SHAME ON YOU.
I should have known better than to let her join us.
UH... SUNG HEE, IT'S... GETTING LATE AND WE BETTER... CALL IT A NIGHT.
I HAVE PLENTY OF OTHER STORIES.
REALLY? I WOULD LOVE TO HEAR THEM!

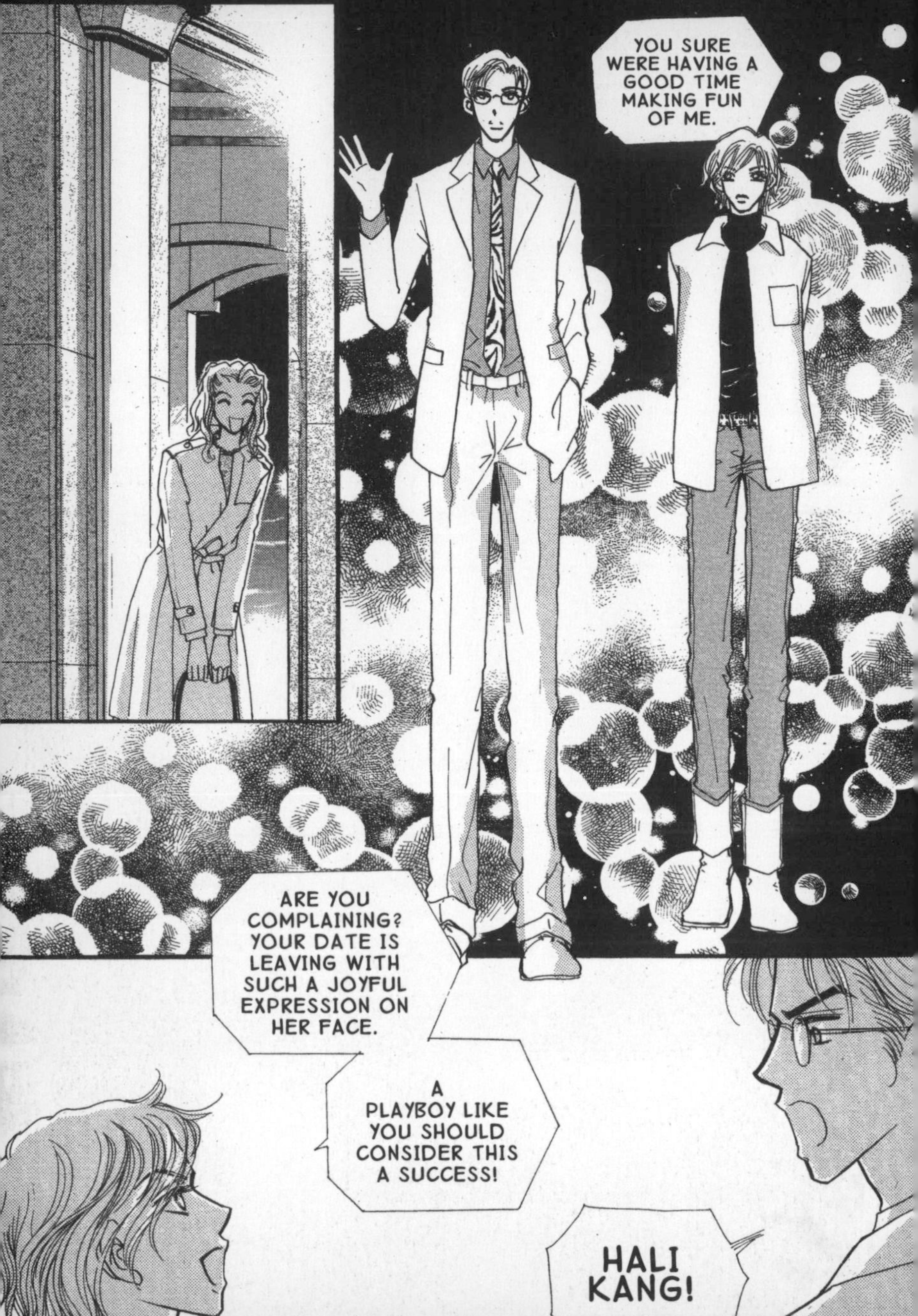
YOU SURE WERE HAVING A GOOD TIME MAKING FUN OF ME.
ARE YOU COMPLAINING? YOUR DATE IS LEAVING WITH SUCH A JOYFUL EXPRESSION ON HER FACE.
A PLAYBOY LIKE YOU SHOULD CONSIDER THIS A SUCCESS!
HALI KANG!

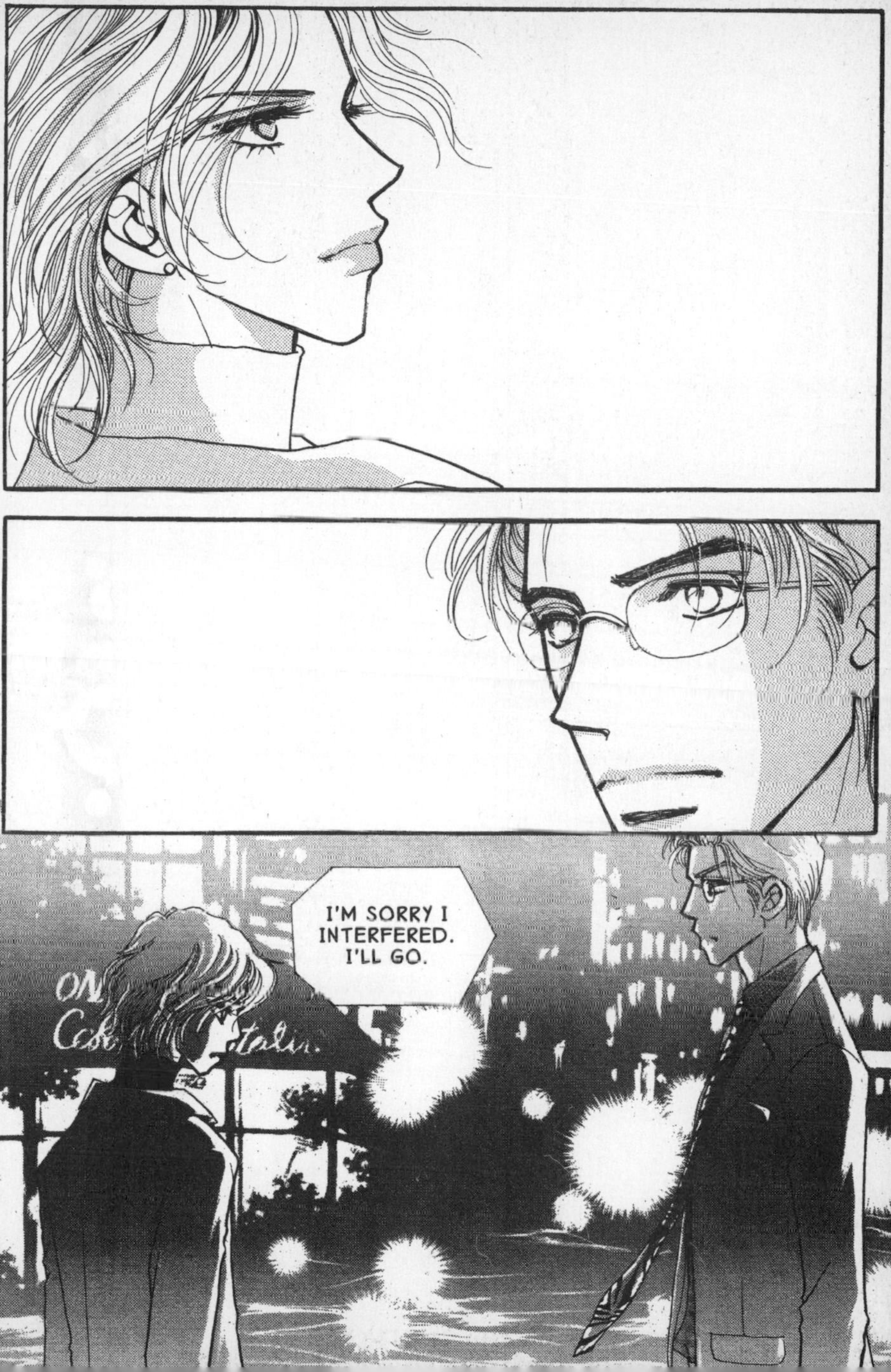
I'M SORRY I INTERFERED. I'LL GO.

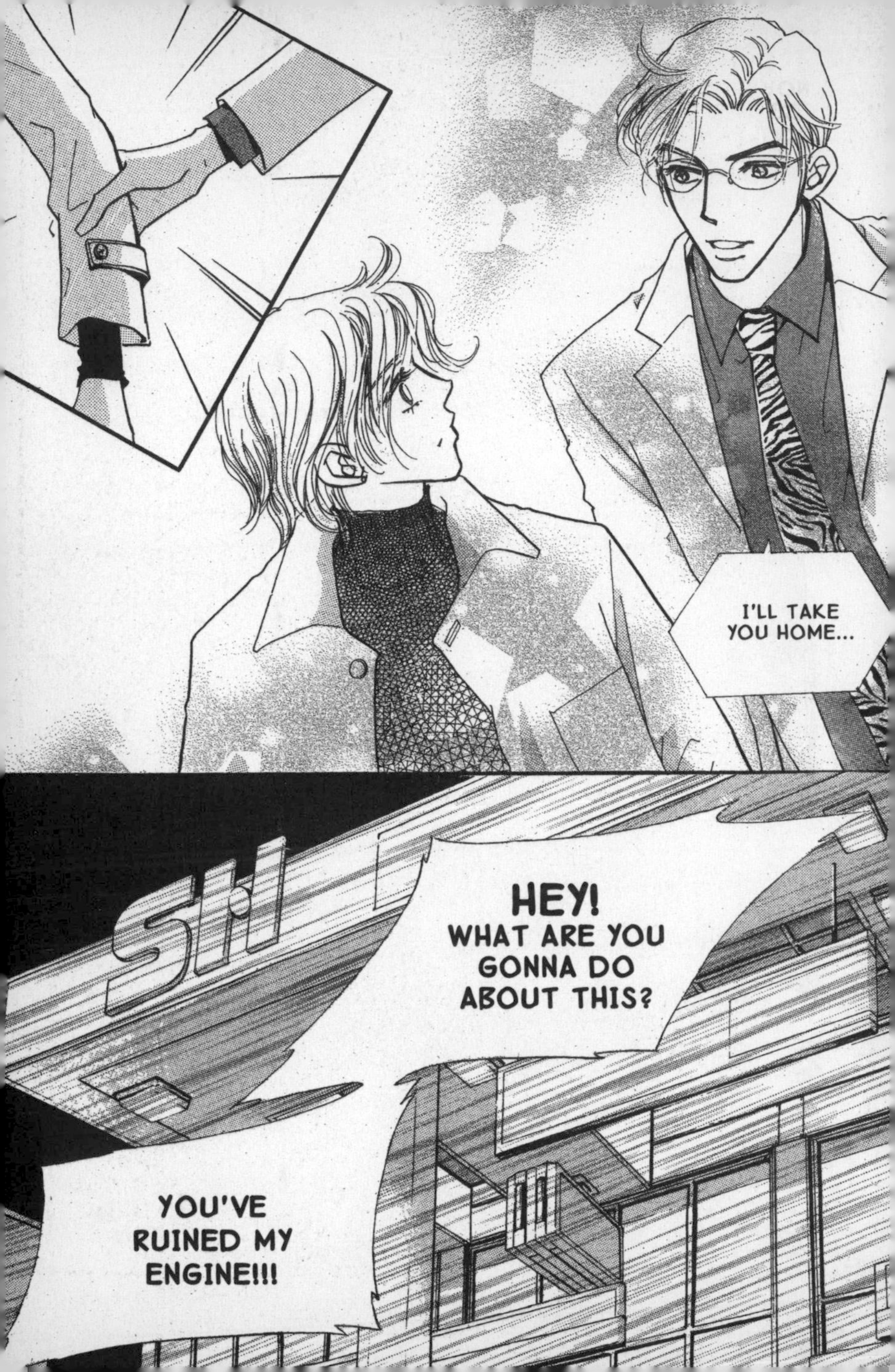
I'LL TAKE YOU HOME...
HEY! WHAT ARE YOU GONNA DO ABOUT THIS?
YOU'VE RUINED MY ENGINE!!!

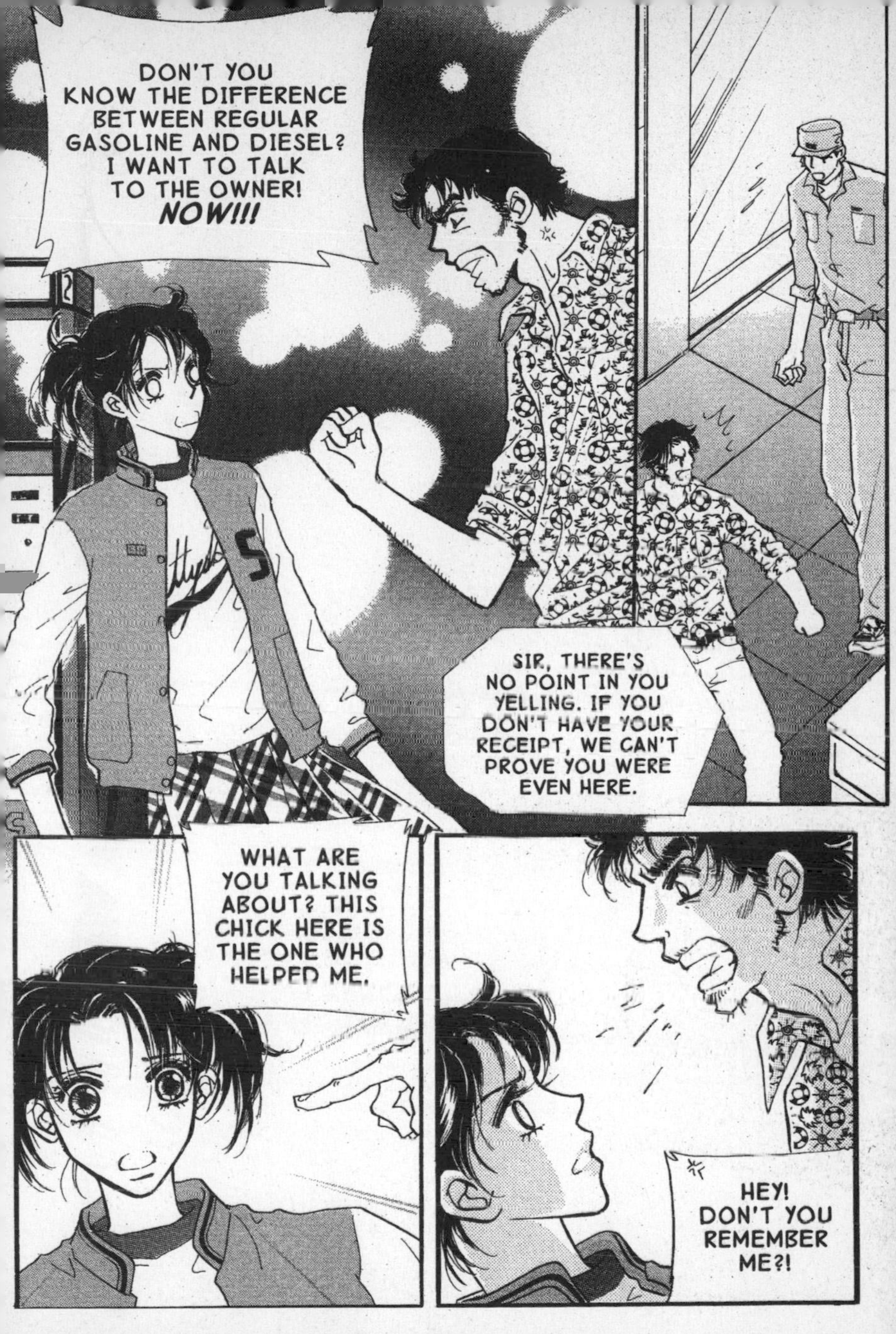
DON'T YOU KNOW THE DIFFERENCE BETWEEN REGULAR GASOLINE AND DIESEL? I WANT TO TALK TO THE OWNER! NOW!!!
SIR, THERE'S NO POINT IN YOU YELLING. IF YOU DON'T HAVE YOUR RECEIPT, WE CAN'T PROVE YOU WERE EVEN HERE.
WHAT ARE YOU TALKING ABOUT? THIS CHICK HERE IS THE ONE WHO HELPED ME.
HEY! DON'T YOU REMEMBER ME?!

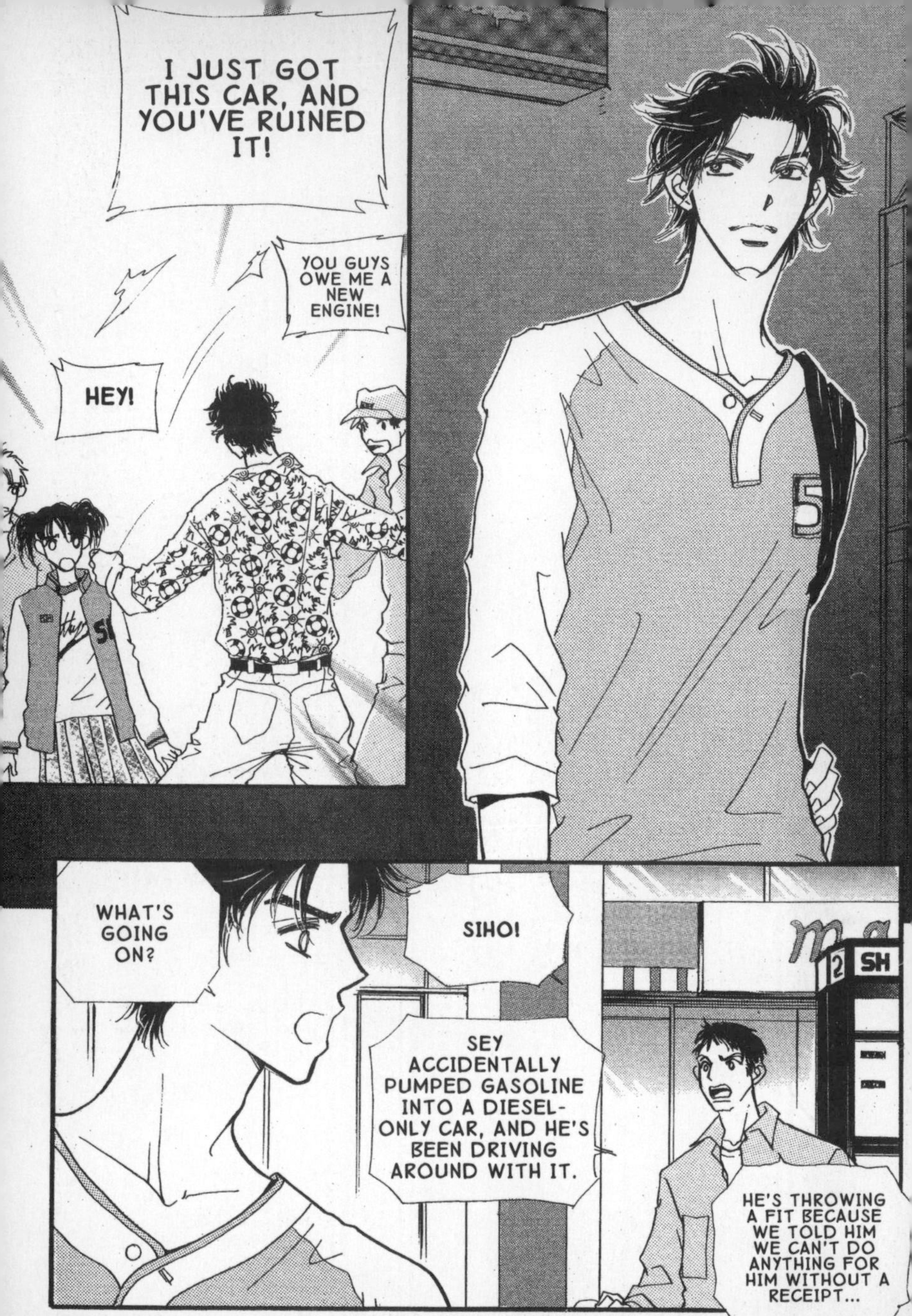
I JUST GOT THIS CAR, AND YOU'VE RUINED IT!
YOU GUYS OWE ME A NEW ENGINE!
HEY!
WHAT'S GOING ON?
SIHO!
SEY ACCIDENTALLY PUMPED GASOLINE INTO A DIESEL-ONLY CAR, AND HE'S BEEN DRIVING AROUND WITH IT.
HE'S THROWING A FIT BECAUSE WE TOLD HIM WE CAN'T DO ANYTHING FOR HIM WITHOUT A RECEIPT...

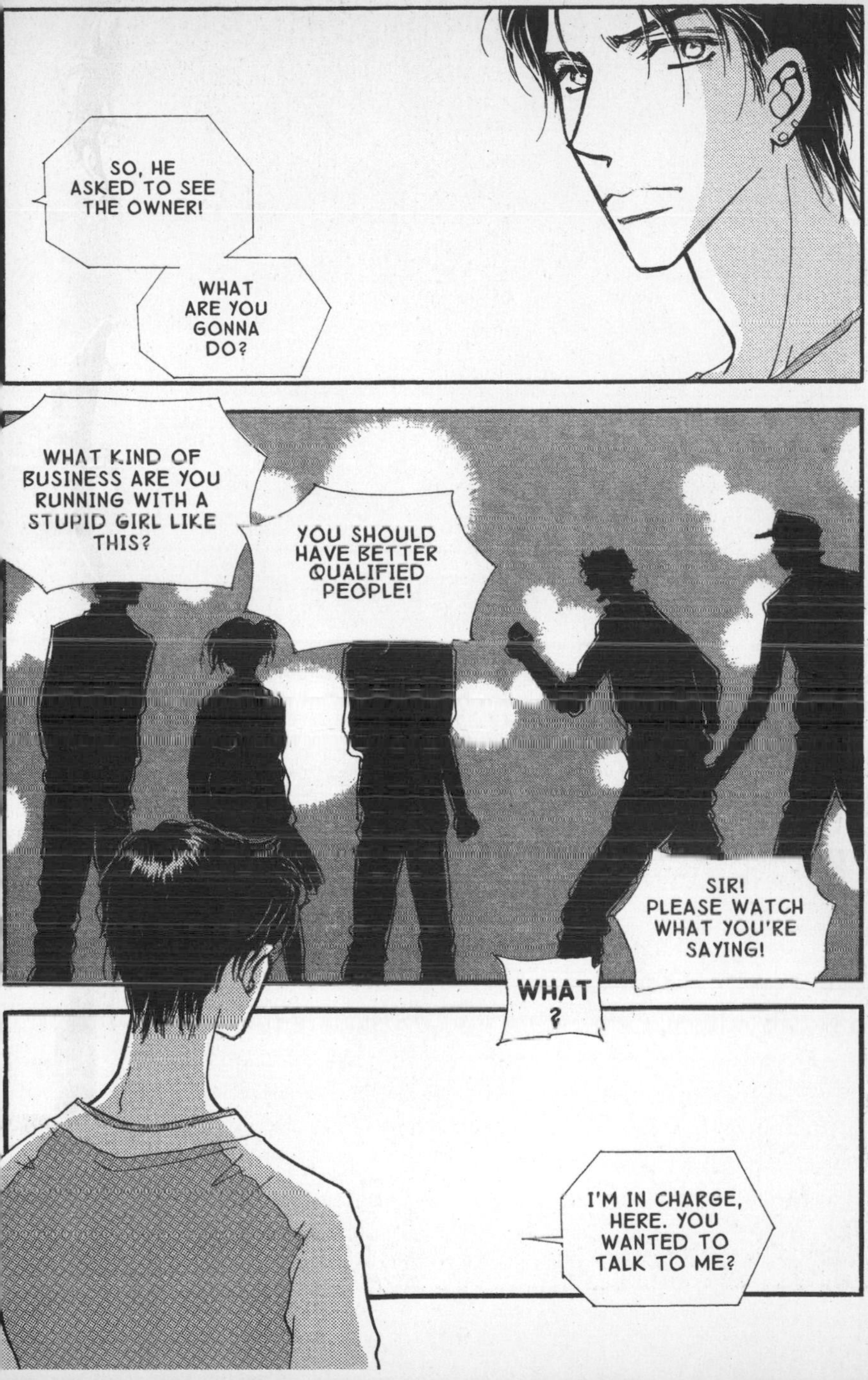
SO, HE ASKED TO SEE THE OWNER!
WHAT ARE YOU GONNA DO?
WHAT KIND OF BUSINESS ARE YOU RUNNING WITH A STUPID GIRL LIKE THIS?
YOU SHOULD HAVE BETTER QUALIFIED PEOPLE!
SIR! PLEASE WATCH WHAT YOU'RE SAYING!
WHAT?
I'M IN CHARGE, HERE. YOU WANTED TO TALK TO ME?

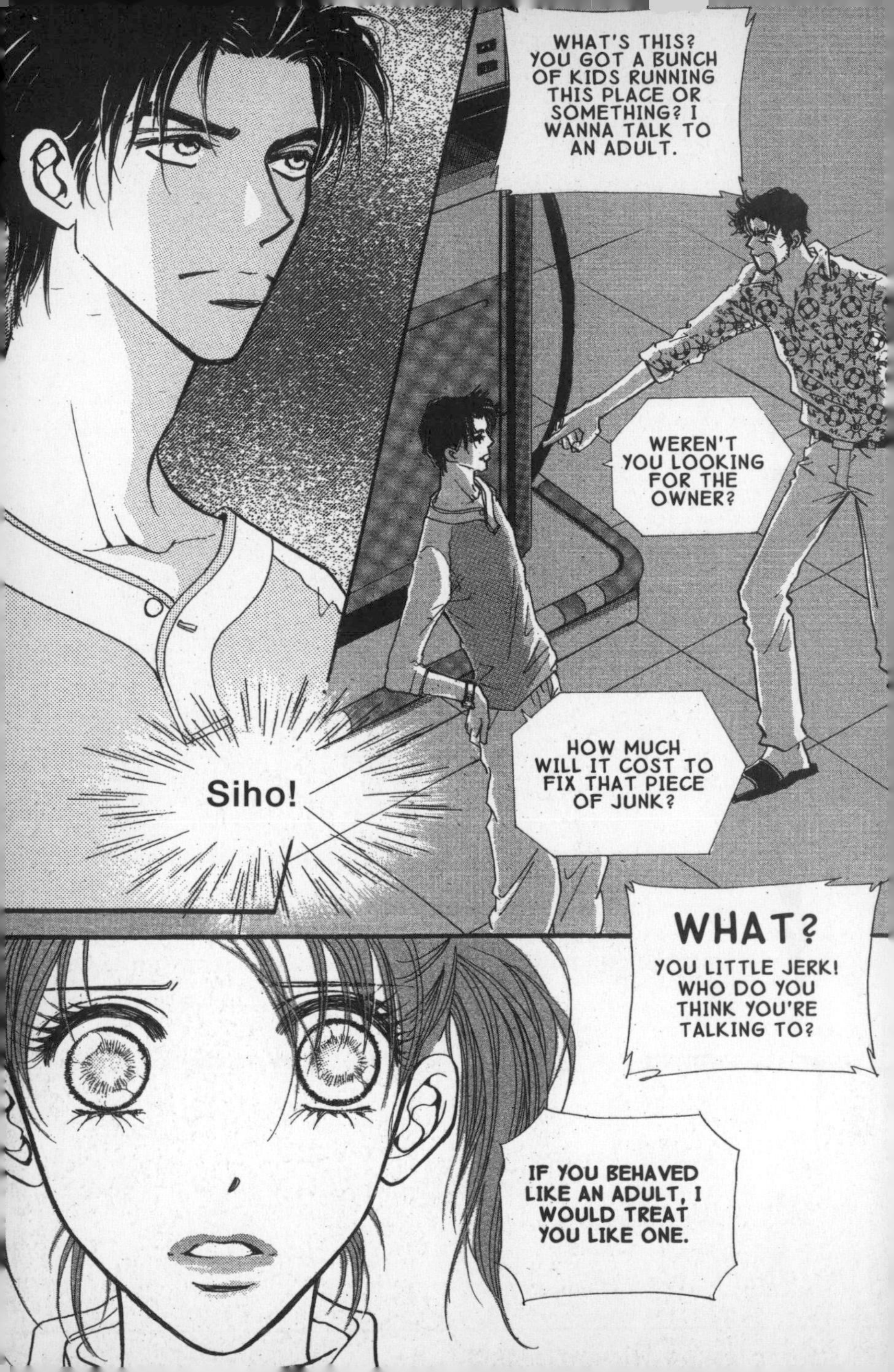
Siho!
WHAT'S THIS? YOU GOT A BUNCH OF KIDS RUNNING THIS PLACE OR SOMETHING? I WANNA TALK TO AN ADULT.
WEREN'T YOU LOOKING FOR THE OWNER?
HOW MUCH WILL IT COST TO FIX THAT PIECE OF JUNK?
WHAT? YOU LITTLE JERK! WHO DO YOU THINK YOU'RE TALKING TO?
IF YOU BEHAVED LIKE AN ADULT, I WOULD TREAT YOU LIKE ONE.

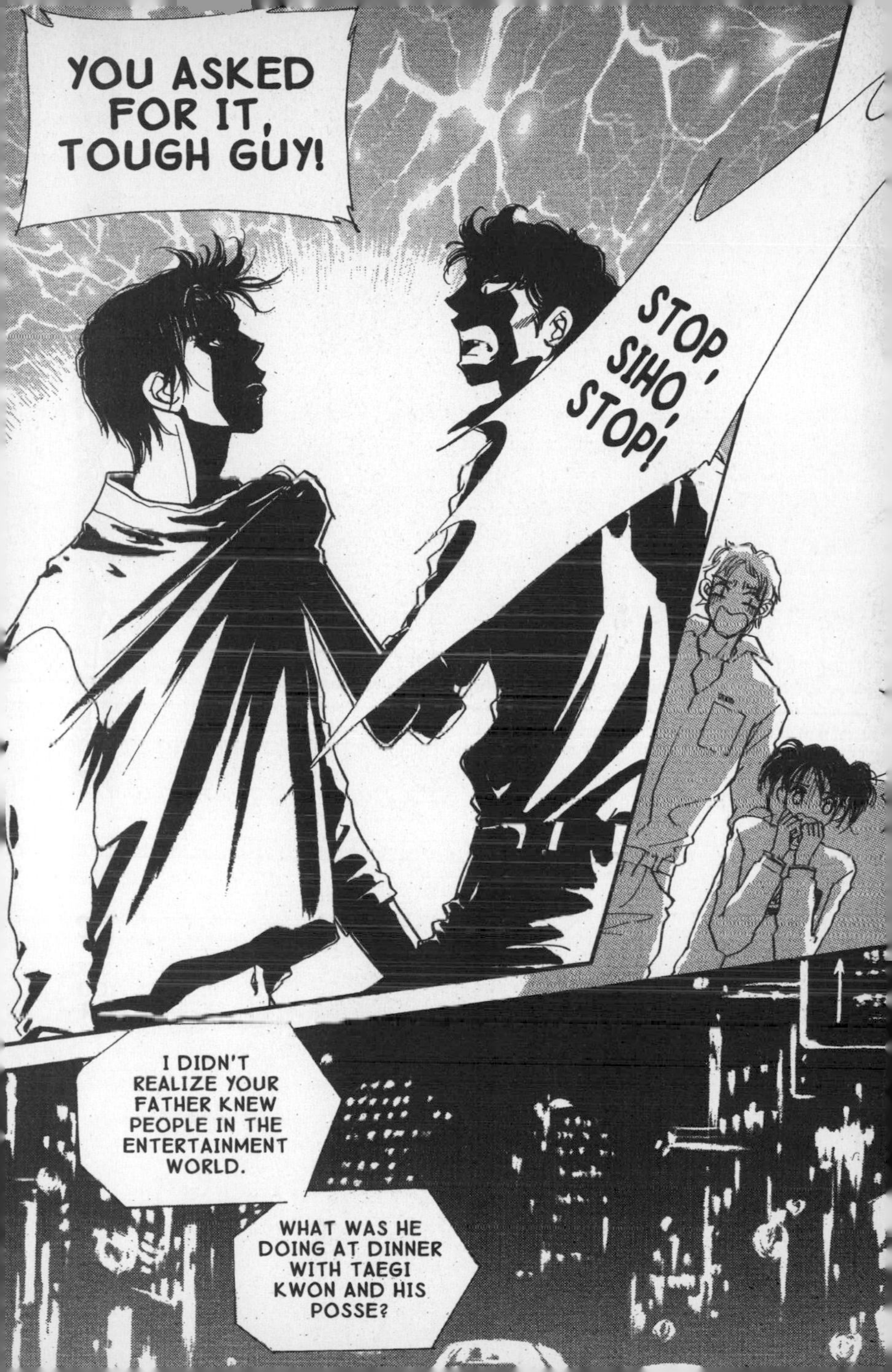
YOU ASKED FOR IT, TOUGH GUY!
STOP, SIHO, STOP!
I DIDN'T REALIZE YOUR FATHER KNEW PEOPLE IN THE ENTERTAINMENT WORLD.
WHAT WAS HE DOING AT DINNER WITH TAEGI KWON AND HIS POSSE?

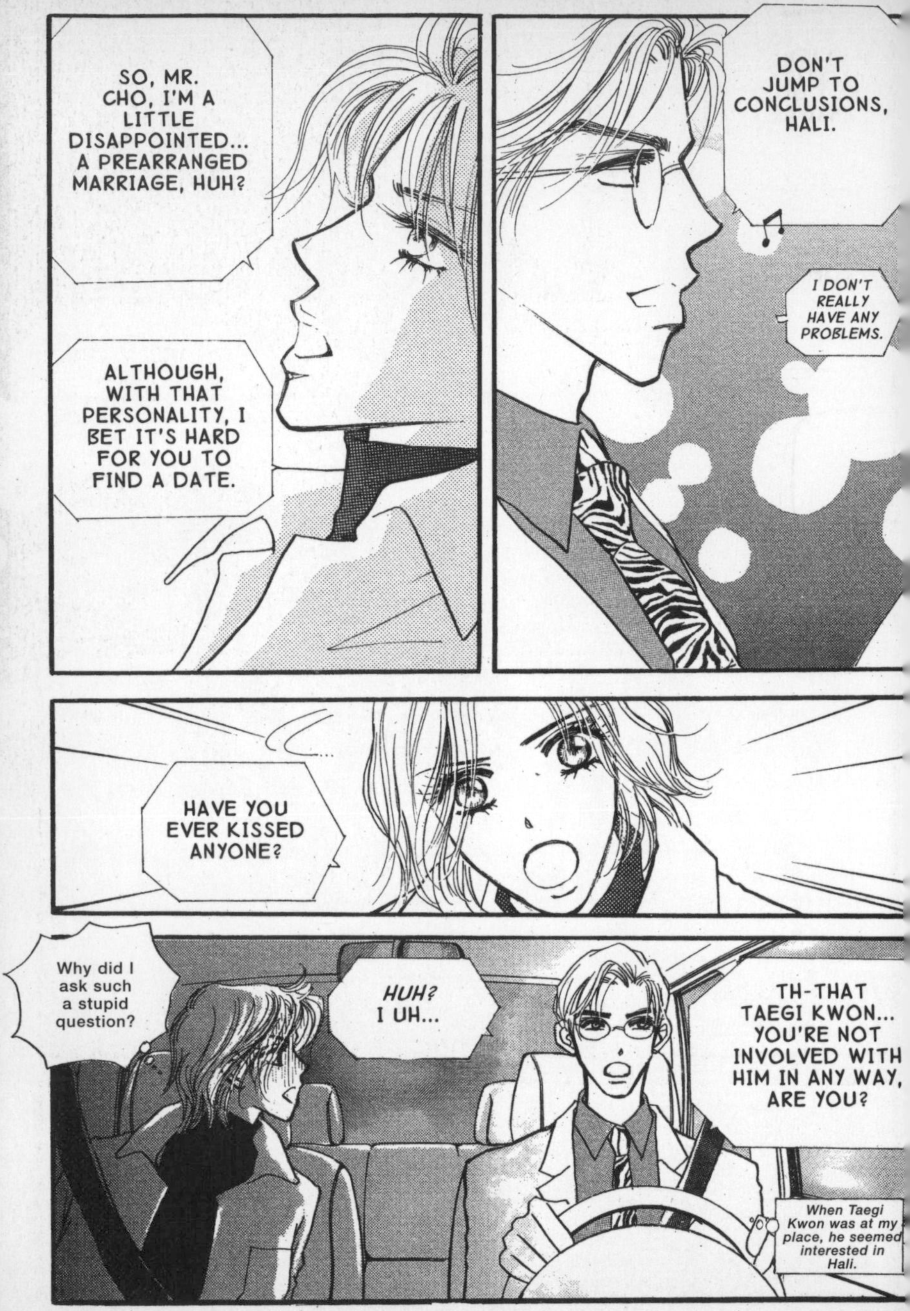
SO, MR. CHO, I'M A LITTLE DISAPPOINTED... A PREARRANGED MARRIAGE, HUH?
ALTHOUGH, WITH THAT PERSONALITY, I BET IT'S HARD FOR YOU TO FIND A DATE.
DON'T JUMP TO CONCLUSIONS, HALI.
I DON'T REALLY HAVE ANY PROBLEMS.
HAVE YOU EVER KISSED ANYONE?
Why did I ask such a stupid question?
HUH? I UH...
TH-THAT TAEGI KWON... YOU'RE NOT INVOLVED WITH HIM IN ANY WAY, ARE YOU?
When Taegi Kwon was at my place, he seemed interested in Hali.

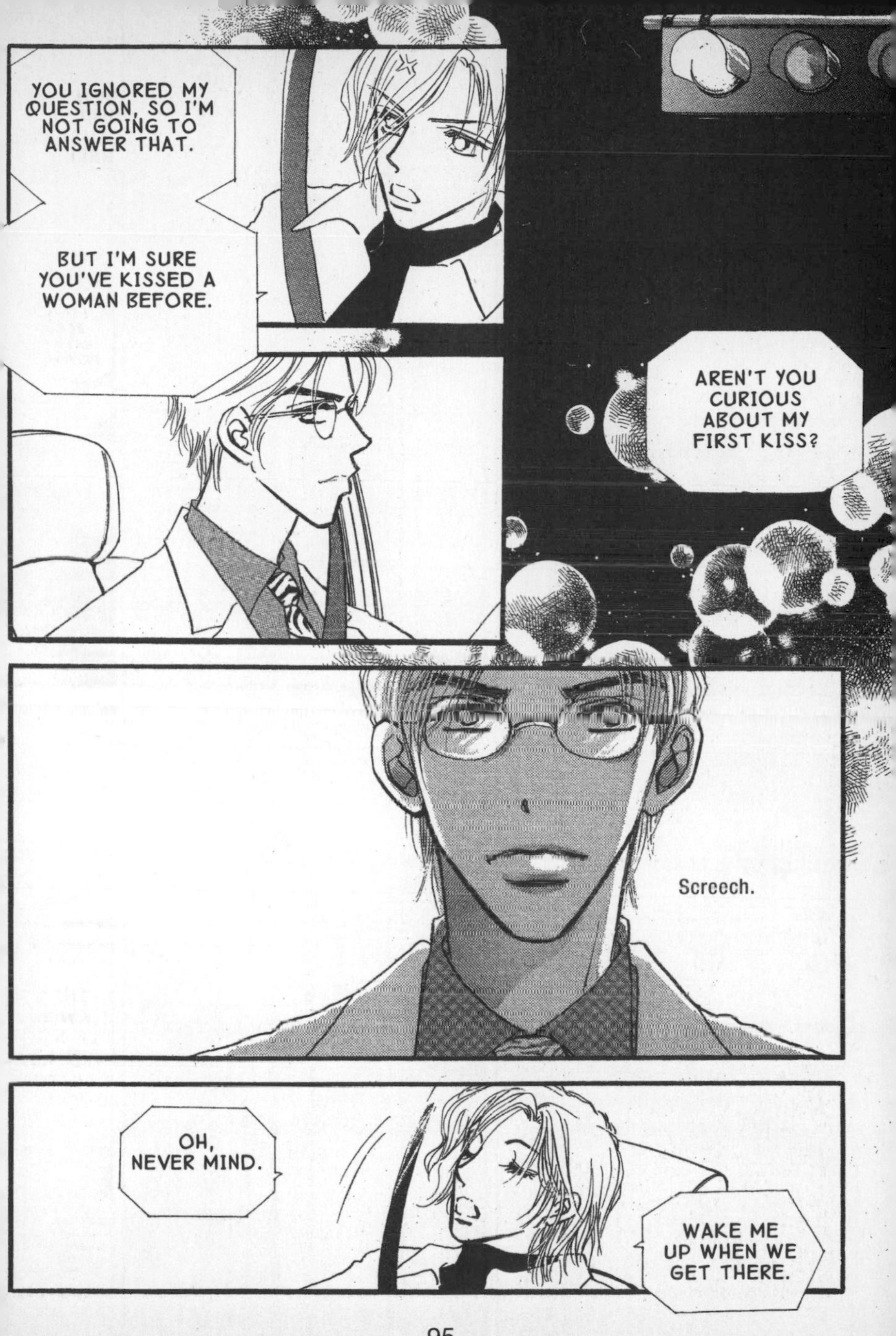
YOU IGNORED MY QUESTION, SO I'M NOT GOING TO ANSWER THAT.
BUT I'M SURE YOU'VE KISSED A WOMAN BEFORE.
AREN'T YOU CURIOUS ABOUT MY FIRST KISS?
Screech.
OH, NEVER MIND.
WAKE ME UP WHEN WE GET THERE.

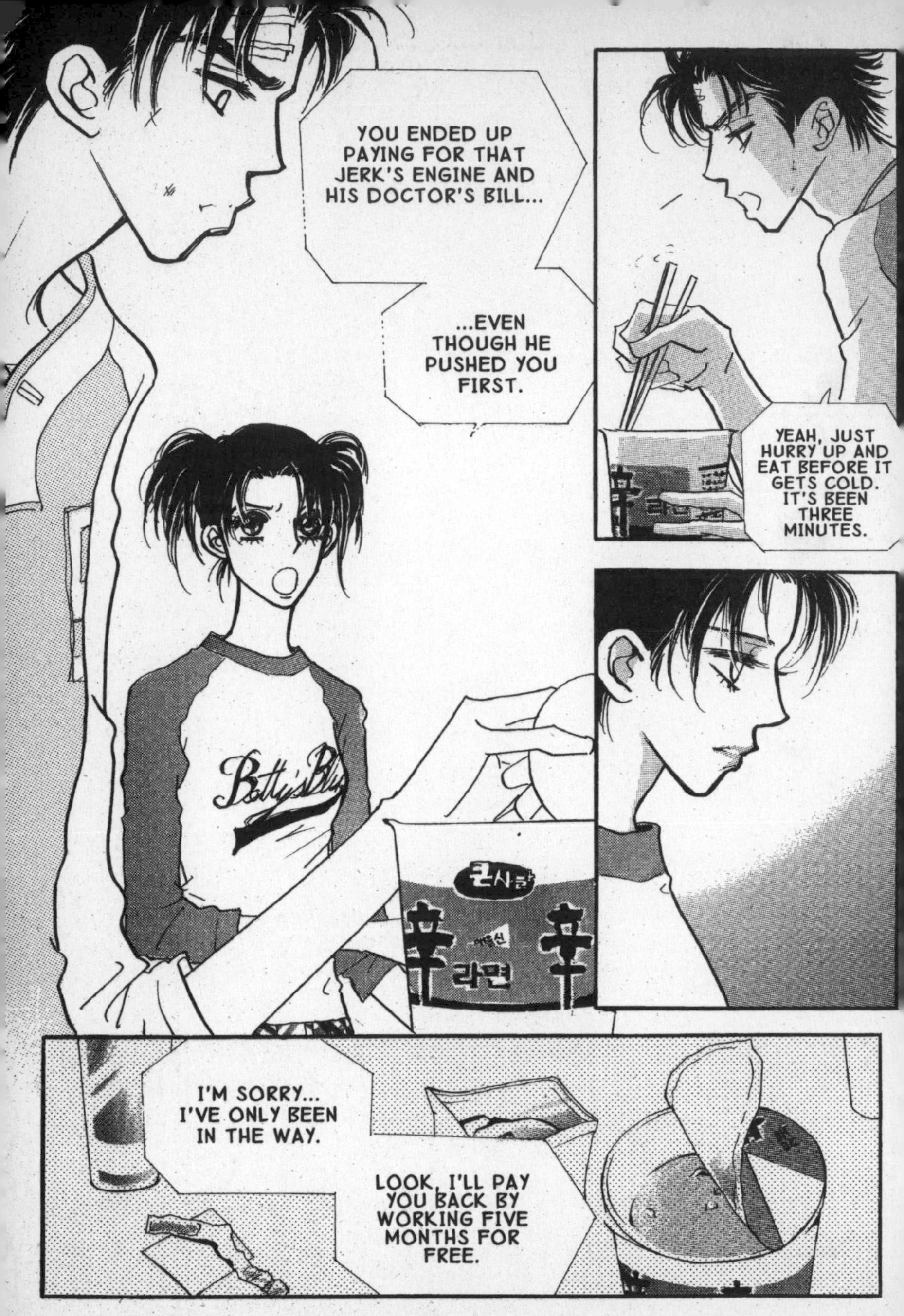
YOU ENDED UP PAYING FOR THAT JERK'S ENGINE AND HIS DOCTOR'S BILL...
...EVEN THOUGH HE PUSHED YOU FIRST.
YEAH, JUST HURRY UP AND EAT BEFORE IT GETS COLD. IT'S BEEN THREE MINUTES.
I'M SORRY... I'VE ONLY BEEN IN THE WAY.
LOOK, I'LL PAY YOU BACK BY WORKING FIVE MONTHS FOR FREE.

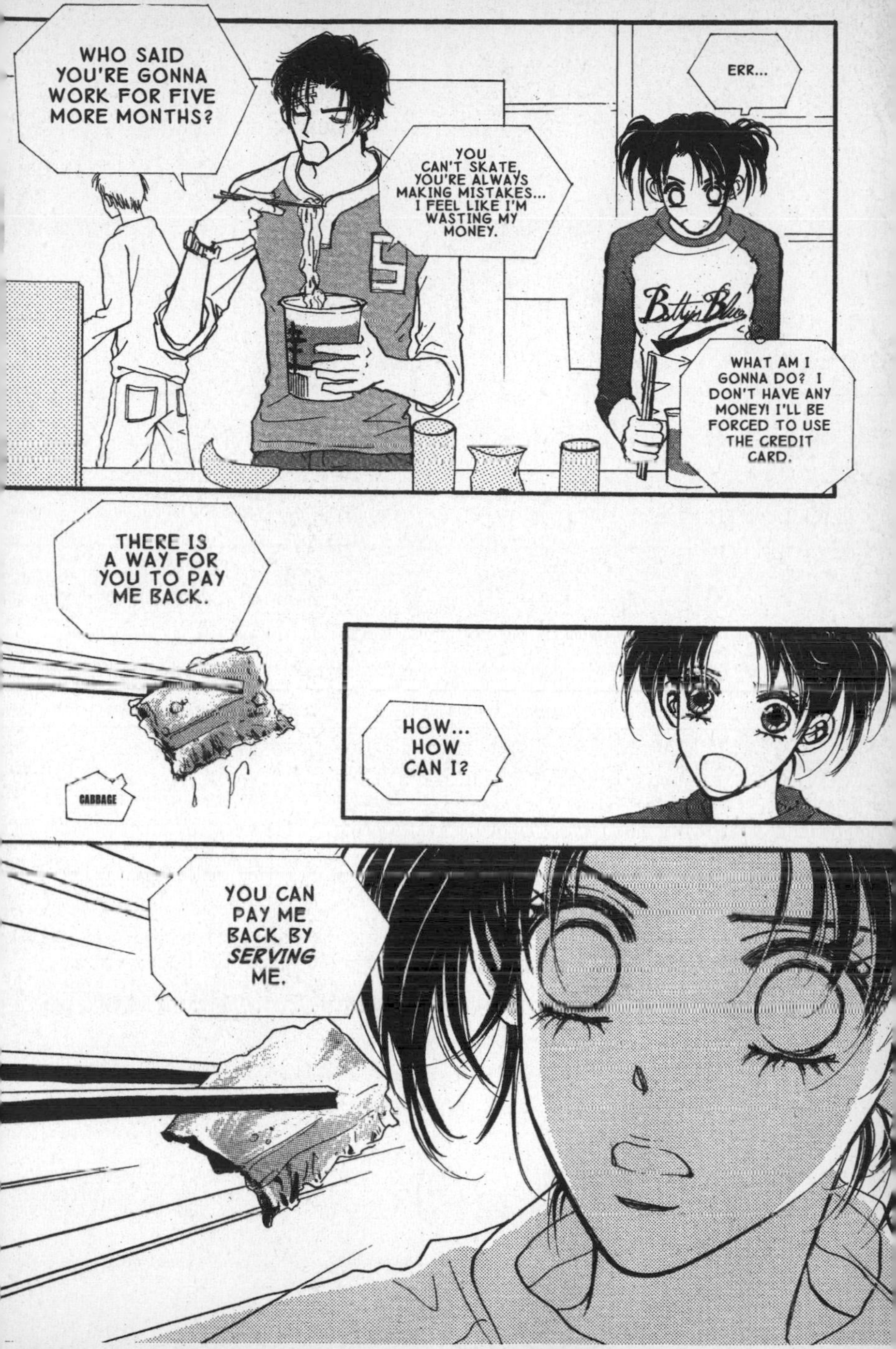
WHO SAID YOU'RE GONNA WORK FOR FIVE MORE MONTHS?
YOU CAN'T SKATE, YOU'RE ALWAYS MAKING MISTAKES... I FEEL LIKE I'M WASTING MY MONEY.
ERR...
WHAT AM I GONNA DO? I DON'T HAVE ANY MONEY! I'LL BE FORCED TO USE THE CREDIT CARD.
THERE IS A WAY FOR YOU TO PAY ME BACK.
CABBAGE
HOW... HOW CAN I?
YOU CAN PAY ME BACK BY *SERVING* ME.

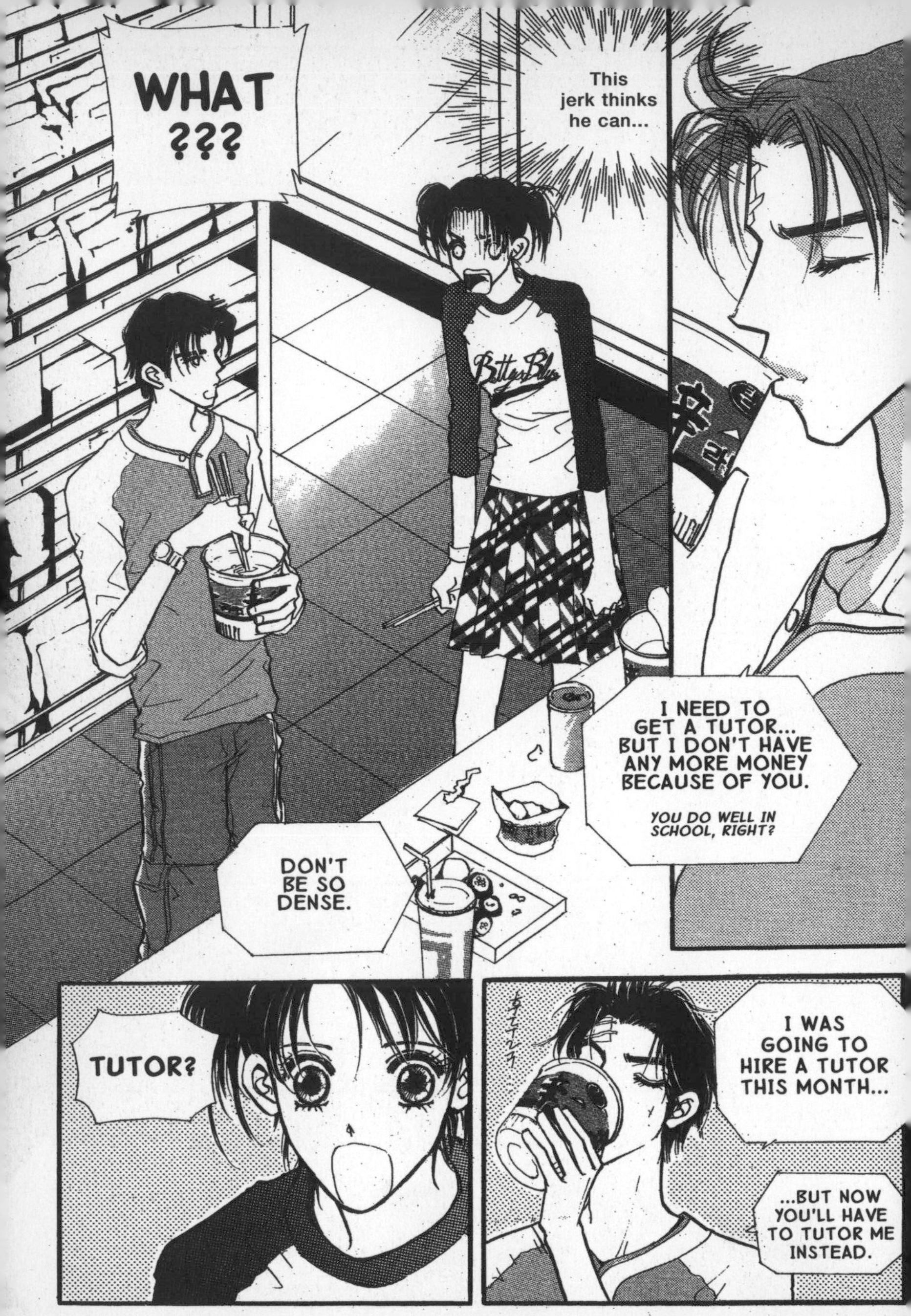
WHAT ???
This jerk thinks he can...
DON'T BE SO DENSE.
I NEED TO GET A TUTOR... BUT I DON'T HAVE ANY MORE MONEY BECAUSE OF YOU.
YOU DO WELL IN SCHOOL, RIGHT?
TUTOR?
I WAS GOING TO HIRE A TUTOR THIS MONTH...
...BUT NOW YOU'LL HAVE TO TUTOR ME INSTEAD.

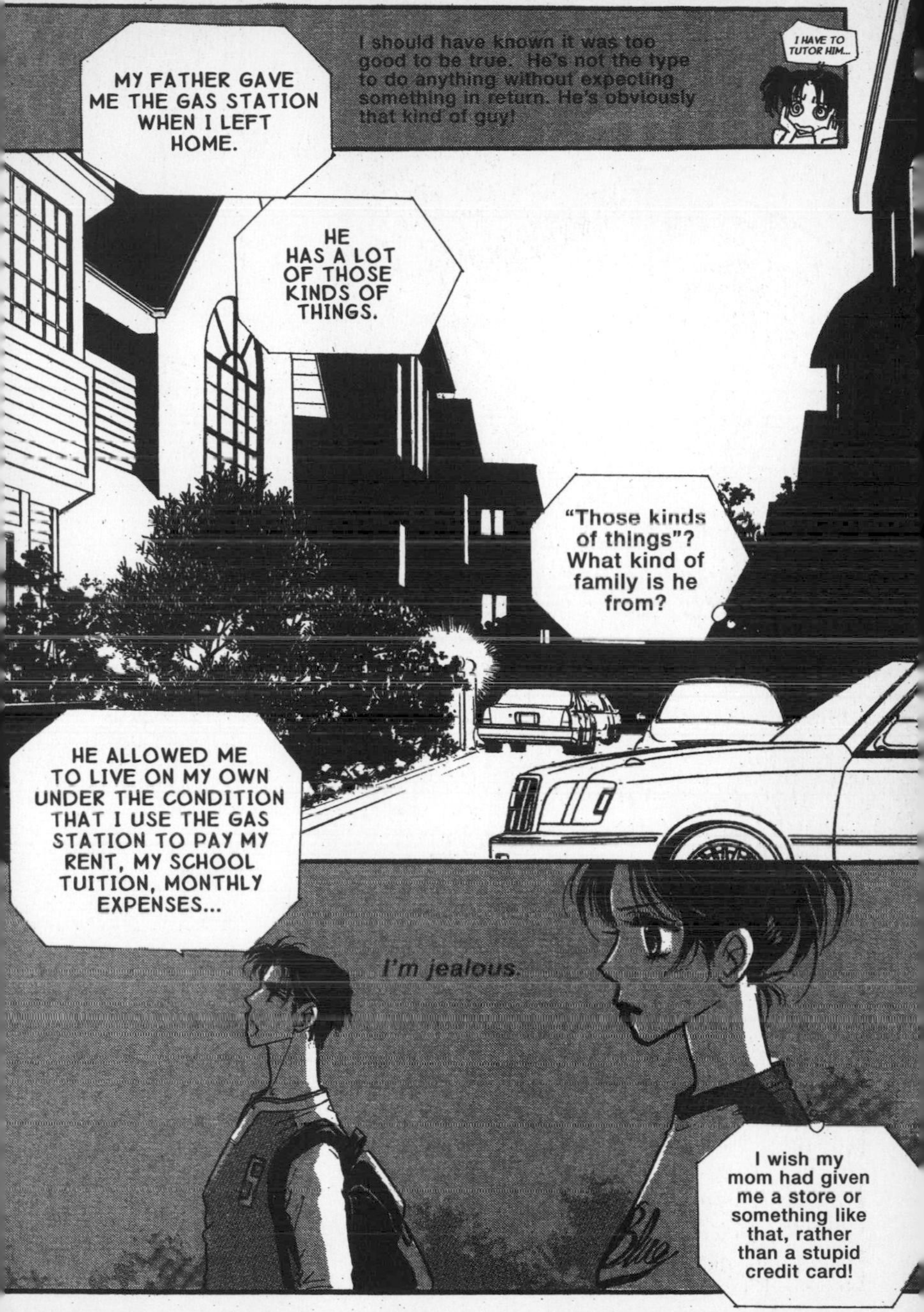
MY FATHER GAVE ME THE GAS STATION WHEN I LEFT HOME.
I should have known it was too good to be true. He's not the type to do anything without expecting something in return. He's obviously that kind of guy!
I HAVE TO TUTOR HIM...
HE HAS A LOT OF THOSE KINDS OF THINGS.
"Those kinds of things"? What kind of family is he from?
HE ALLOWED ME TO LIVE ON MY OWN UNDER THE CONDITION THAT I USE THE GAS STATION TO PAY MY RENT, MY SCHOOL TUITION, MONTHLY EXPENSES...
I'm jealous.
I wish my mom had given me a store or something like that, rather than a stupid credit card!

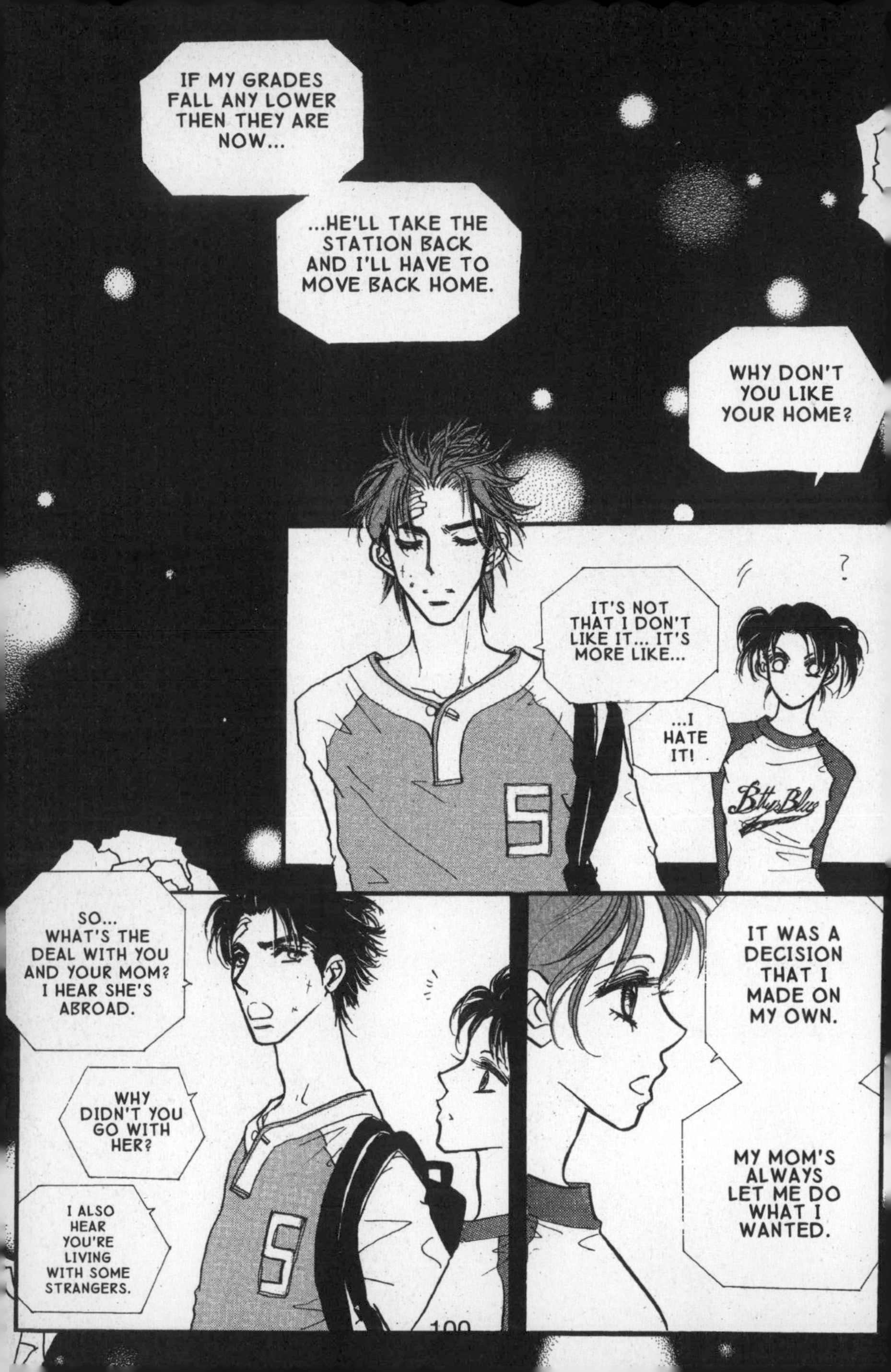
IF MY GRADES FALL ANY LOWER THEN THEY ARE NOW...
...HE'LL TAKE THE STATION BACK AND I'LL HAVE TO MOVE BACK HOME.
WHY DON'T YOU LIKE YOUR HOME?
IT'S NOT THAT I DON'T LIKE IT... IT'S MORE LIKE...
...I HATE IT!
?
SO... WHAT'S THE DEAL WITH YOU AND YOUR MOM? I HEAR SHE'S ABROAD.
WHY DIDN'T YOU GO WITH HER?
I ALSO HEAR YOU'RE LIVING WITH SOME STRANGERS.
IT WAS A DECISION THAT I MADE ON MY OWN.
MY MOM'S ALWAYS LET ME DO WHAT I WANTED.

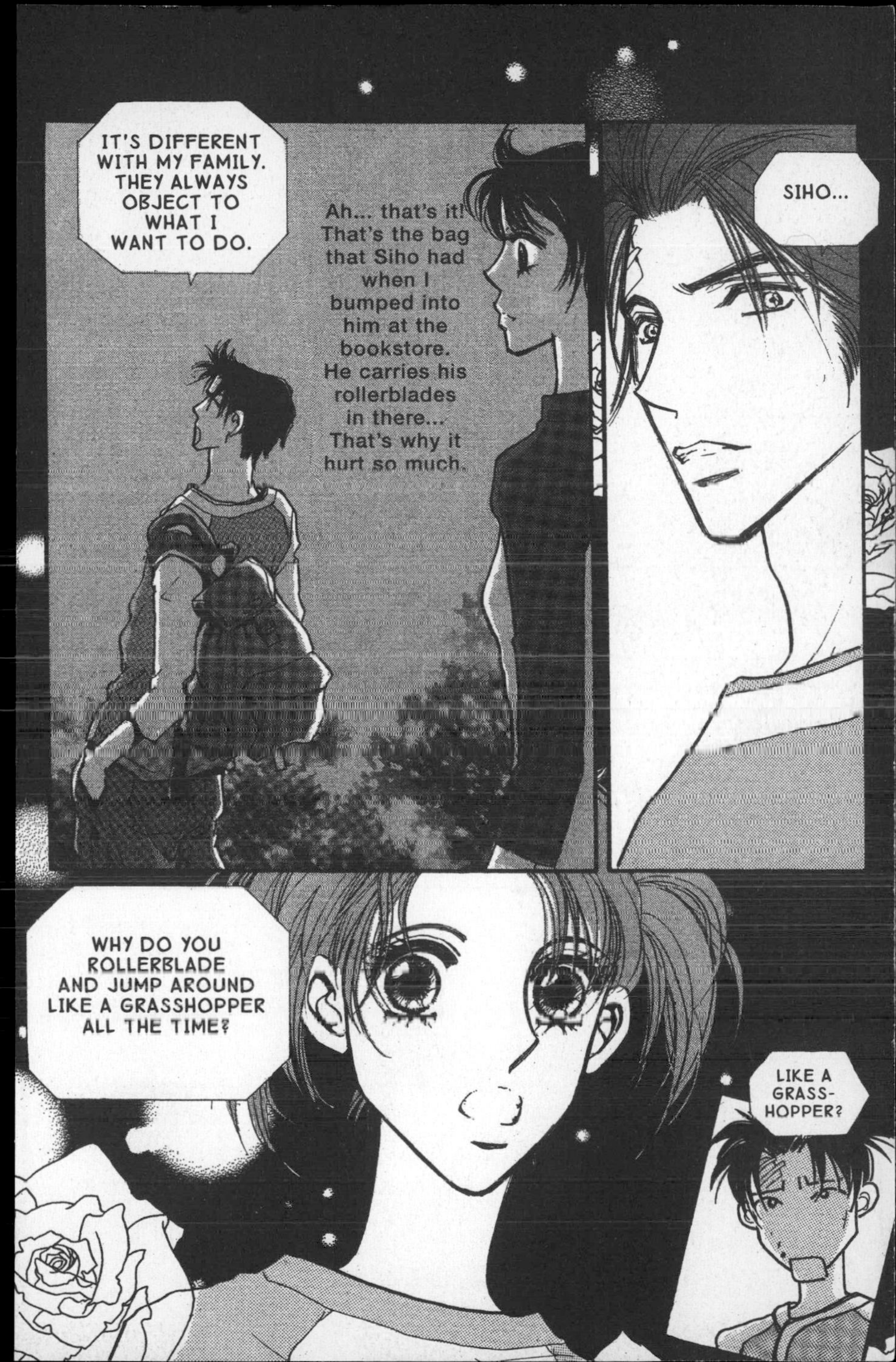
IT'S DIFFERENT WITH MY FAMILY. THEY ALWAYS OBJECT TO WHAT I WANT TO DO.
Ah... that's it! That's the bag that Siho had when I bumped into him at the bookstore. He carries his rollerblades in there... That's why it hurt so much.
SIHO...
WHY DO YOU ROLLERBLADE AND JUMP AROUND LIKE A GRASSHOPPER ALL THE TIME?
LIKE A GRASS-HOPPER?

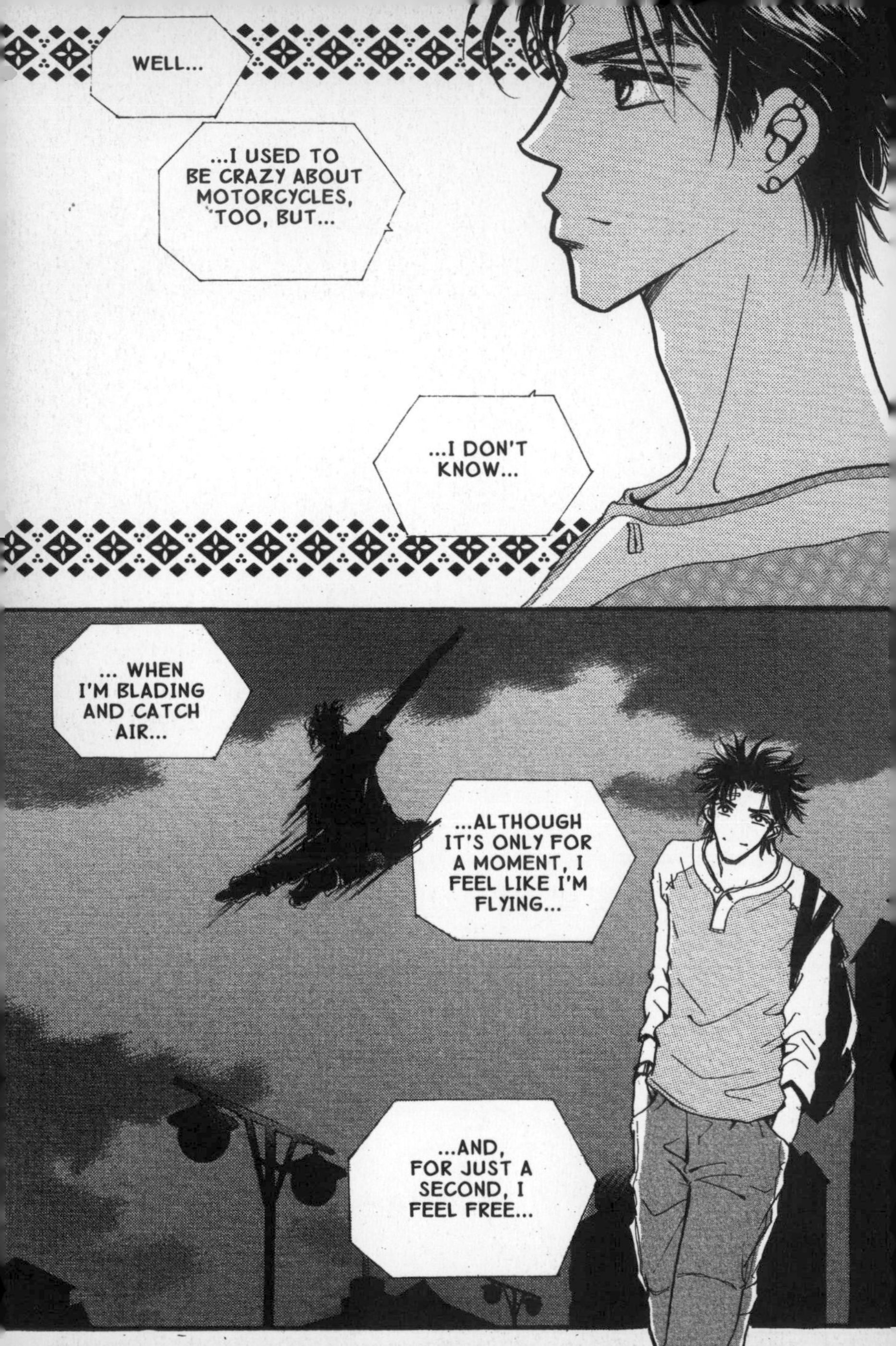
WELL...
...I USED TO BE CRAZY ABOUT MOTORCYCLES, TOO, BUT...
...I DON'T KNOW...
... WHEN I'M BLADING AND CATCH AIR...
...ALTHOUGH IT'S ONLY FOR A MOMENT, I FEEL LIKE I'M FLYING...
...AND, FOR JUST A SECOND, I FEEL FREE...

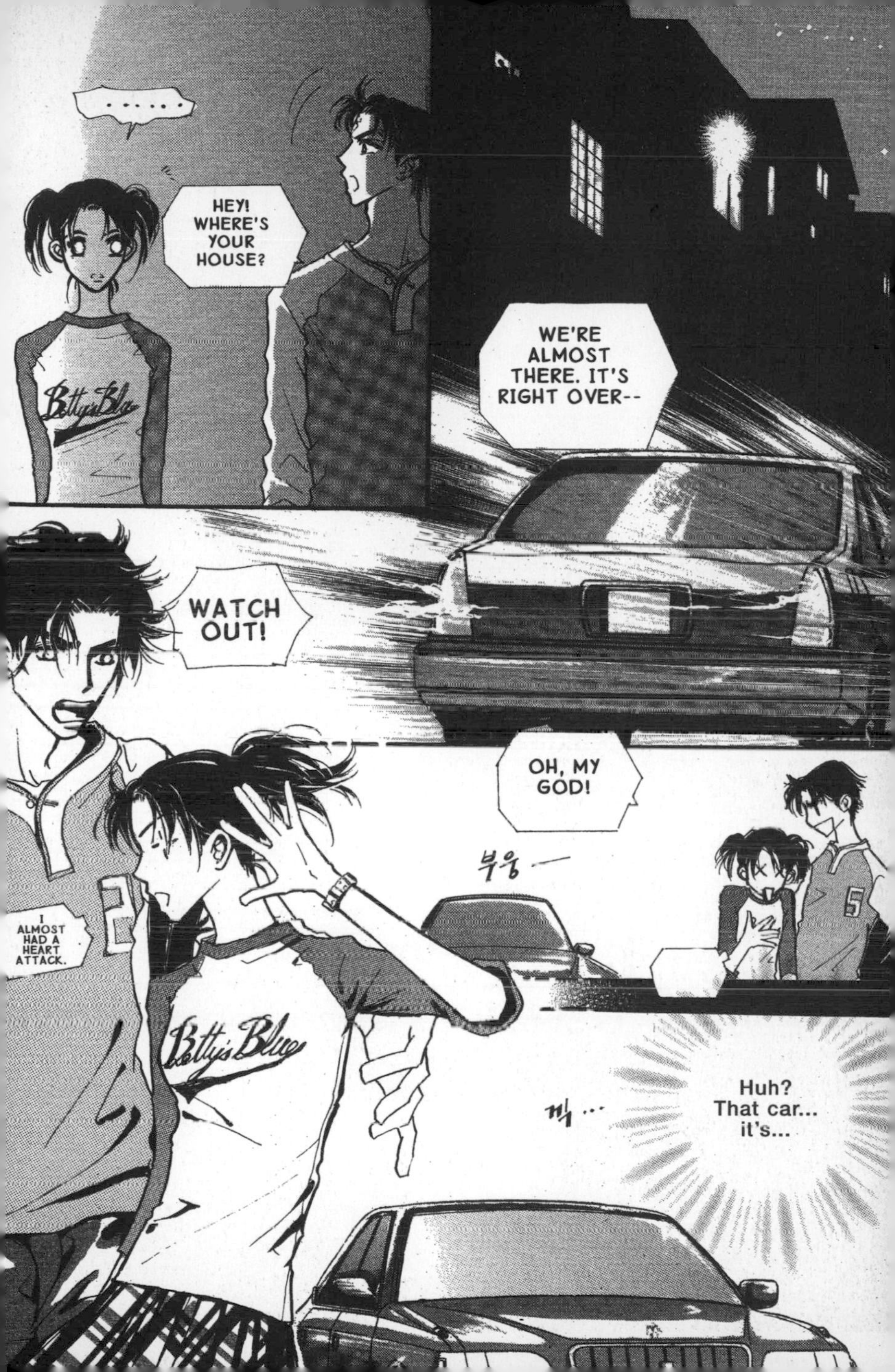

......
HEY! WHERE'S YOUR HOUSE?
WE'RE ALMOST THERE. IT'S RIGHT OVER--
WATCH OUT!
OH, MY GOD!
부웅 —
I ALMOST HAD A HEART ATTACK.
Huh? That car... it's...

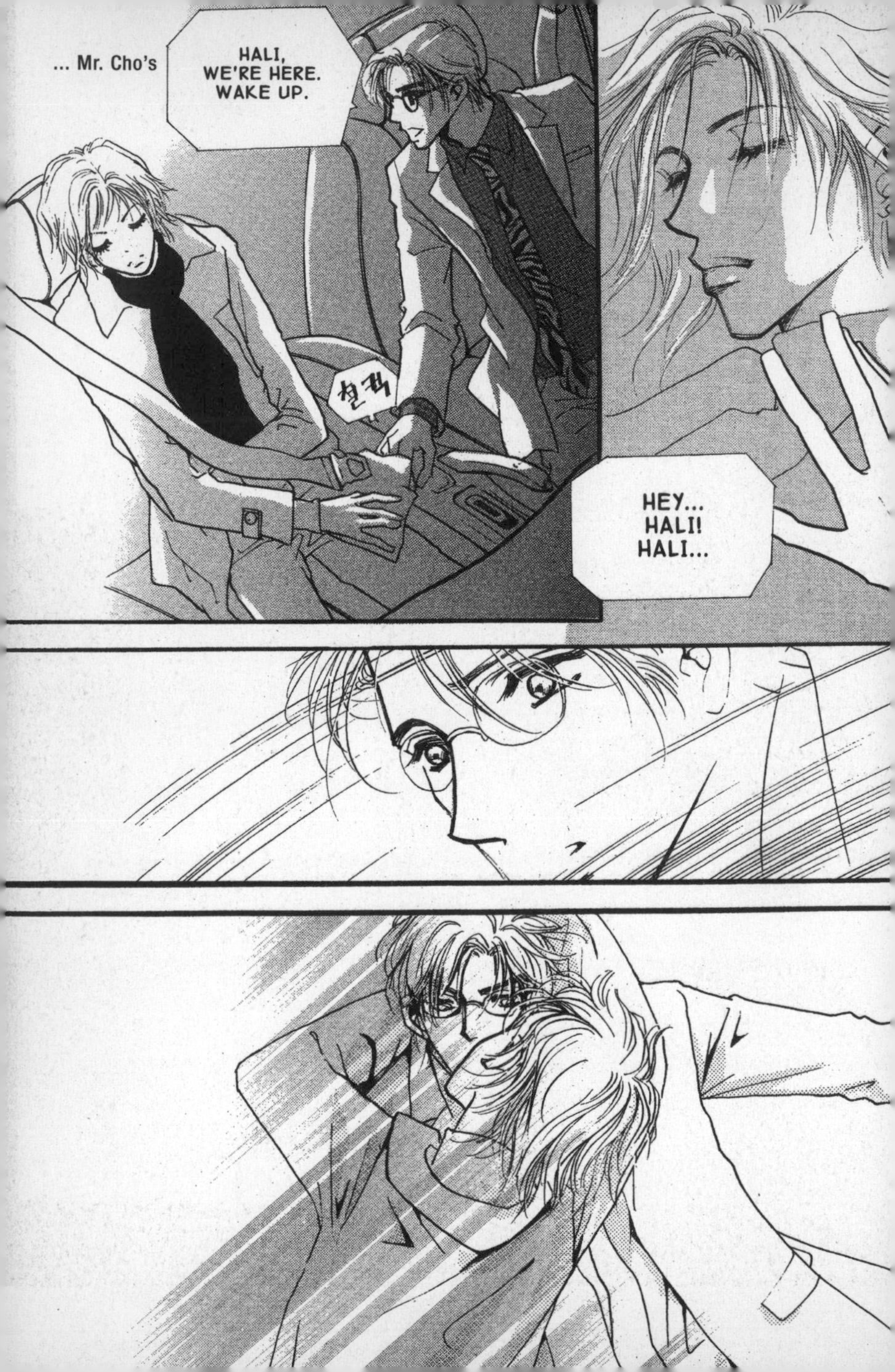
... Mr. Cho's
HALI, WE'RE HERE. WAKE UP.
철컥
HEY... HALI! HALI...

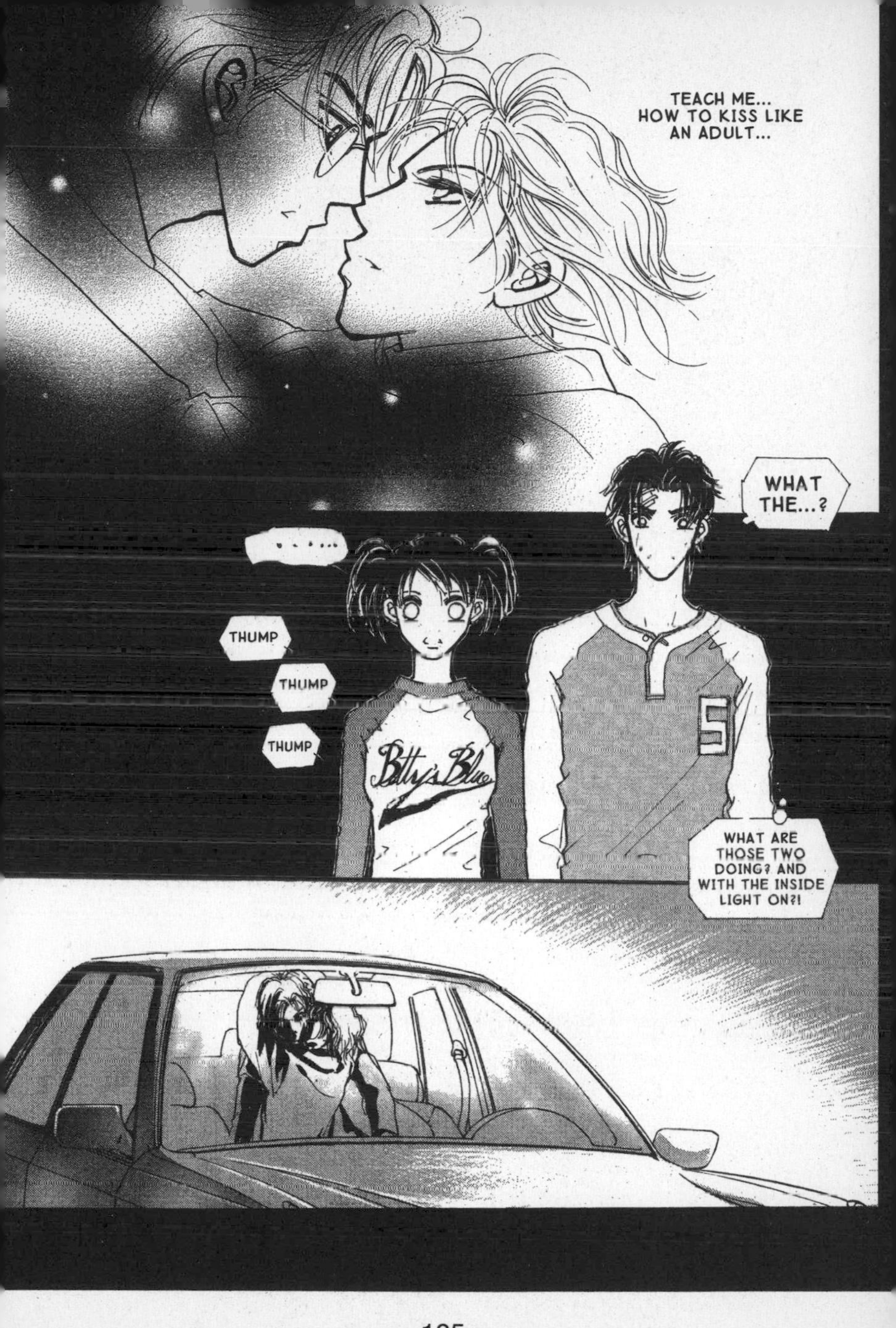
TEACH ME... HOW TO KISS LIKE AN ADULT...
......
THUMP
THUMP
THUMP
WHAT THE...?
WHAT ARE THOSE TWO DOING? AND WITH THE INSIDE LIGHT ON?!

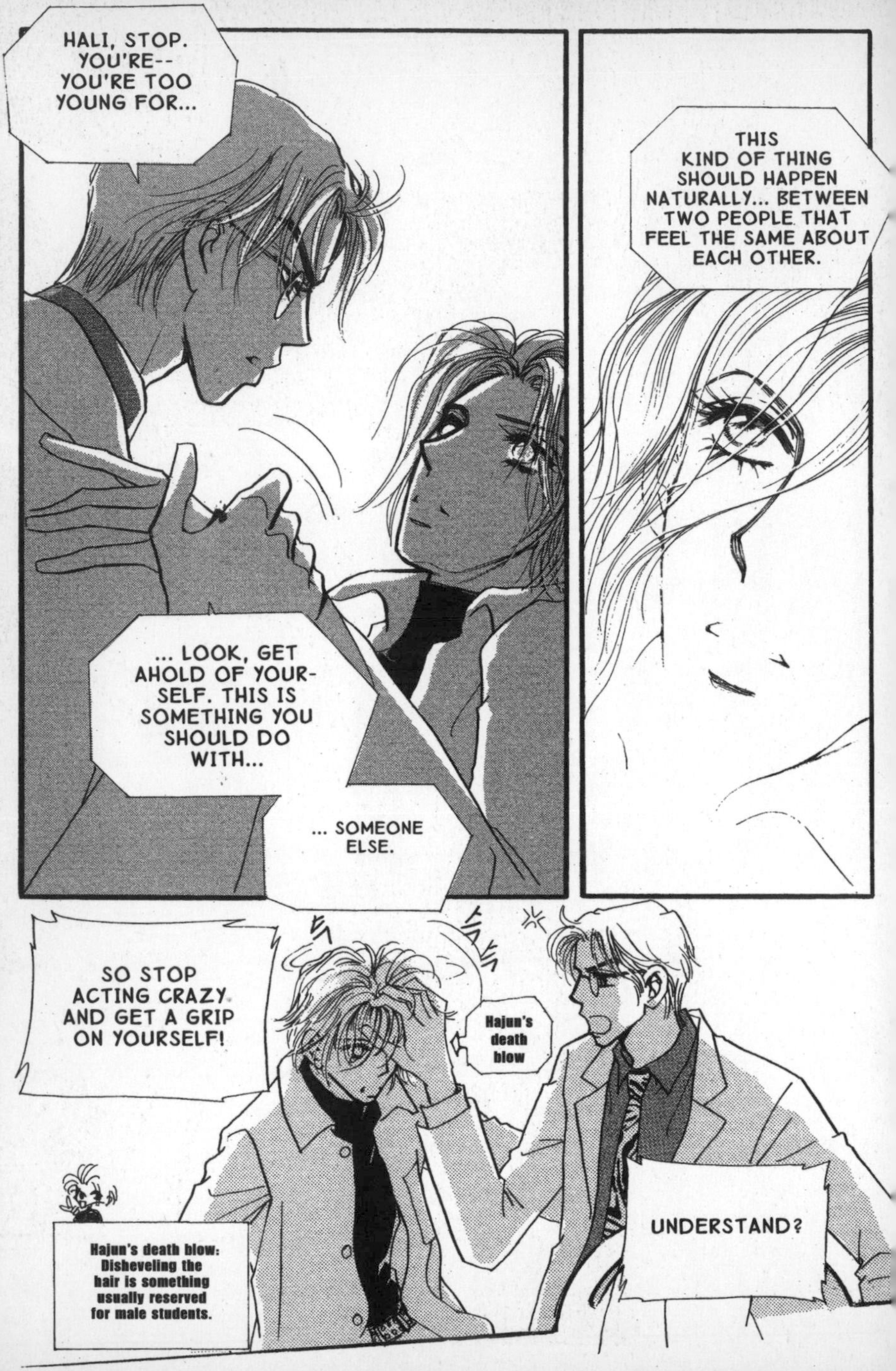
HALI, STOP. YOU'RE-- YOU'RE TOO YOUNG FOR...
... LOOK, GET AHOLD OF YOURSELF. THIS IS SOMETHING YOU SHOULD DO WITH...
... SOMEONE ELSE.
THIS KIND OF THING SHOULD HAPPEN NATURALLY... BETWEEN TWO PEOPLE THAT FEEL THE SAME ABOUT EACH OTHER.
SO STOP ACTING CRAZY AND GET A GRIP ON YOURSELF!
Hajun's death blow
Hajun's death blow: Disheveling the hair is something usually reserved for male students.
UNDERSTAND?

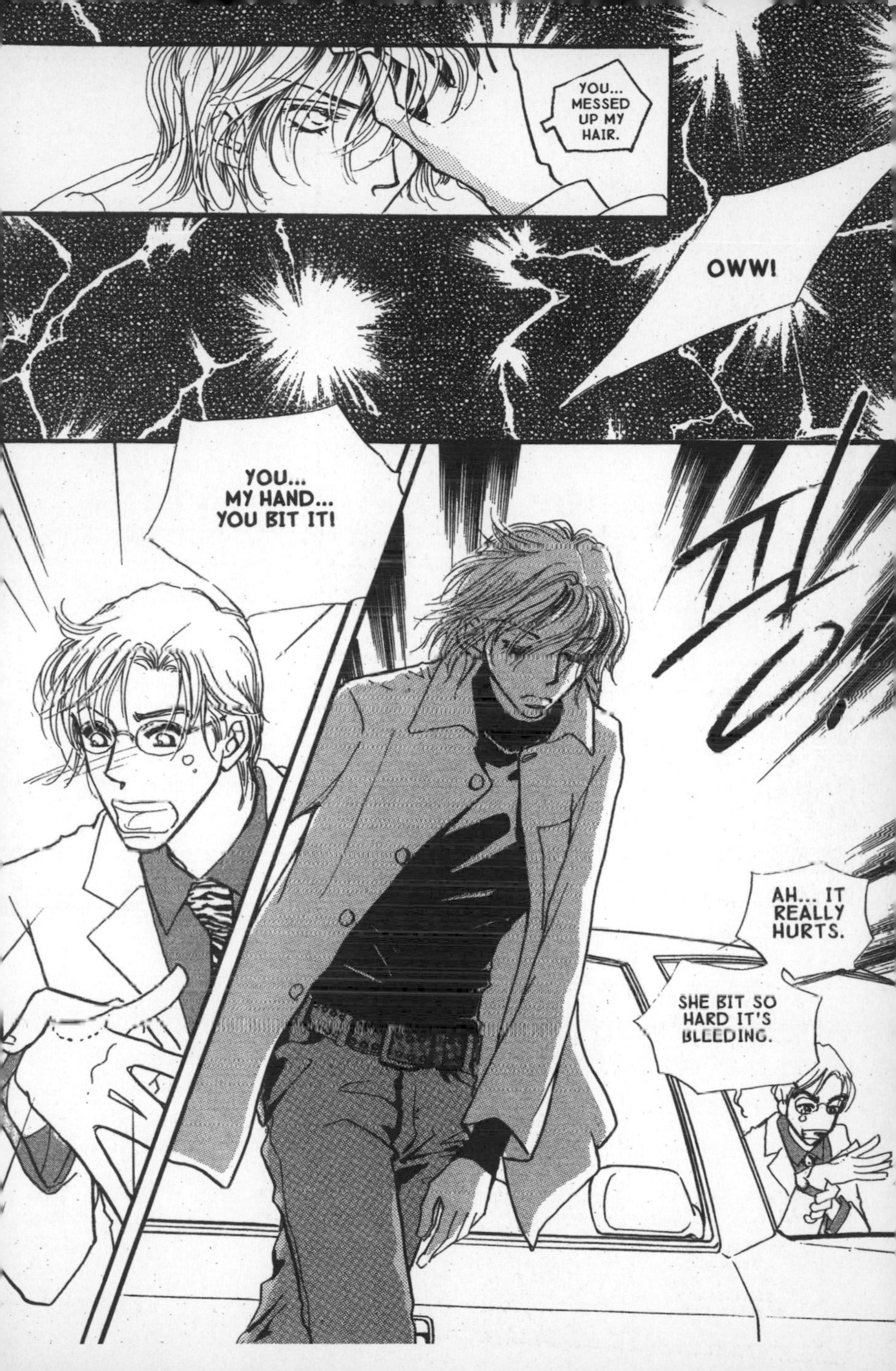
YOU... MESSED UP MY HAIR.
OWW!
YOU... MY HAND... YOU BIT IT!
AH... IT REALLY HURTS.
SHE BIT SO HARD IT'S BLEEDING.

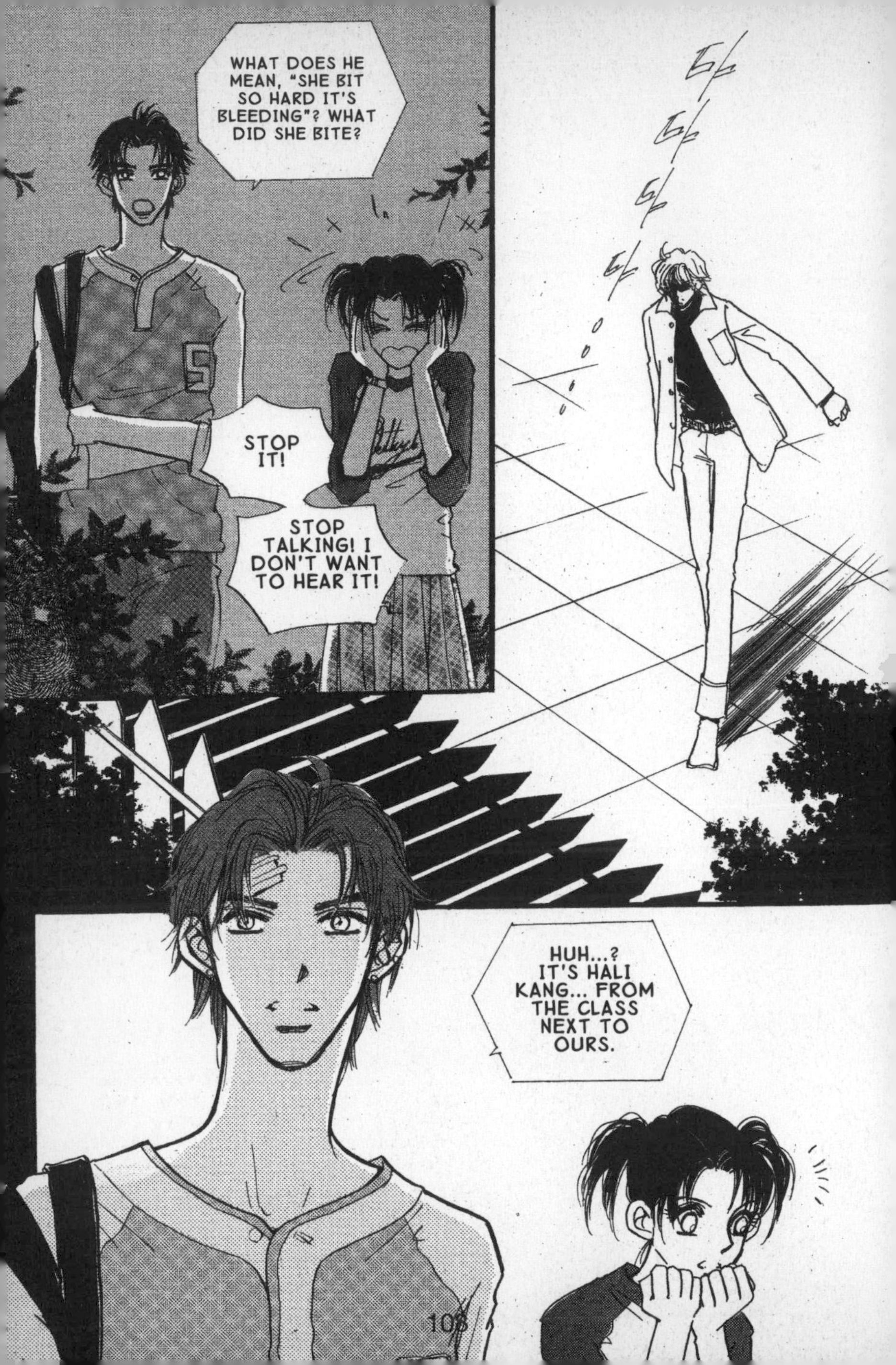
WHAT DOES HE MEAN, "SHE BIT SO HARD IT'S BLEEDING"? WHAT DID SHE BITE?
STOP IT!
STOP TALKING! I DON'T WANT TO HEAR IT!
HUH...? IT'S HALI KANG... FROM THE CLASS NEXT TO OURS.

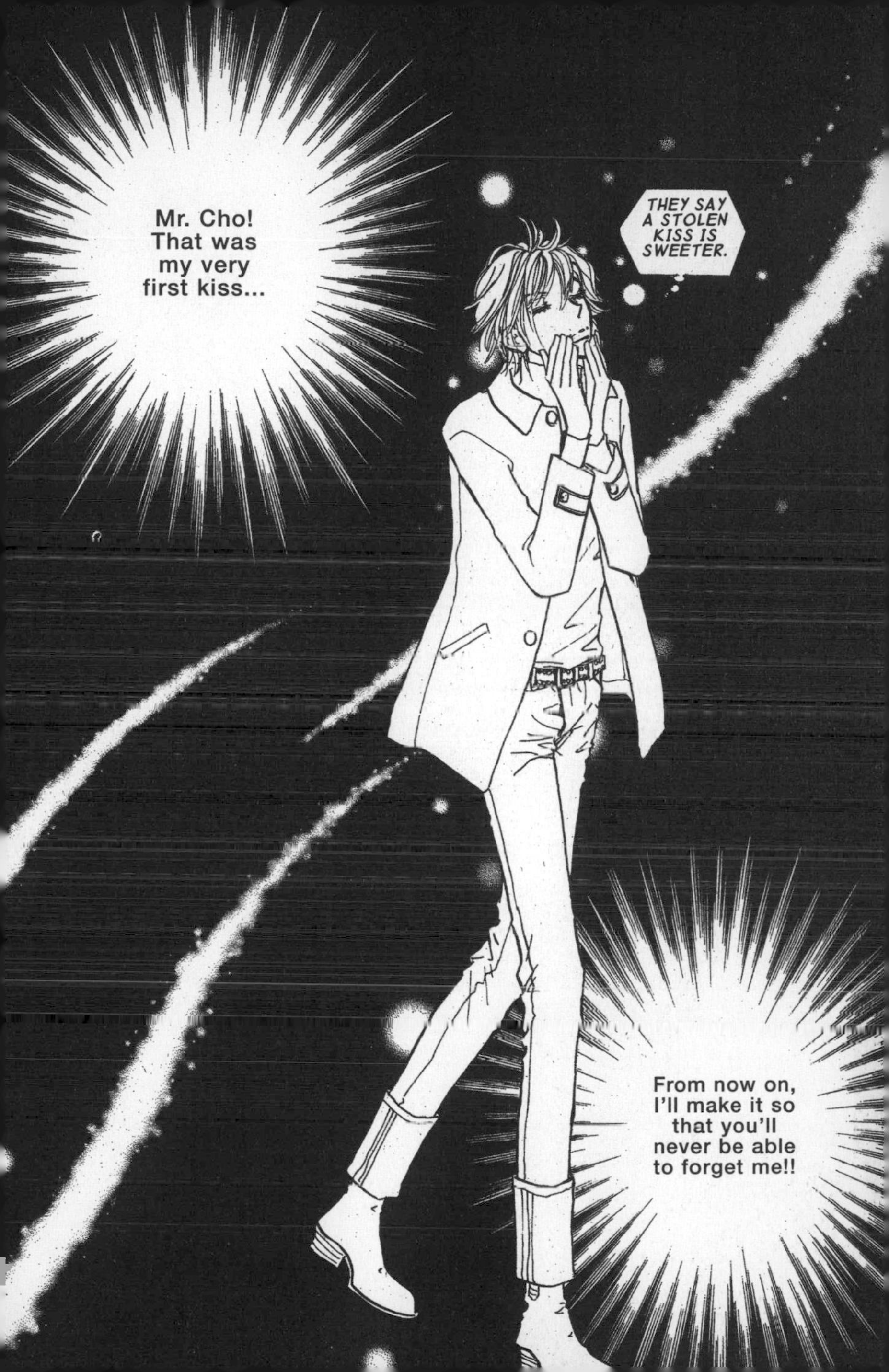
Mr. Cho! That was my very first kiss...
THEY SAY A STOLEN KISS IS SWEETER.
From now on, I'll make it so that you'll never be able to forget me!!

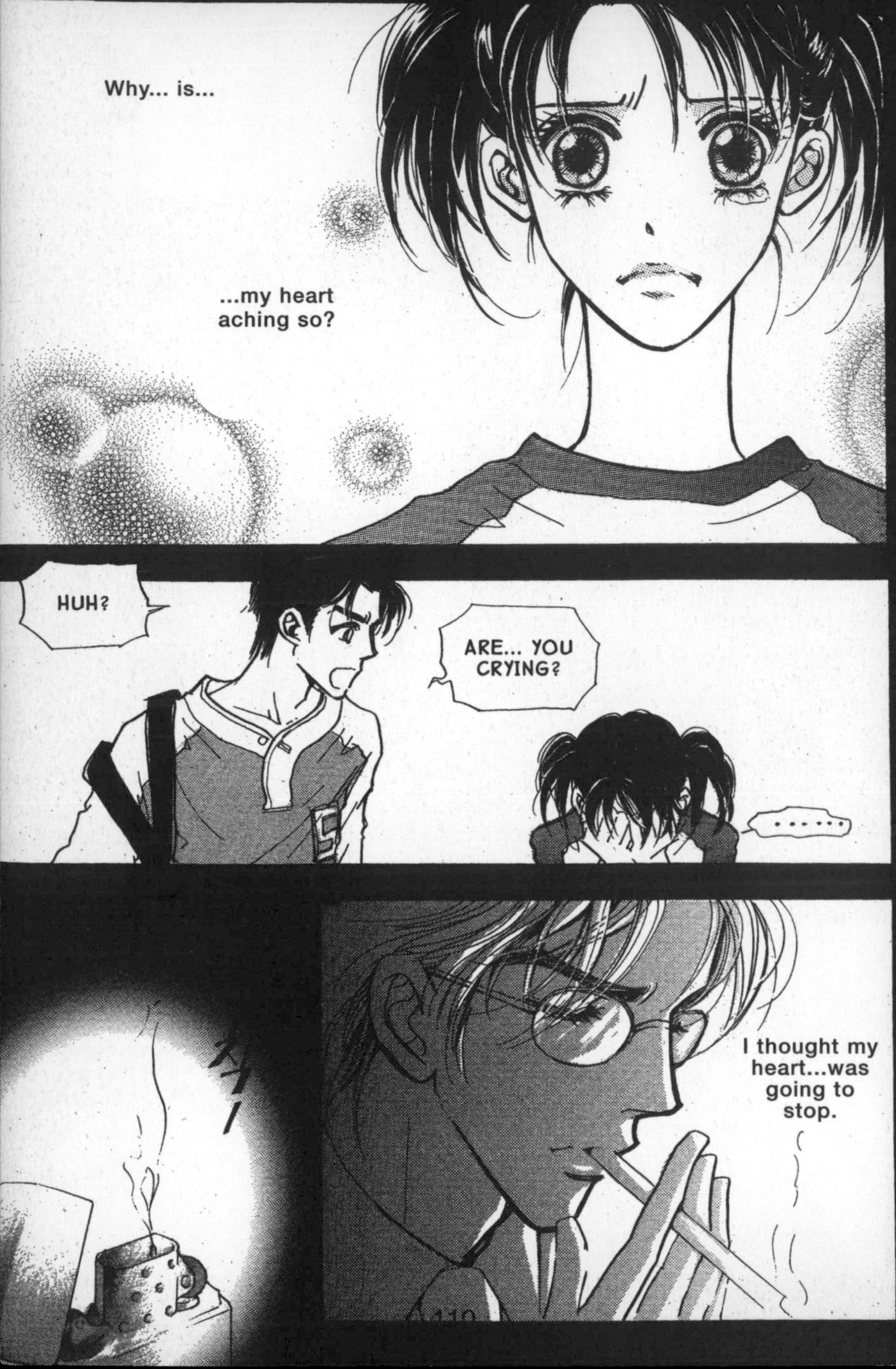
Why... is...
...my heart aching so?
HUH?
ARE... YOU CRYING?
......
I thought my heart...was going to stop.

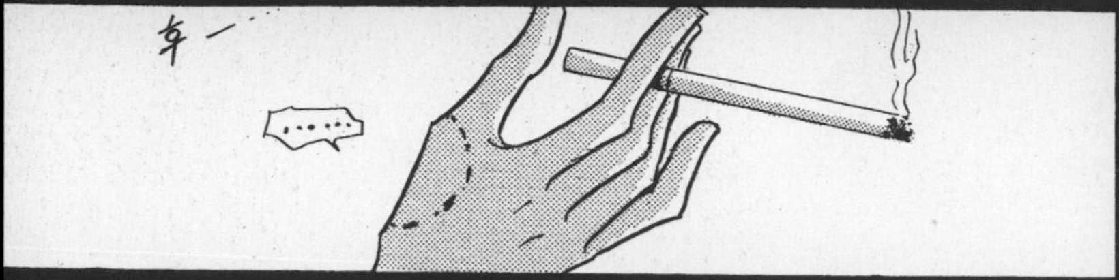

......

That girl...

I wonder...

...what she's planning.

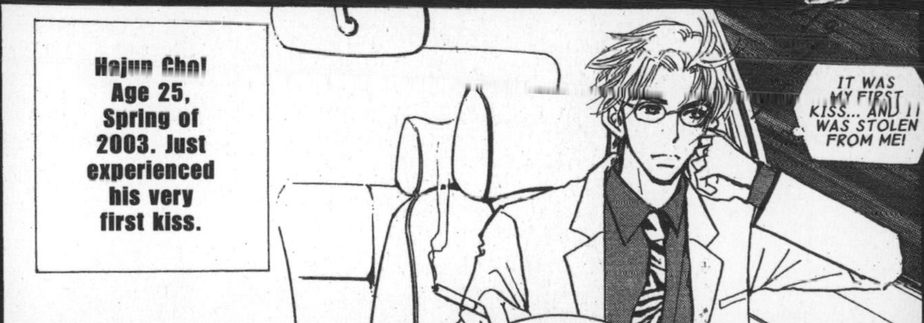

Hajun Choi Age 25, Spring of 2003. Just experienced his very first kiss.
IT WAS MY FIRST KISS... AND IT WAS STOLEN FROM ME!

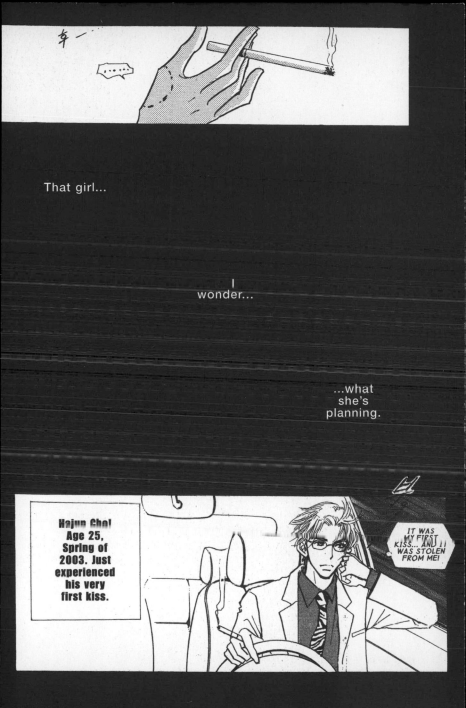

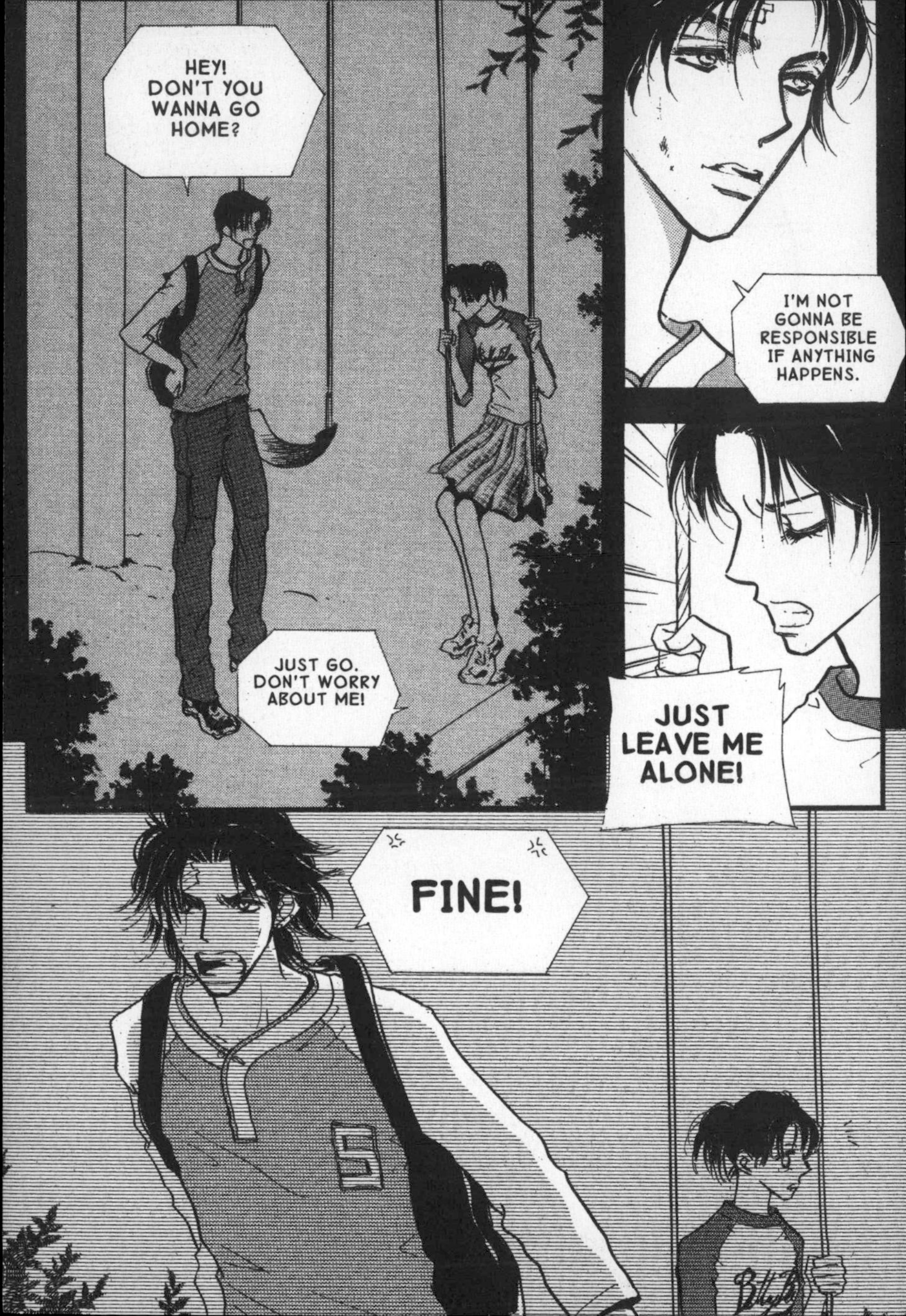
HEY! DON'T YOU WANNA GO HOME?
JUST GO. DON'T WORRY ABOUT ME!
I'M NOT GONNA BE RESPONSIBLE IF ANYTHING HAPPENS.
JUST LEAVE ME ALONE!
FINE!

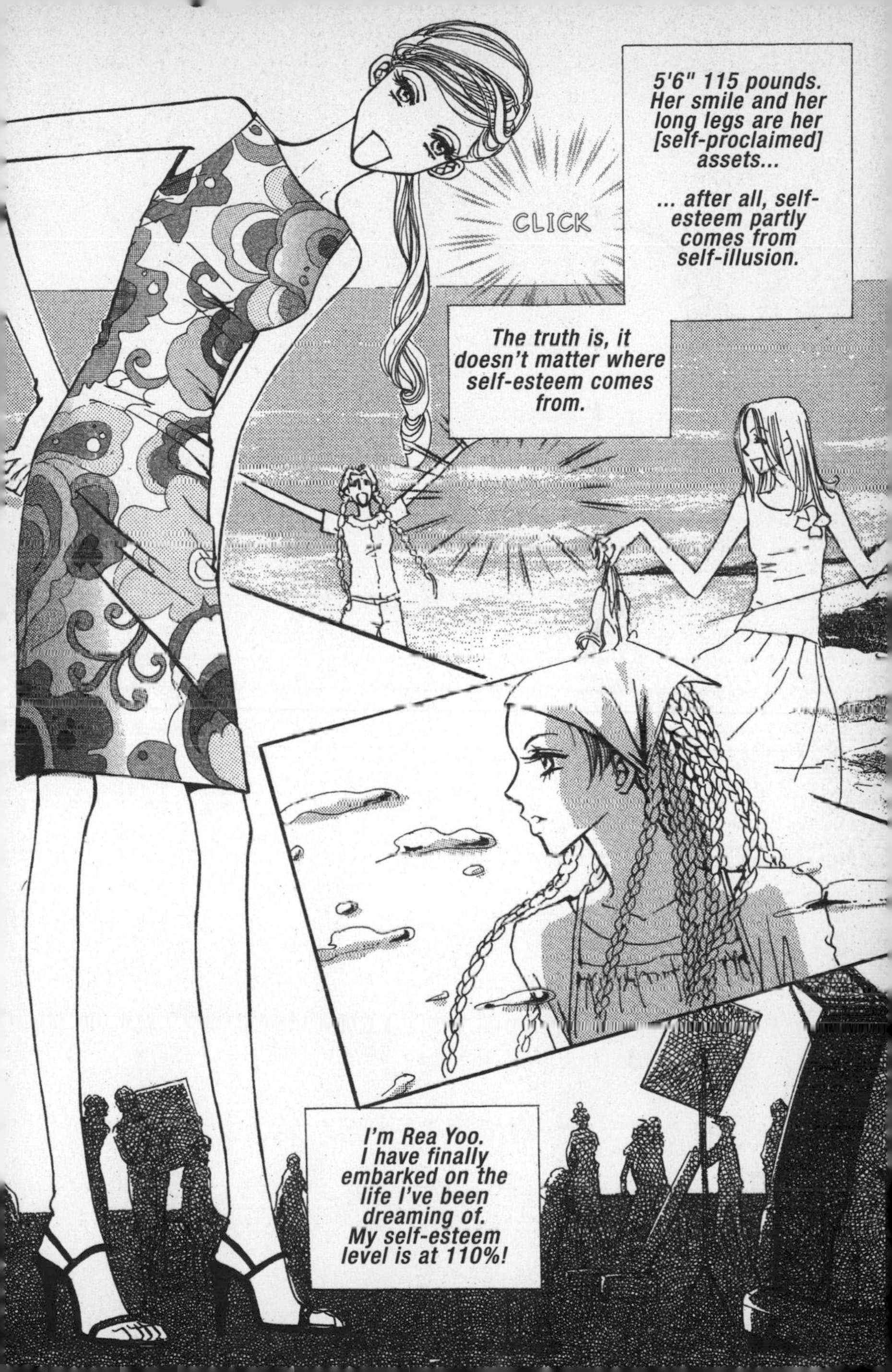
5'6" 115 pounds. Her smile and her long legs are her [self-proclaimed] assets...
... after all, self-esteem partly comes from self-illusion.
CLICK
The truth is, it doesn't matter where self-esteem comes from.
I'm Rea Yoo. I have finally embarked on the life I've been dreaming of. My self-esteem level is at 110%!

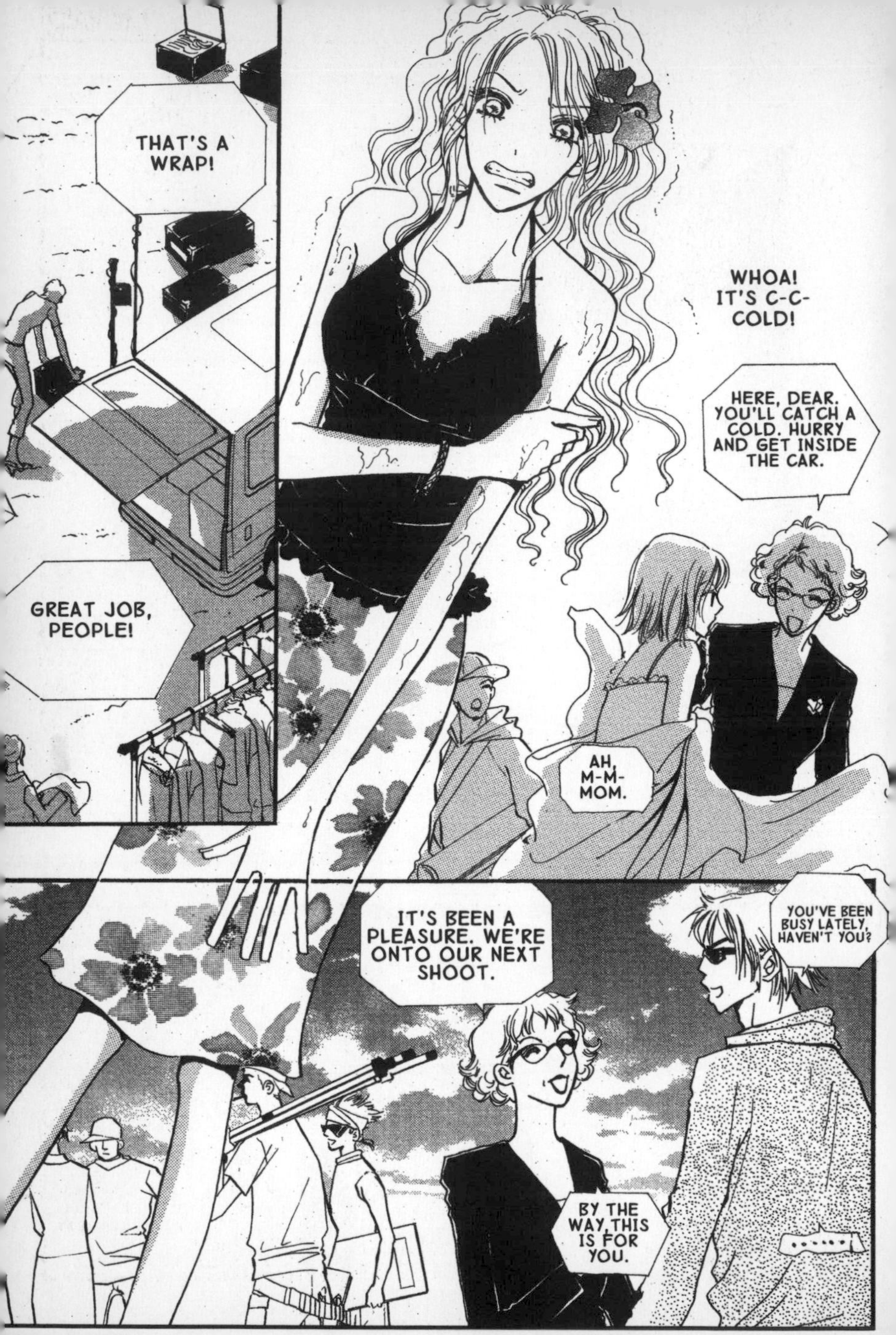
THAT'S A WRAP!
GREAT JOB, PEOPLE!
WHOA! IT'S C-C-COLD!
HERE, DEAR. YOU'LL CATCH A COLD. HURRY AND GET INSIDE THE CAR.
AH, M-M-MOM.
IT'S BEEN A PLEASURE. WE'RE ONTO OUR NEXT SHOOT.
YOU'VE BEEN BUSY LATELY, HAVEN'T YOU?
BY THE WAY, THIS IS FOR YOU.
......

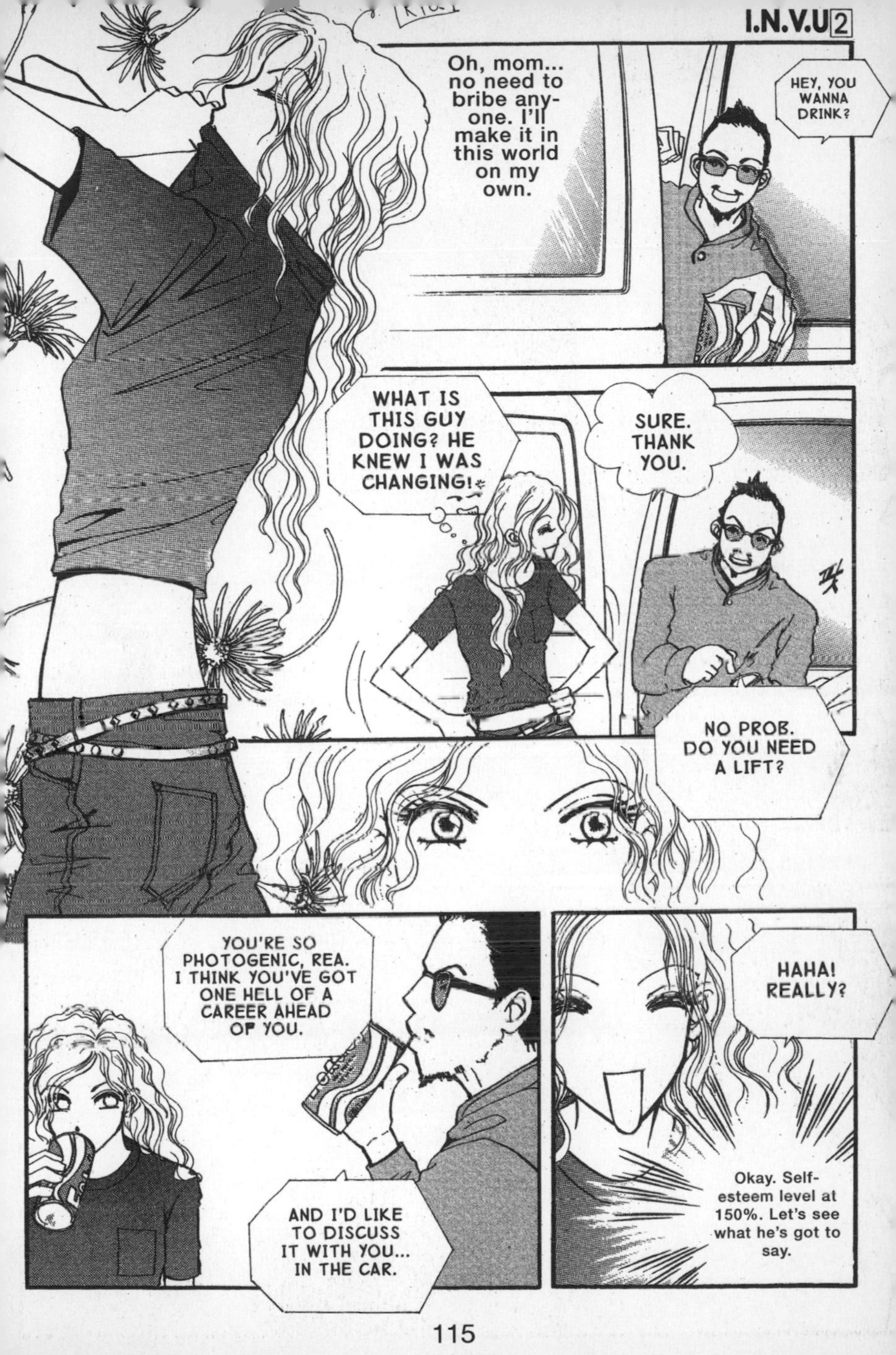
Oh, mom... no need to bribe any-one. I'll make it in this world on my own.
HEY, YOU WANNA DRINK?
WHAT IS THIS GUY DOING? HE KNEW I WAS CHANGING!
SURE. THANK YOU.
NO PROB. DO YOU NEED A LIFT?
YOU'RE SO PHOTOGENIC, REA. I THINK YOU'VE GOT ONE HELL OF A CAREER AHEAD OF YOU.
AND I'D LIKE TO DISCUSS IT WITH YOU... IN THE CAR.
HAHA! REALLY?
Okay. Self-esteem level at 150%. Let's see what he's got to say.

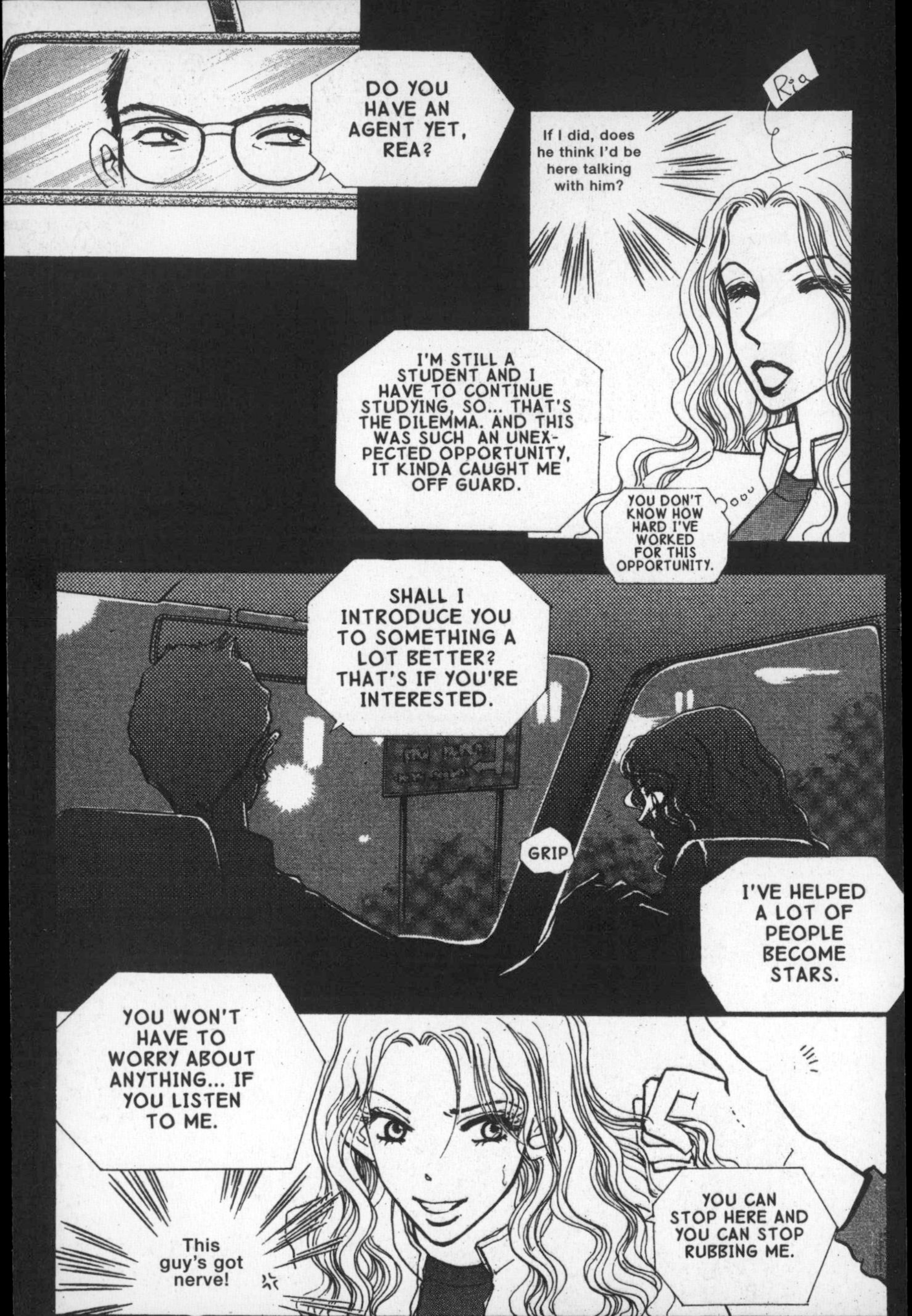
DO YOU HAVE AN AGENT YET, REA?
Ria
If I did, does he think I'd be here talking with him?
I'M STILL A STUDENT AND I HAVE TO CONTINUE STUDYING, SO... THAT'S THE DILEMMA. AND THIS WAS SUCH AN UNEXPECTED OPPORTUNITY, IT KINDA CAUGHT ME OFF GUARD.
YOU DON'T KNOW HOW HARD I'VE WORKED FOR THIS OPPORTUNITY.
SHALL I INTRODUCE YOU TO SOMETHING A LOT BETTER? THAT'S IF YOU'RE INTERESTED.
GRIP
I'VE HELPED A LOT OF PEOPLE BECOME STARS.
YOU WON'T HAVE TO WORRY ABOUT ANYTHING... IF YOU LISTEN TO ME.
This guy's got nerve!
YOU CAN STOP HERE AND YOU CAN STOP RUBBING ME.

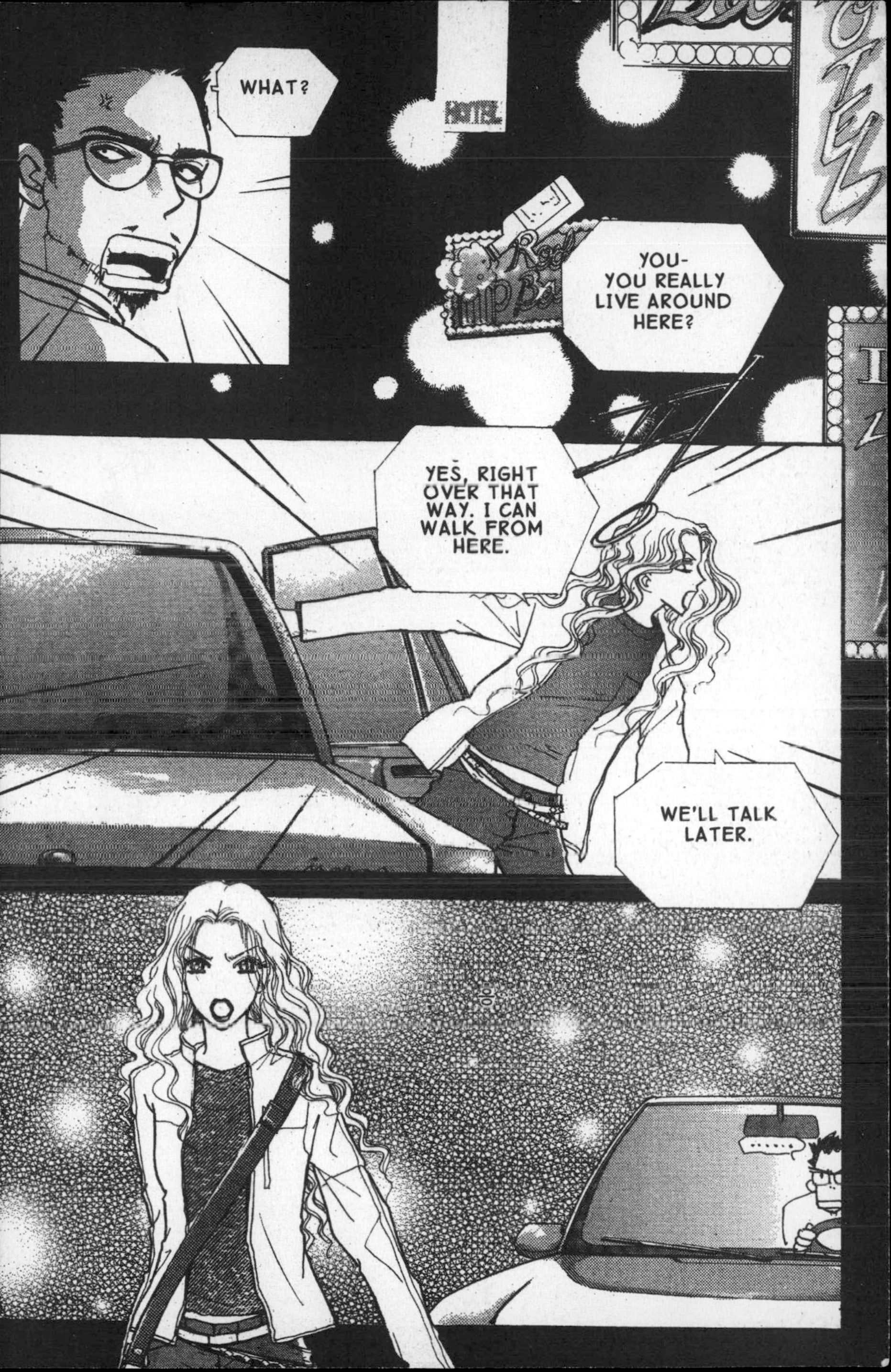
WHAT?
HOTEL
YOU-
YOU REALLY
LIVE AROUND
HERE?
YES, RIGHT
OVER THAT
WAY. I CAN
WALK FROM
HERE.
WE'LL TALK
LATER.
......

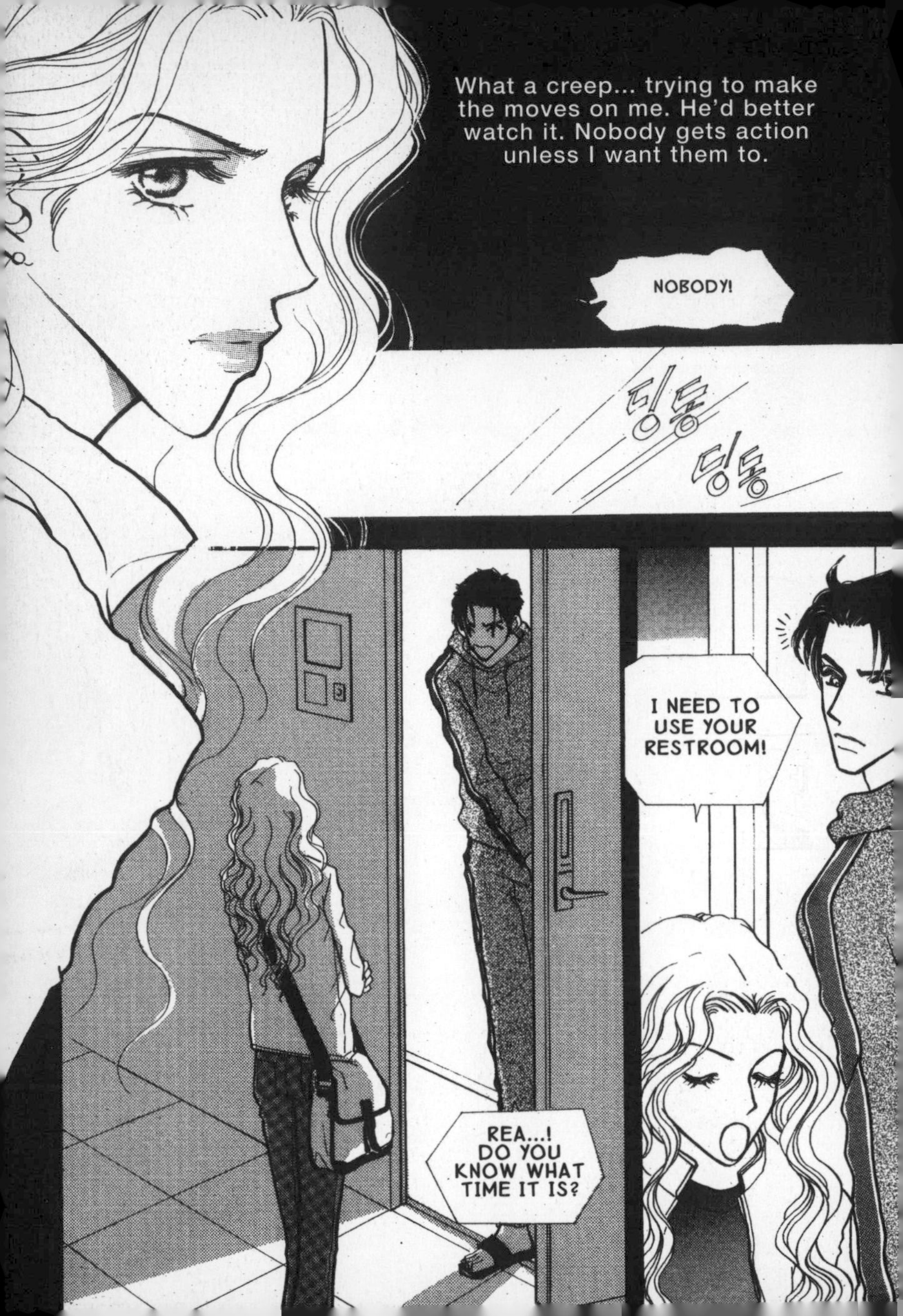
What a creep... trying to make the moves on me. He'd better watch it. Nobody gets action unless I want them to.
NOBODY!
딩동
딩동
REA...! DO YOU KNOW WHAT TIME IT IS?
I NEED TO USE YOUR RESTROOM!

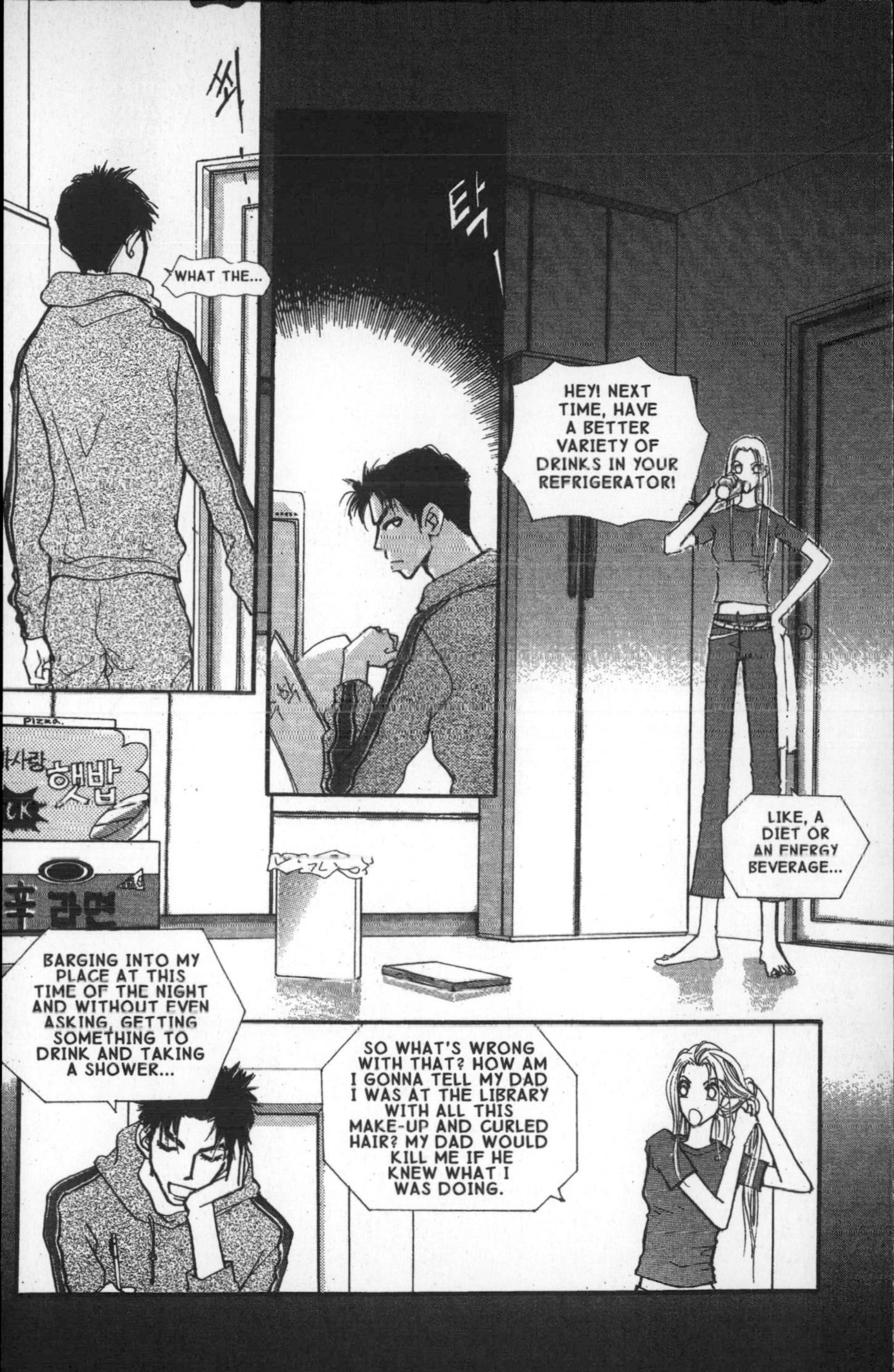

쏴
WHAT THE...
탁
HEY! NEXT TIME, HAVE A BETTER VARIETY OF DRINKS IN YOUR REFRIGERATOR!
LIKE, A DIET OR AN ENERGY BEVERAGE...
BARGING INTO MY PLACE AT THIS TIME OF THE NIGHT AND WITHOUT EVEN ASKING, GETTING SOMETHING TO DRINK AND TAKING A SHOWER...
SO WHAT'S WRONG WITH THAT? HOW AM I GONNA TELL MY DAD I WAS AT THE LIBRARY WITH ALL THIS MAKE-UP AND CURLED HAIR? MY DAD WOULD KILL ME IF HE KNEW WHAT I WAS DOING.

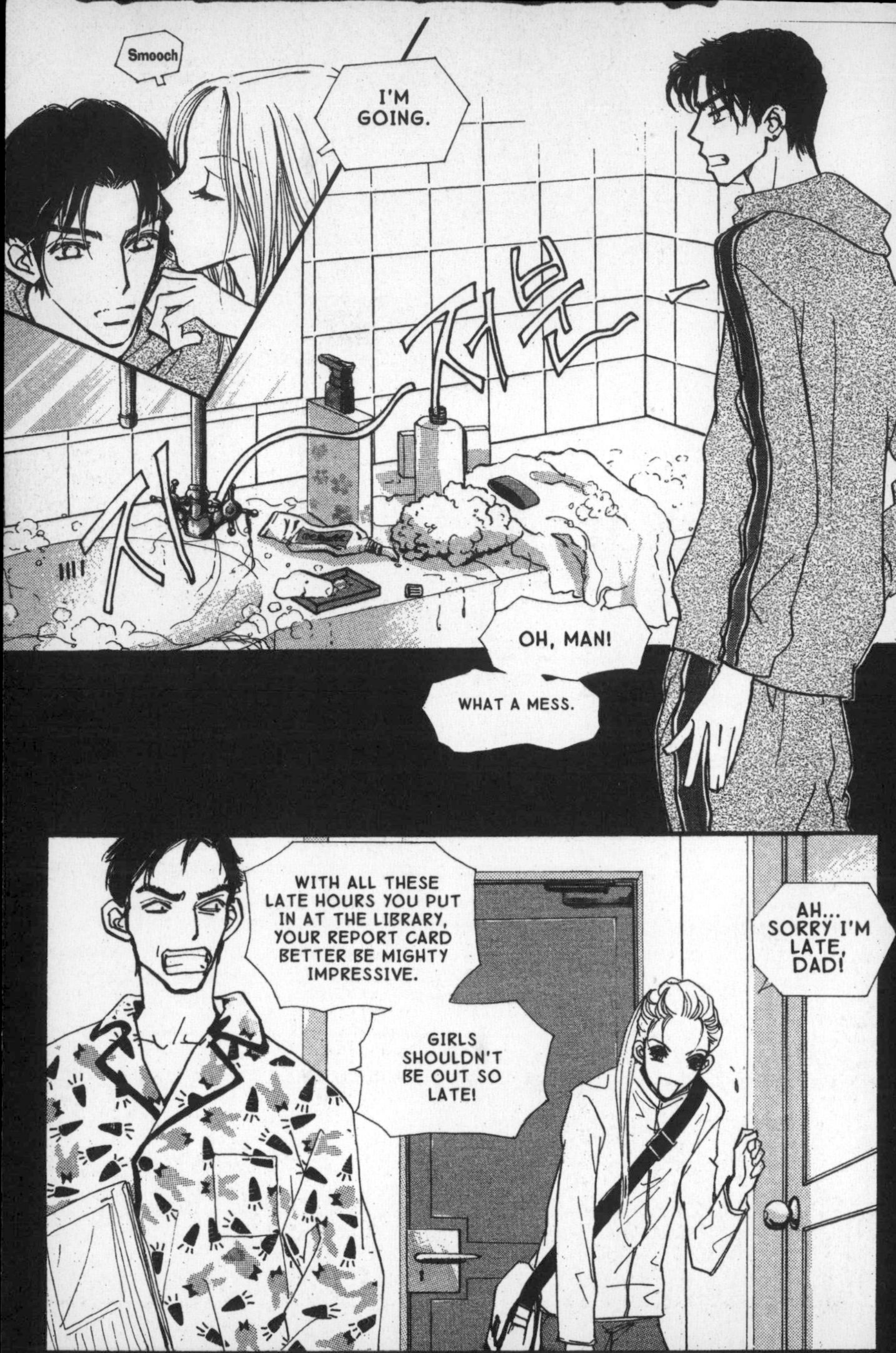
Smooch
I'M GOING.
지
저분~
OH, MAN!
WHAT A MESS.
WITH ALL THESE LATE HOURS YOU PUT IN AT THE LIBRARY, YOUR REPORT CARD BETTER BE MIGHTY IMPRESSIVE.
GIRLS SHOULDN'T BE OUT SO LATE!
AH... SORRY I'M LATE, DAD!

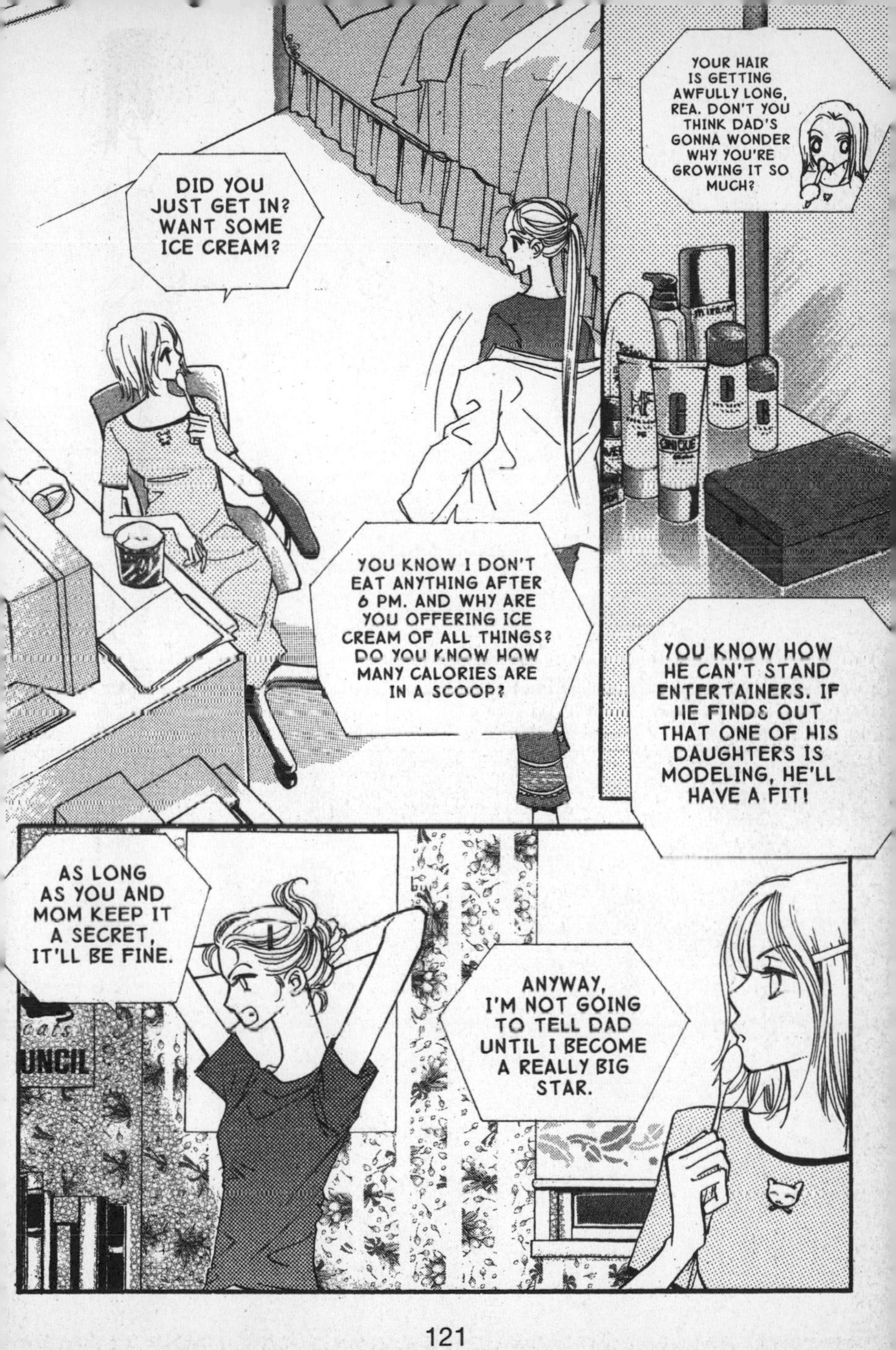
DID YOU JUST GET IN? WANT SOME ICE CREAM?
YOU KNOW I DON'T EAT ANYTHING AFTER 6 PM. AND WHY ARE YOU OFFERING ICE CREAM OF ALL THINGS? DO YOU KNOW HOW MANY CALORIES ARE IN A SCOOP?
YOUR HAIR IS GETTING AWFULLY LONG, REA. DON'T YOU THINK DAD'S GONNA WONDER WHY YOU'RE GROWING IT SO MUCH?
YOU KNOW HOW HE CAN'T STAND ENTERTAINERS. IF HE FINDS OUT THAT ONE OF HIS DAUGHTERS IS MODELING, HE'LL HAVE A FIT!
AS LONG AS YOU AND MOM KEEP IT A SECRET, IT'LL BE FINE.
ANYWAY, I'M NOT GOING TO TELL DAD UNTIL I BECOME A REALLY BIG STAR.

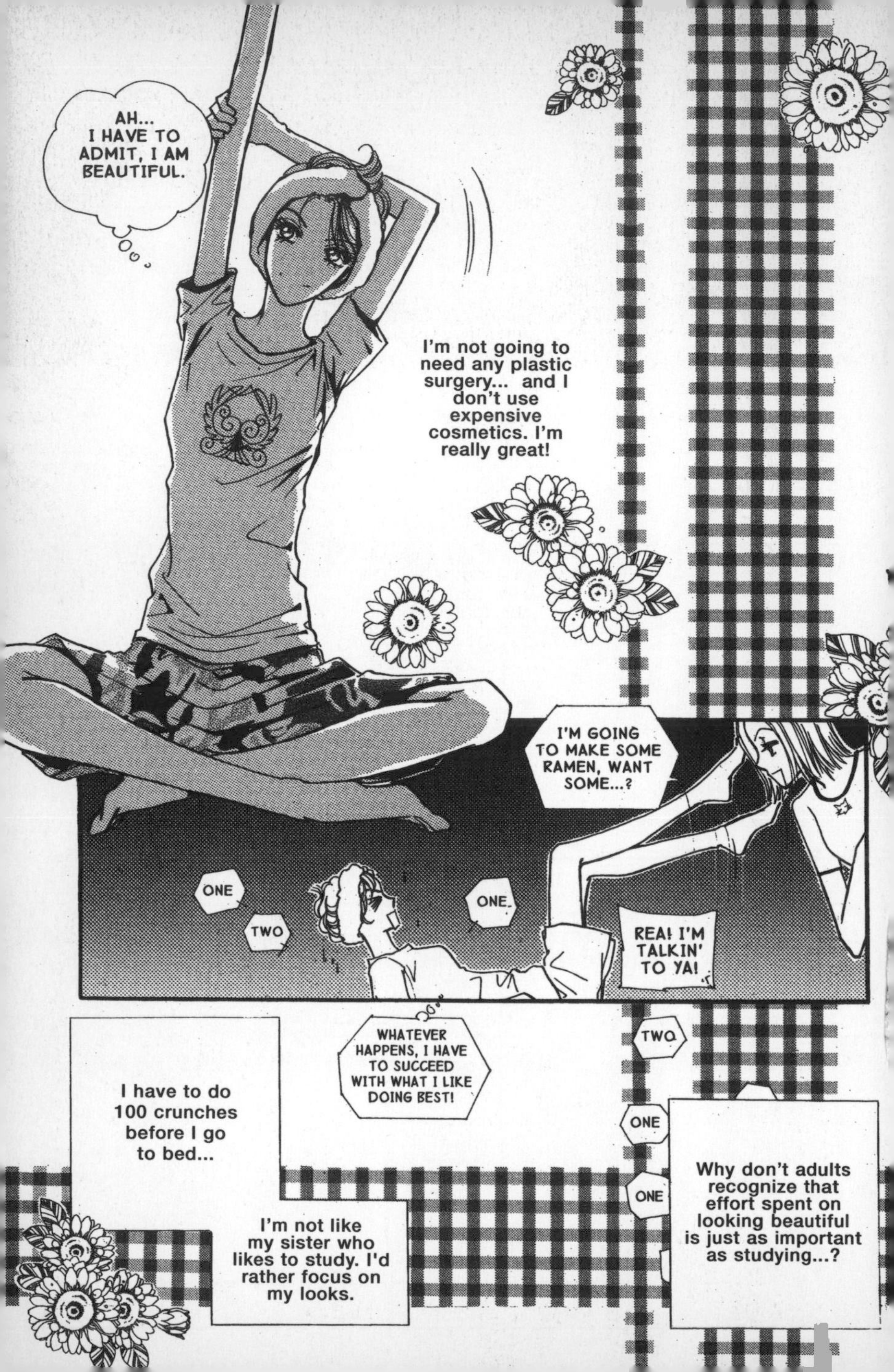
AH... I HAVE TO ADMIT, I AM BEAUTIFUL.
I'm not going to need any plastic surgery... and I don't use expensive cosmetics. I'm really great!
I'M GOING TO MAKE SOME RAMEN, WANT SOME...?
ONE
TWO
ONE
REA! I'M TALKIN' TO YA!
I have to do 100 crunches before I go to bed...
I'm not like my sister who likes to study. I'd rather focus on my looks.
WHATEVER HAPPENS, I HAVE TO SUCCEED WITH WHAT I LIKE DOING BEST!
TWO
ONE
ONE
Why don't adults recognize that effort spent on looking beautiful is just as important as studying...?

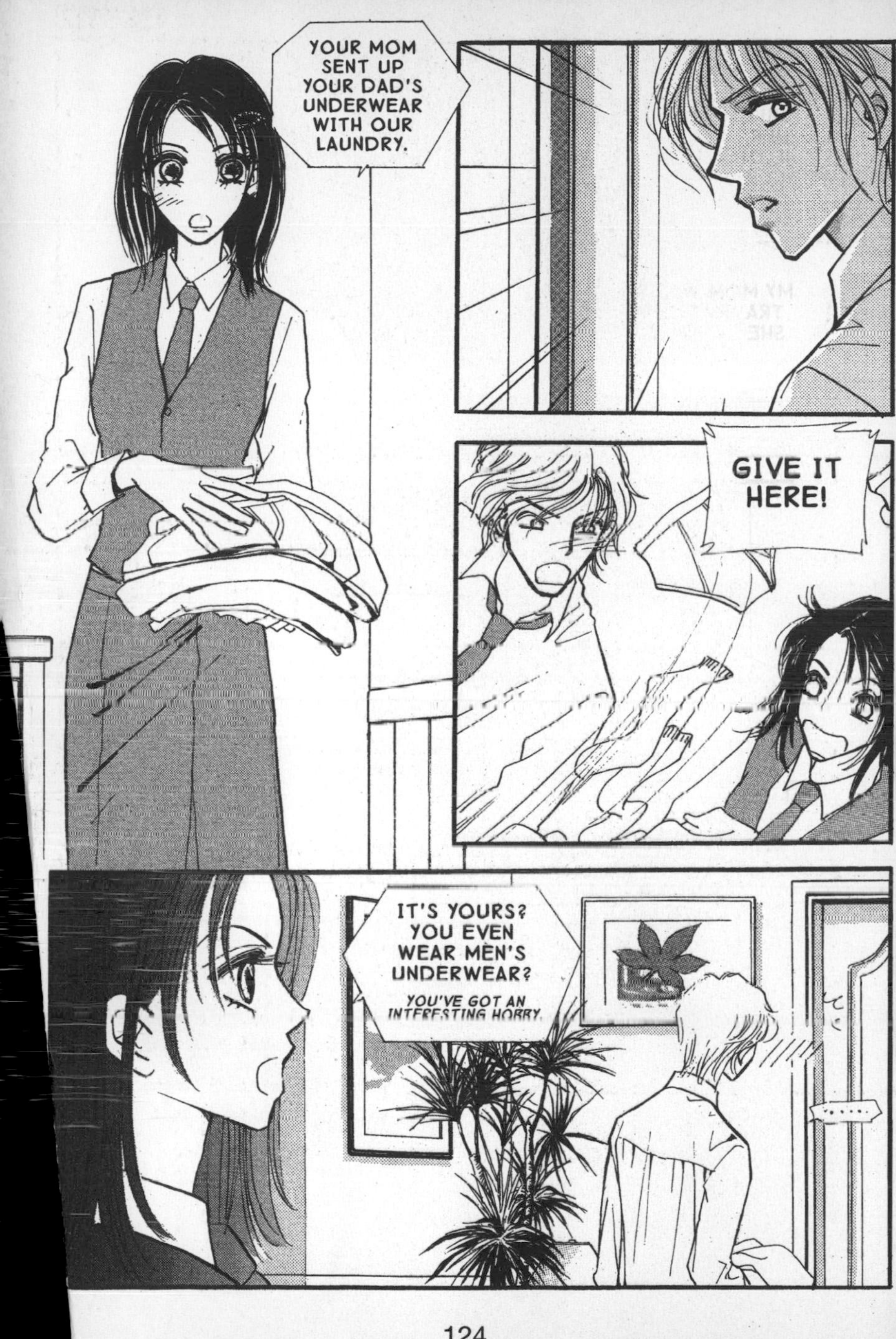
YOUR MOM SENT UP YOUR DAD'S UNDERWEAR WITH OUR LAUNDRY.
GIVE IT HERE!
IT'S YOURS? YOU EVEN WEAR MEN'S UNDERWEAR?
YOU'VE GOT AN INTERESTING HOBBY.
.....

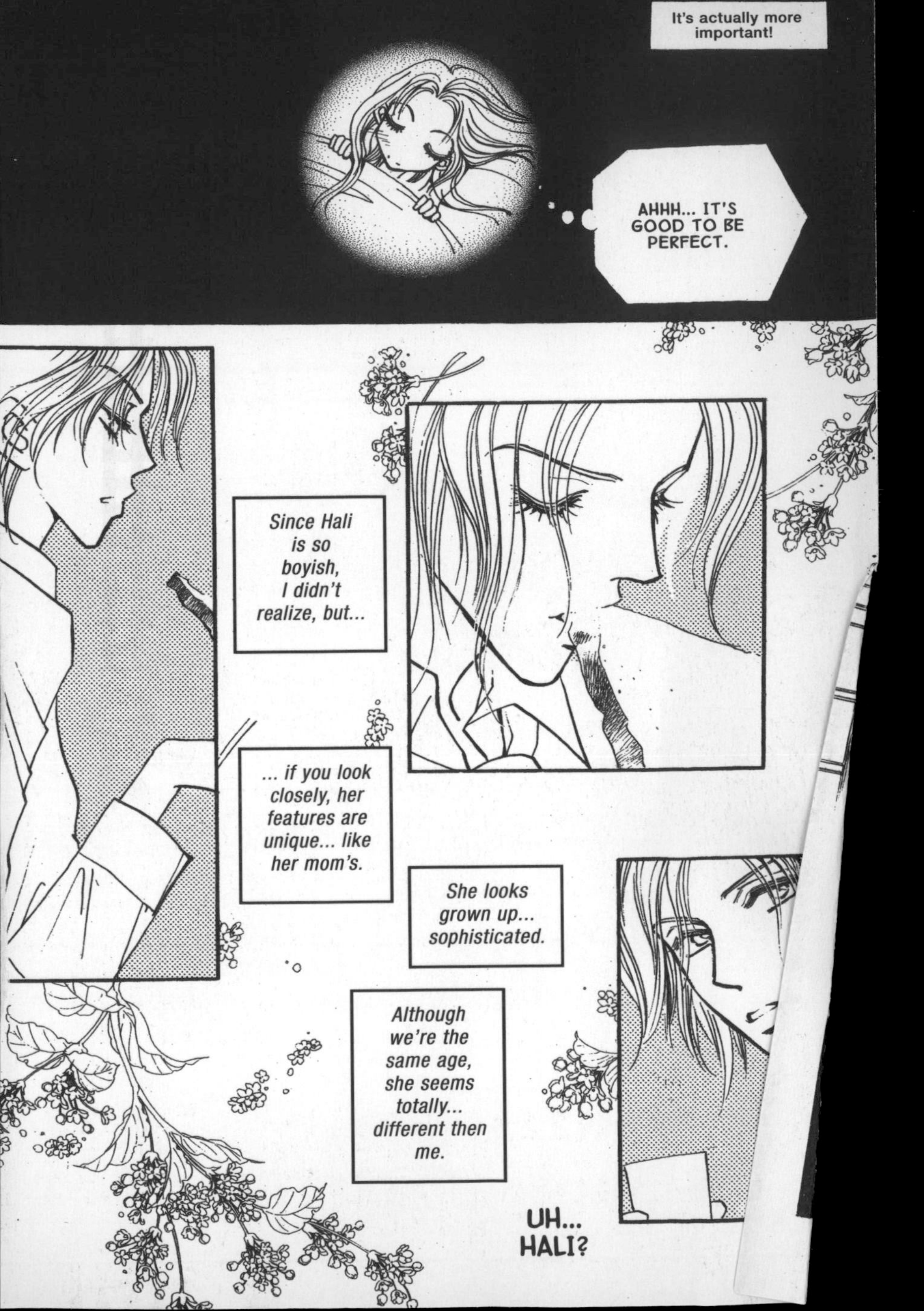
It's actually more important!
AHHH... IT'S GOOD TO BE PERFECT.
Since Hali is so boyish, I didn't realize, but...
... if you look closely, her features are unique... like her mom's.
She looks grown up... sophisticated.
Although we're the same age, she seems totally... different then me.
UH... HALI?

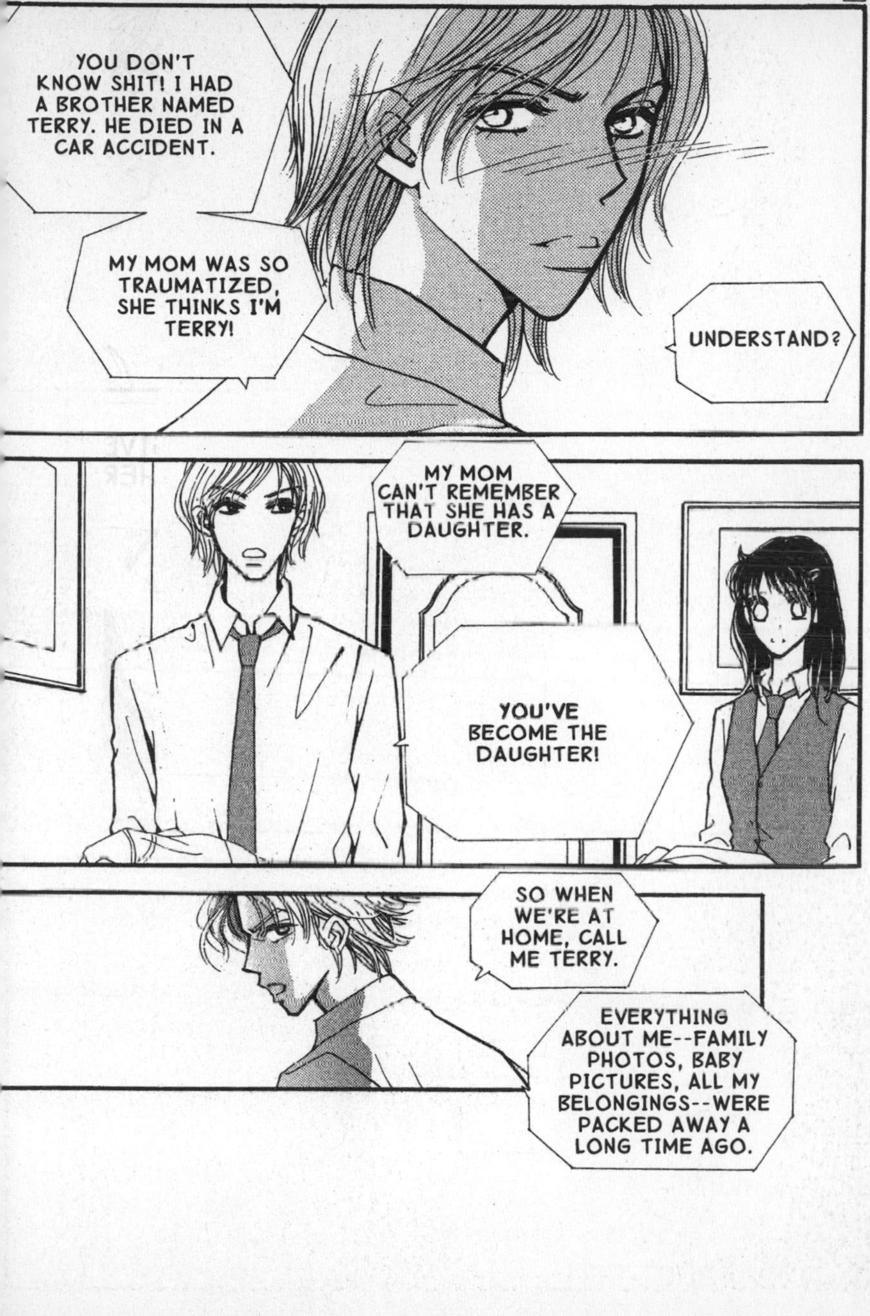
YOU DON'T KNOW SHIT! I HAD A BROTHER NAMED TERRY. HE DIED IN A CAR ACCIDENT.
MY MOM WAS SO TRAUMATIZED, SHE THINKS I'M TERRY!
UNDERSTAND?
MY MOM CAN'T REMEMBER THAT SHE HAS A DAUGHTER.
YOU'VE BECOME THE DAUGHTER!
SO WHEN WE'RE AT HOME, CALL ME TERRY.
EVERYTHING ABOUT ME--FAMILY PHOTOS, BABY PICTURES, ALL MY BELONGINGS--WERE PACKED AWAY A LONG TIME AGO.

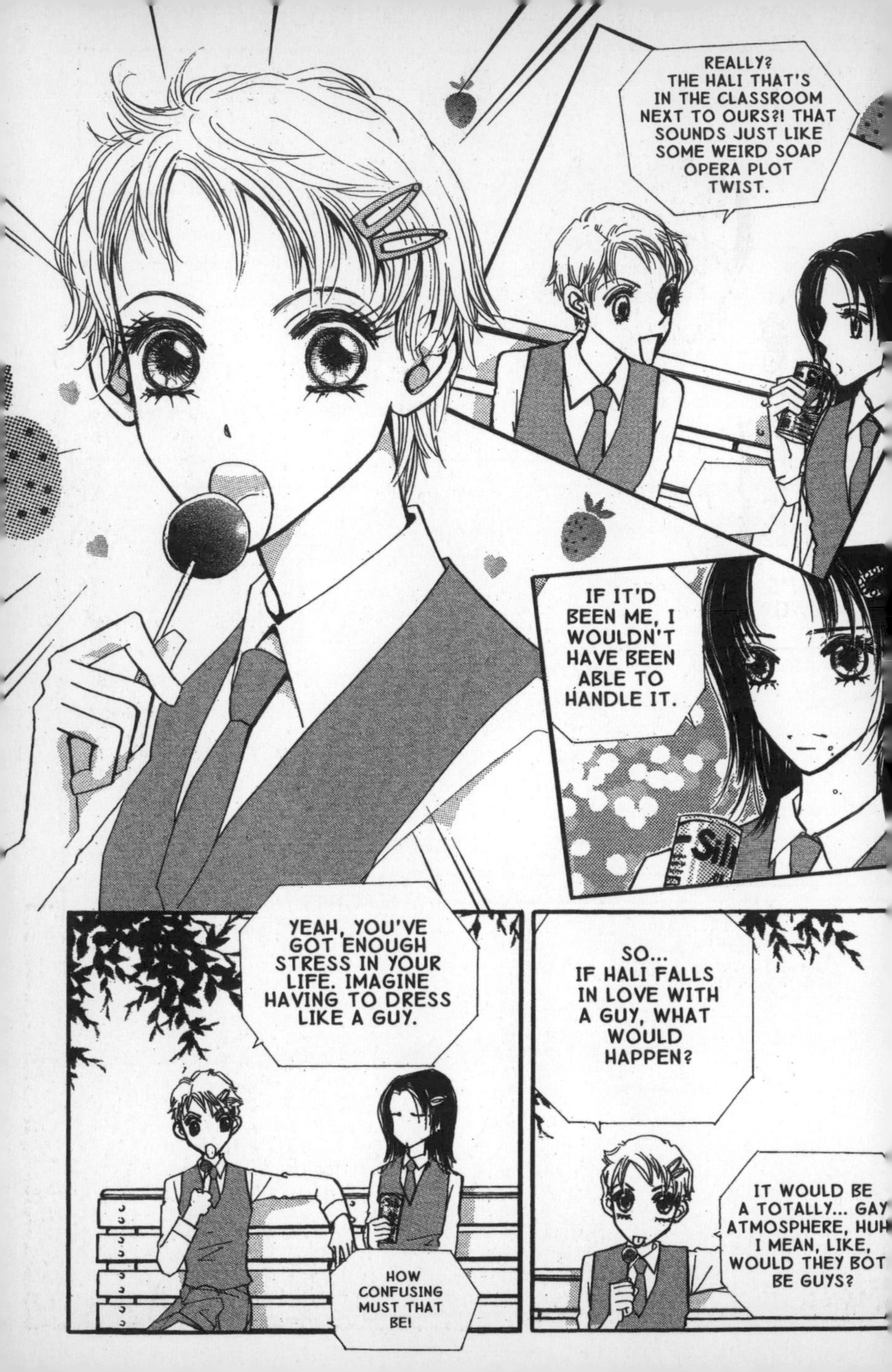
REALLY? THE HALI THAT'S IN THE CLASSROOM NEXT TO OURS?! THAT SOUNDS JUST LIKE SOME WEIRD SOAP OPERA PLOT TWIST.
IF IT'D BEEN ME, I WOULDN'T HAVE BEEN ABLE TO HANDLE IT.
YEAH, YOU'VE GOT ENOUGH STRESS IN YOUR LIFE. IMAGINE HAVING TO DRESS LIKE A GUY.
HOW CONFUSING MUST THAT BE!
SO... IF HALI FALLS IN LOVE WITH A GUY, WHAT WOULD HAPPEN?
IT WOULD BE A TOTALLY... GAY ATMOSPHERE, HUH I MEAN, LIKE, WOULD THEY BOT BE GUYS?

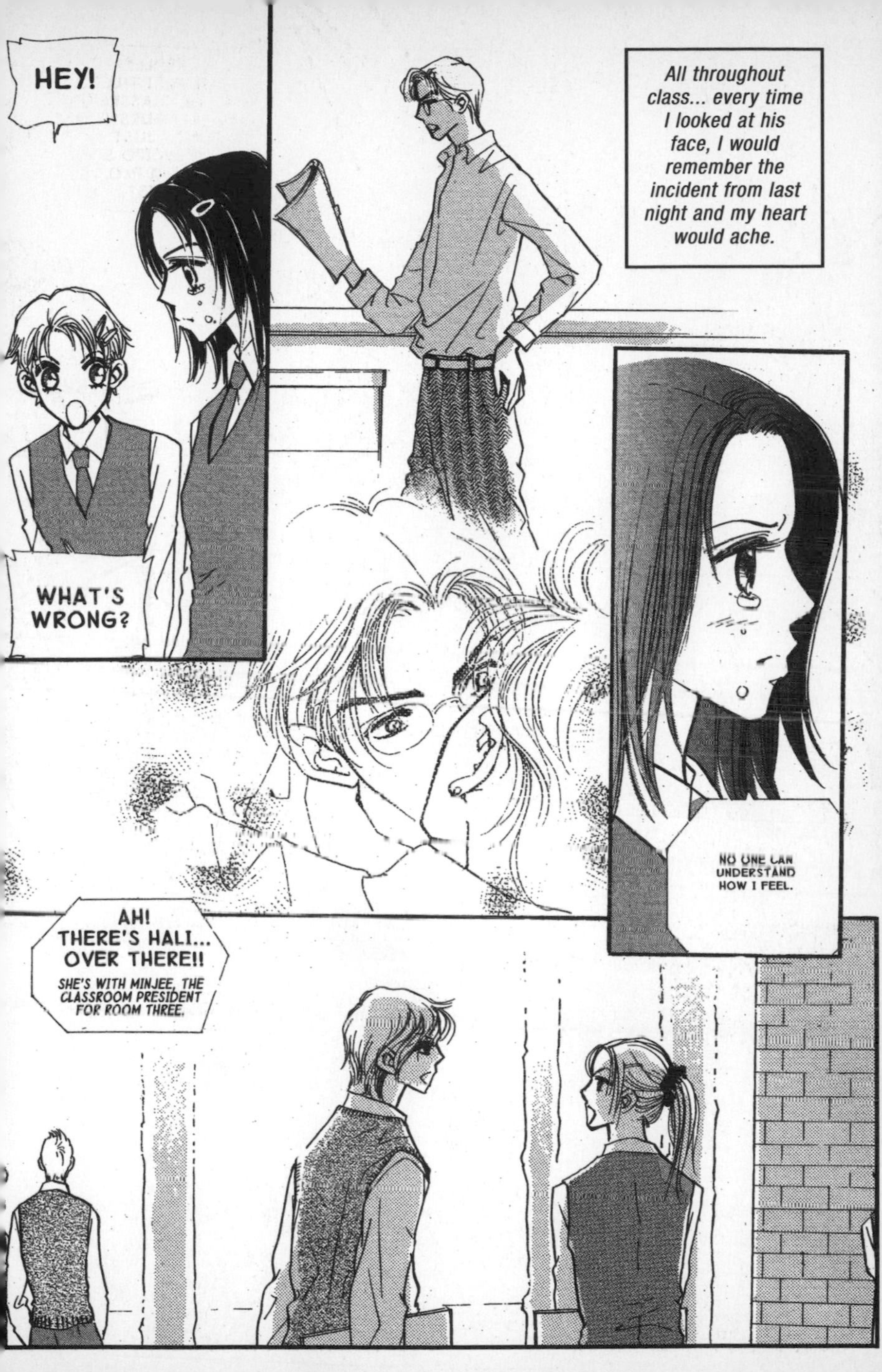
HEY!
WHAT'S WRONG?
All throughout class... every time I looked at his face, I would remember the incident from last night and my heart would ache.
NO ONE CAN UNDERSTAND HOW I FEEL.
AH! THERE'S HALI... OVER THERE!!
SHE'S WITH MINJEE, THE CLASSROOM PRESIDENT FOR ROOM THREE.

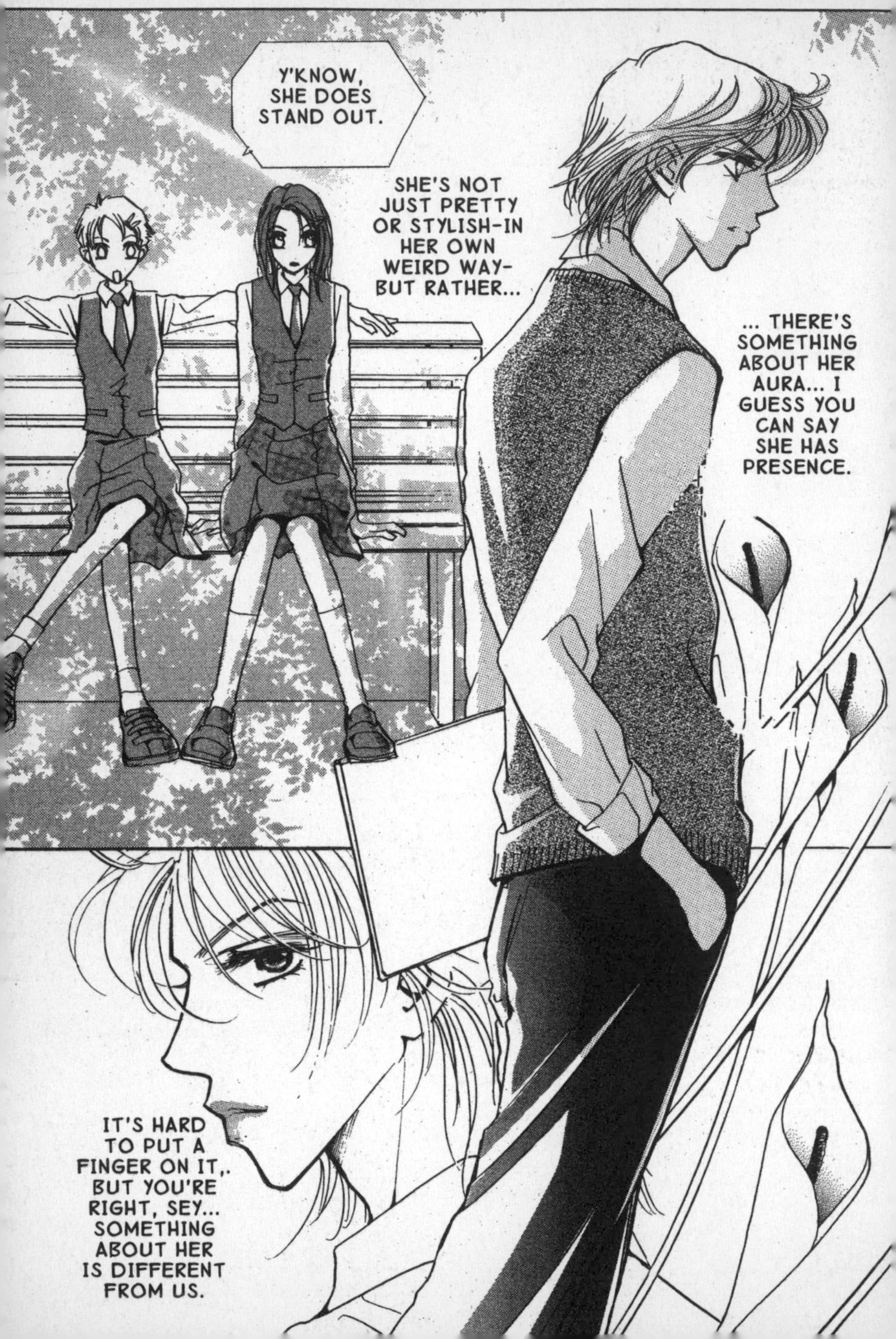
Y'KNOW, SHE DOES STAND OUT.
SHE'S NOT JUST PRETTY OR STYLISH-IN HER OWN WEIRD WAY-BUT RATHER...
... THERE'S SOMETHING ABOUT HER AURA... I GUESS YOU CAN SAY SHE HAS PRESENCE.
IT'S HARD TO PUT A FINGER ON IT,. BUT YOU'RE RIGHT, SEY... SOMETHING ABOUT HER IS DIFFERENT FROM US.

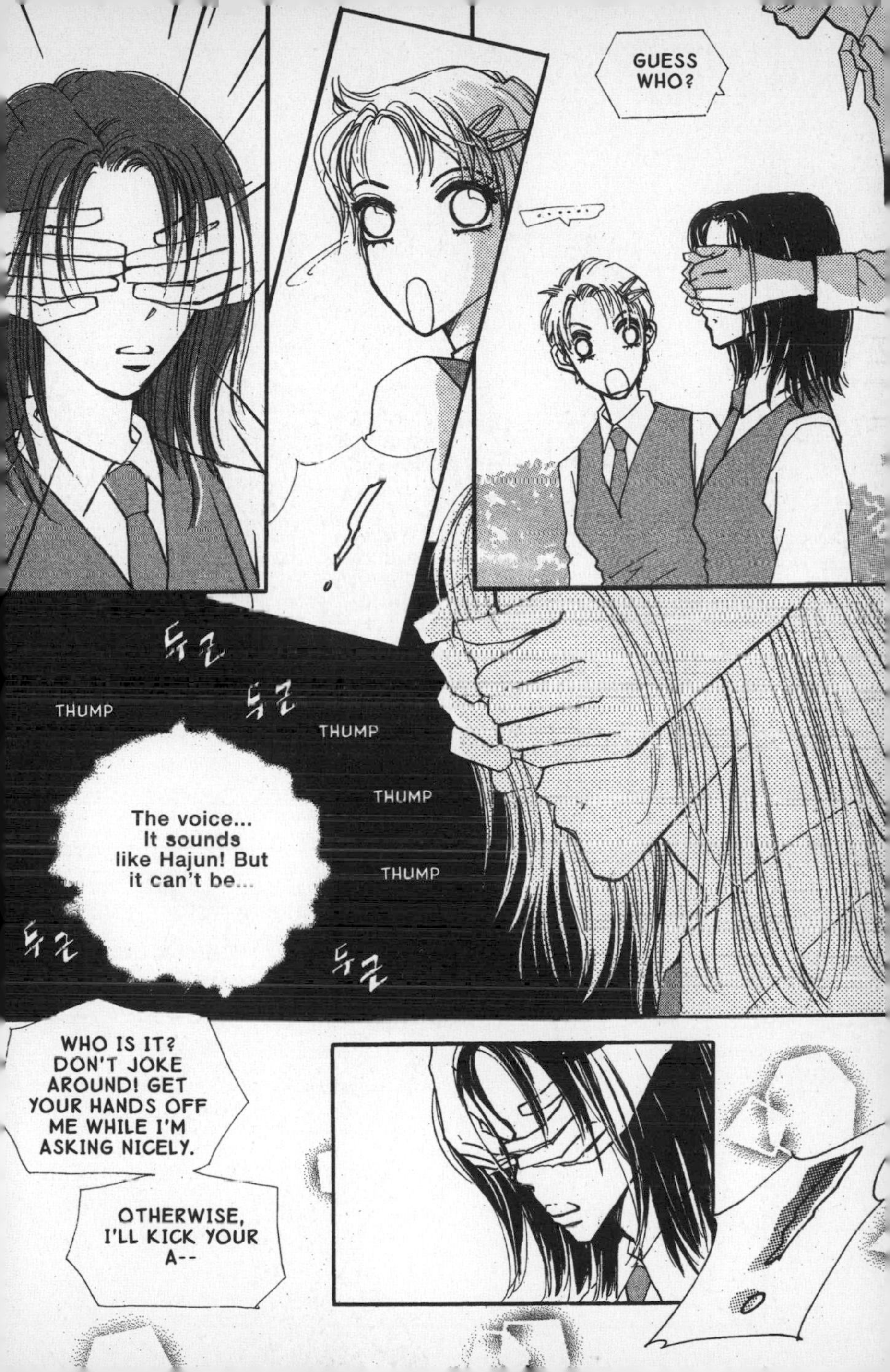
GUESS WHO?
......
두근
THUMP
두근
THUMP
THUMP
The voice... It sounds like Hajun! But it can't be...
THUMP
두근
두근
WHO IS IT? DON'T JOKE AROUND! GET YOUR HANDS OFF ME WHILE I'M ASKING NICELY.
OTHERWISE, I'LL KICK YOUR A--

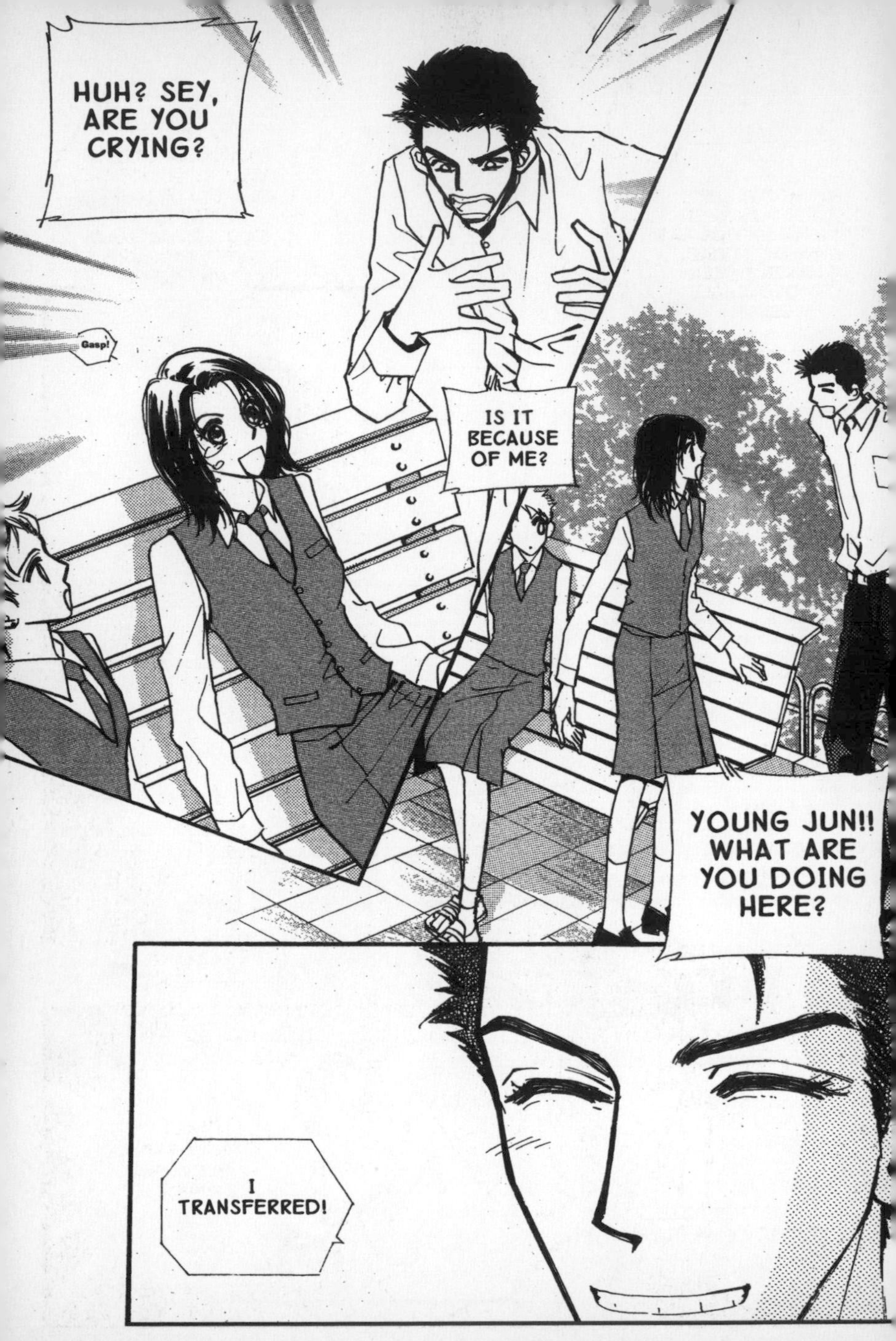
HUH? SEY, ARE YOU CRYING?
Gasp!
IS IT BECAUSE OF ME?
YOUNG JUN!! WHAT ARE YOU DOING HERE?
I TRANSFERRED!

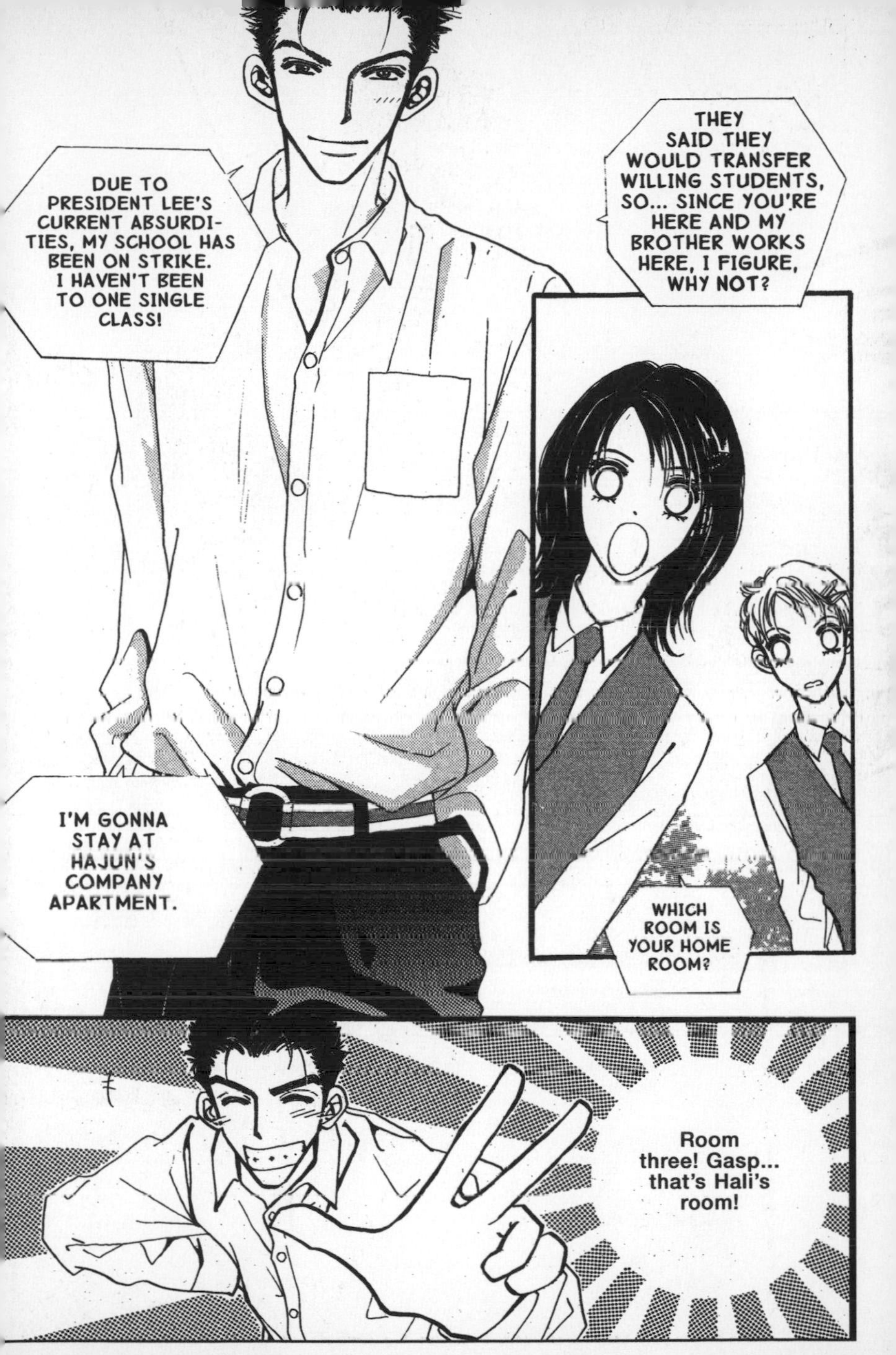
DUE TO PRESIDENT LEE'S CURRENT ABSURDITIES, MY SCHOOL HAS BEEN ON STRIKE. I HAVEN'T BEEN TO ONE SINGLE CLASS!
THEY SAID THEY WOULD TRANSFER WILLING STUDENTS, SO... SINCE YOU'RE HERE AND MY BROTHER WORKS HERE, I FIGURE, WHY NOT?
I'M GONNA STAY AT HAJUN'S COMPANY APARTMENT.
WHICH ROOM IS YOUR HOME ROOM?
Room three! Gasp... that's Hali's room!

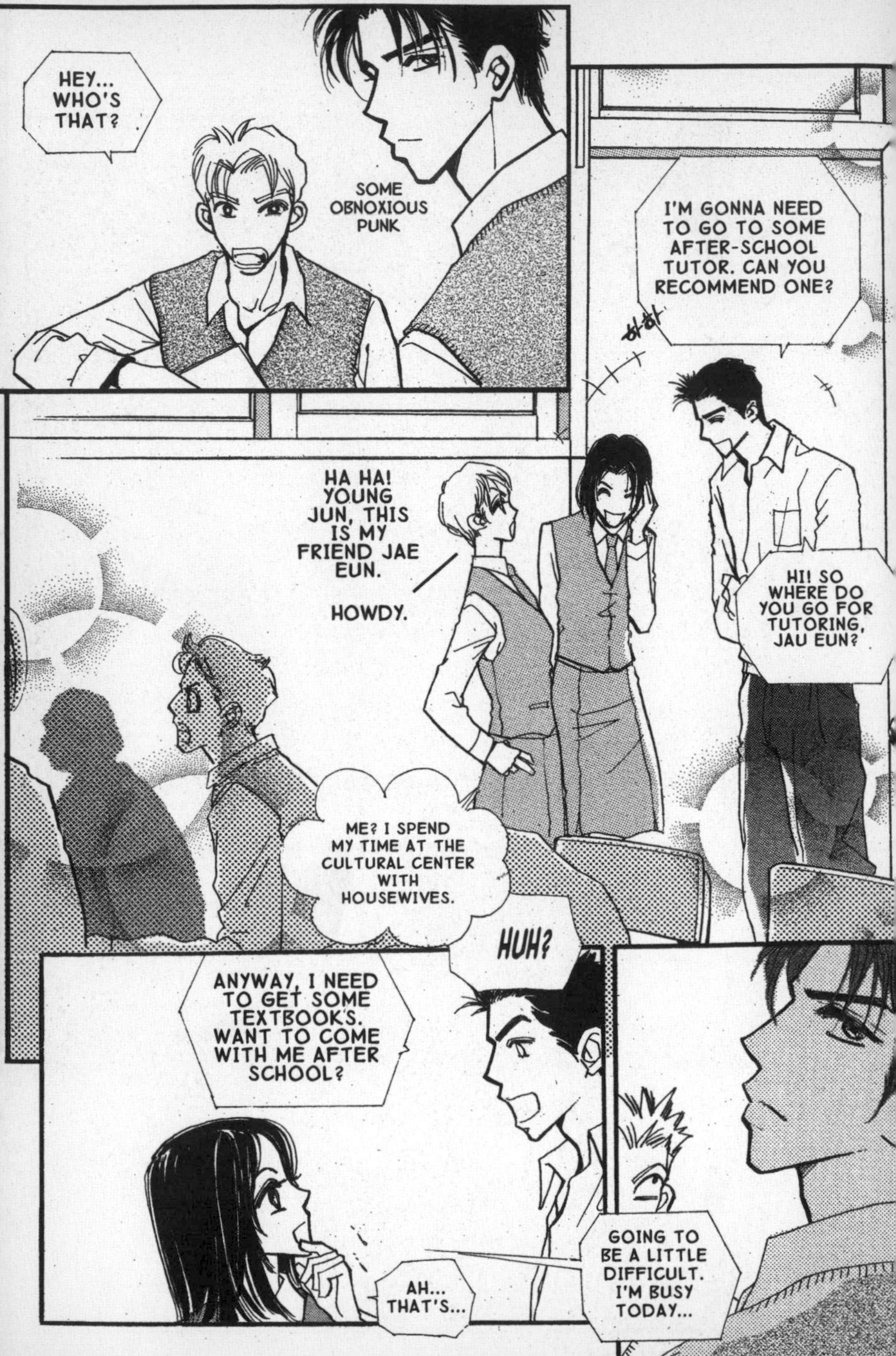
HEY... WHO'S THAT?
SOME OBNOXIOUS PUNK
I'M GONNA NEED TO GO TO SOME AFTER-SCHOOL TUTOR. CAN YOU RECOMMEND ONE?
하하
HA HA! YOUNG JUN, THIS IS MY FRIEND JAE EUN.
HOWDY.
HI! SO WHERE DO YOU GO FOR TUTORING, JAU EUN?
ME? I SPEND MY TIME AT THE CULTURAL CENTER WITH HOUSEWIVES.
HUH?
ANYWAY, I NEED TO GET SOME TEXTBOOKS. WANT TO COME WITH ME AFTER SCHOOL?
AH... THAT'S...
GOING TO BE A LITTLE DIFFICULT. I'M BUSY TODAY...

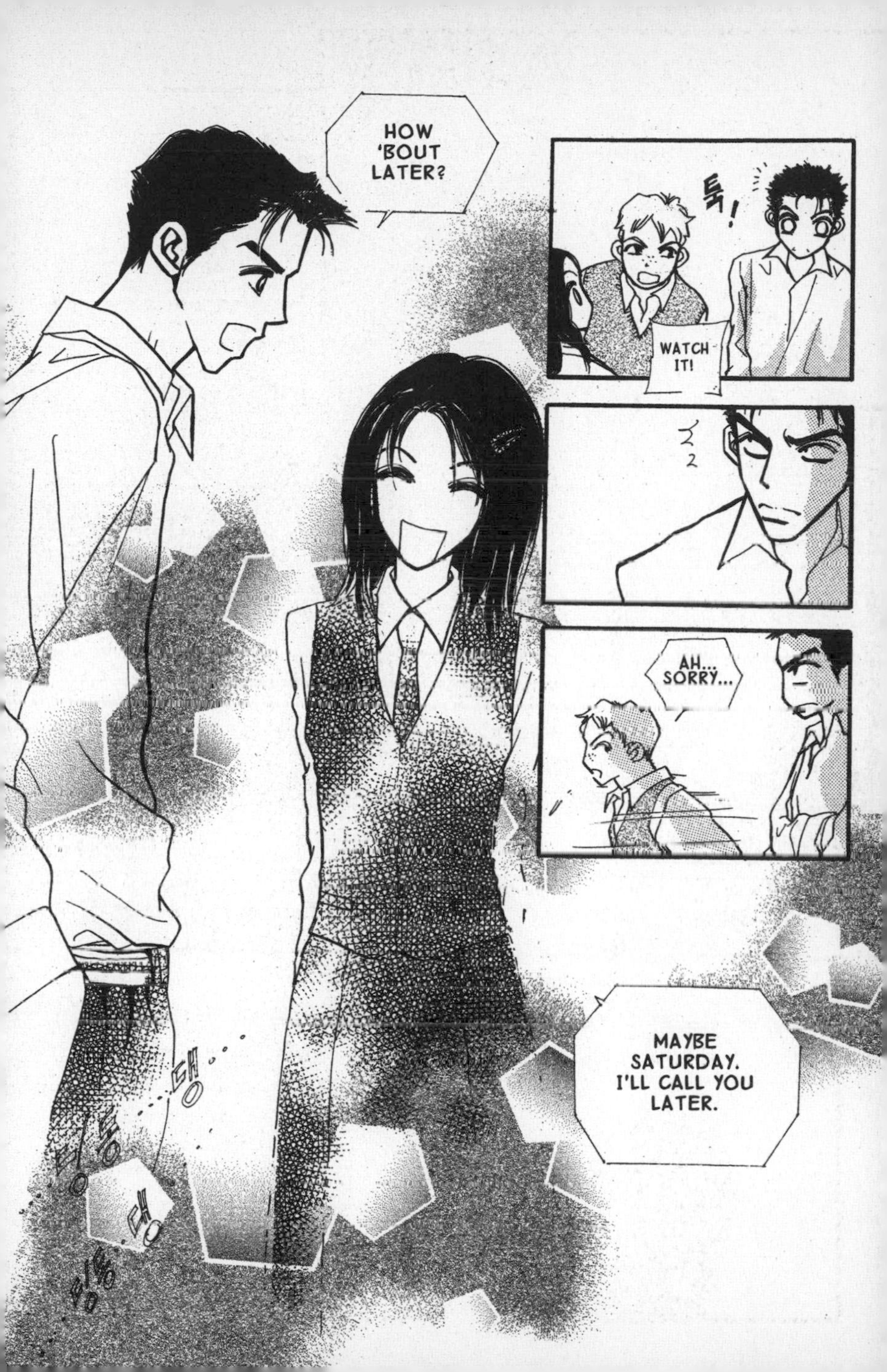
HOW 'BOUT LATER?
MAYBE SATURDAY. I'LL CALL YOU LATER.
툭!
WATCH IT!
AH... SORRY...

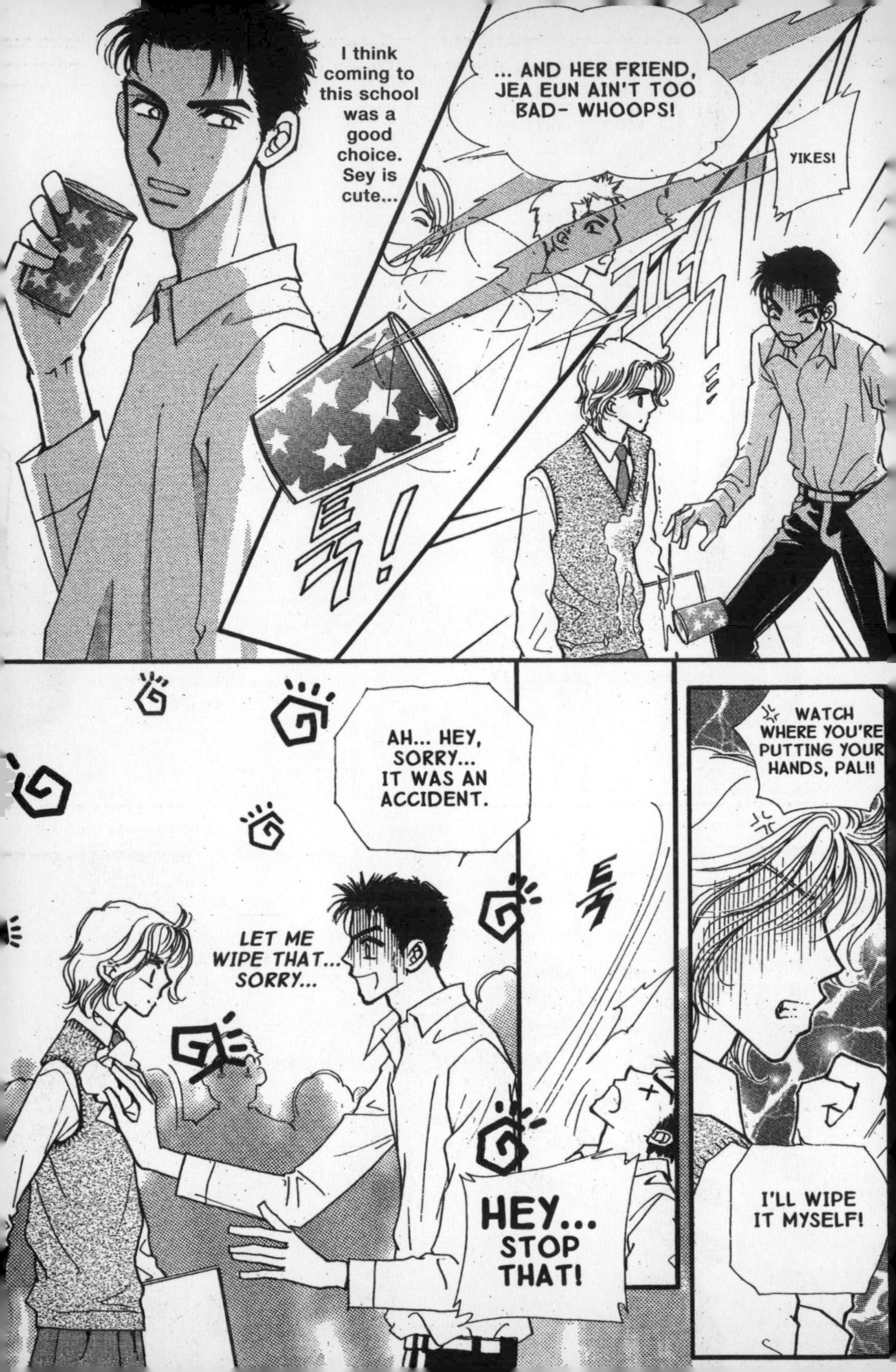
I think coming to this school was a good choice. Sey is cute...
... AND HER FRIEND, JEA EUN AIN'T TOO BAD- WHOOPS!
YIKES!
AH... HEY, SORRY... IT WAS AN ACCIDENT.
LET ME WIPE THAT... SORRY...
HEY... STOP THAT!
WATCH WHERE YOU'RE PUTTING YOUR HANDS, PAL!!
I'LL WIPE IT MYSELF!

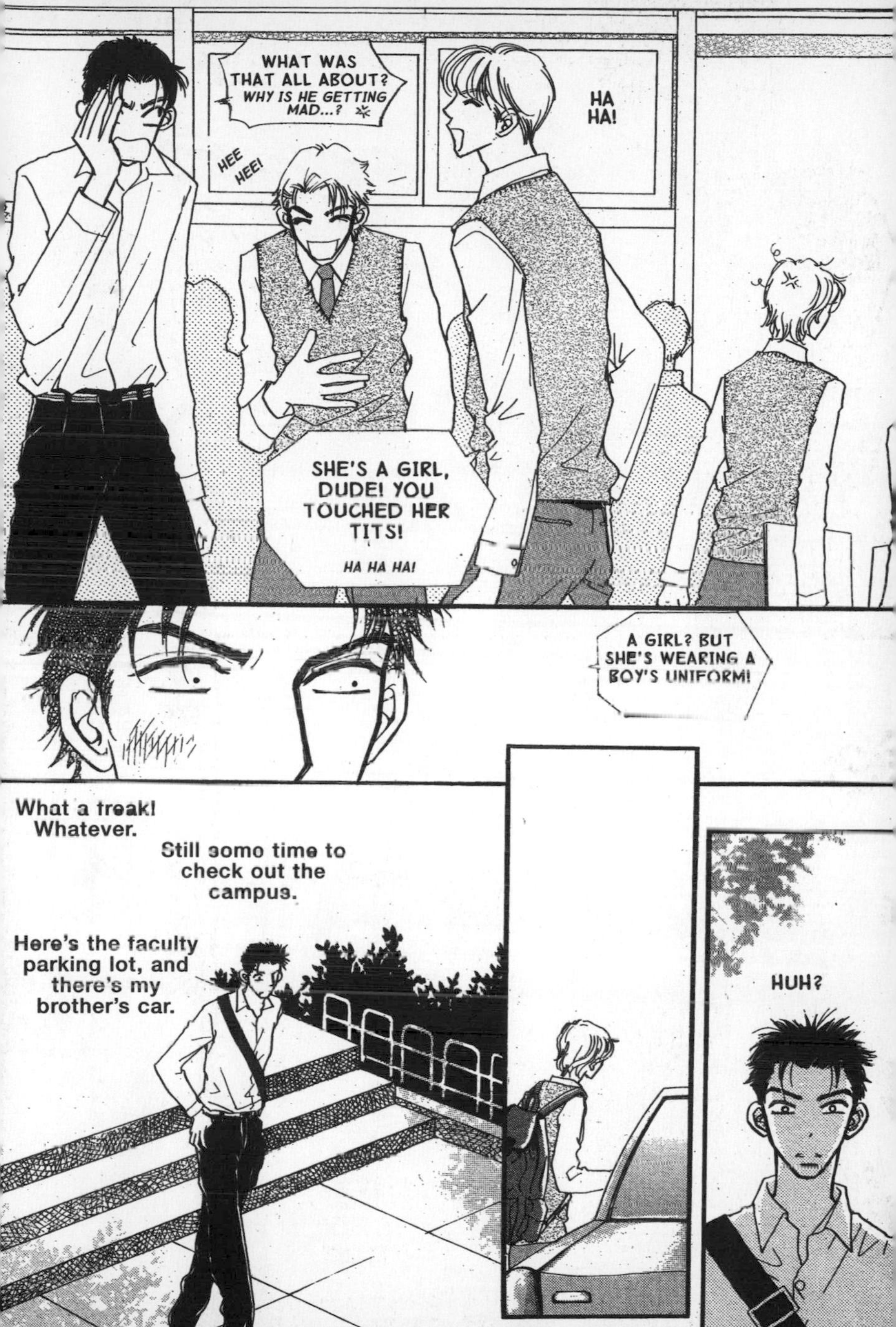

WHAT WAS THAT ALL ABOUT? WHY IS HE GETTING MAD...?
HEE HEE!
HA HA!
SHE'S A GIRL, DUDE! YOU TOUCHED HER TITS!
HA HA HA!
A GIRL? BUT SHE'S WEARING A BOY'S UNIFORM!
What a freak! Whatever.
Still some time to check out the campus.
Here's the faculty parking lot, and there's my brother's car.
HUH?

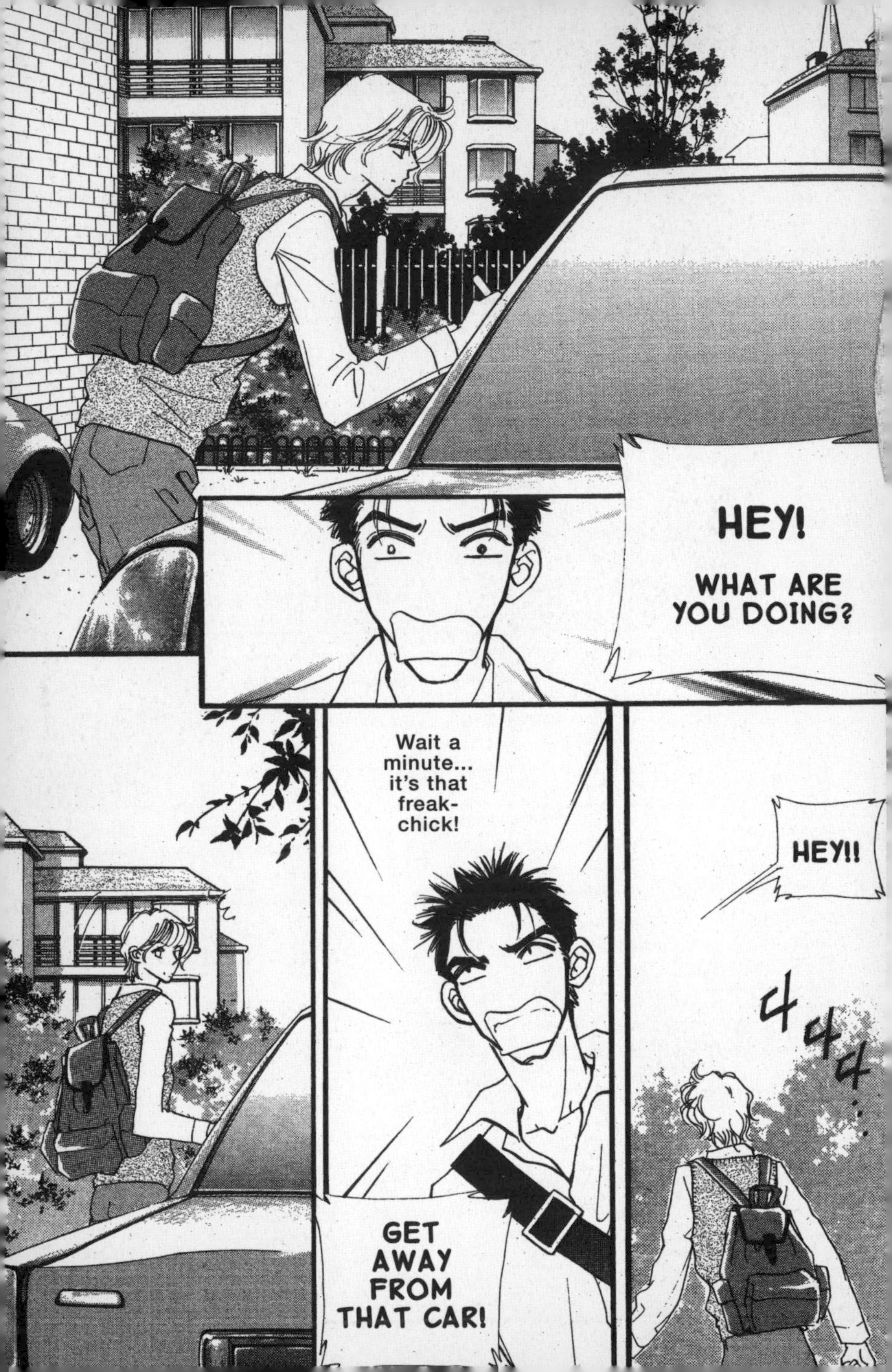
HEY!
WHAT ARE YOU DOING?
Wait a minute... it's that freak-chick!
GET AWAY FROM THAT CAR!
HEY!!

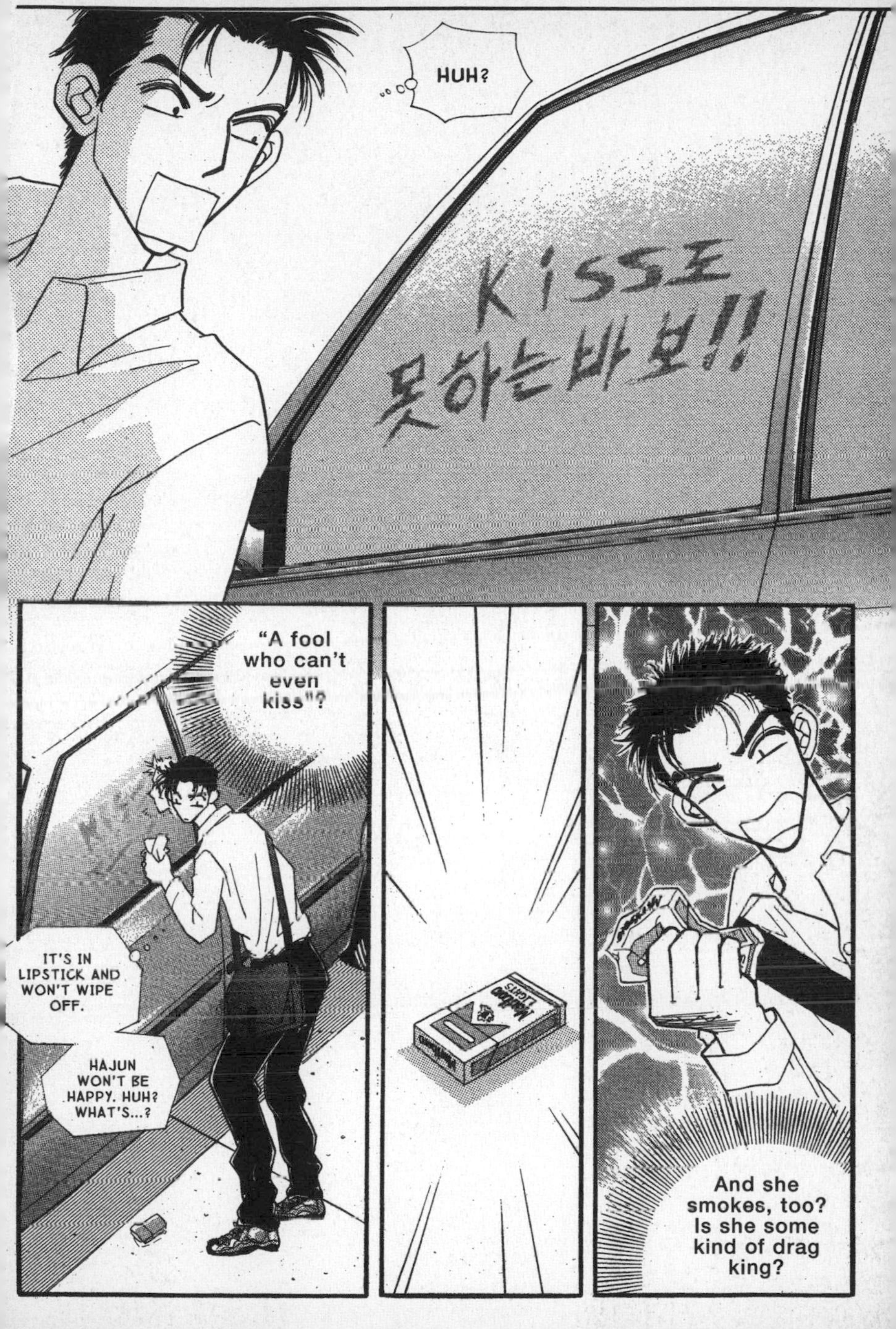
HUH?
KiSS도
못하는바보!!
"A fool who can't even kiss"?
IT'S IN LIPSTICK AND WON'T WIPE OFF.
HAJUN WON'T BE HAPPY. HUH? WHAT'S...?
And she smokes, too? Is she some kind of drag king?

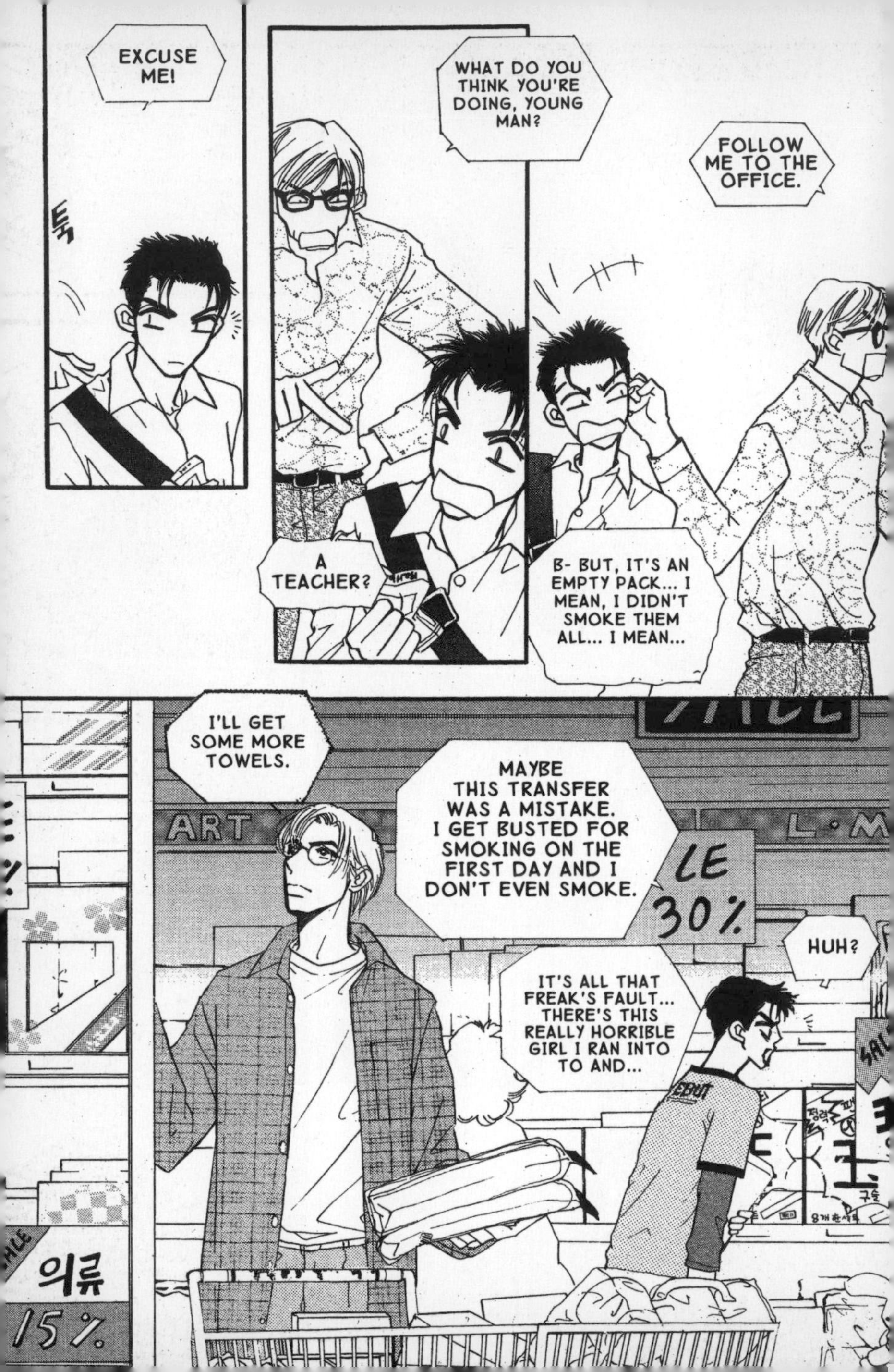
EXCUSE ME!
툭
WHAT DO YOU THINK YOU'RE DOING, YOUNG MAN?
A TEACHER?
FOLLOW ME TO THE OFFICE.
B- BUT, IT'S AN EMPTY PACK... I MEAN, I DIDN'T SMOKE THEM ALL... I MEAN...
I'LL GET SOME MORE TOWELS.
ART
MAYBE THIS TRANSFER WAS A MISTAKE. I GET BUSTED FOR SMOKING ON THE FIRST DAY AND I DON'T EVEN SMOKE.
LE 30%
HUH?
IT'S ALL THAT FREAK'S FAULT... THERE'S THIS REALLY HORRIBLE GIRL I RAN INTO TO AND...
의류
15%

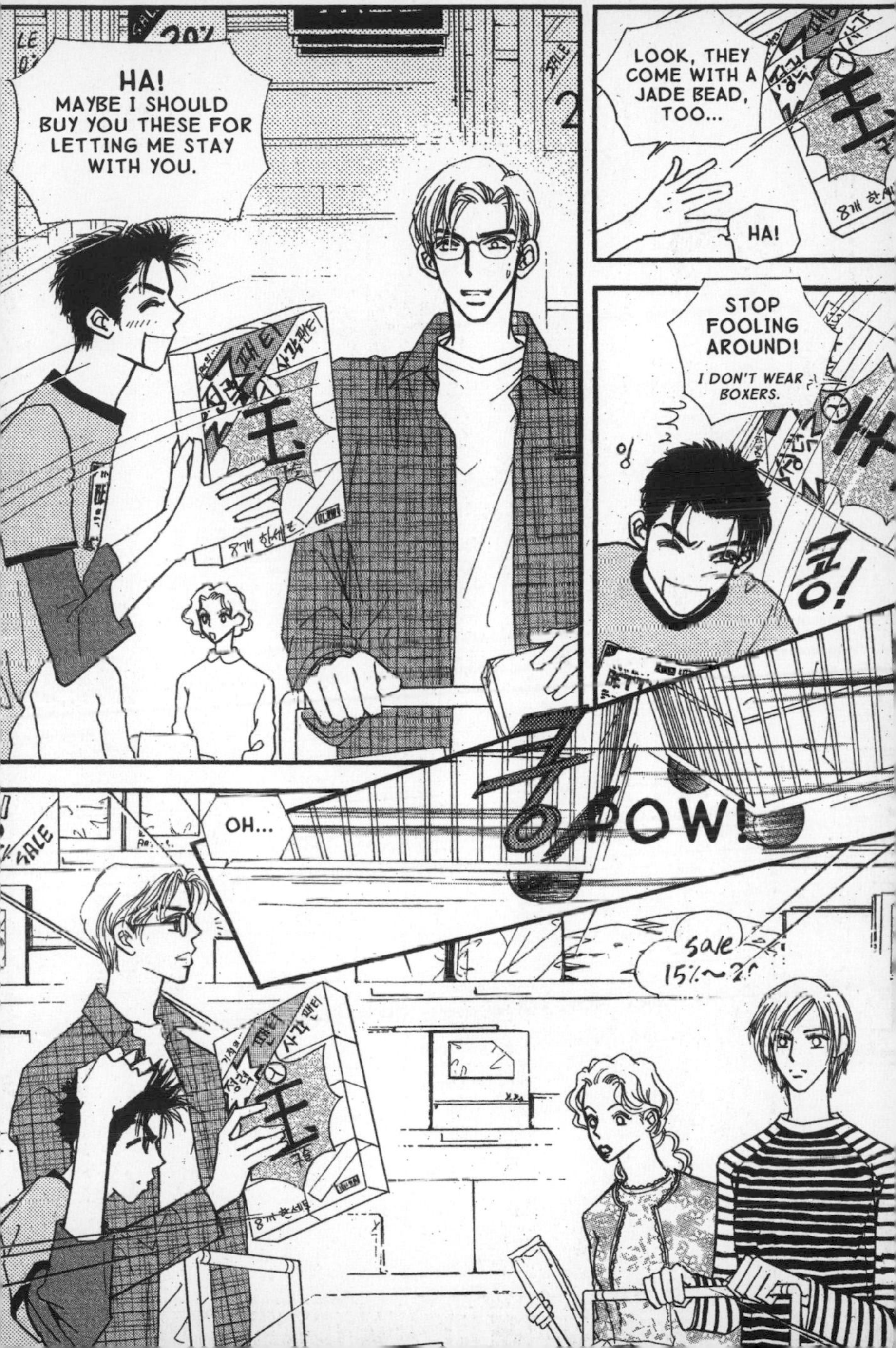
HA!
MAYBE I SHOULD BUY YOU THESE FOR LETTING ME STAY WITH YOU.
LOOK, THEY COME WITH A JADE BEAD, TOO...
HA!
STOP FOOLING AROUND!
I DON'T WEAR BOXERS.
콩!
POW!
OH...

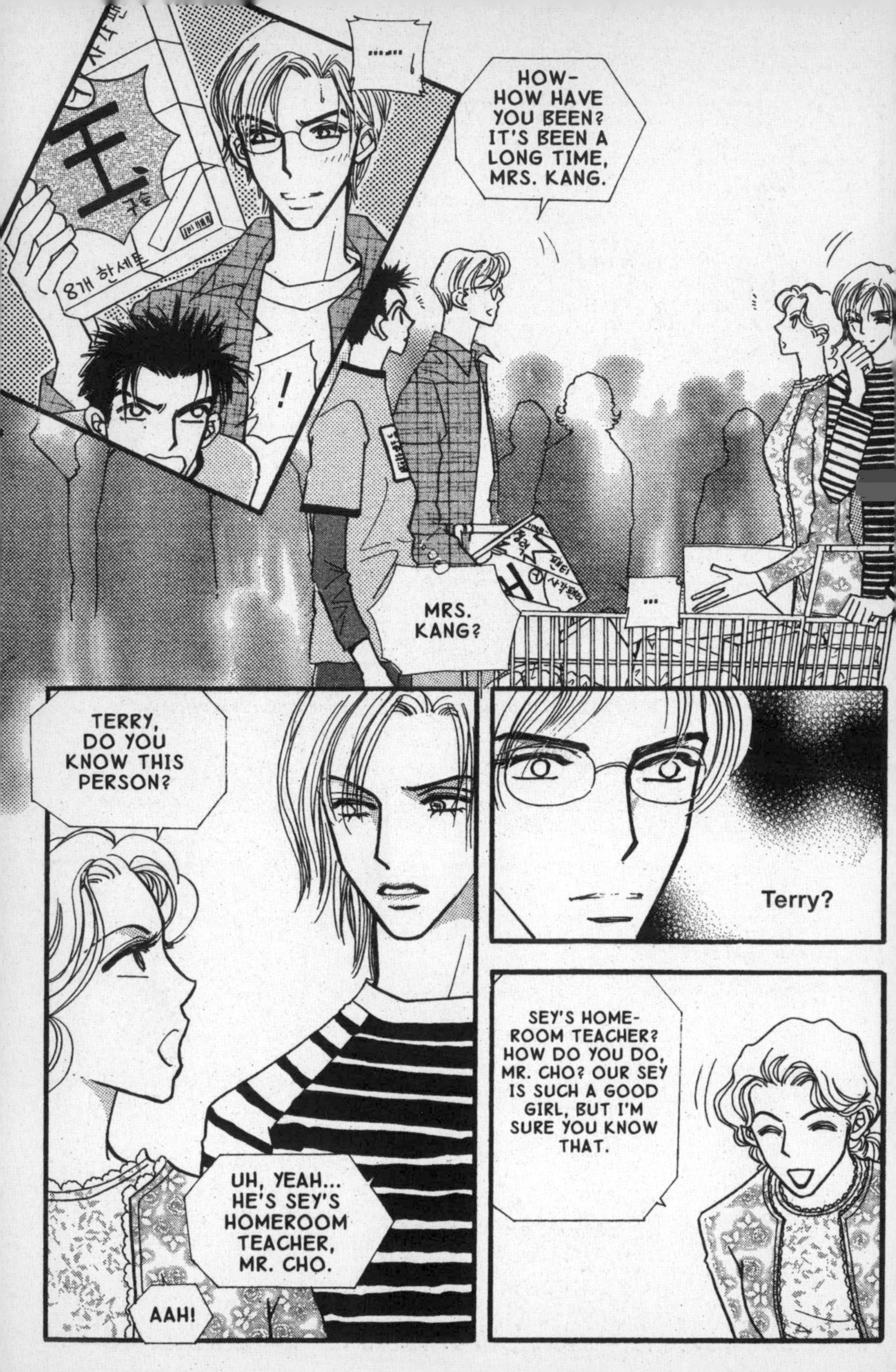
8개 한세트
......!
HOW-HOW HAVE YOU BEEN? IT'S BEEN A LONG TIME, MRS. KANG.
!
MRS. KANG?
...
TERRY, DO YOU KNOW THIS PERSON?
UH, YEAH... HE'S SEY'S HOMEROOM TEACHER, MR. CHO.
AAH!
Terry?
SEY'S HOME-ROOM TEACHER? HOW DO YOU DO, MR. CHO? OUR SEY IS SUCH A GOOD GIRL, BUT I'M SURE YOU KNOW THAT.

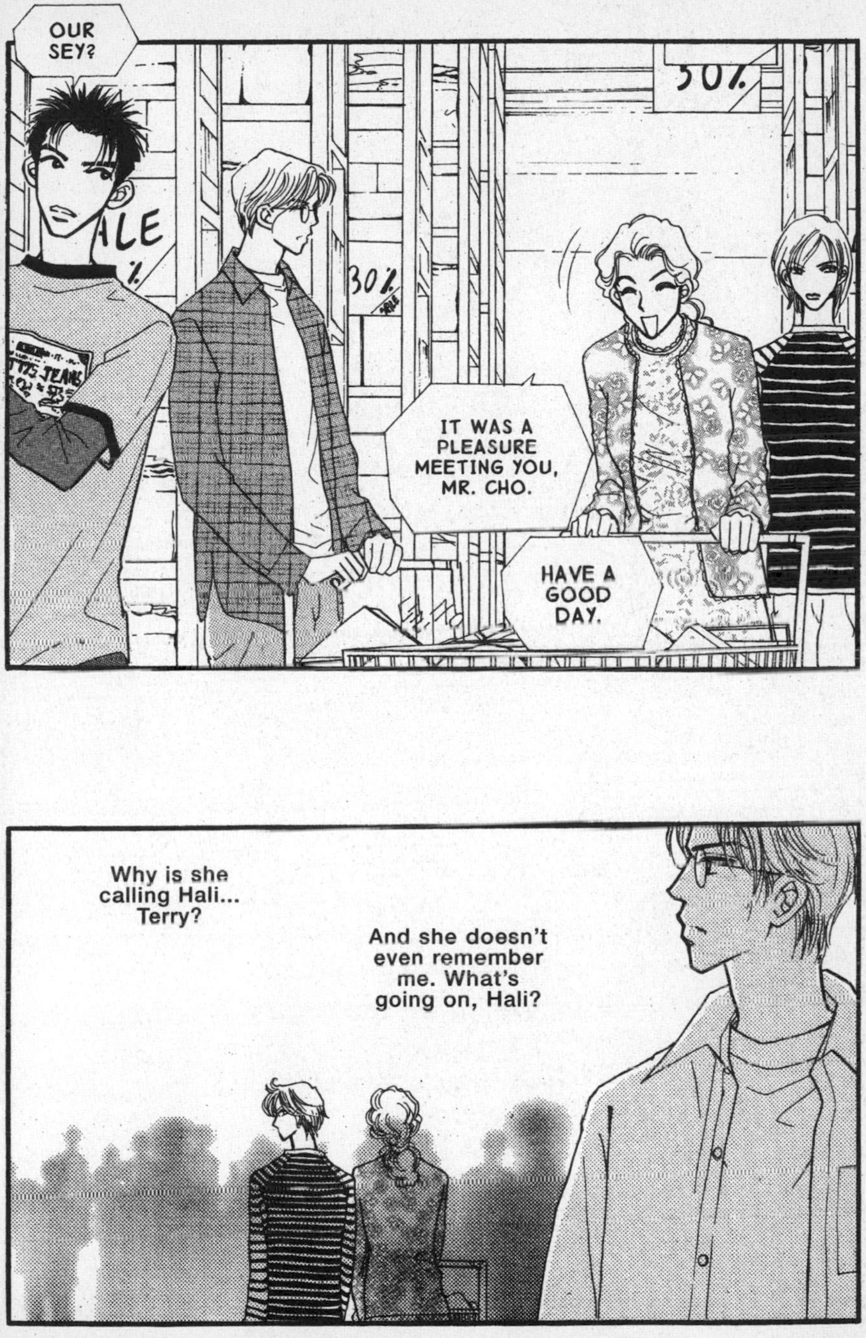
OUR SEY?
30%
IT WAS A PLEASURE MEETING YOU, MR. CHO.
HAVE A GOOD DAY.
Why is she calling Hali... Terry?
And she doesn't even remember me. What's going on, Hali?

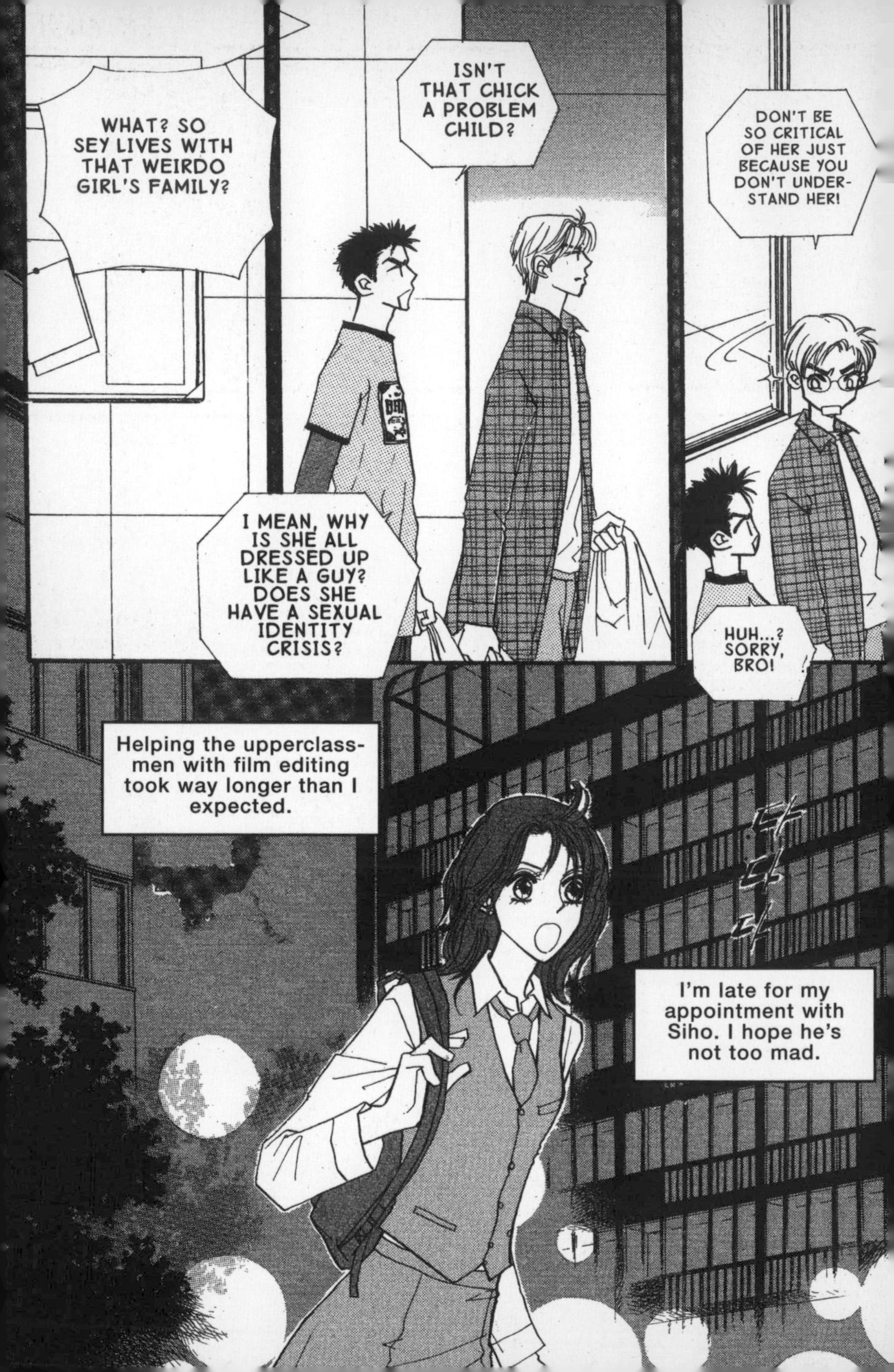
WHAT? SO SEY LIVES WITH THAT WEIRDO GIRL'S FAMILY?
ISN'T THAT CHICK A PROBLEM CHILD?
I MEAN, WHY IS SHE ALL DRESSED UP LIKE A GUY? DOES SHE HAVE A SEXUAL IDENTITY CRISIS?
DON'T BE SO CRITICAL OF HER JUST BECAUSE YOU DON'T UNDER-STAND HER!
HUH...? SORRY, BRO!
Helping the upperclass-men with film editing took way longer than I expected.
I'm late for my appointment with Siho. I hope he's not too mad.

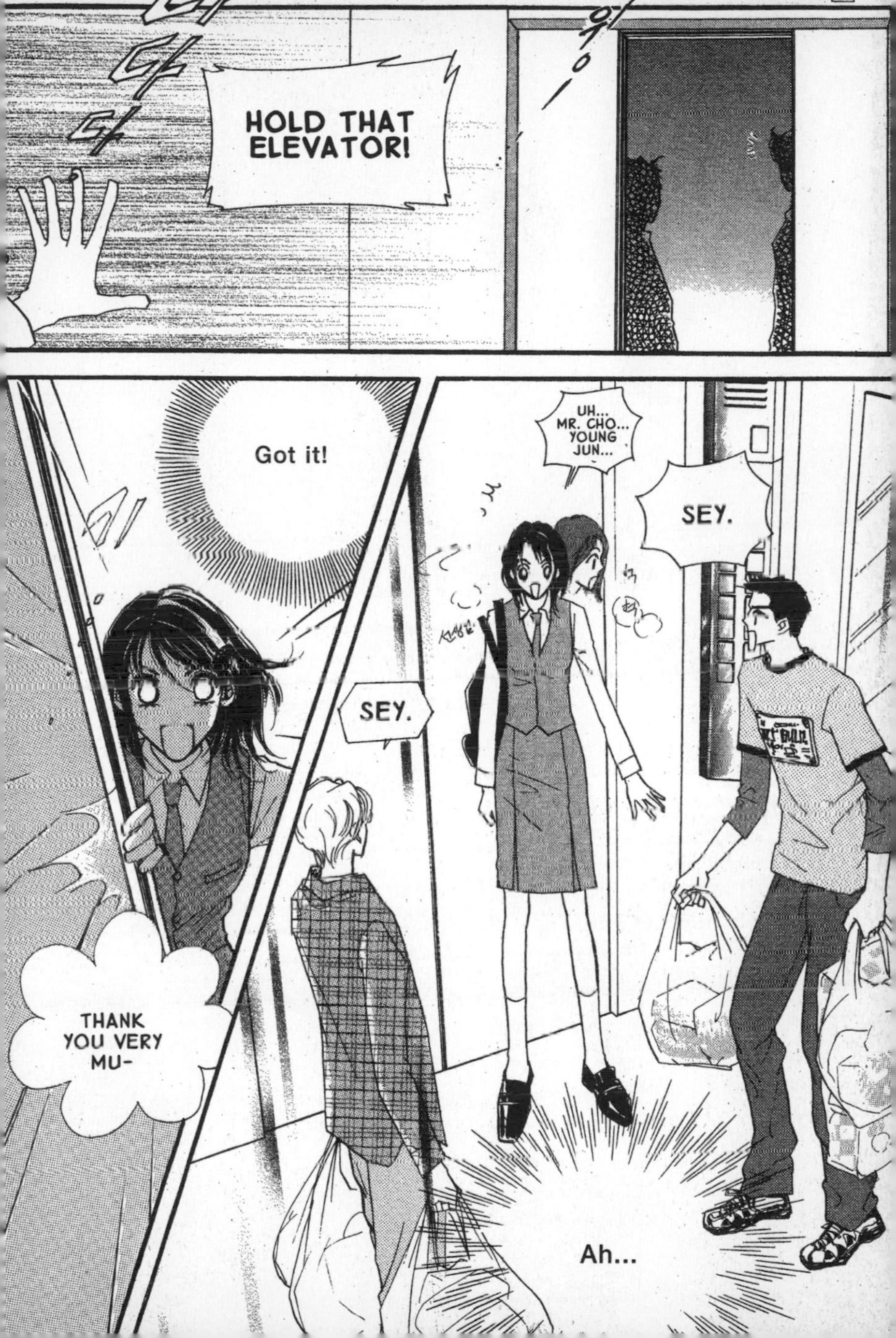
HOLD THAT ELEVATOR!
Got it!
THANK YOU VERY MU-
UH... MR. CHO... YOUNG JUN...
SEY.
SEY.
Ah...

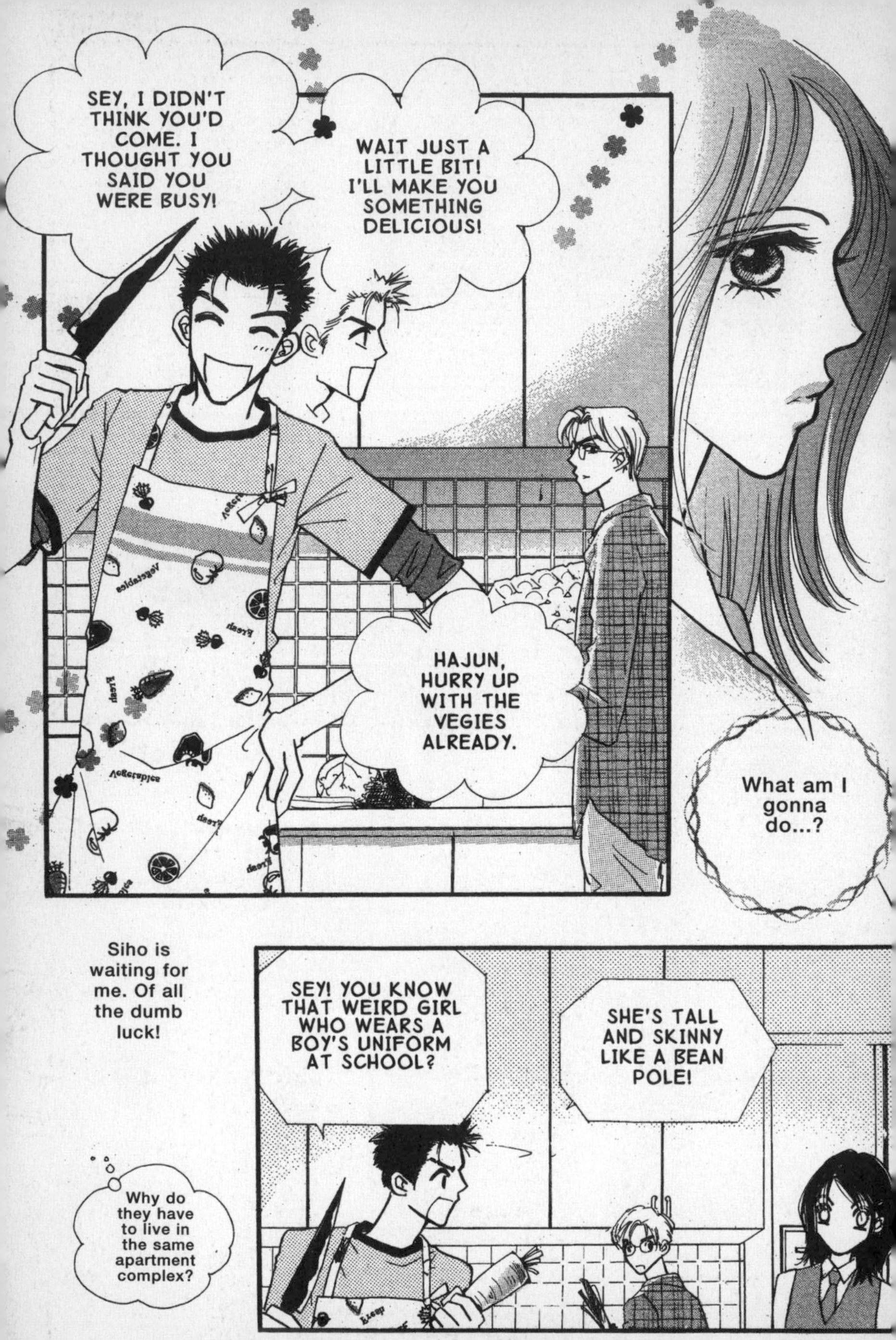
SEY, I DIDN'T THINK YOU'D COME. I THOUGHT YOU SAID YOU WERE BUSY!
WAIT JUST A LITTLE BIT! I'LL MAKE YOU SOMETHING DELICIOUS!
HAJUN, HURRY UP WITH THE VEGIES ALREADY.
What am I gonna do...?
Siho is waiting for me. Of all the dumb luck!
Why do they have to live in the same apartment complex?
SEY! YOU KNOW THAT WEIRD GIRL WHO WEARS A BOY'S UNIFORM AT SCHOOL?
SHE'S TALL AND SKINNY LIKE A BEAN POLE!

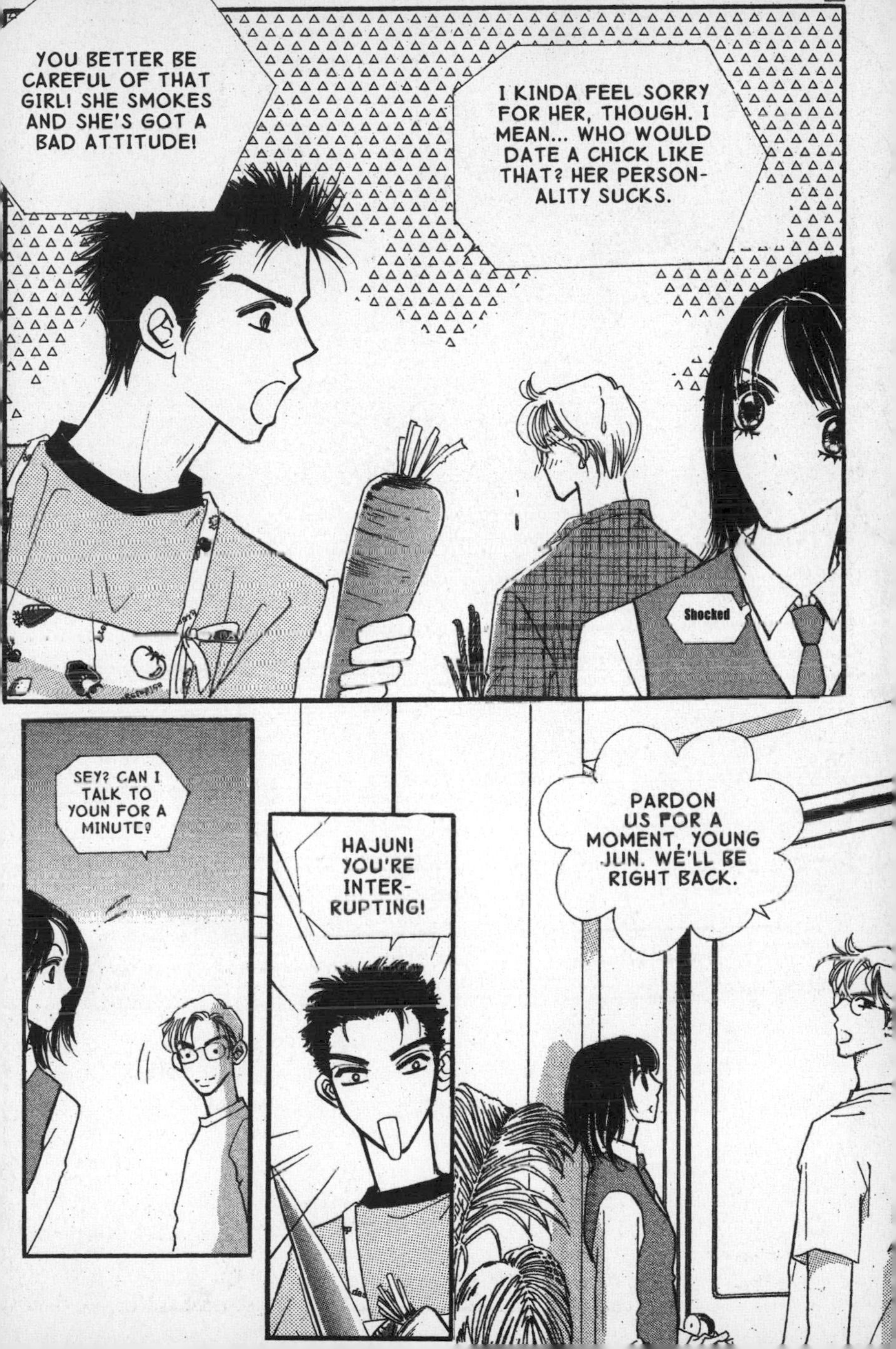
YOU BETTER BE CAREFUL OF THAT GIRL! SHE SMOKES AND SHE'S GOT A BAD ATTITUDE!
I KINDA FEEL SORRY FOR HER, THOUGH. I MEAN... WHO WOULD DATE A CHICK LIKE THAT? HER PERSON-ALITY SUCKS.
Shocked
SEY? CAN I TALK TO YOUN FOR A MINUTE?
HAJUN! YOU'RE INTER-RUPTING!
PARDON US FOR A MOMENT, YOUNG JUN. WE'LL BE RIGHT BACK.

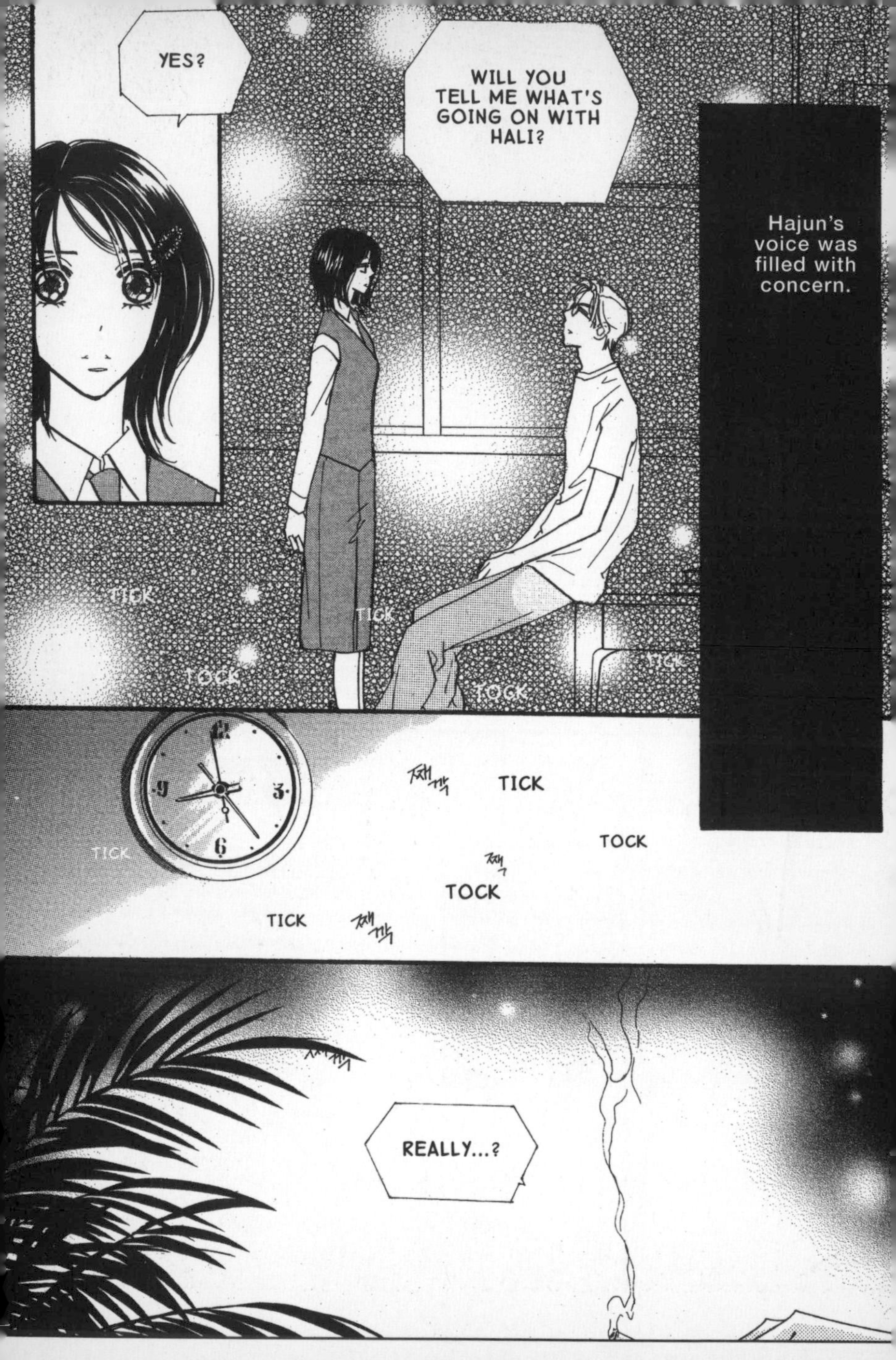
YES?
WILL YOU TELL ME WHAT'S GOING ON WITH HALI?
TICK
TICK
TOCK
TICK
TOCK
Hajun's voice was filled with concern.
TICK
째깍
TICK
TOCK
째깍
TOCK
TICK
째깍
REALLY...?

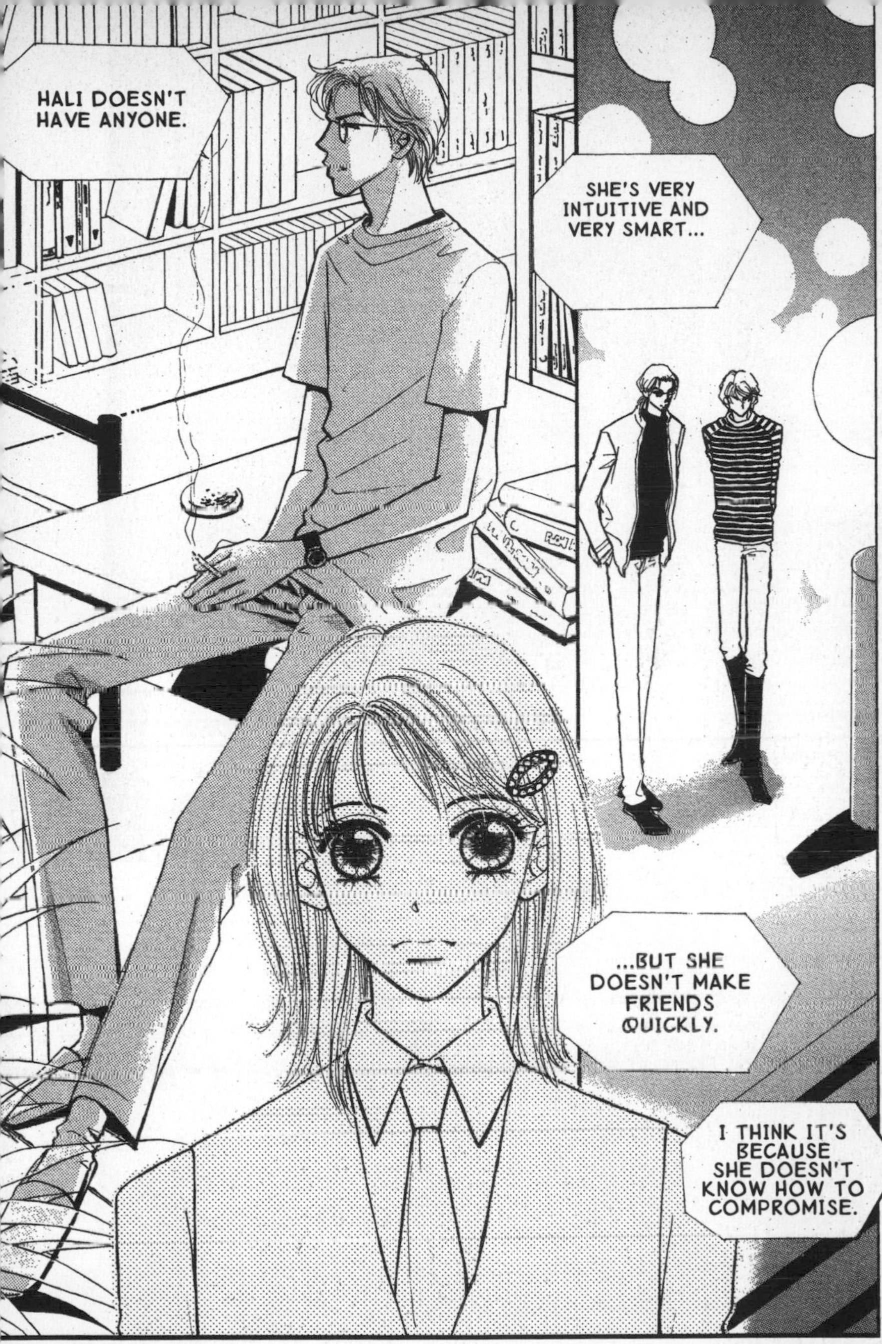
HALI DOESN'T HAVE ANYONE.
SHE'S VERY INTUITIVE AND VERY SMART...
...BUT SHE DOESN'T MAKE FRIENDS QUICKLY.
I THINK IT'S BECAUSE SHE DOESN'T KNOW HOW TO COMPROMISE.

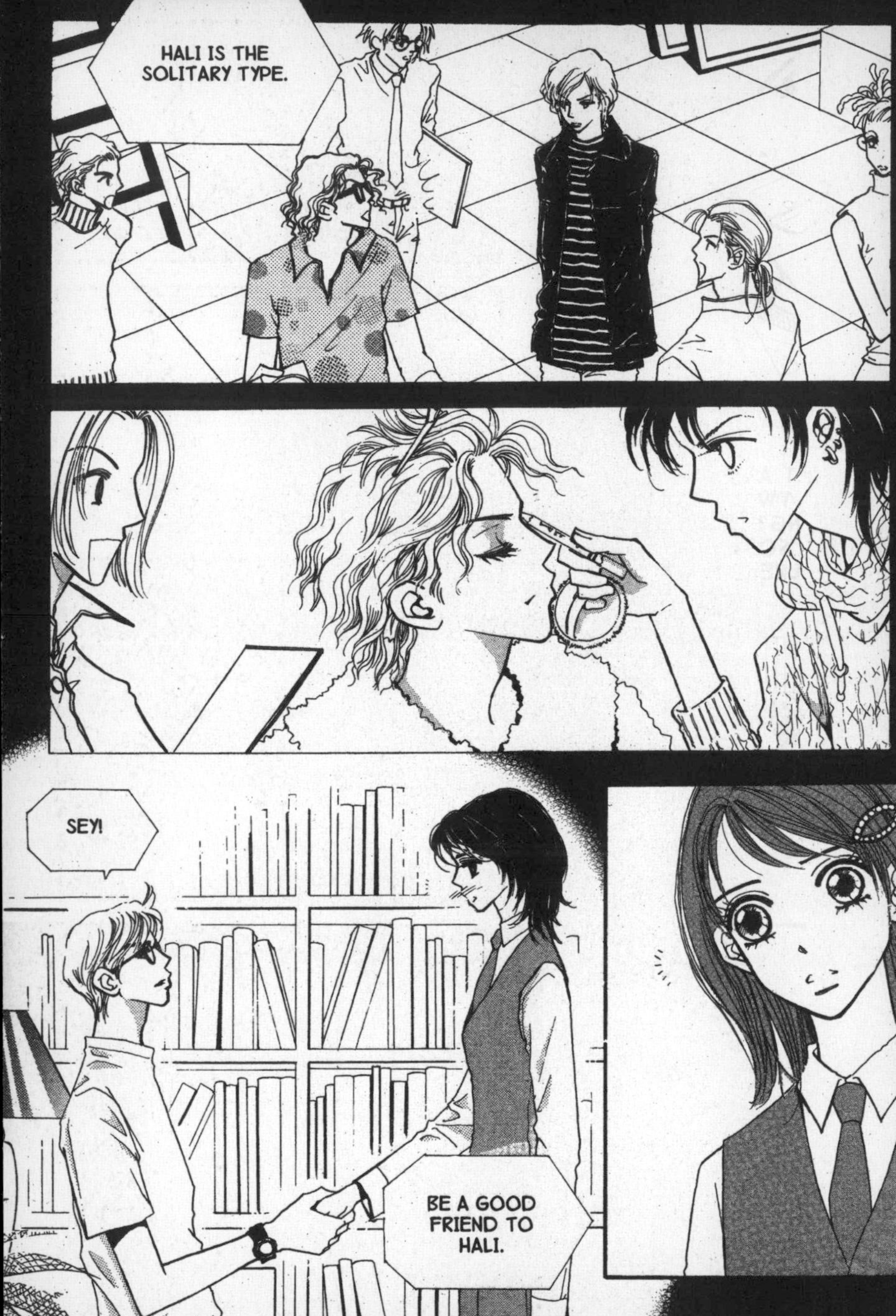
HALI IS THE SOLITARY TYPE.
SEY!
BE A GOOD FRIEND TO HALI.

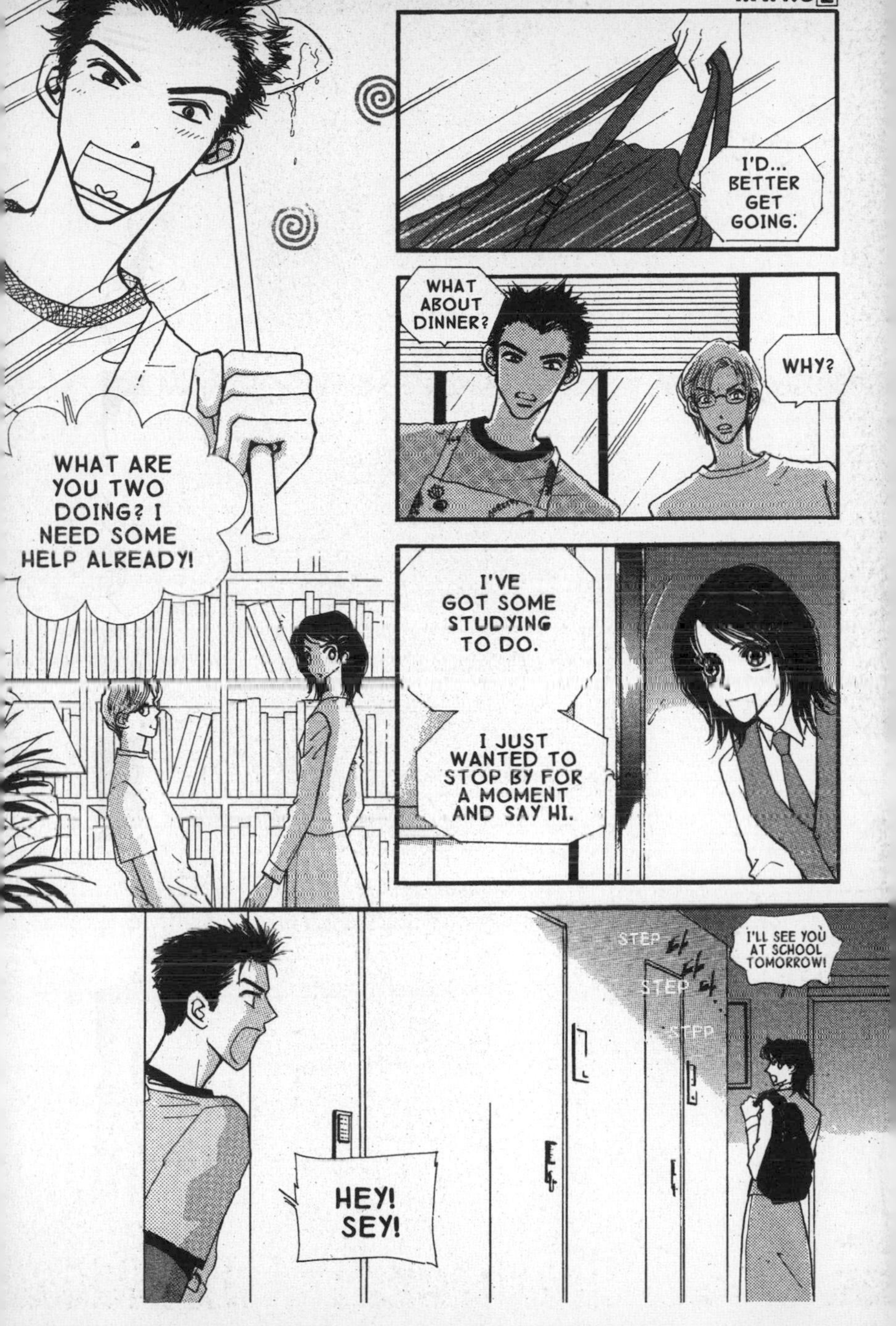
WHAT ARE YOU TWO DOING? I NEED SOME HELP ALREADY!
I'D... BETTER GET GOING.
WHAT ABOUT DINNER?
WHY?
I'VE GOT SOME STUDYING TO DO.
I JUST WANTED TO STOP BY FOR A MOMENT AND SAY HI.
STEP
STEP
STEP
I'LL SEE YOU AT SCHOOL TOMORROW!
HEY! SEY!

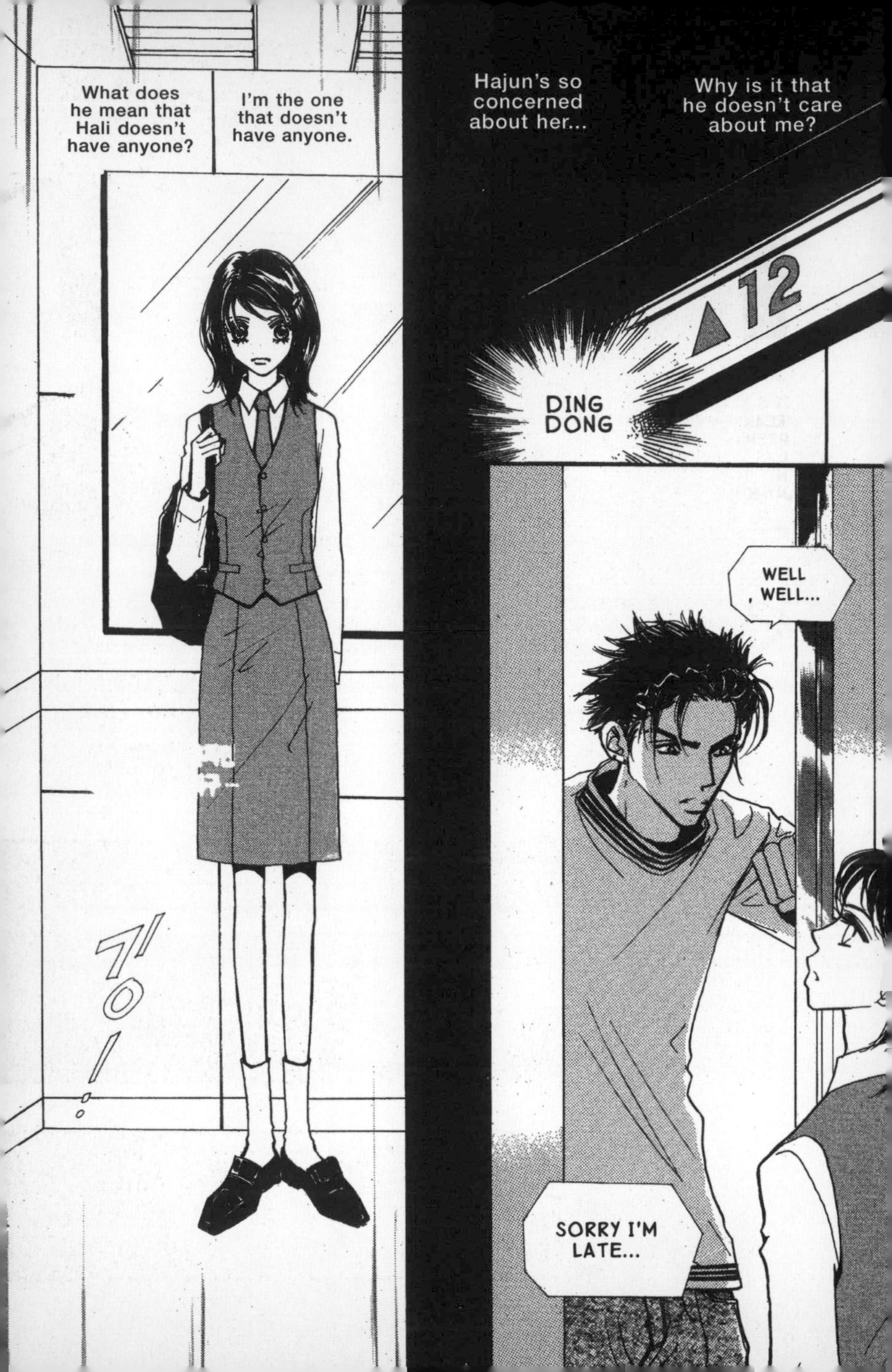
What does he mean that Hali doesn't have anyone?
I'm the one that doesn't have anyone.
Hajun's so concerned about her...
Why is it that he doesn't care about me?
▲12
DING DONG
WELL, WELL...
SORRY I'M LATE...

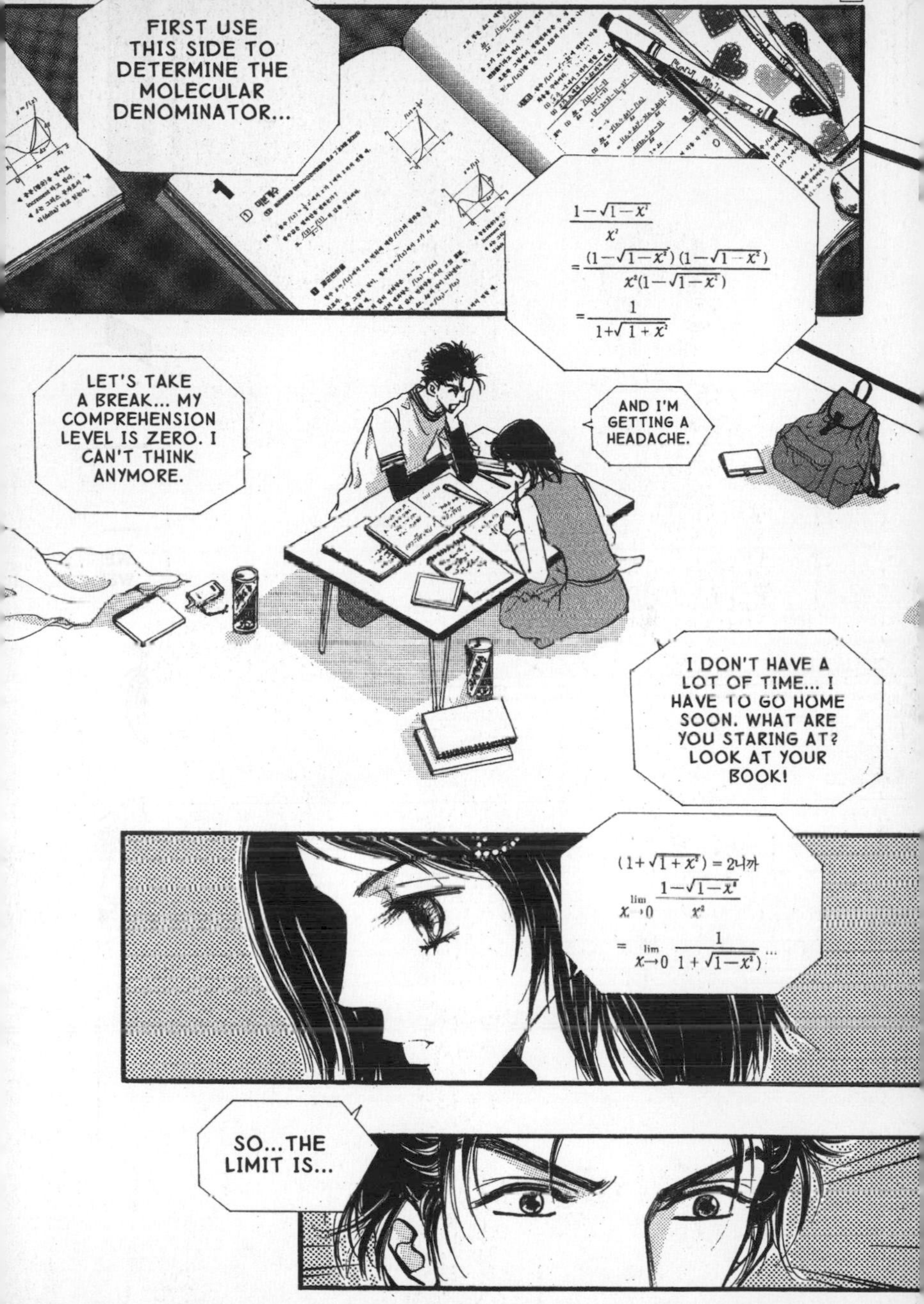
FIRST USE THIS SIDE TO DETERMINE THE MOLECULAR DENOMINATOR...
$\frac{1-\sqrt{1-x^2}}{x^2} = \frac{(1-\sqrt{1-x^2})(1-\sqrt{1-x^2})}{x^2(1-\sqrt{1-x^2})} = \frac{1}{1+\sqrt{1+x^2}}$
LET'S TAKE A BREAK... MY COMPREHENSION LEVEL IS ZERO. I CAN'T THINK ANYMORE.
AND I'M GETTING A HEADACHE.
I DON'T HAVE A LOT OF TIME... I HAVE TO GO HOME SOON. WHAT ARE YOU STARING AT? LOOK AT YOUR BOOK!
$(1+\sqrt{1+x^2}) = 2$니까
$\lim_{x\to 0} \frac{1-\sqrt{1-x^2}}{x^2} = \lim_{x\to 0} \frac{1}{1+\sqrt{1-x^2})}$...
SO...THE LIMIT IS...

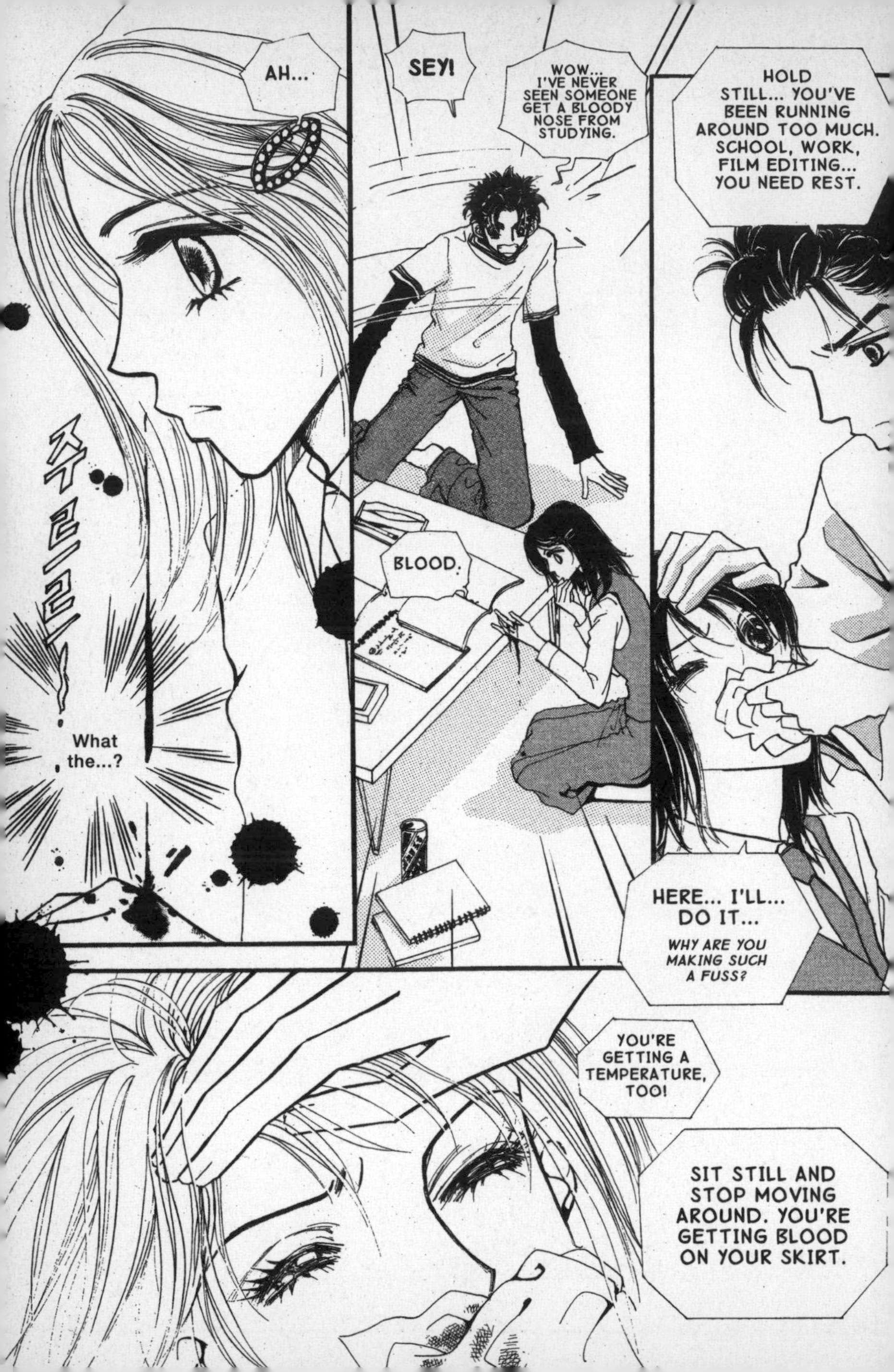
AH...
주르르
What the...?
SEY!
WOW... I'VE NEVER SEEN SOMEONE GET A BLOODY NOSE FROM STUDYING.
BLOOD.
HOLD STILL... YOU'VE BEEN RUNNING AROUND TOO MUCH. SCHOOL, WORK, FILM EDITING... YOU NEED REST.
HERE... I'LL... DO IT...
WHY ARE YOU MAKING SUCH A FUSS?
YOU'RE GETTING A TEMPERATURE, TOO!
SIT STILL AND STOP MOVING AROUND. YOU'RE GETTING BLOOD ON YOUR SKIRT.

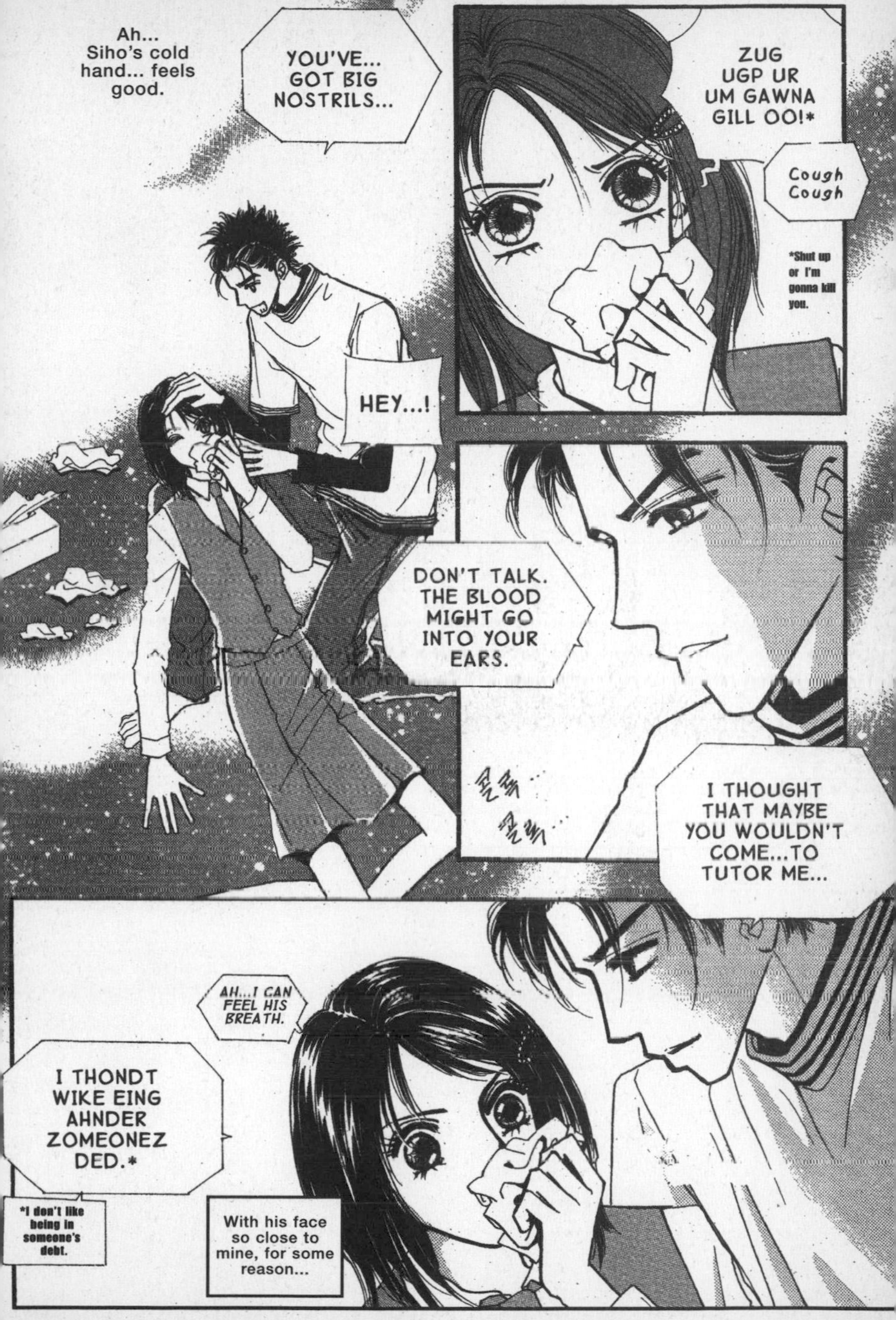
Ah... Siho's cold hand... feels good.
YOU'VE... GOT BIG NOSTRILS...
HEY...!
ZUG UGP UR UM GAWNA GILL OO!*
Cough Cough
*Shut up or I'm gonna kill you.
DON'T TALK. THE BLOOD MIGHT GO INTO YOUR EARS.
I THOUGHT THAT MAYBE YOU WOULDN'T COME...TO TUTOR ME...
AH...I CAN FEEL HIS BREATH.
I THONDT WIKE EING AHNDER ZOMEONEZ DED.*
*I don't like being in someone's debt.
With his face so close to mine, for some reason...

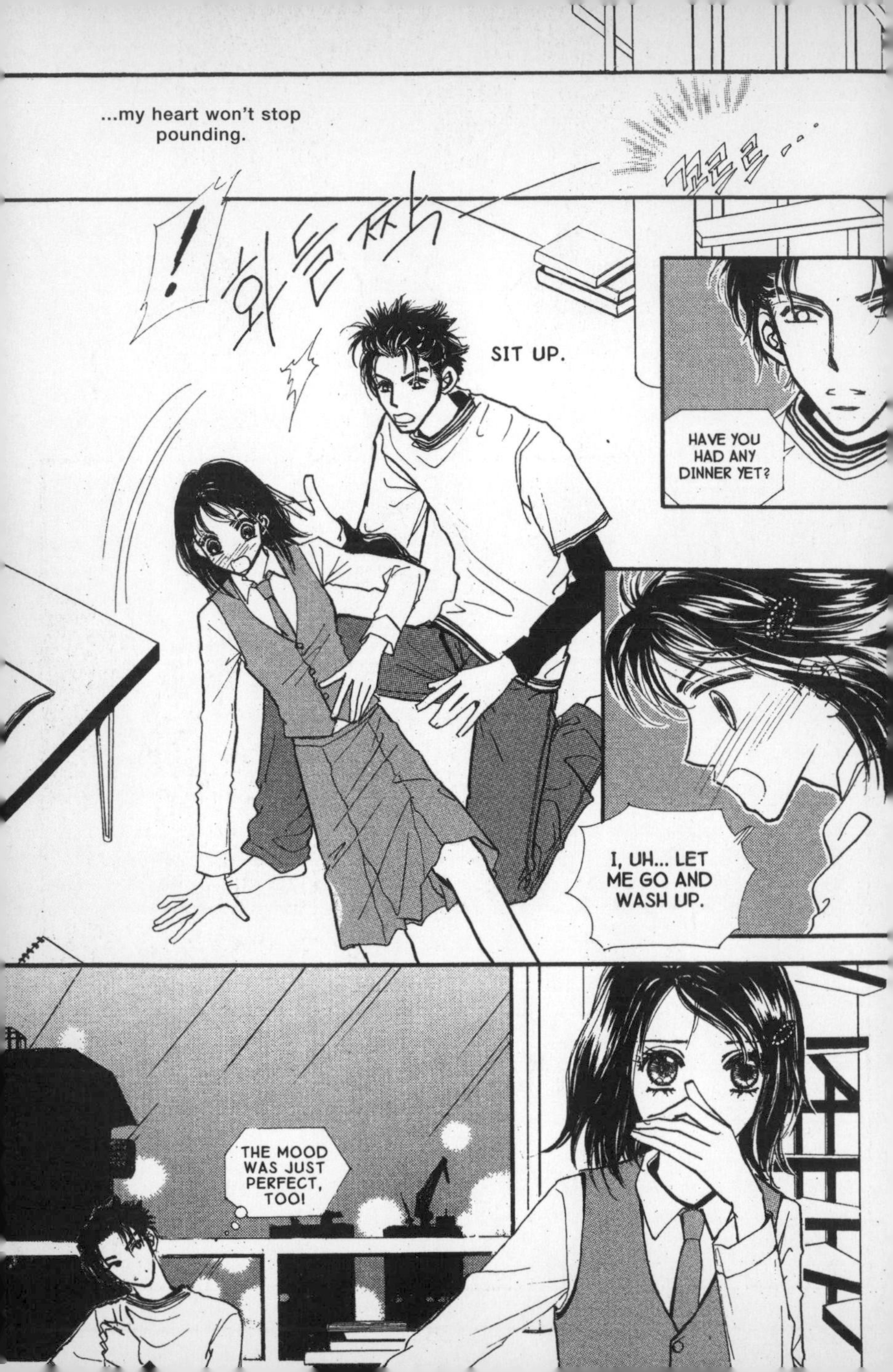
...my heart won't stop pounding.
꼬르르...
!
화들짝
SIT UP.
HAVE YOU HAD ANY DINNER YET?
I, UH... LET ME GO AND WASH UP.
THE MOOD WAS JUST PERFECT, TOO!

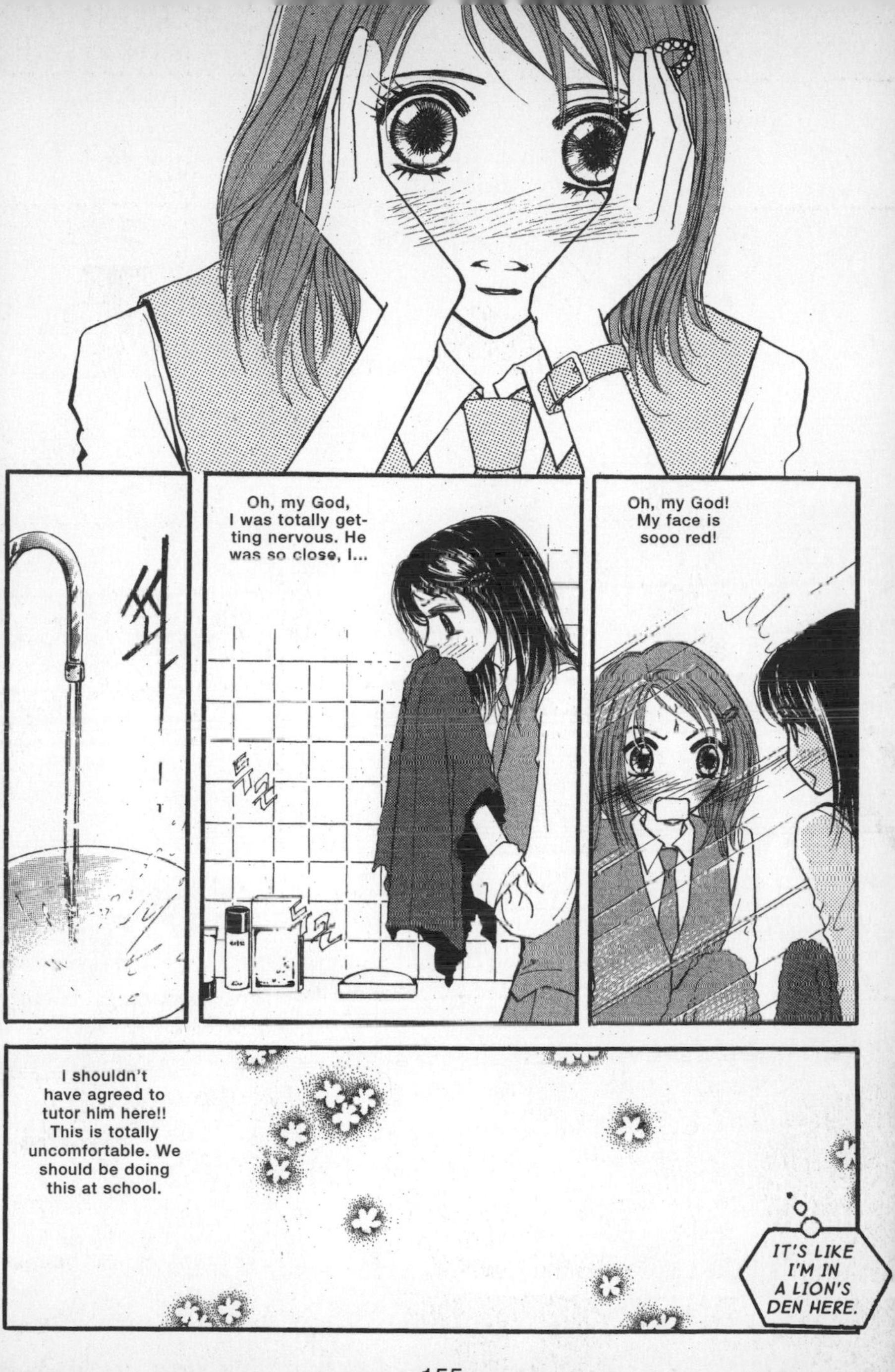
Oh, my God,
I was totally get-
ting nervous. He
was so close, I...
Oh, my God!
My face is
sooo red!
I shouldn't
have agreed to
tutor him here!!
This is totally
uncomfortable. We
should be doing
this at school.
IT'S LIKE
I'M IN
A LION'S
DEN HERE.

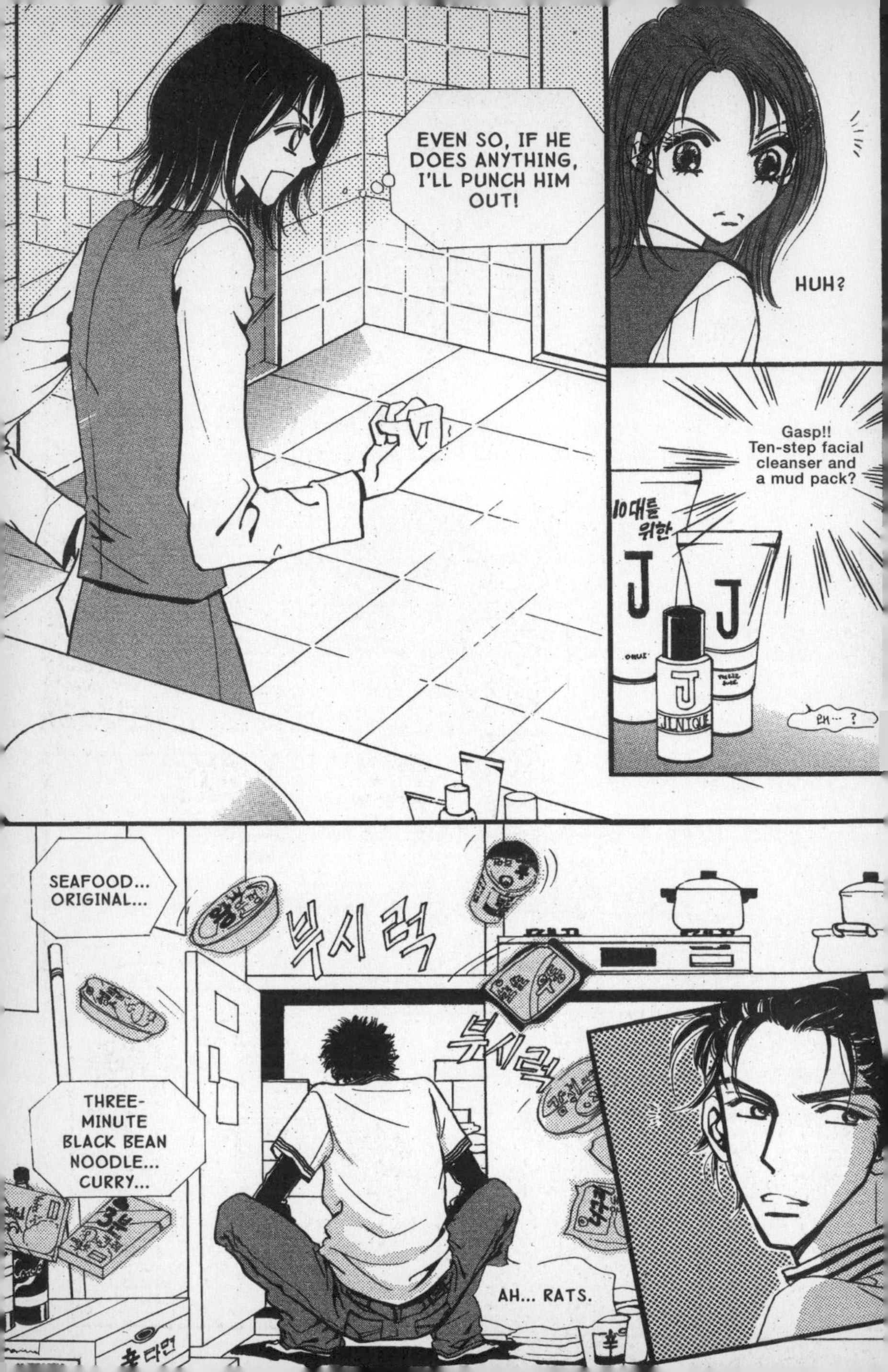
EVEN SO, IF HE DOES ANYTHING, I'LL PUNCH HIM OUT!
HUH?
Gasp!! Ten-step facial cleanser and a mud pack?
10대를 위한
JINIQUE
왜…?
SEAFOOD... ORIGINAL...
부시럭
THREE-MINUTE BLACK BEAN NOODLE... CURRY...
부시럭
AH... RATS.

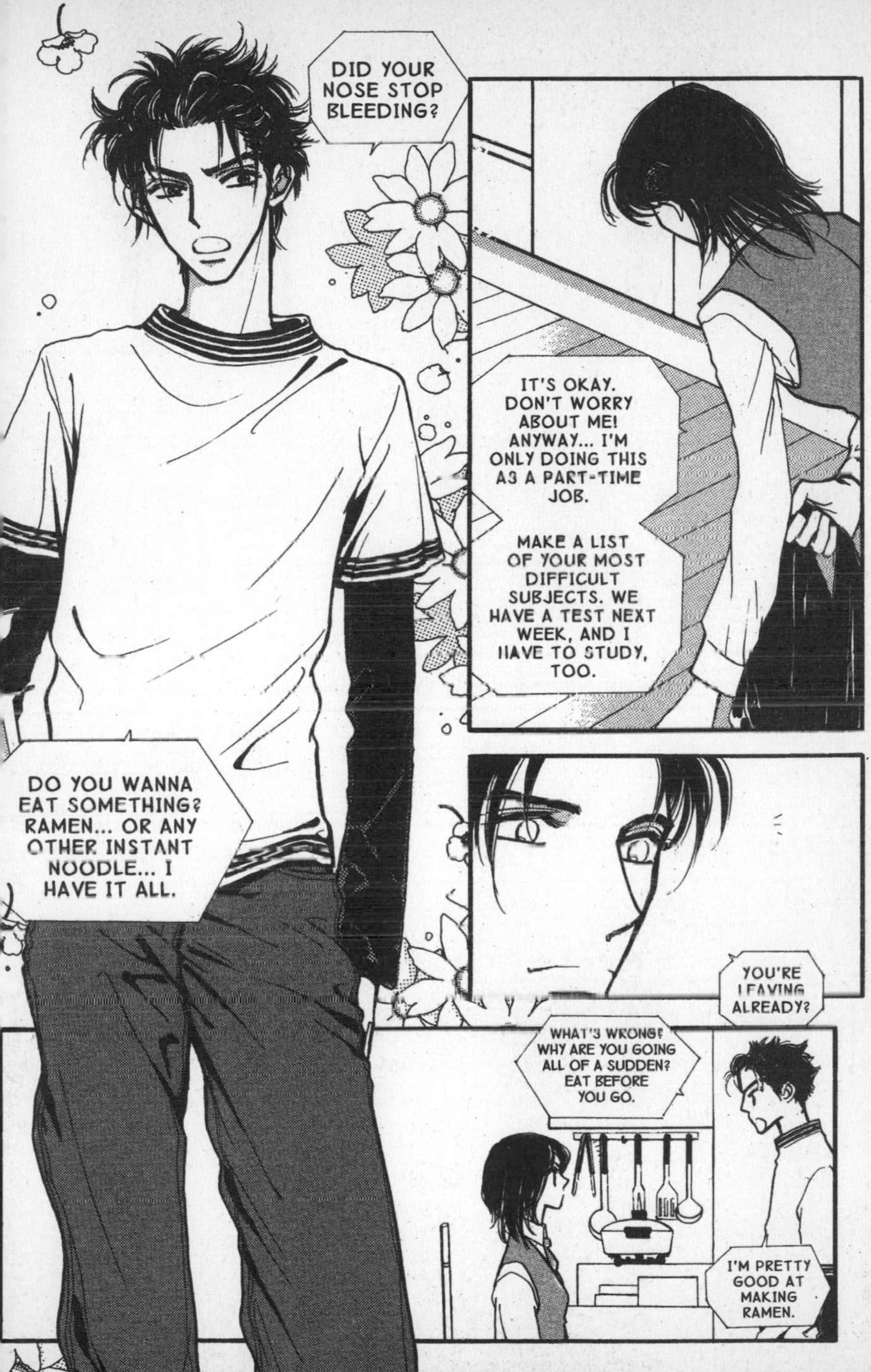
DID YOUR NOSE STOP BLEEDING?
DO YOU WANNA EAT SOMETHING? RAMEN... OR ANY OTHER INSTANT NOODLE... I HAVE IT ALL.
IT'S OKAY. DON'T WORRY ABOUT ME! ANYWAY... I'M ONLY DOING THIS AS A PART-TIME JOB.
MAKE A LIST OF YOUR MOST DIFFICULT SUBJECTS. WE HAVE A TEST NEXT WEEK, AND I HAVE TO STUDY, TOO.
YOU'RE LEAVING ALREADY?
WHAT'S WRONG? WHY ARE YOU GOING ALL OF A SUDDEN? EAT BEFORE YOU GO.
I'M PRETTY GOOD AT MAKING RAMEN.

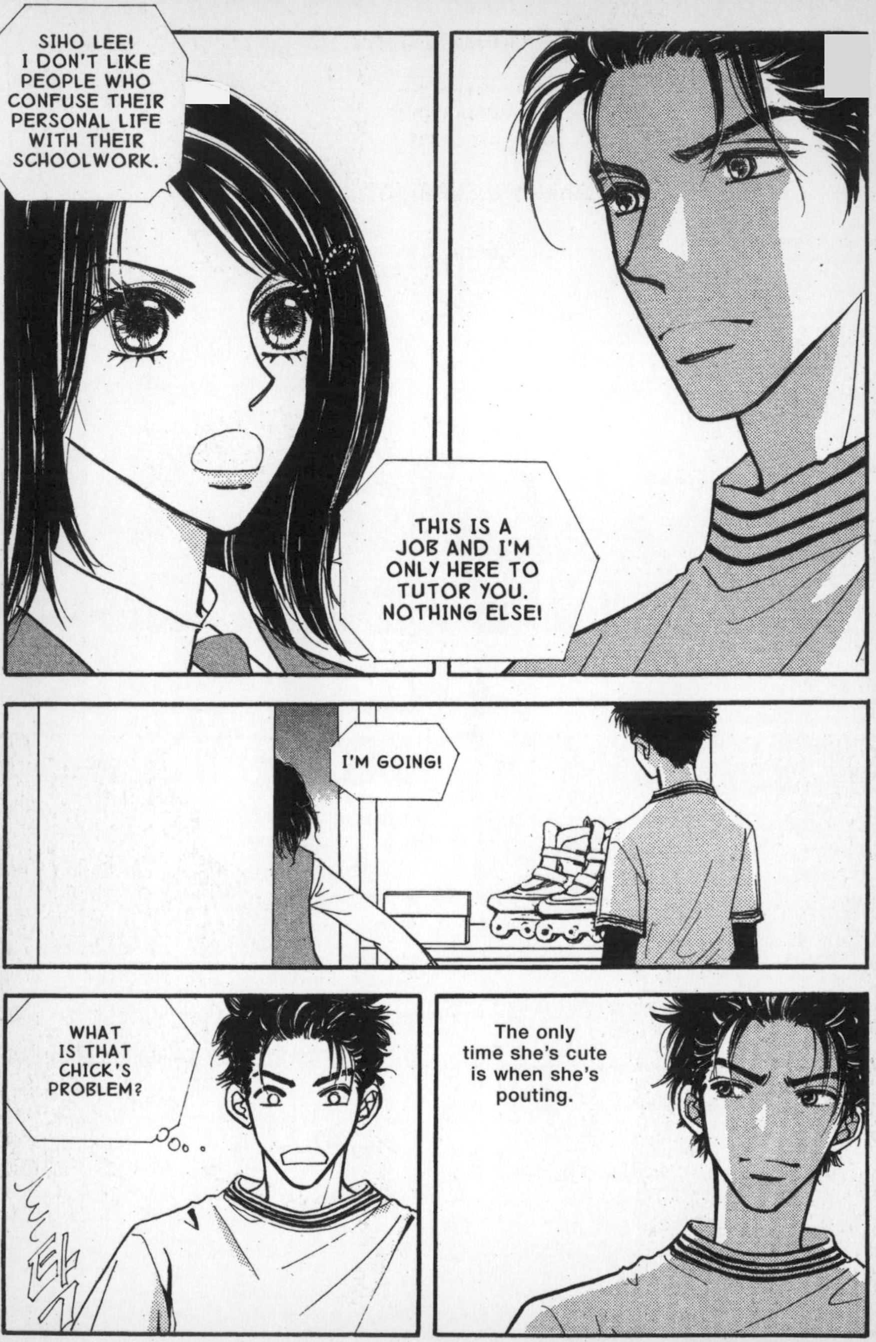

SIHO LEE! I DON'T LIKE PEOPLE WHO CONFUSE THEIR PERSONAL LIFE WITH THEIR SCHOOLWORK.
THIS IS A JOB AND I'M ONLY HERE TO TUTOR YOU. NOTHING ELSE!
I'M GOING!
WHAT IS THAT CHICK'S PROBLEM?
The only time she's cute is when she's pouting.

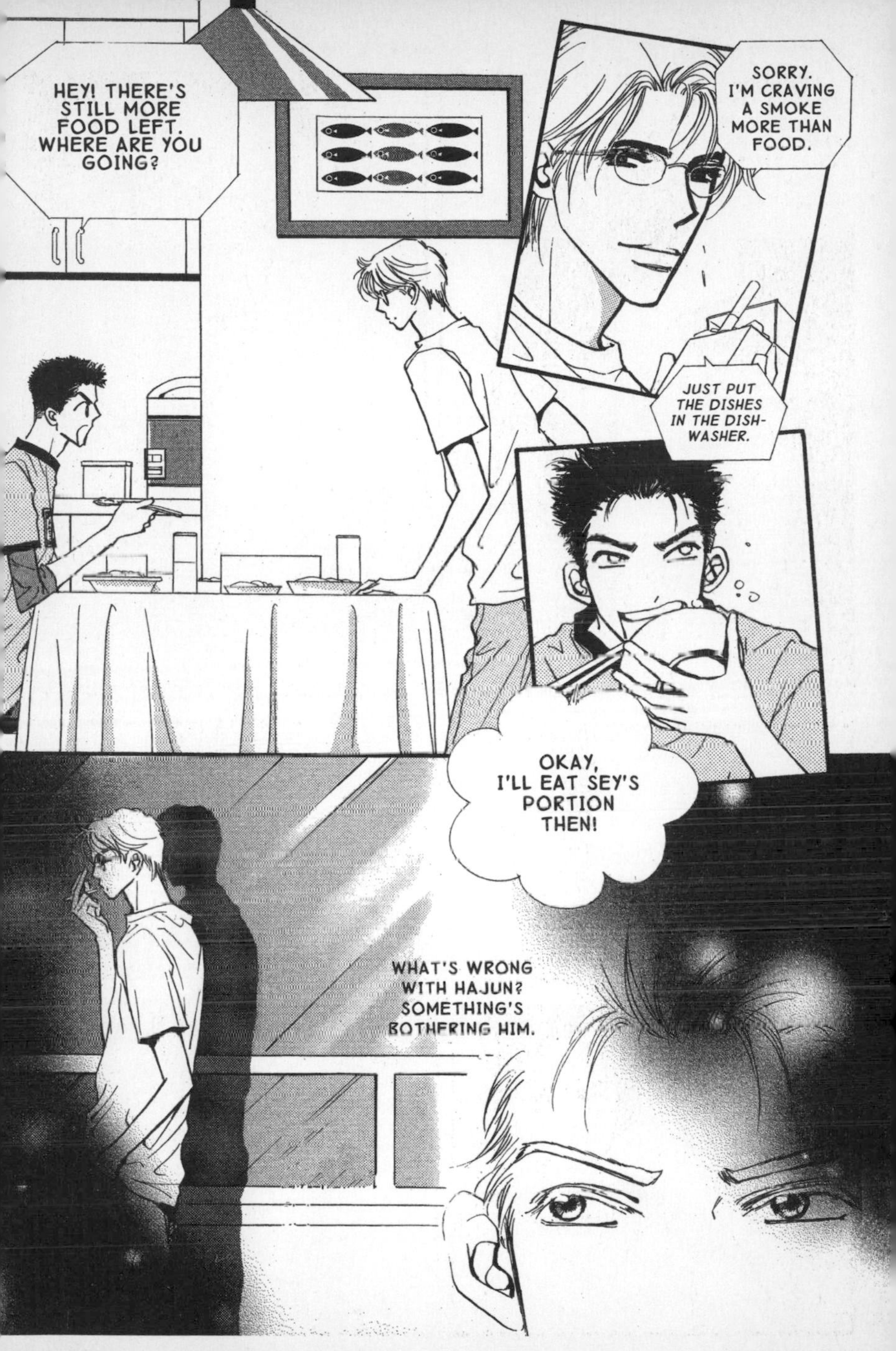
HEY! THERE'S STILL MORE FOOD LEFT. WHERE ARE YOU GOING?
SORRY. I'M CRAVING A SMOKE MORE THAN FOOD.
JUST PUT THE DISHES IN THE DISH-WASHER.
OKAY, I'LL EAT SEY'S PORTION THEN!
WHAT'S WRONG WITH HAJUN? SOMETHING'S BOTHERING HIM.

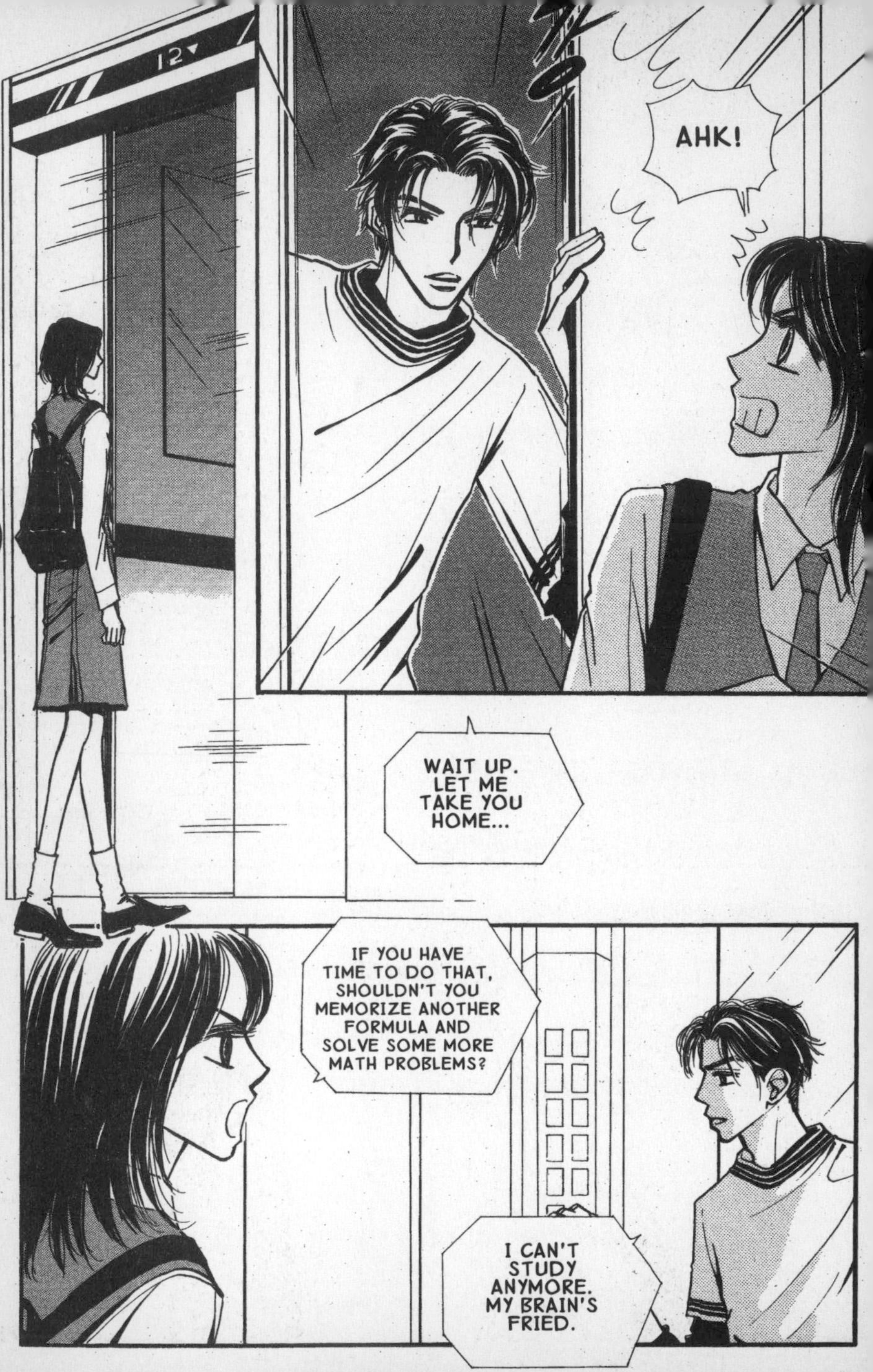
AHK!
WAIT UP. LET ME TAKE YOU HOME...
IF YOU HAVE TIME TO DO THAT, SHOULDN'T YOU MEMORIZE ANOTHER FORMULA AND SOLVE SOME MORE MATH PROBLEMS?
I CAN'T STUDY ANYMORE. MY BRAIN'S FRIED.

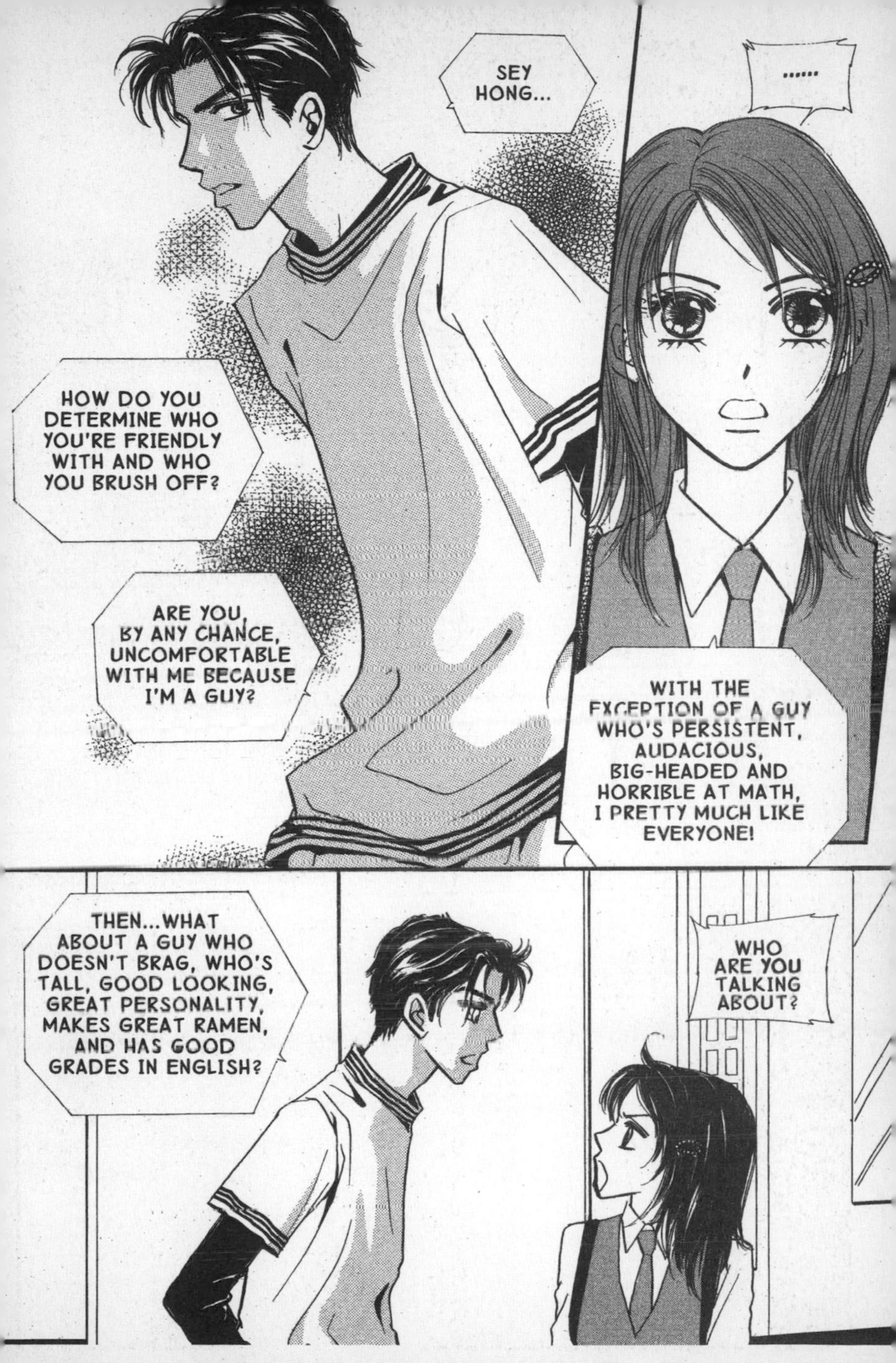
SEY HONG...
......
HOW DO YOU DETERMINE WHO YOU'RE FRIENDLY WITH AND WHO YOU BRUSH OFF?
ARE YOU, BY ANY CHANCE, UNCOMFORTABLE WITH ME BECAUSE I'M A GUY?
WITH THE EXCEPTION OF A GUY WHO'S PERSISTENT, AUDACIOUS, BIG-HEADED AND HORRIBLE AT MATH, I PRETTY MUCH LIKE EVERYONE!
THEN...WHAT ABOUT A GUY WHO DOESN'T BRAG, WHO'S TALL, GOOD LOOKING, GREAT PERSONALITY, MAKES GREAT RAMEN, AND HAS GOOD GRADES IN ENGLISH?
WHO ARE YOU TALKING ABOUT?

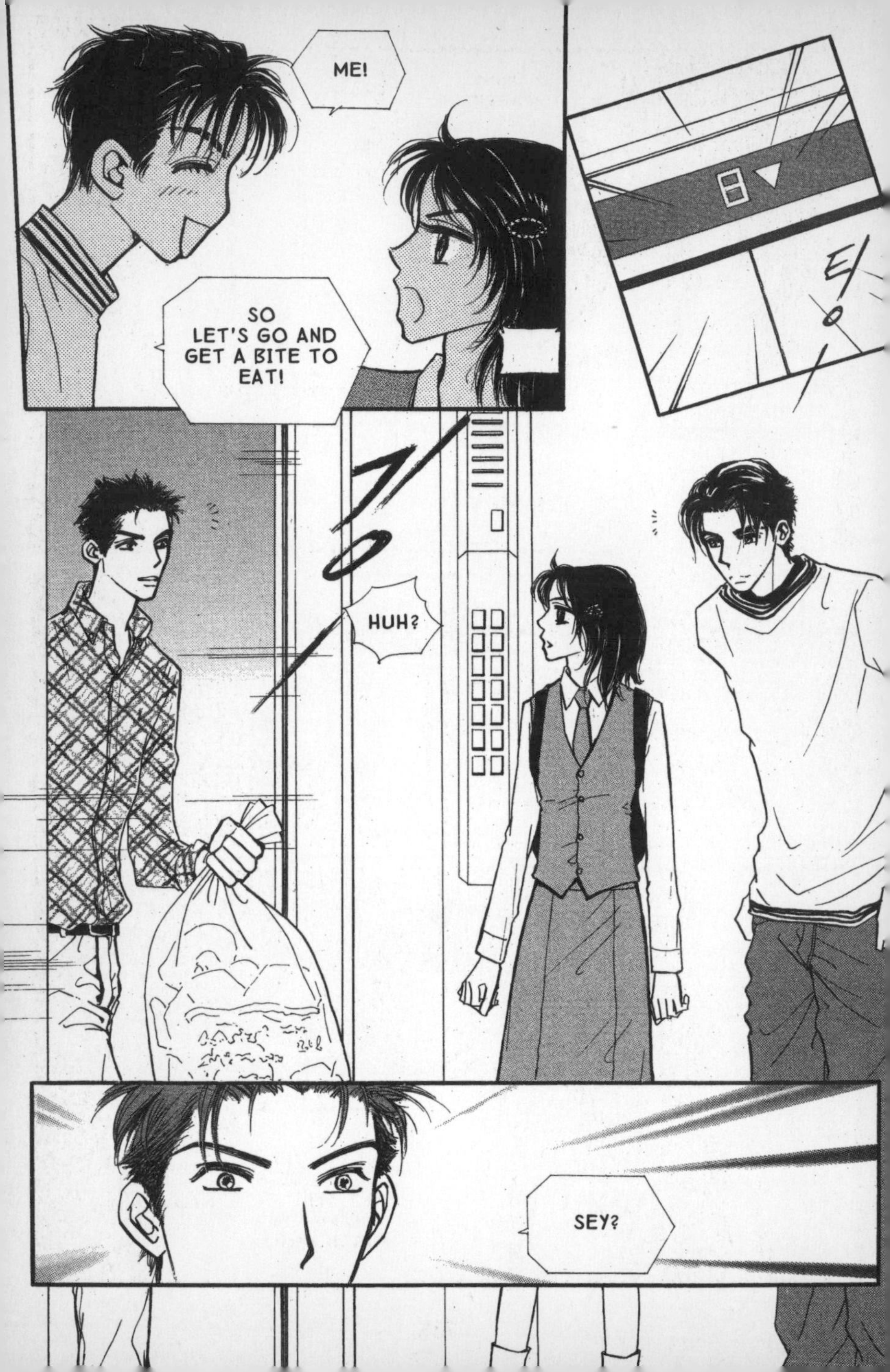
ME!
SO LET'S GO AND GET A BITE TO EAT!
HUH?
SEY?

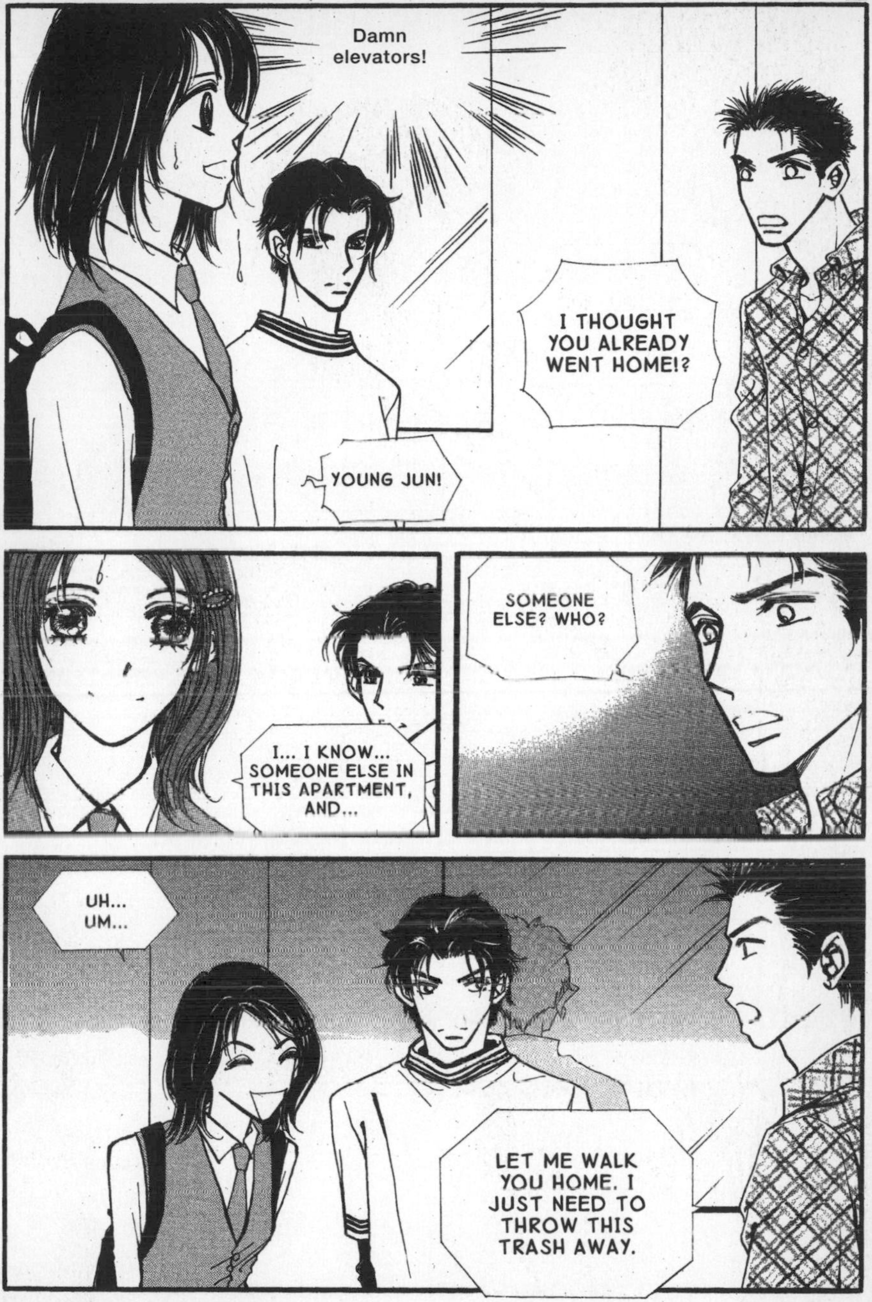
Damn elevators!
I THOUGHT YOU ALREADY WENT HOME!?
YOUNG JUN!
I... I KNOW... SOMEONE ELSE IN THIS APARTMENT, AND...
SOMEONE ELSE? WHO?
UH... UM...
LET ME WALK YOU HOME. I JUST NEED TO THROW THIS TRASH AWAY.

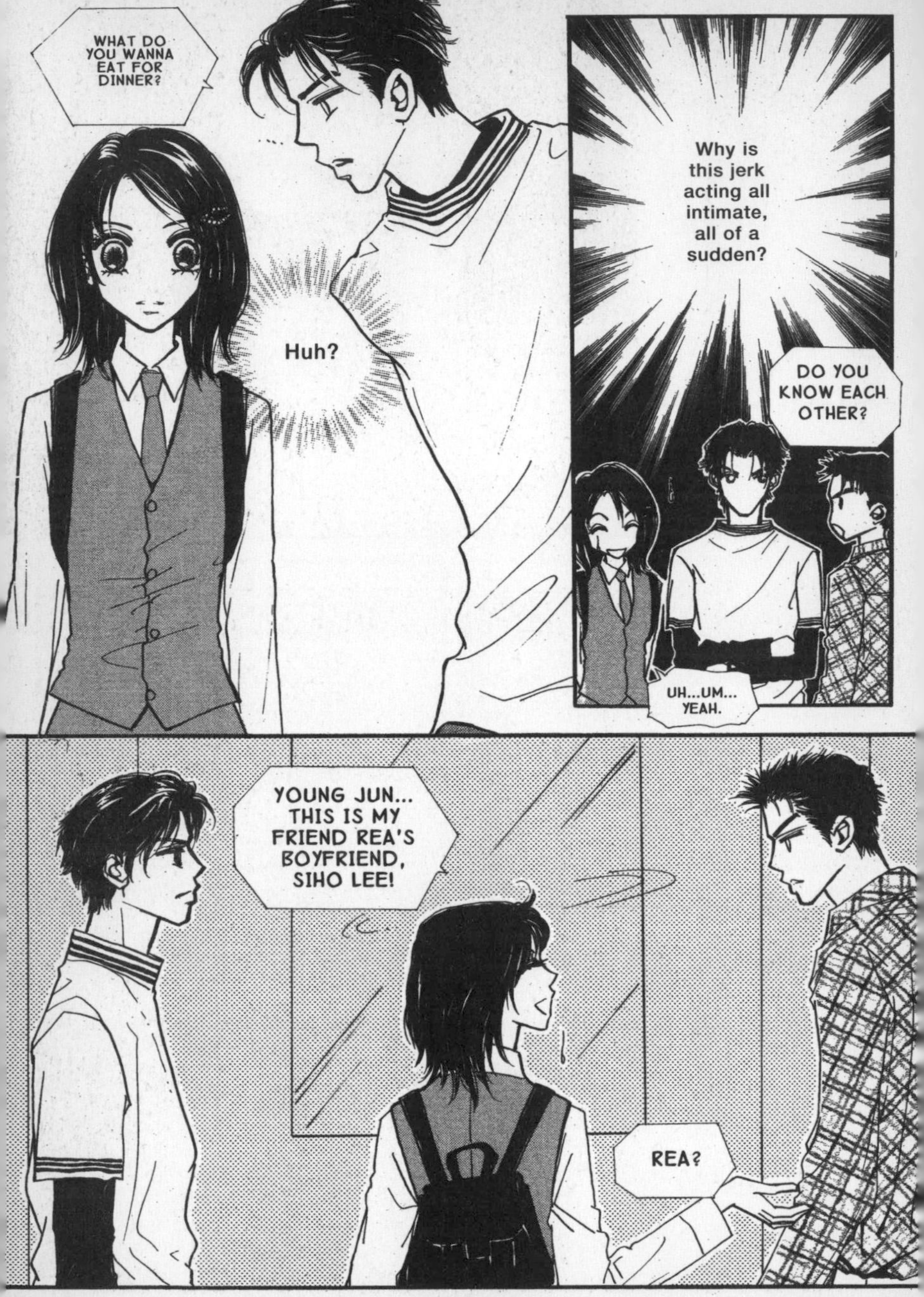
WHAT DO YOU WANNA EAT FOR DINNER?
...
Huh?
Why is this jerk acting all intimate, all of a sudden?
DO YOU KNOW EACH OTHER?
UH...UM... YEAH.
YOUNG JUN... THIS IS MY FRIEND REA'S BOYFRIEND, SIHO LEE!
REA?

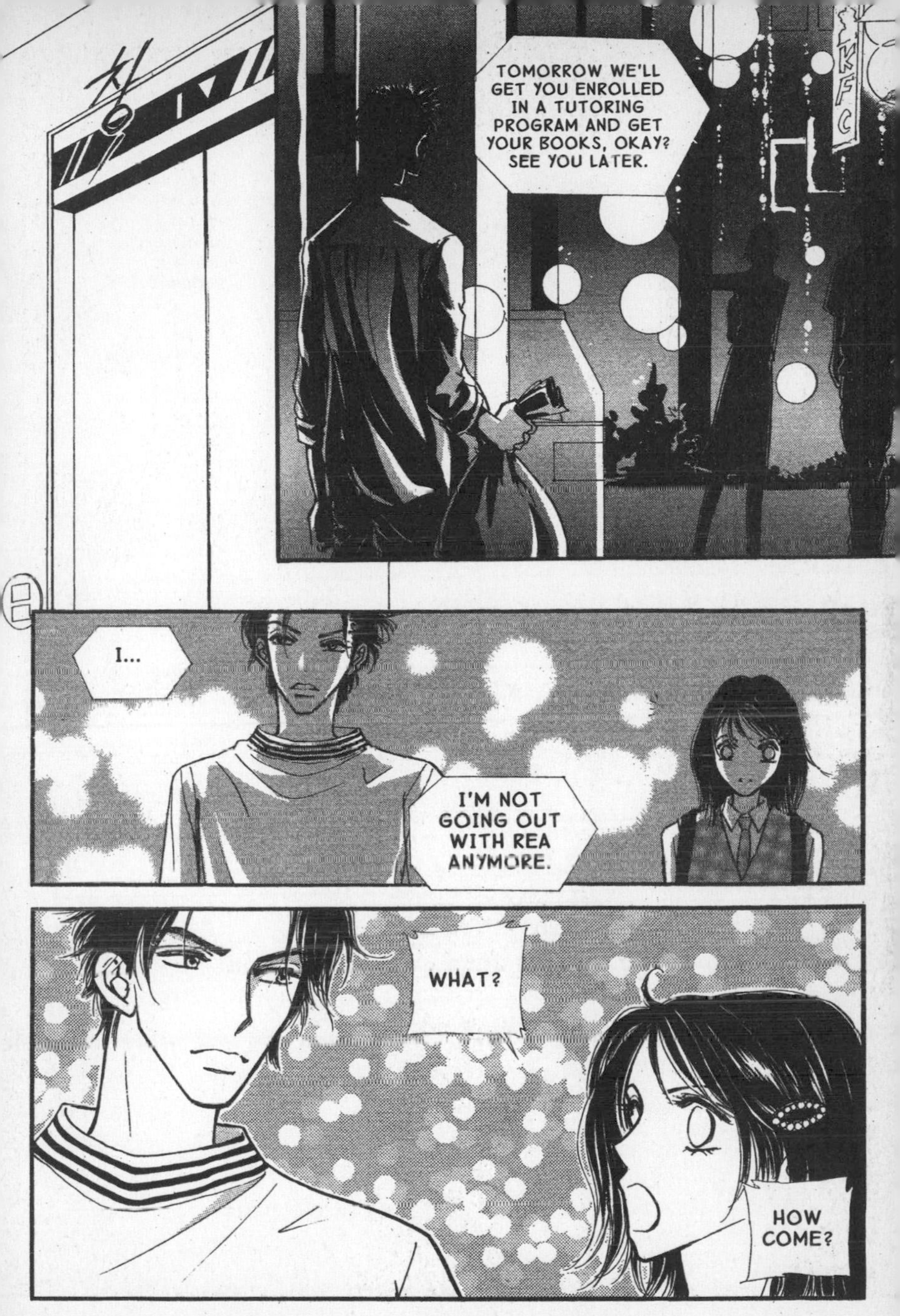
찰
TOMORROW WE'LL GET YOU ENROLLED IN A TUTORING PROGRAM AND GET YOUR BOOKS, OKAY? SEE YOU LATER.
I...
I'M NOT GOING OUT WITH REA ANYMORE.
WHAT?
HOW COME?

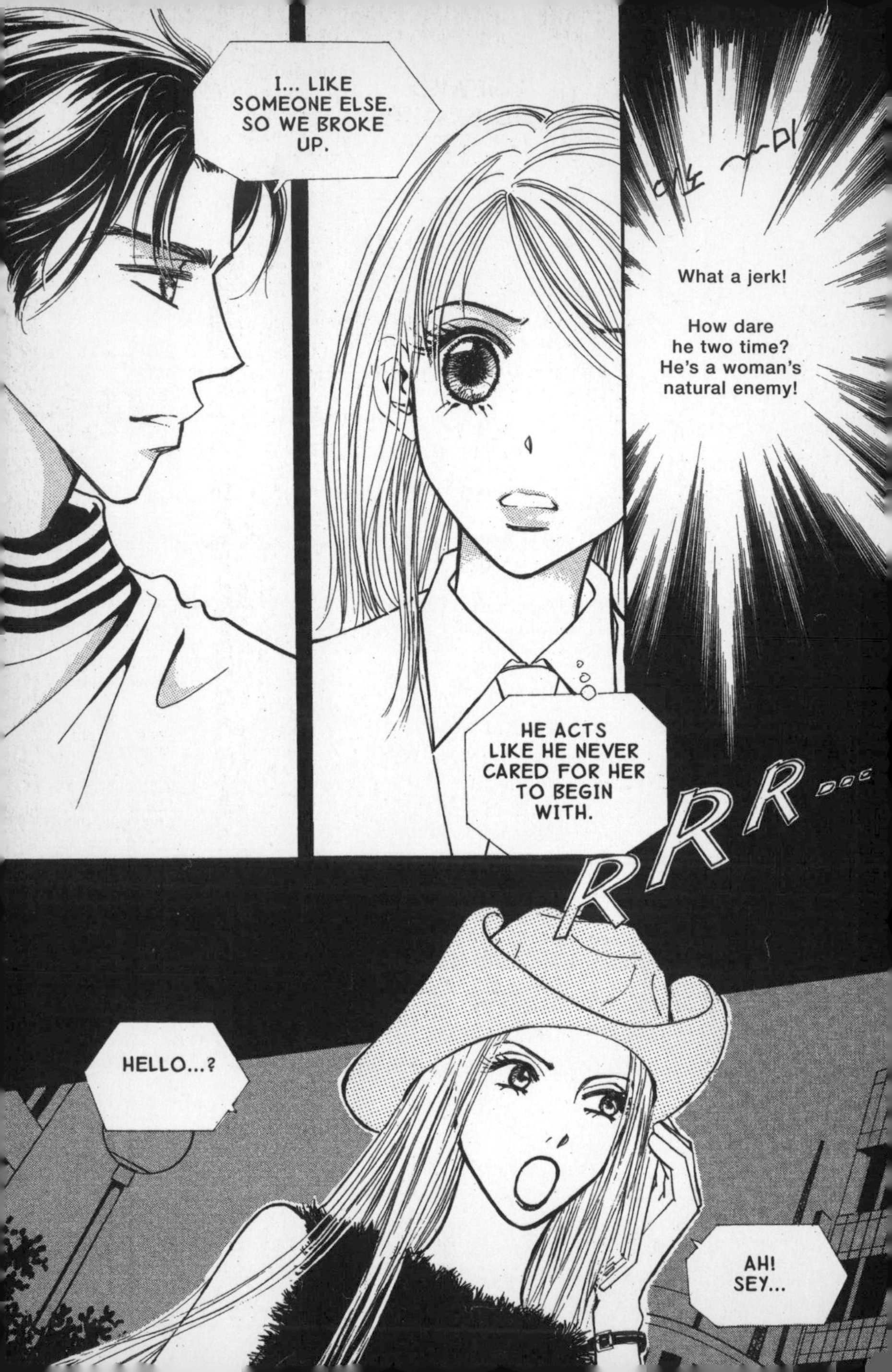
I... LIKE SOMEONE ELSE. SO WE BROKE UP.
HE ACTS LIKE HE NEVER CARED FOR HER TO BEGIN WITH.
What a jerk!
How dare he two time? He's a woman's natural enemy!
RRRR...
HELLO...?
AH! SEY...

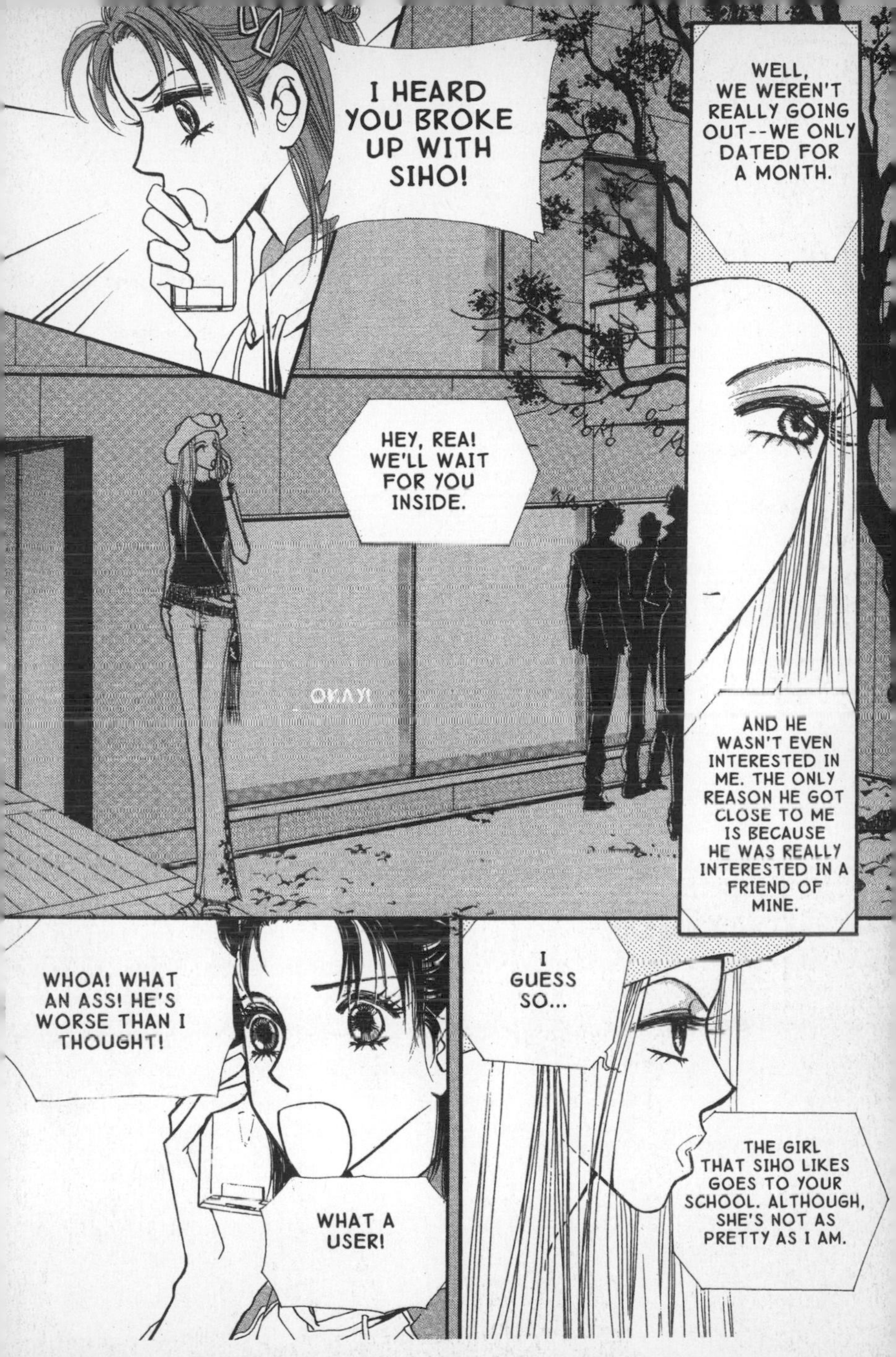
I HEARD YOU BROKE UP WITH SIHO!
HEY, REA! WE'LL WAIT FOR YOU INSIDE.
OKAY!
WELL, WE WEREN'T REALLY GOING OUT--WE ONLY DATED FOR A MONTH.
AND HE WASN'T EVEN INTERESTED IN ME. THE ONLY REASON HE GOT CLOSE TO ME IS BECAUSE HE WAS REALLY INTERESTED IN A FRIEND OF MINE.
WHOA! WHAT AN ASS! HE'S WORSE THAN I THOUGHT!
WHAT A USER!
I GUESS SO...
THE GIRL THAT SIHO LIKES GOES TO YOUR SCHOOL. ALTHOUGH, SHE'S NOT AS PRETTY AS I AM.

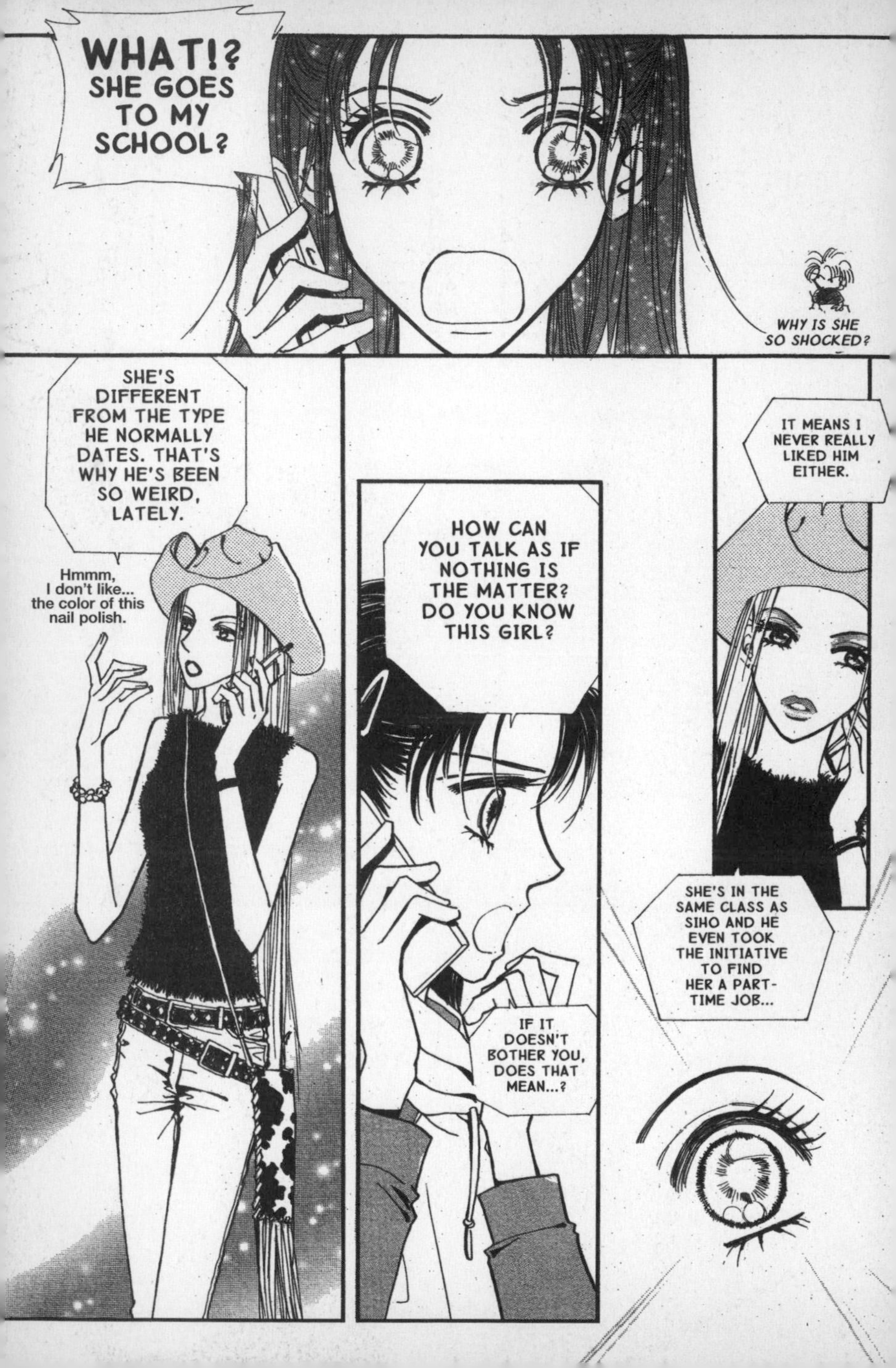
WHAT!? SHE GOES TO MY SCHOOL?
WHY IS SHE SO SHOCKED?
SHE'S DIFFERENT FROM THE TYPE HE NORMALLY DATES. THAT'S WHY HE'S BEEN SO WEIRD, LATELY.
Hmmm, I don't like... the color of this nail polish.
HOW CAN YOU TALK AS IF NOTHING IS THE MATTER? DO YOU KNOW THIS GIRL?
IF IT DOESN'T BOTHER YOU, DOES THAT MEAN...?
IT MEANS I NEVER REALLY LIKED HIM EITHER.
SHE'S IN THE SAME CLASS AS SIHO AND HE EVEN TOOK THE INITIATIVE TO FIND HER A PART-TIME JOB...

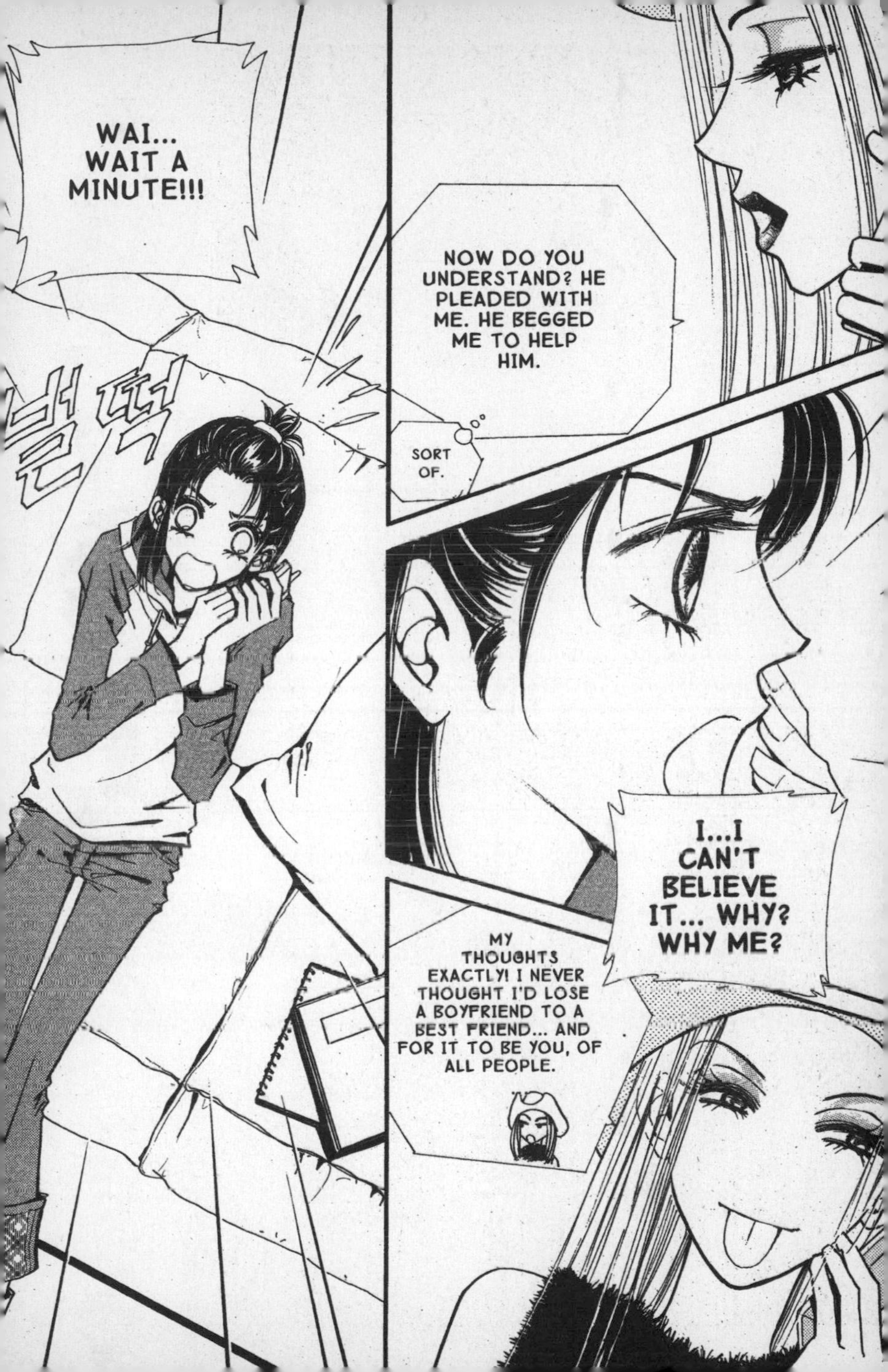
WAI... WAIT A MINUTE!!!
벌떡
NOW DO YOU UNDERSTAND? HE PLEADED WITH ME. HE BEGGED ME TO HELP HIM.
SORT OF.
I...I CAN'T BELIEVE IT... WHY? WHY ME?
MY THOUGHTS EXACTLY! I NEVER THOUGHT I'D LOSE A BOYFRIEND TO A BEST FRIEND... AND FOR IT TO BE YOU, OF ALL PEOPLE.

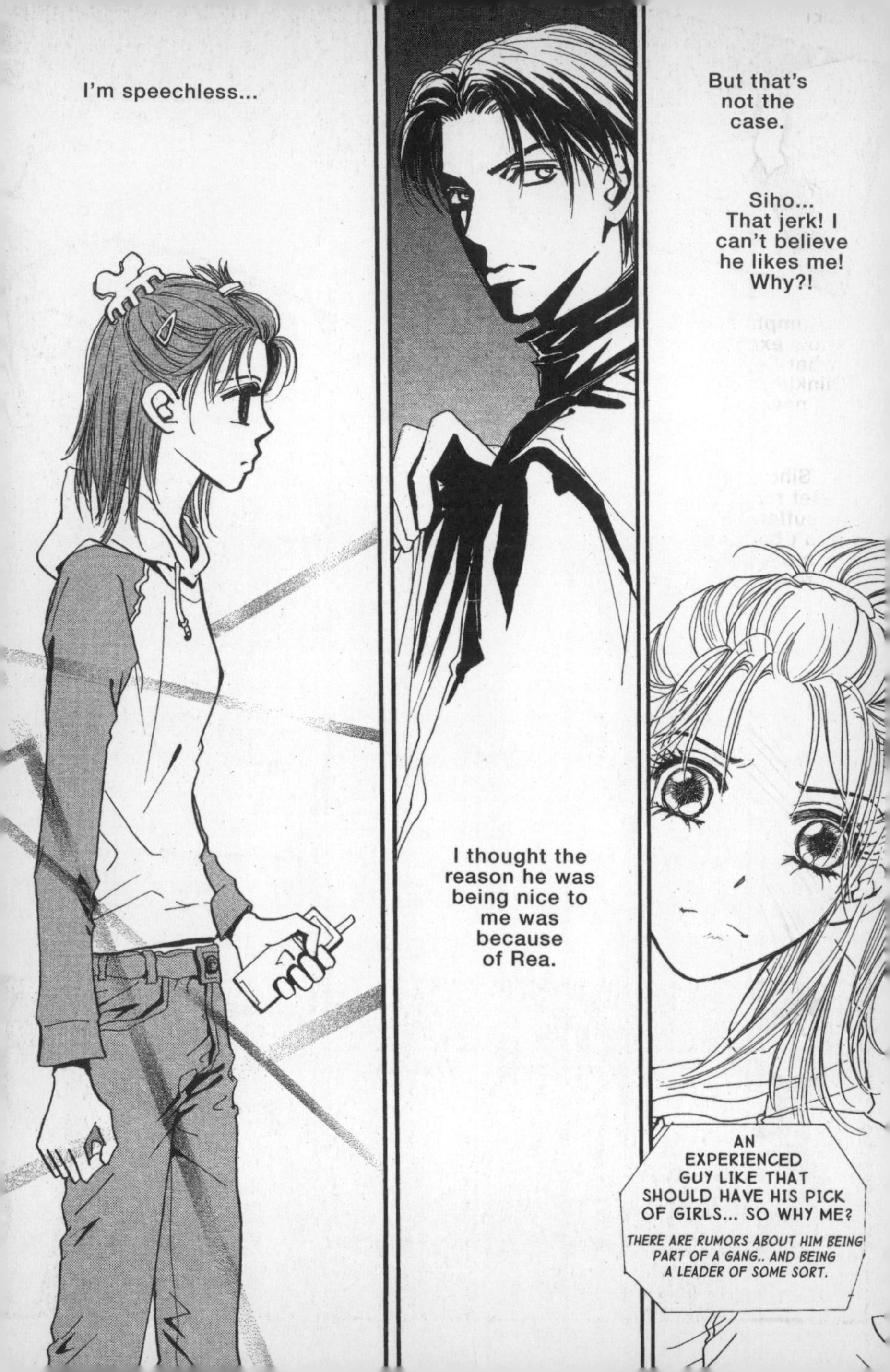
I'm speechless...
But that's not the case.
Siho... That jerk! I can't believe he likes me! Why?!
I thought the reason he was being nice to me was because of Rea.
AN EXPERIENCED GUY LIKE THAT SHOULD HAVE HIS PICK OF GIRLS... SO WHY ME?
THERE ARE RUMORS ABOUT HIM BEING PART OF A GANG.. AND BEING A LEADER OF SOME SORT.

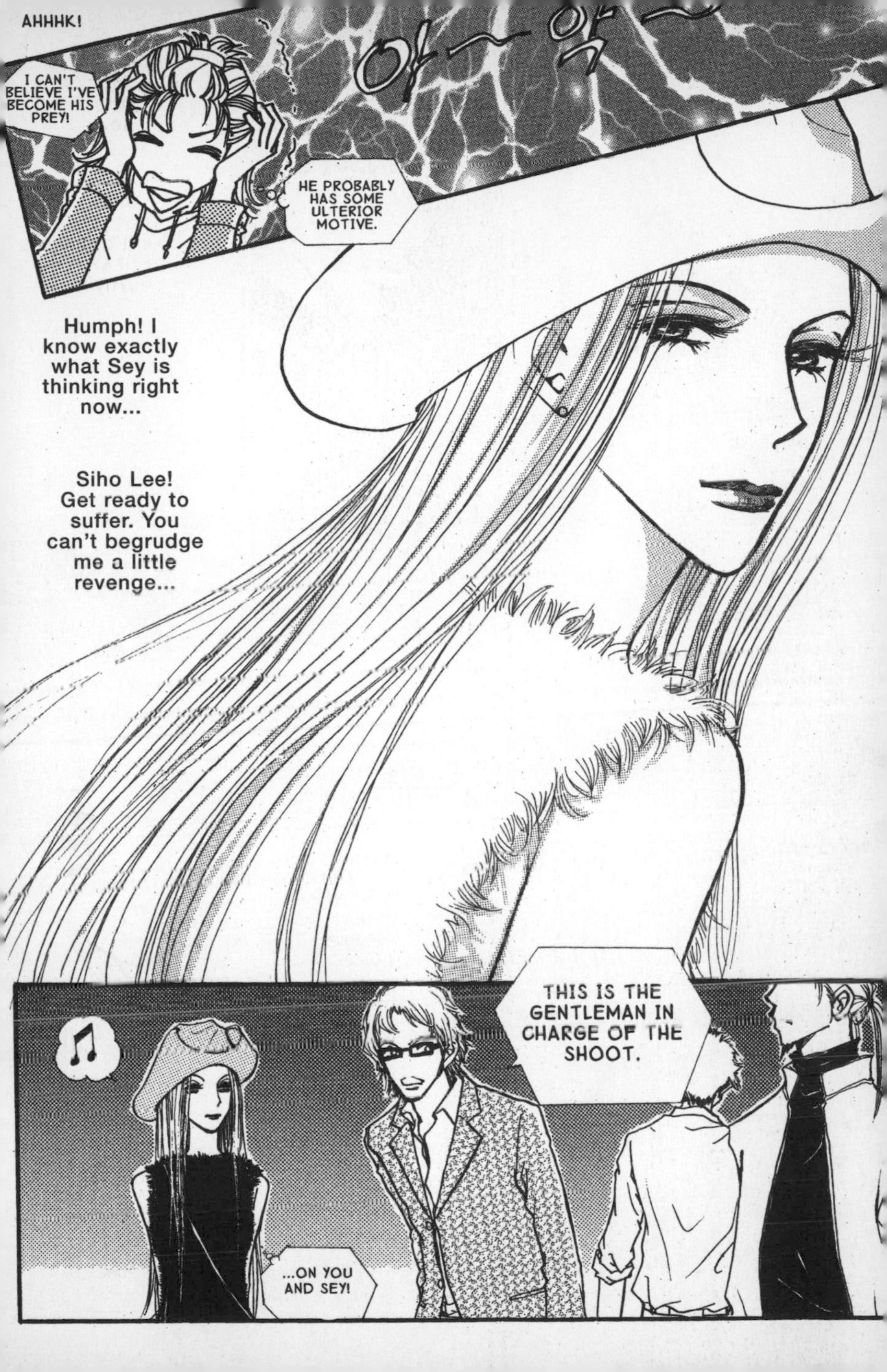
AHHHK!
I CAN'T BELIEVE I'VE BECOME HIS PREY!
HE PROBABLY HAS SOME ULTERIOR MOTIVE.
Humph! I know exactly what Sey is thinking right now...
Siho Lee! Get ready to suffer. You can't begrudge me a little revenge...
...ON YOU AND SEY!
THIS IS THE GENTLEMAN IN CHARGE OF THE SHOOT.

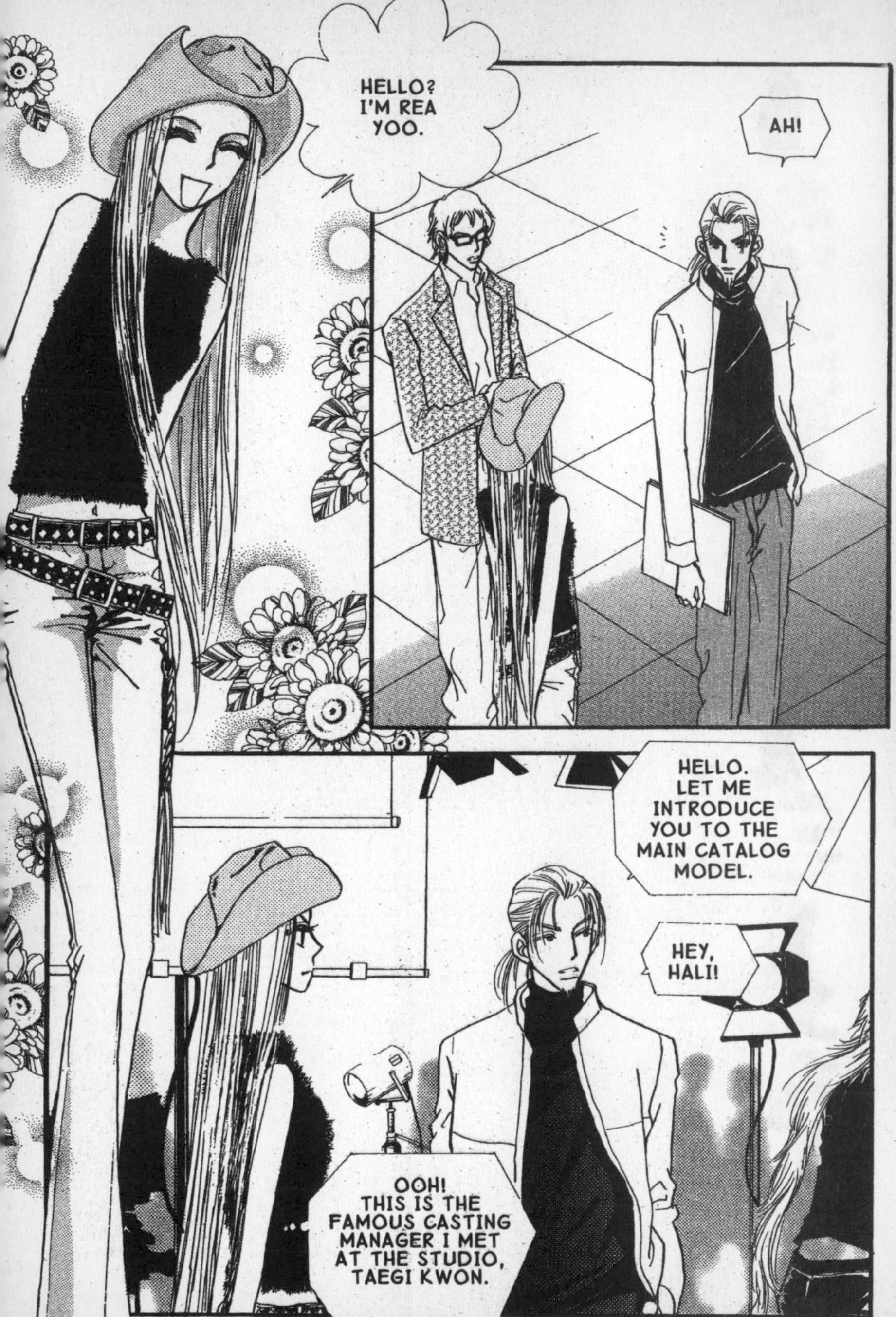
HELLO? I'M REA YOO.
AH!
HELLO. LET ME INTRODUCE YOU TO THE MAIN CATALOG MODEL.
HEY, HALI!
OOH! THIS IS THE FAMOUS CASTING MANAGER I MET AT THE STUDIO, TAEGI KWON.

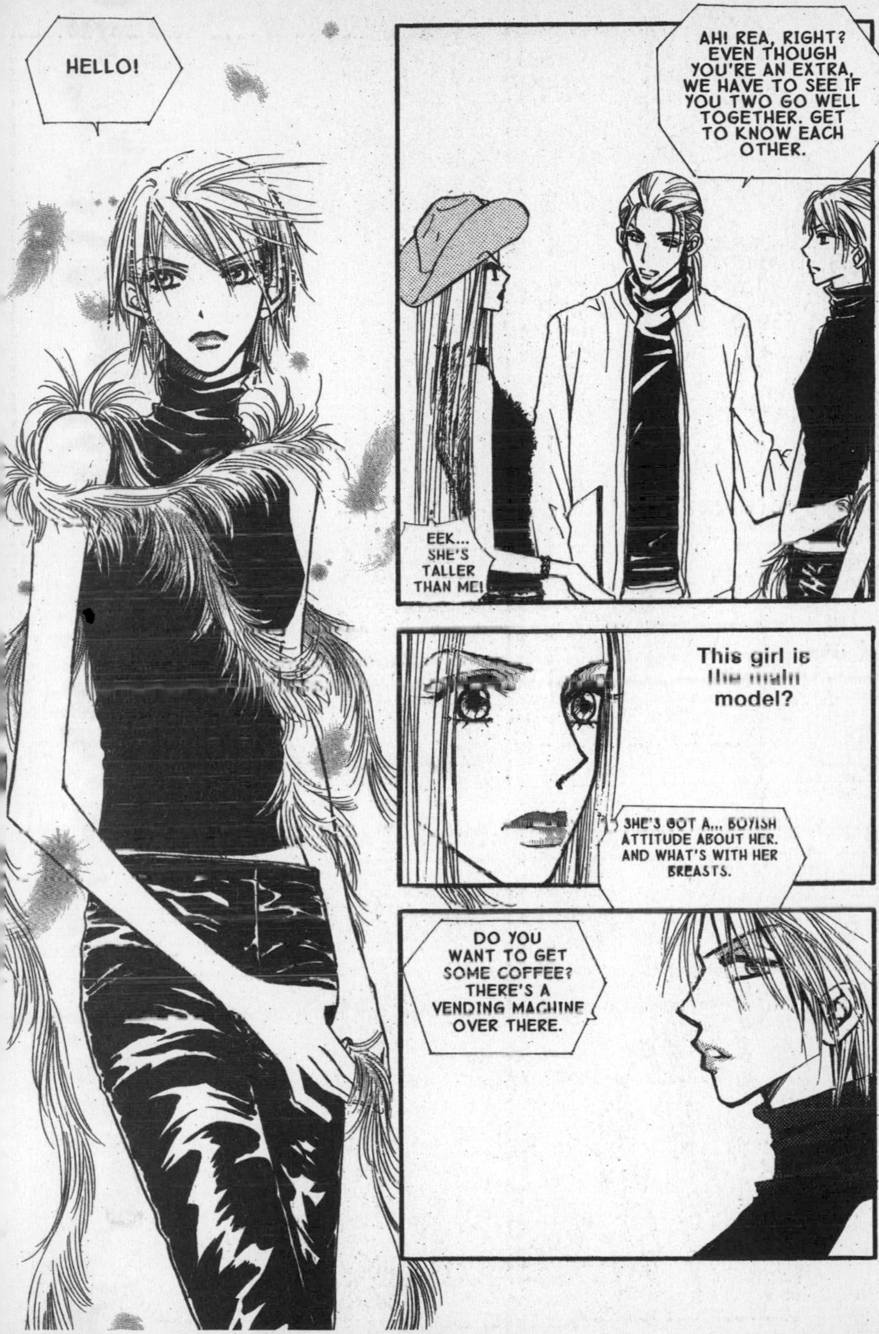
HELLO!
AH! REA, RIGHT? EVEN THOUGH YOU'RE AN EXTRA, WE HAVE TO SEE IF YOU TWO GO WELL TOGETHER. GET TO KNOW EACH OTHER.
EEK... SHE'S TALLER THAN ME!
This girl is the main model?
SHE'S GOT A... BOYISH ATTITUDE ABOUT HER. AND WHAT'S WITH HER BREASTS.
DO YOU WANT TO GET SOME COFFEE? THERE'S A VENDING MACHINE OVER THERE.

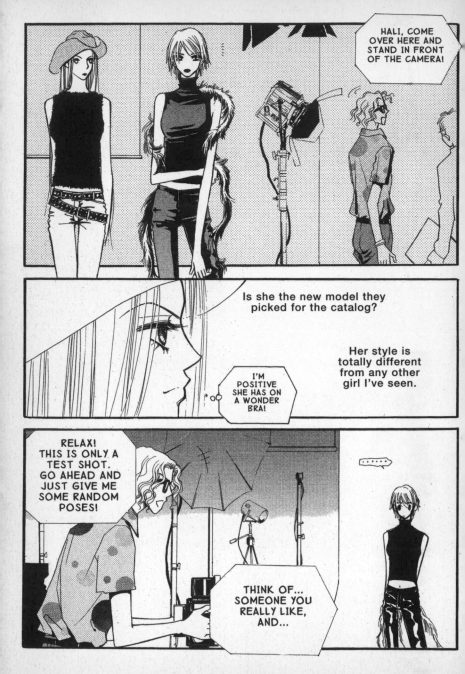

HALI, COME OVER HERE AND STAND IN FRONT OF THE CAMERA!

Is she the new model they picked for the catalog?

I'M POSITIVE SHE HAS ON A WONDER BRA!

Her style is totally different from any other girl I've seen.

RELAX! THIS IS ONLY A TEST SHOT. GO AHEAD AND JUST GIVE ME SOME RANDOM POSES!

THINK OF... SOMEONE YOU REALLY LIKE, AND...

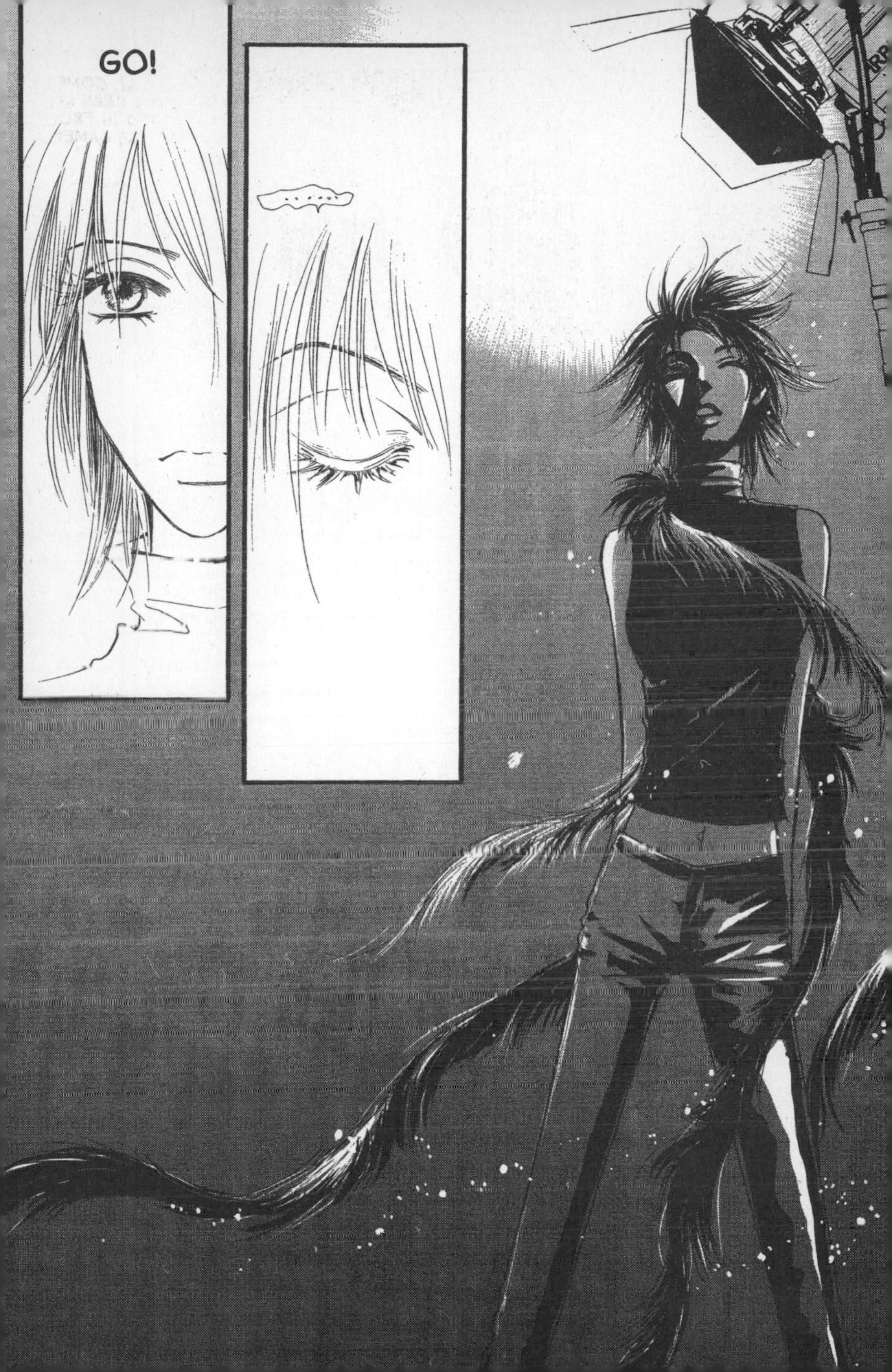
GO!
……

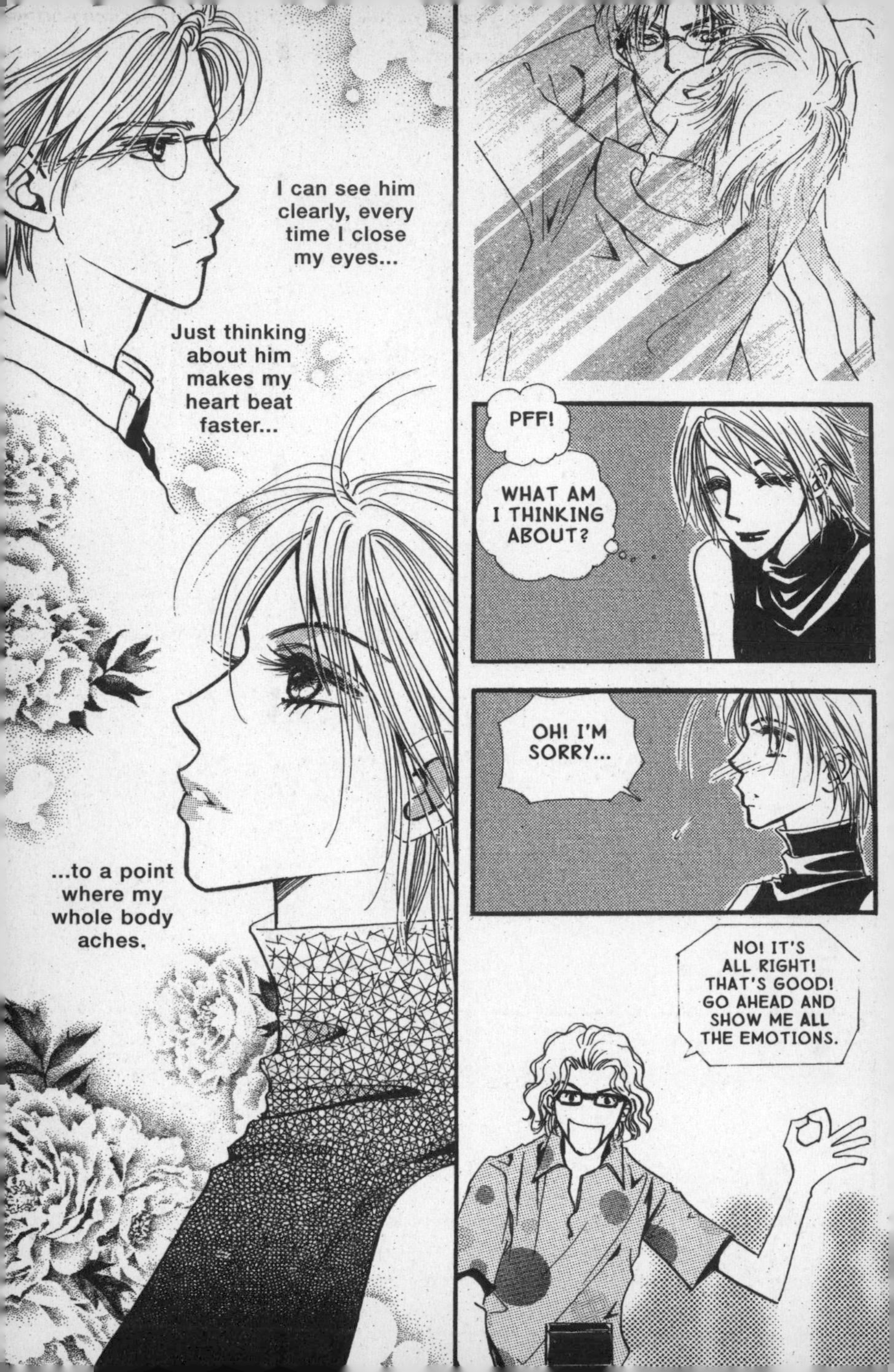
I can see him clearly, every time I close my eyes...
Just thinking about him makes my heart beat faster...
...to a point where my whole body aches.
PFF!
WHAT AM I THINKING ABOUT?
OH! I'M SORRY...
NO! IT'S ALL RIGHT! THAT'S GOOD! GO AHEAD AND SHOW ME ALL THE EMOTIONS.

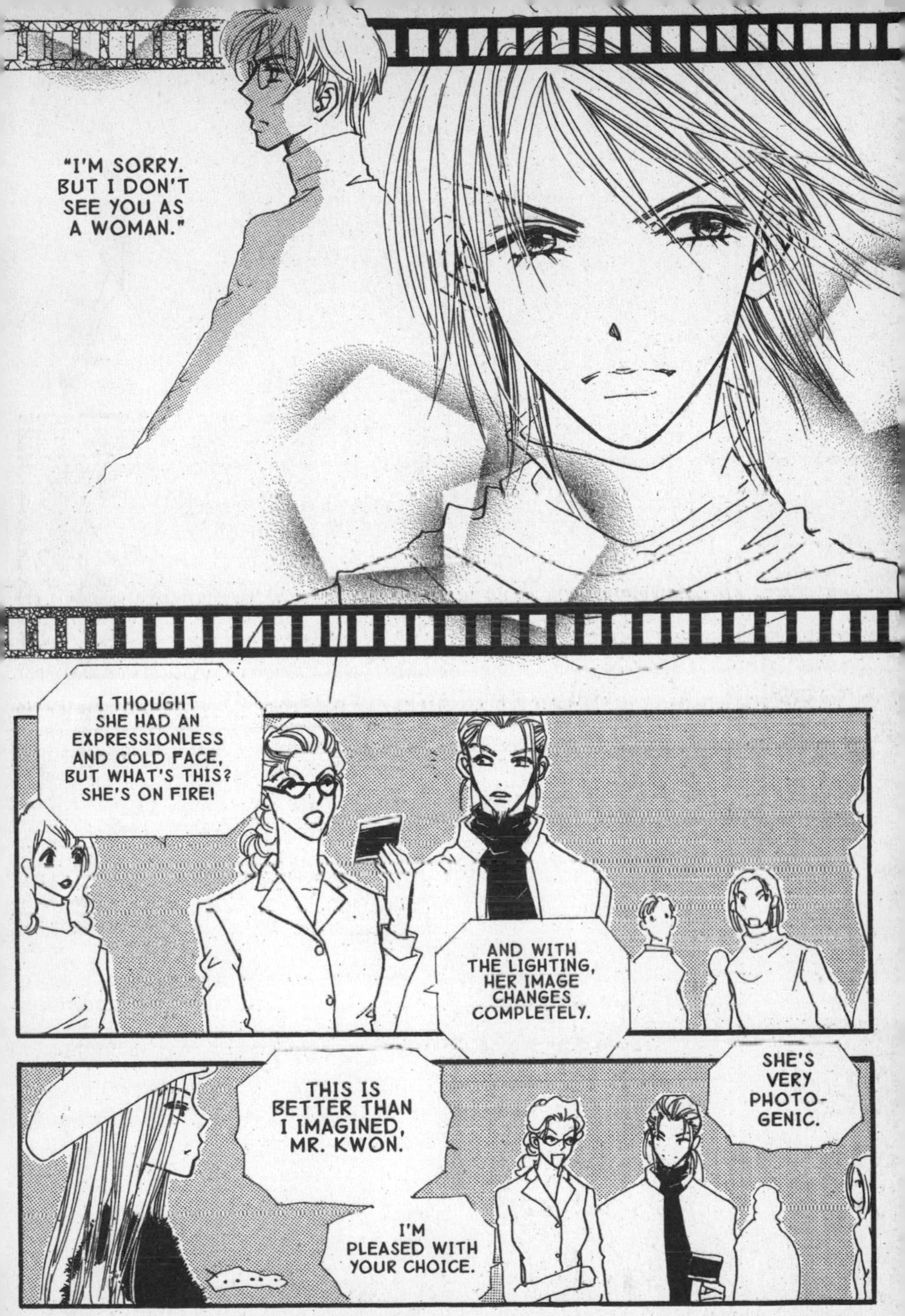
"I'M SORRY. BUT I DON'T SEE YOU AS A WOMAN."
I THOUGHT SHE HAD AN EXPRESSIONLESS AND COLD FACE, BUT WHAT'S THIS? SHE'S ON FIRE!
AND WITH THE LIGHTING, HER IMAGE CHANGES COMPLETELY.
....
THIS IS BETTER THAN I IMAGINED, MR. KWON.
I'M PLEASED WITH YOUR CHOICE.
SHE'S VERY PHOTO-GENIC.

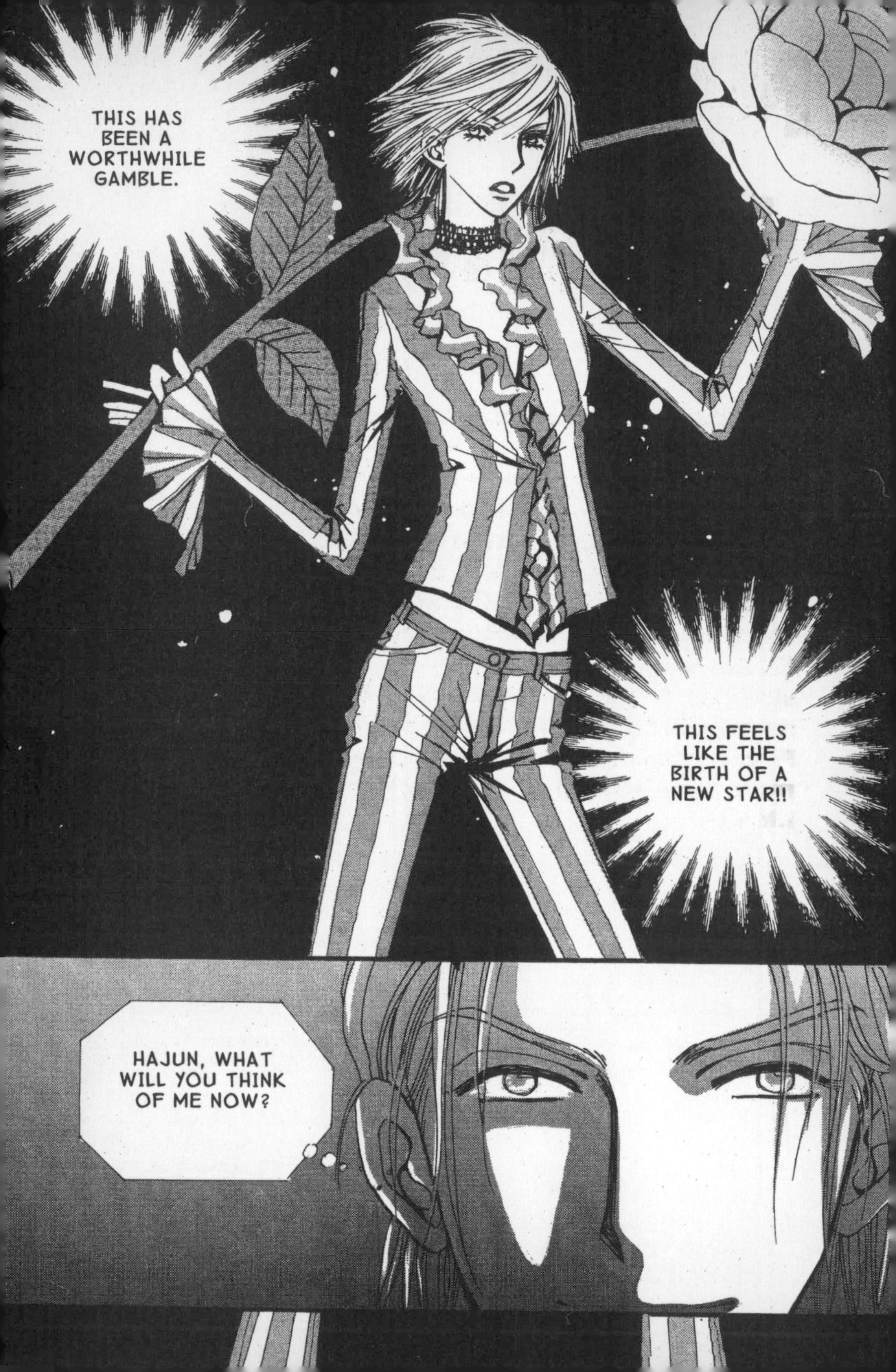
THIS HAS BEEN A WORTHWHILE GAMBLE.
THIS FEELS LIKE THE BIRTH OF A NEW STAR!!
HAJUN, WHAT WILL YOU THINK OF ME NOW?

NEXT IN I.N.V.U.

Now that Sey knows about Hali's double life as Terry, will there be some double crossing—especially since Sey thinks Hali and Mr. Hajun Cho were getting it on? Will Siho ever get a chance to give Sey her first kiss? Now that Hali has taken the first step towards stardom, will there be a collision with the aggressive and devious Rea? And what new recipes for love will Jea Eun learn? Find the answers to these and many more questions in the next volume of I.N.V.U.

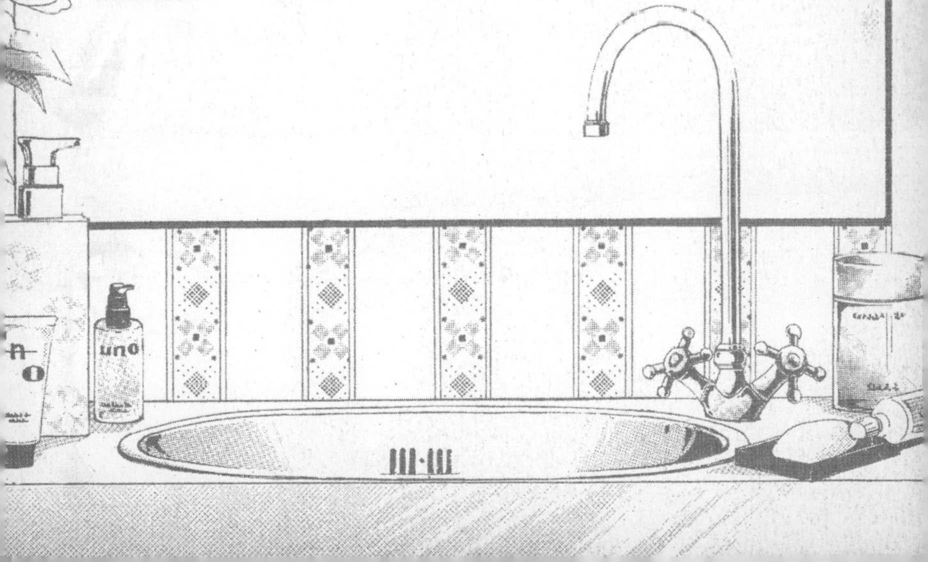
uno

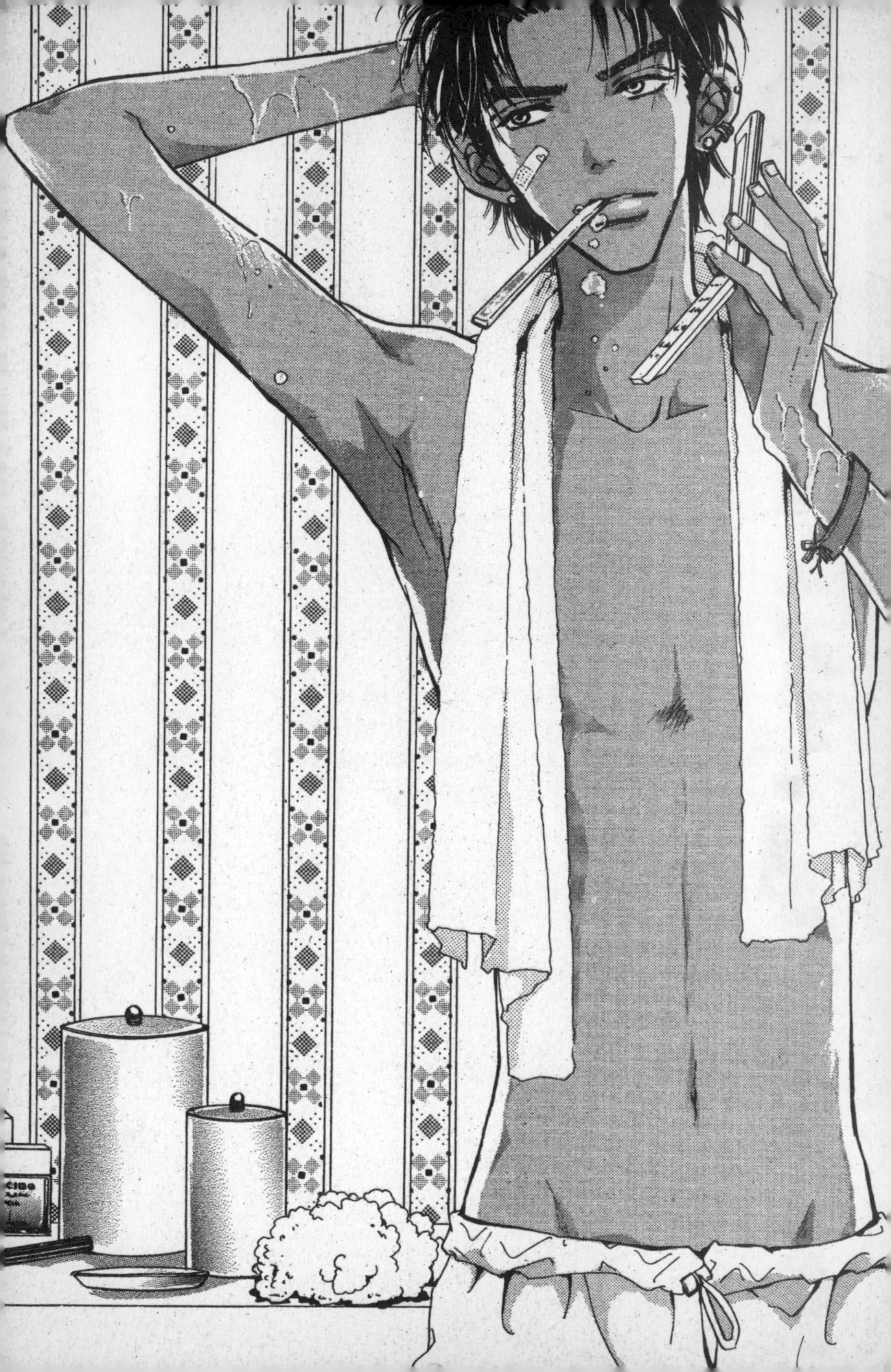

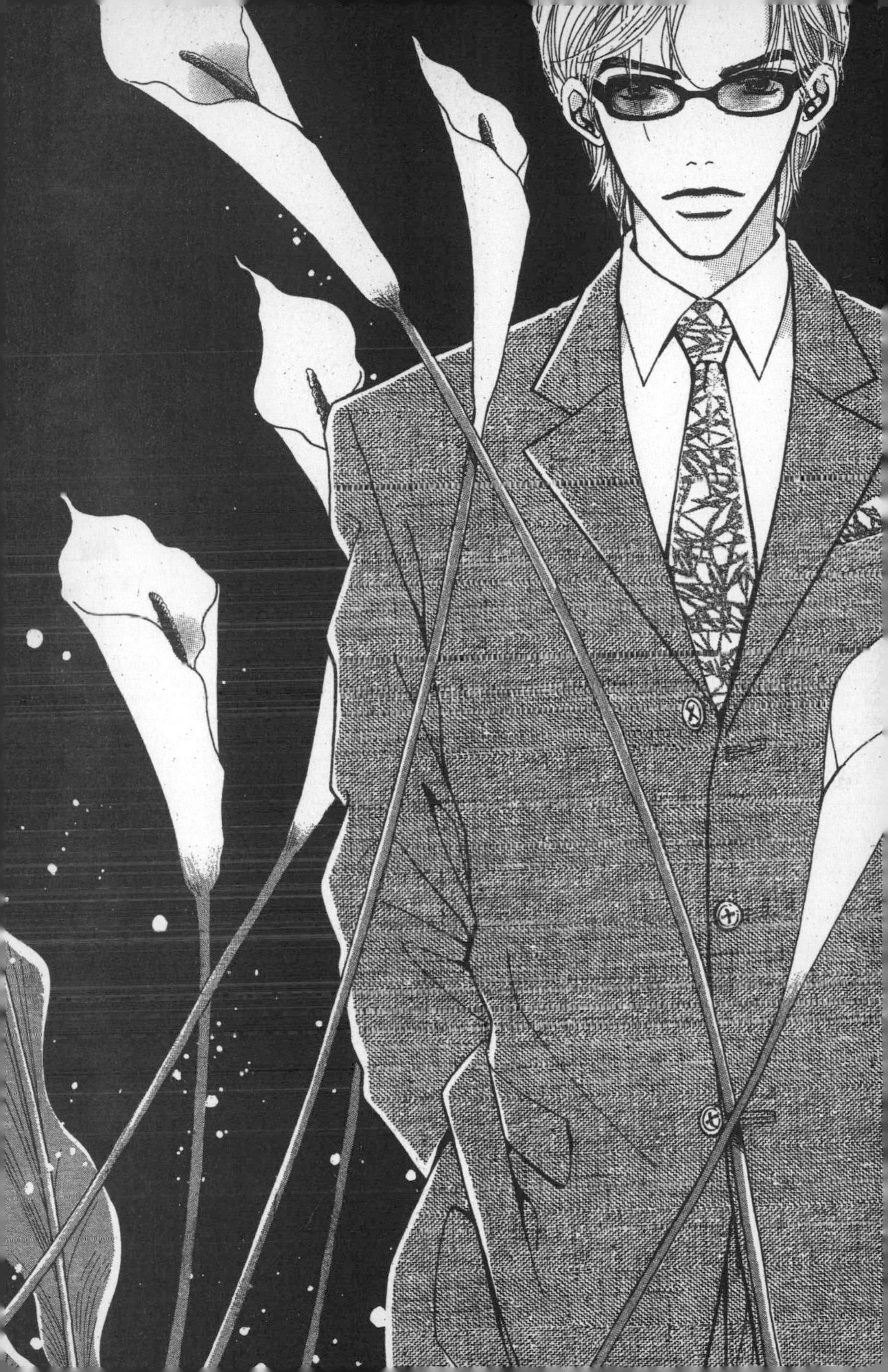